THE
RIME
OF
THE
MODERN
MARINER

THE
RIME
OF
THE
MODERN
MARINER

nick hayes

VIKING

VIKING

Published by the Penguin Group

Penguin Group (USA) Inc., 375 Hudson Street, New York, New York 10014, U.S.A.

Penguin Group (Canada), 90 Eglinton Avenue East, Suite 700
Toronto, Ontario, Canada, M4P 2Y3
(a division of Pearson Penguin Canada Inc.)

Penguin Books Ltd, 80 Strand, London WC2R 0RL, England

Penguin Ireland, 25 St Stevens Green, Dublin 2, Ireland
(a division of Penguin Books Ltd)

Penguin Books Australia Ltd, 250 Camberwell Road,
Camberwell, Victoria 3124, Australia
(a division of Pearson Australia Group Pty Ltd)

Penguin Books India Pvt Ltd, 11 Community Centre,
Panscheel Park, New Delhi - 110 017, India

Penguin Group (NZ), 67 Apollo Drive, Rosedale,
Auckland 0632, New Zealand
(a division of Pearson New Zealand Ltd)

Penguin Books (South Africa) (Pty) Ltd, 24 Sturdee Avenue,
Rosebank, Johannesburg 2196, South Africa

Penguin Books Ltd, Registered Offices:
80 Strand, London WC2R 0RL, England

First American edition
Published in 2012 by Viking Penguin,
a member of Penguin Group (USA) Inc.

1 3 5 7 9 10 8 6 4 2

Copyright © Nick Hayes, 2011
All rights reserved

Published by arrangement with The Random House Group Limited (London)

Excerpt from "When the Ship Comes in" by Bob Dylan. Copyright © 1963, 1964 by
Warner Bros. Inc.; renewed 1991, 1992 by Special Rider Music. All rights reserved.
International copyright secured. Reprinted by permission.

ISBN 978-0-670-02580-0

Printed in the United States of America

Designed by nick hayes

NOV 3 0 2012

ALWAYS LEARNING　　　　　　　　　　　　**PEARSON**

FOR MY FRIENDS

" BUT THEY'LL PINCH THEMSELVES AND SQUEAL,
AND THEY'LL KNOW THAT IT'S FOR REAL,
THE HOUR THAT THE SHIP COMES IN.
"

–BOB DYLAN

PART ONE

HE SWIFTLY SIGNED THE PAPERS

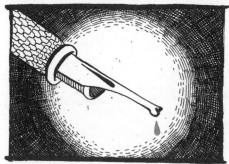

IN THE STUFFY OFFICE AIR...

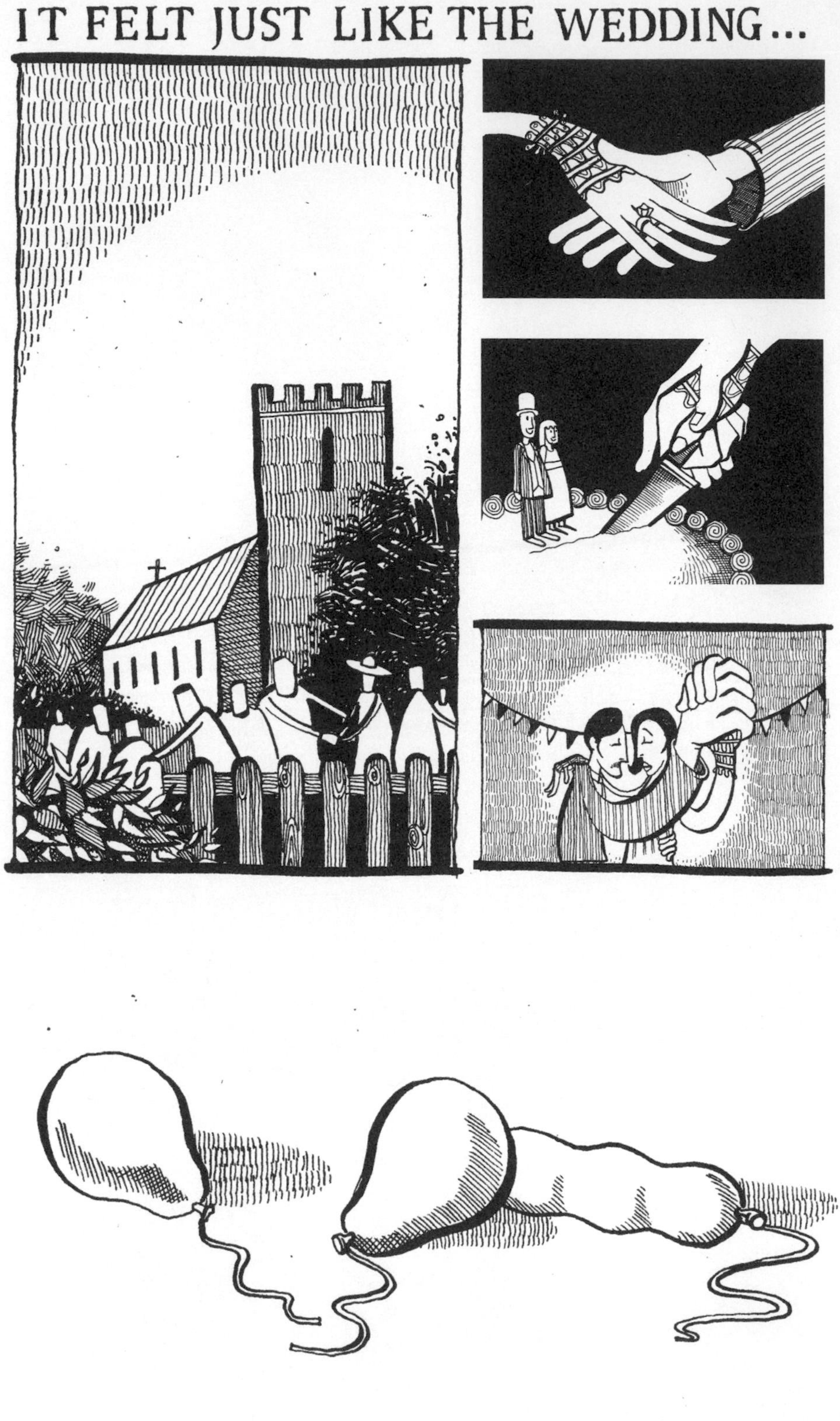
IT FELT JUST LIKE THE WEDDING...

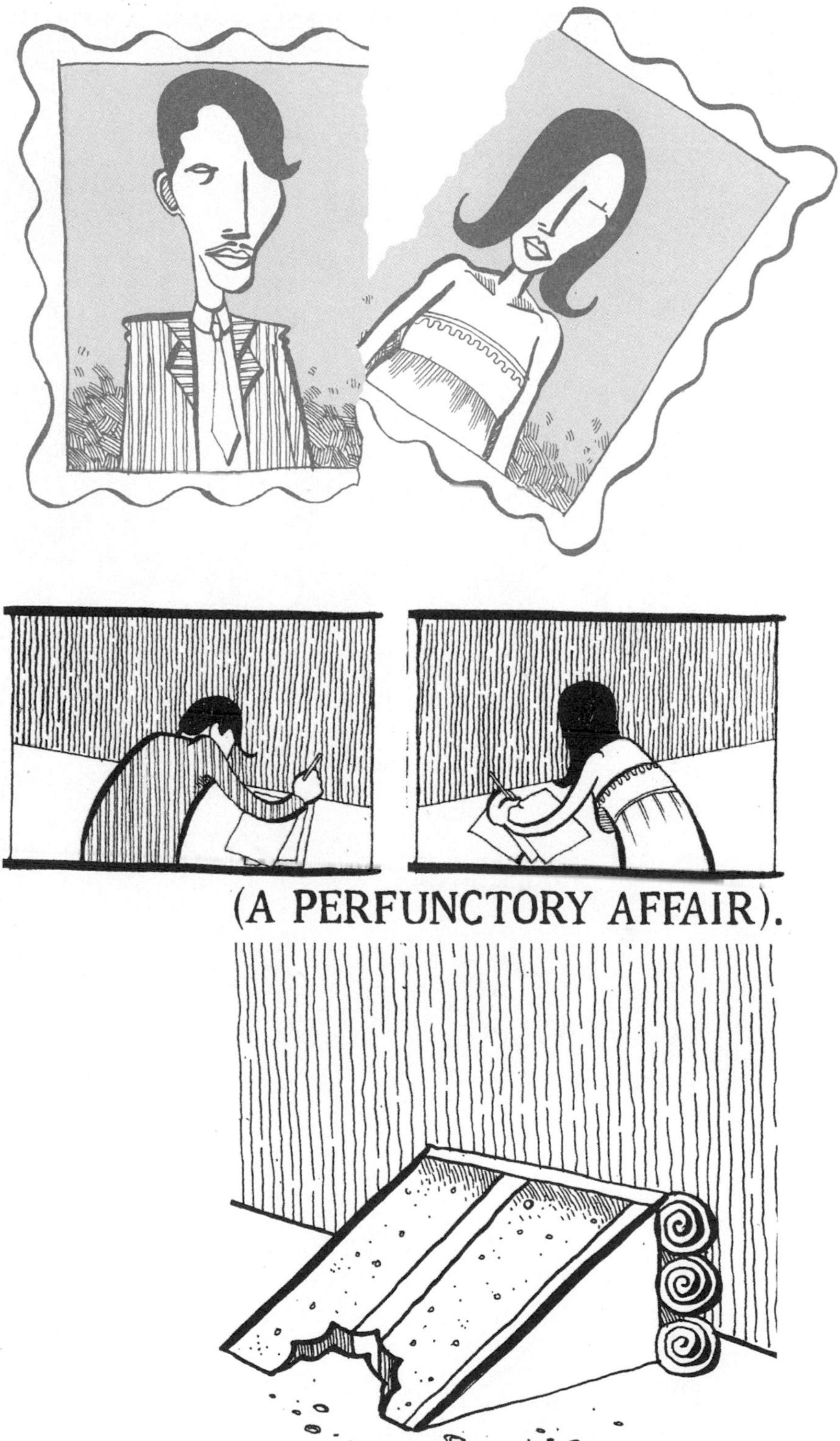
(A PERFUNCTORY AFFAIR).

COCOONED INSIDE AND COSY

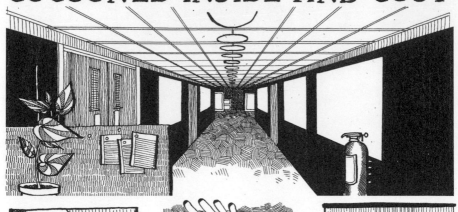

IN THE ARTIFICIAL GLOW

 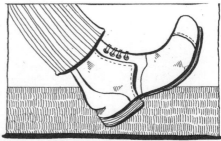

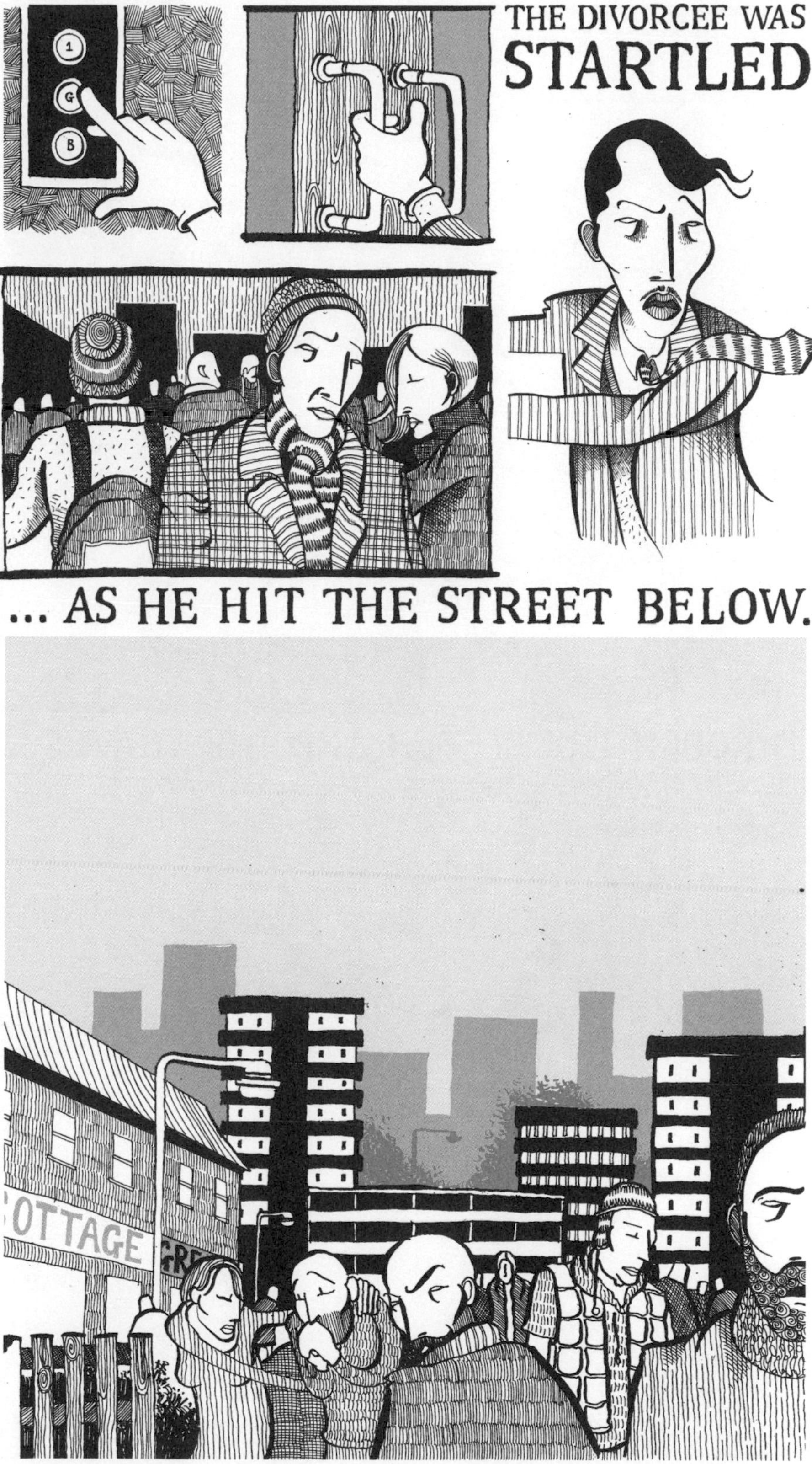
1
G
B
THE DIVORCEE WAS STARTLED
... AS HE HIT THE STREET BELOW.
OTTAGE

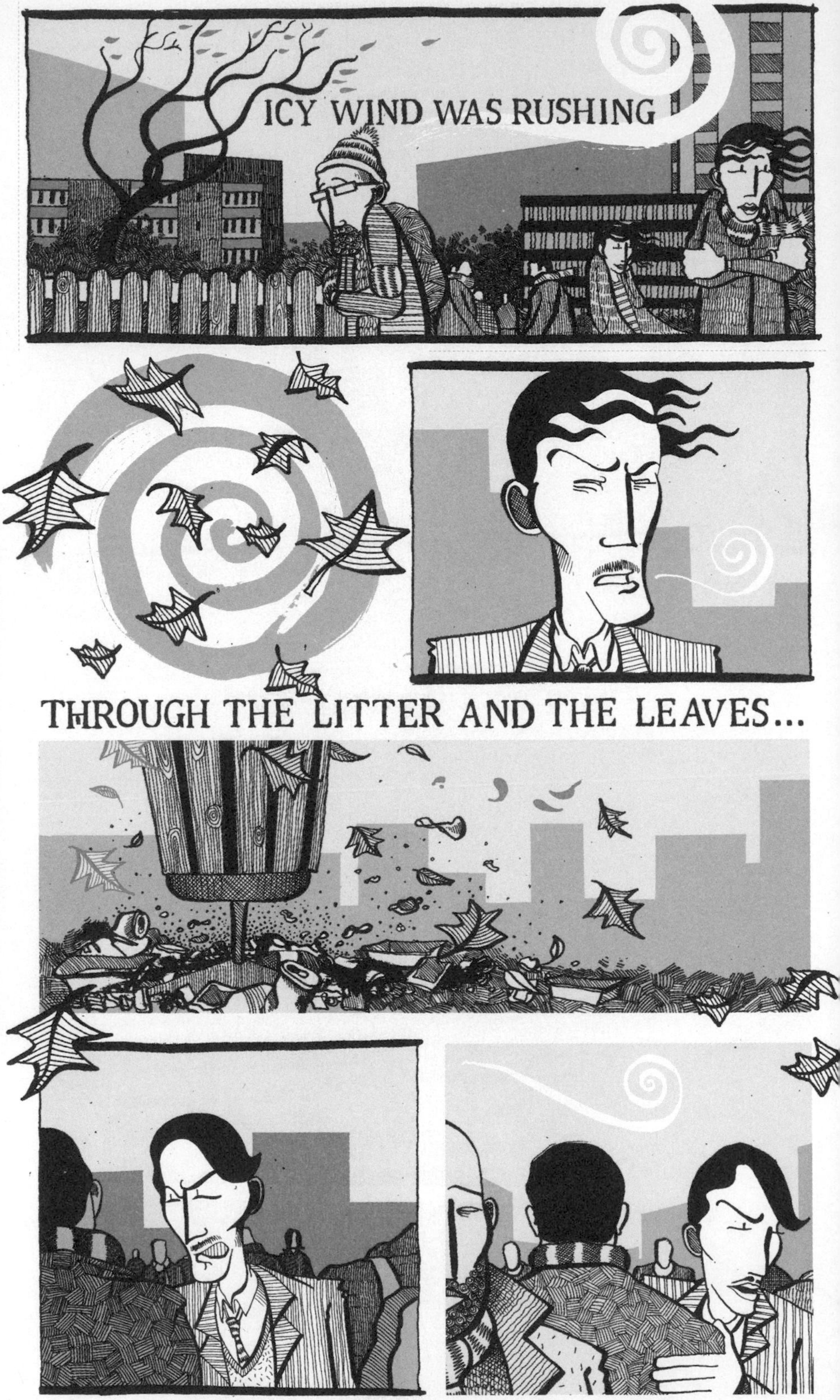
ICY WIND WAS RUSHING
THROUGH THE LITTER AND THE LEAVES...

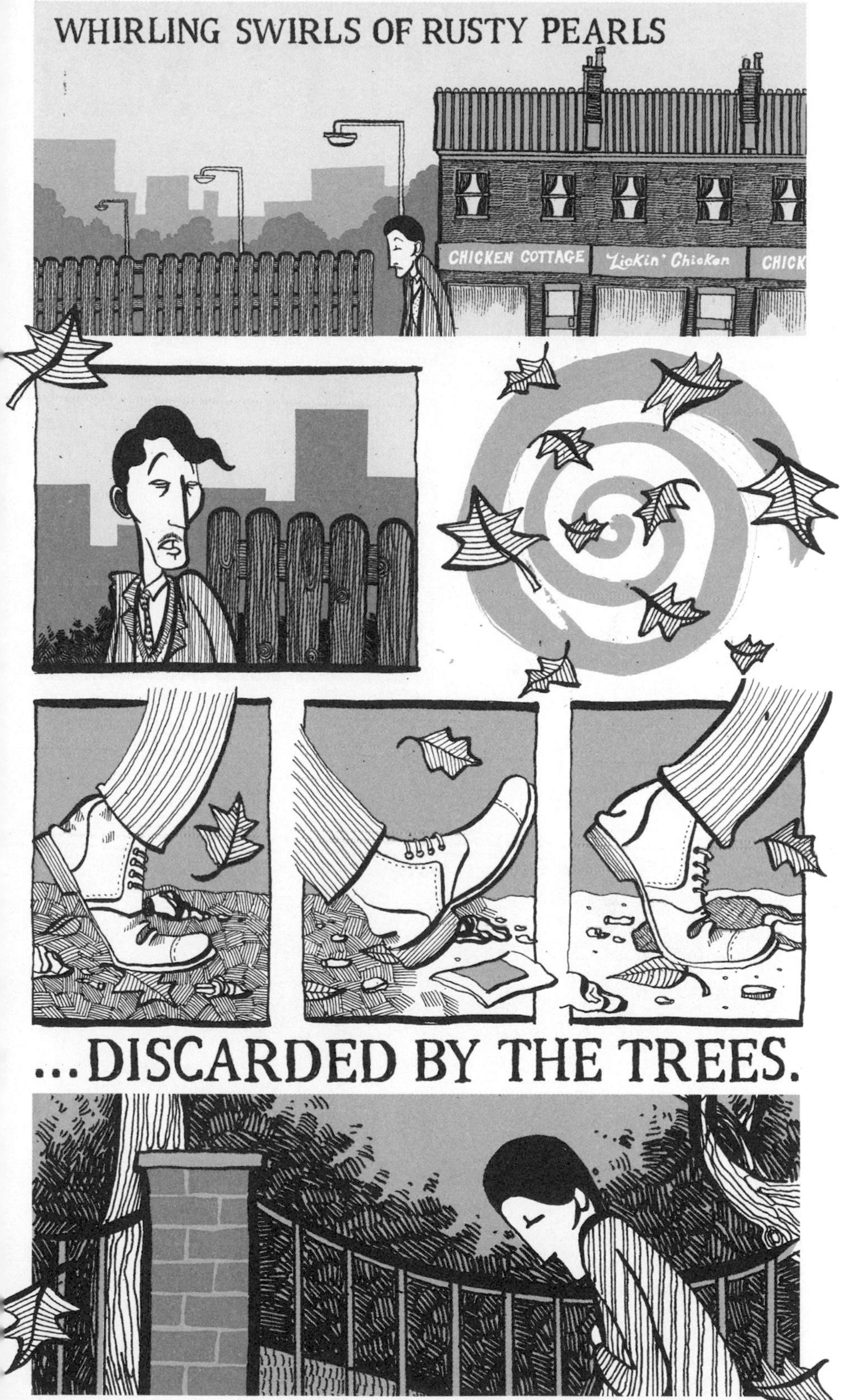
WHIRLING SWIRLS OF RUSTY PEARLS
CHICKEN COTTAGE
Lickin' Chicken
CHICK
...DISCARDED BY THE TREES.

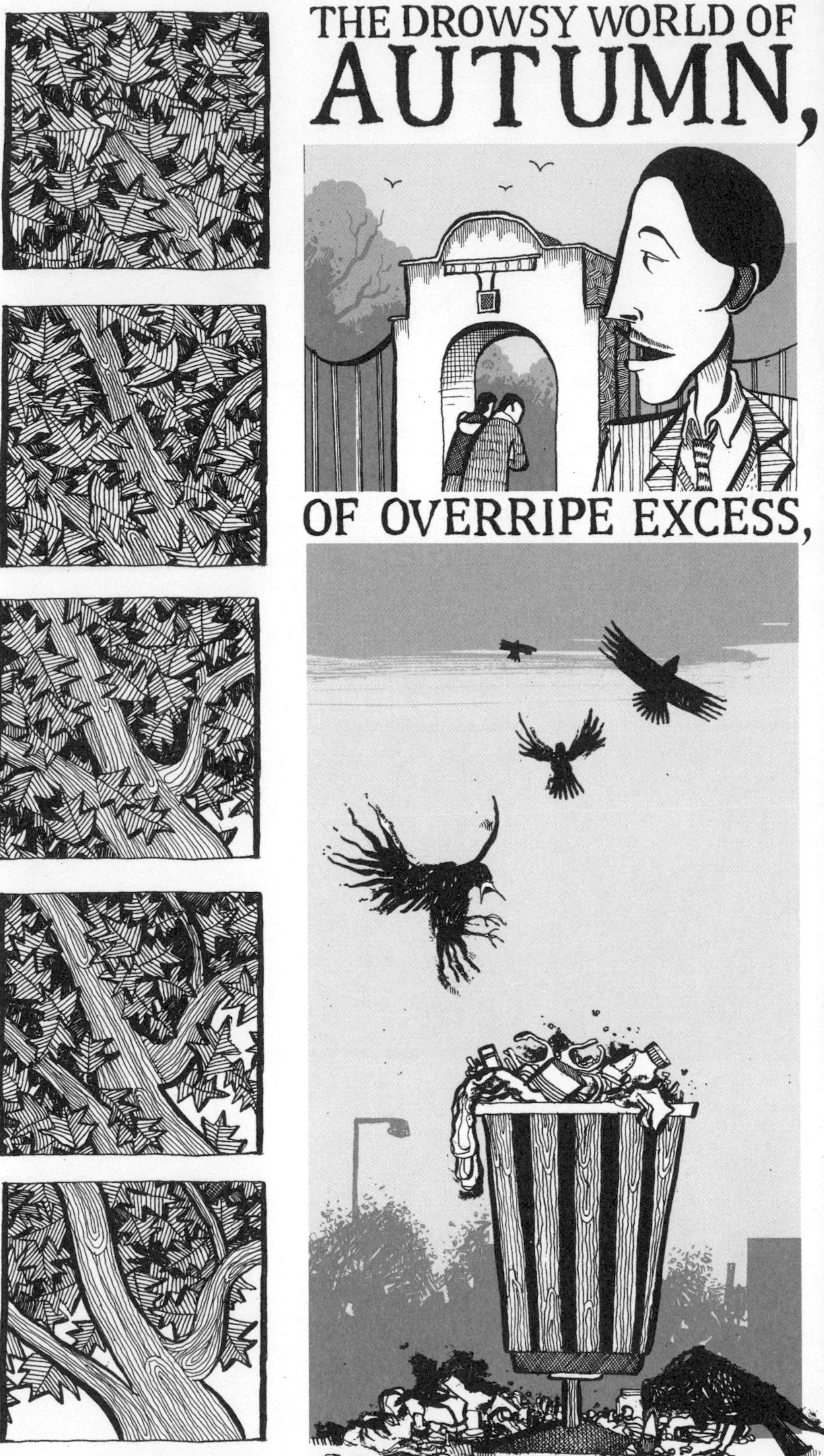
THE DROWSY WORLD OF
AUTUMN,
OF OVERRIPE EXCESS,

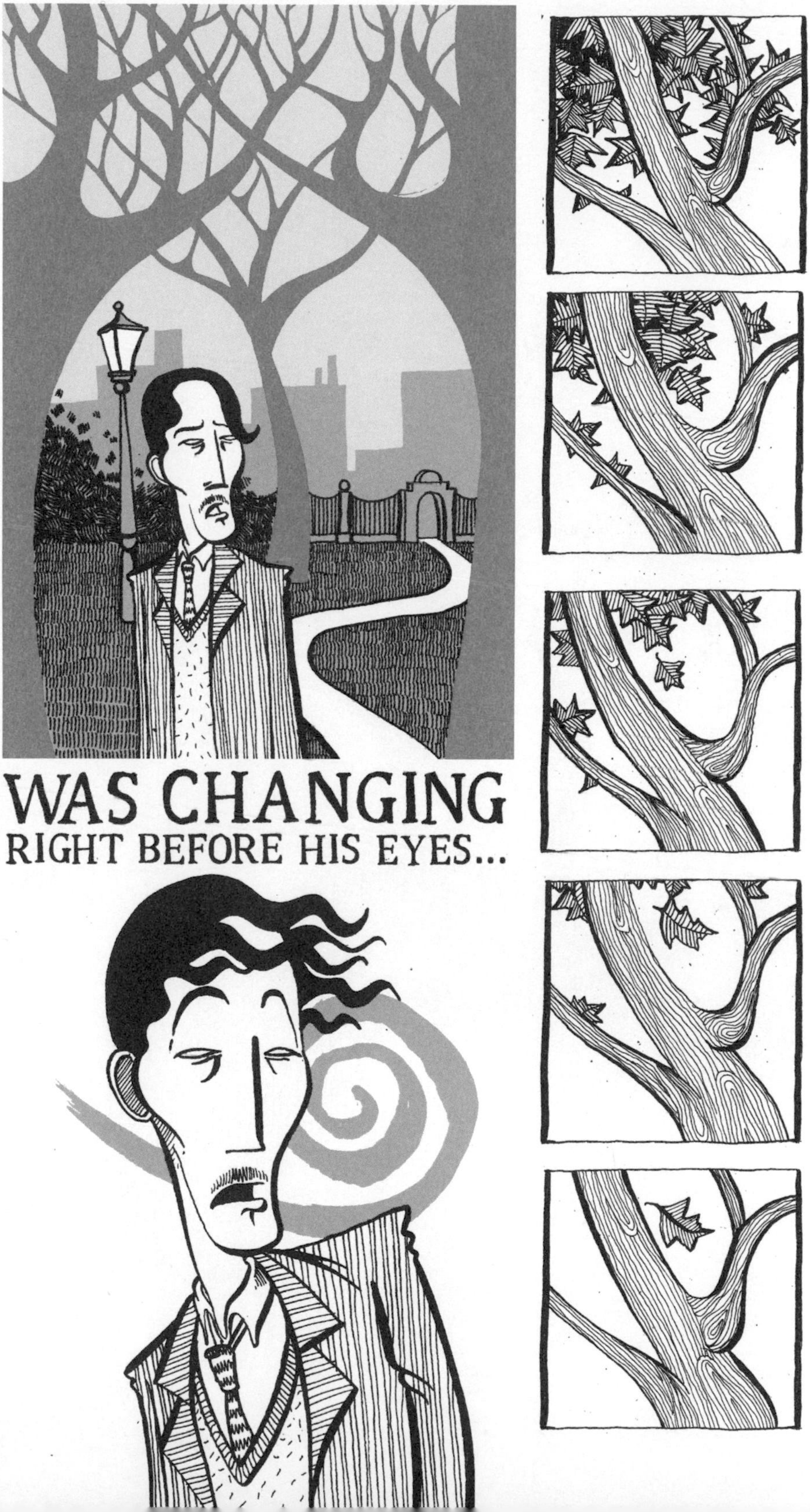
WAS CHANGING
RIGHT BEFORE HIS EYES...

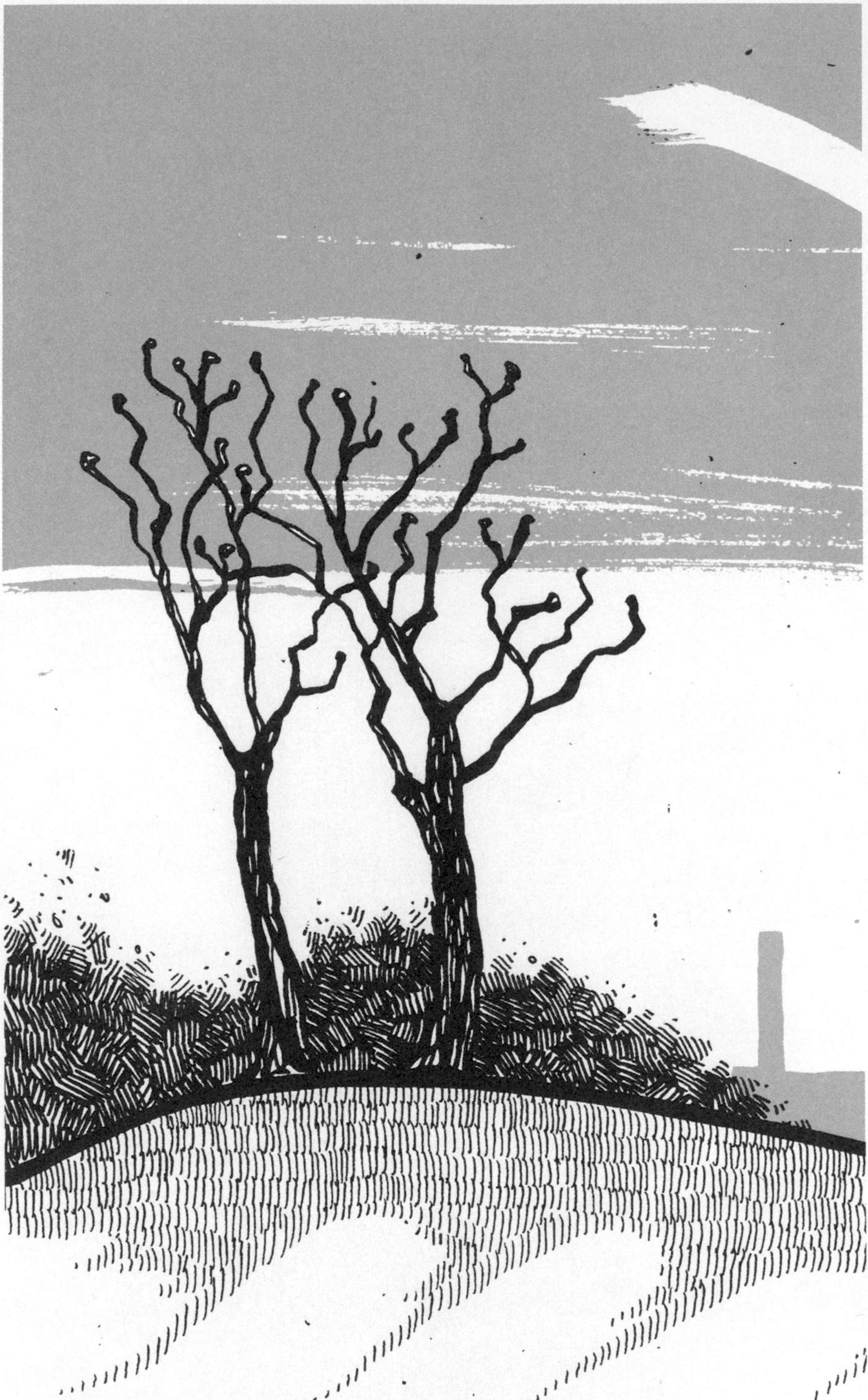

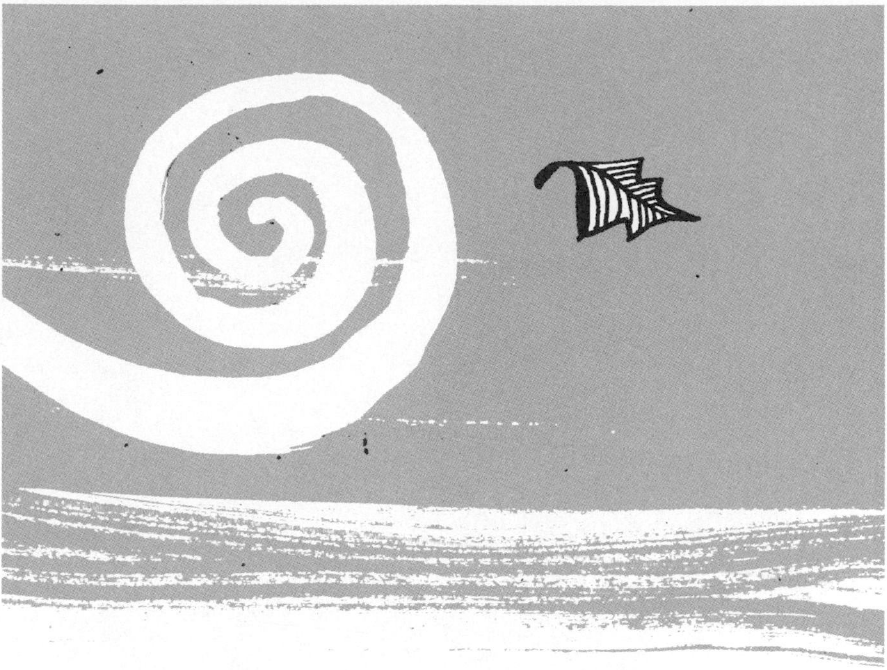

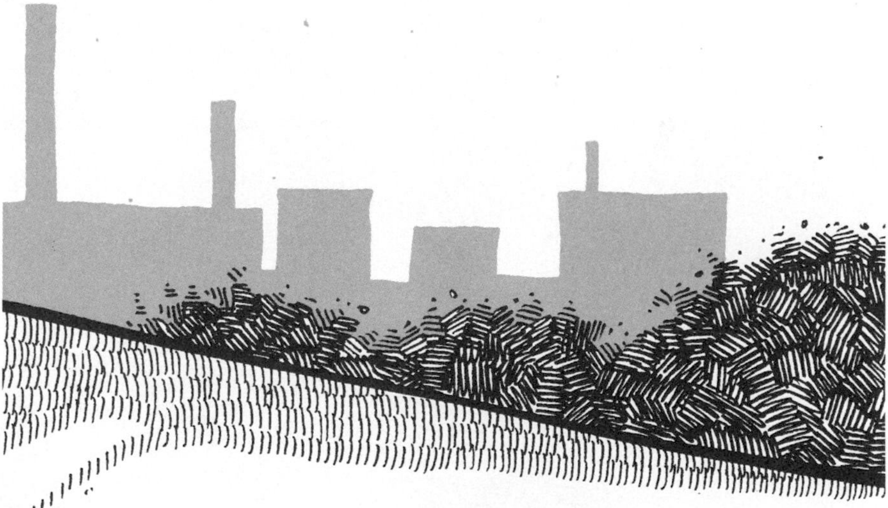

...TO HOARY ABJECTNESS.

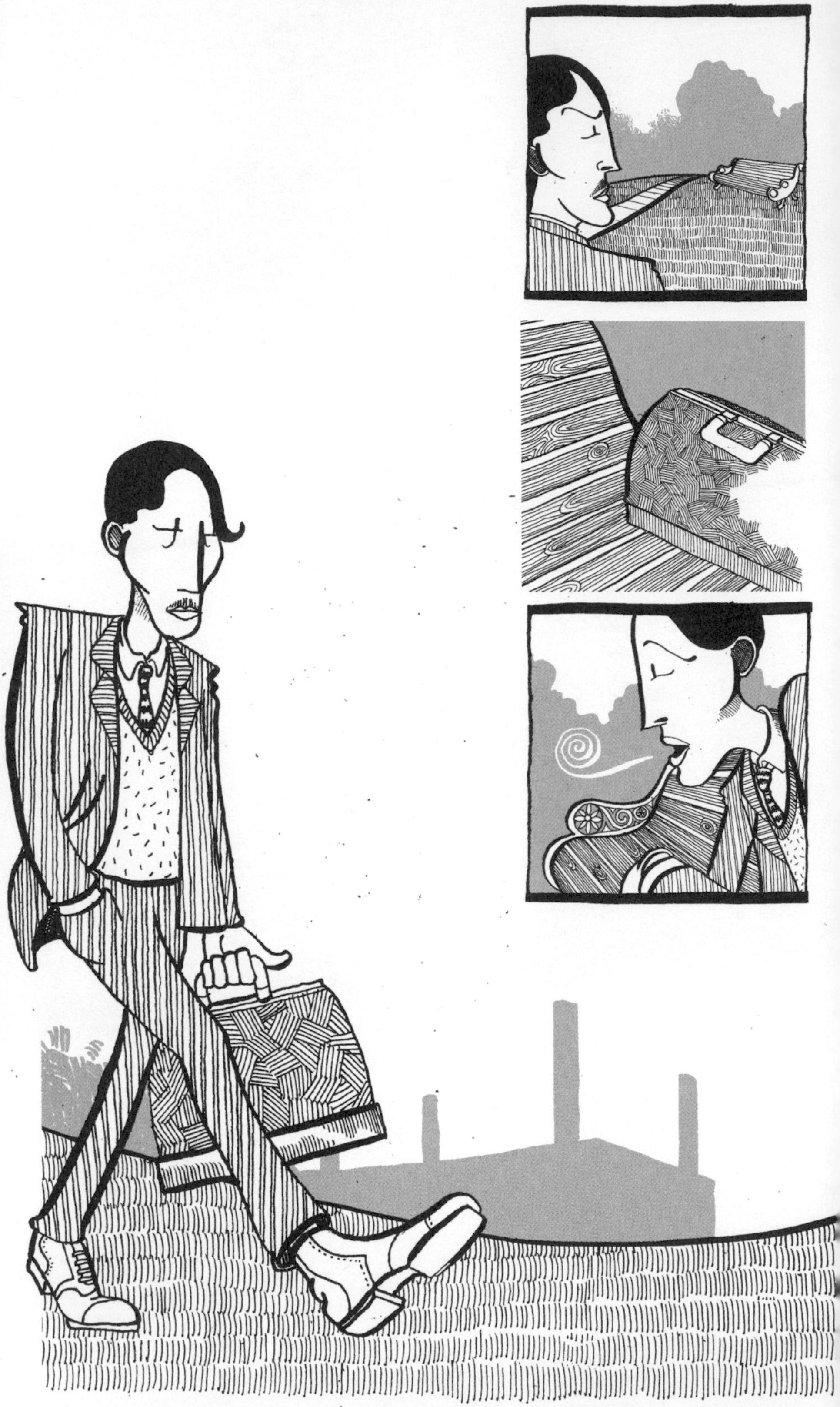

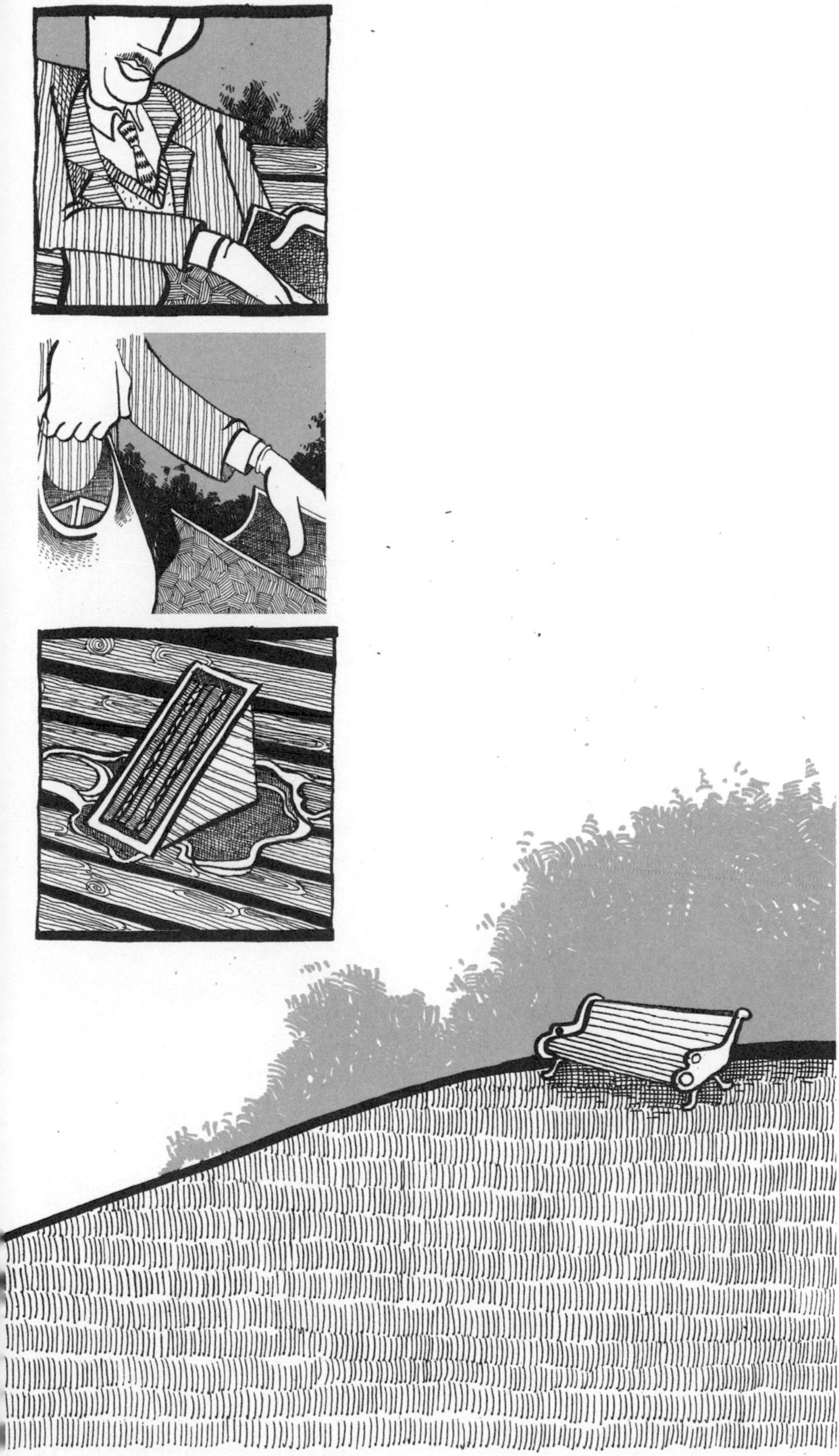

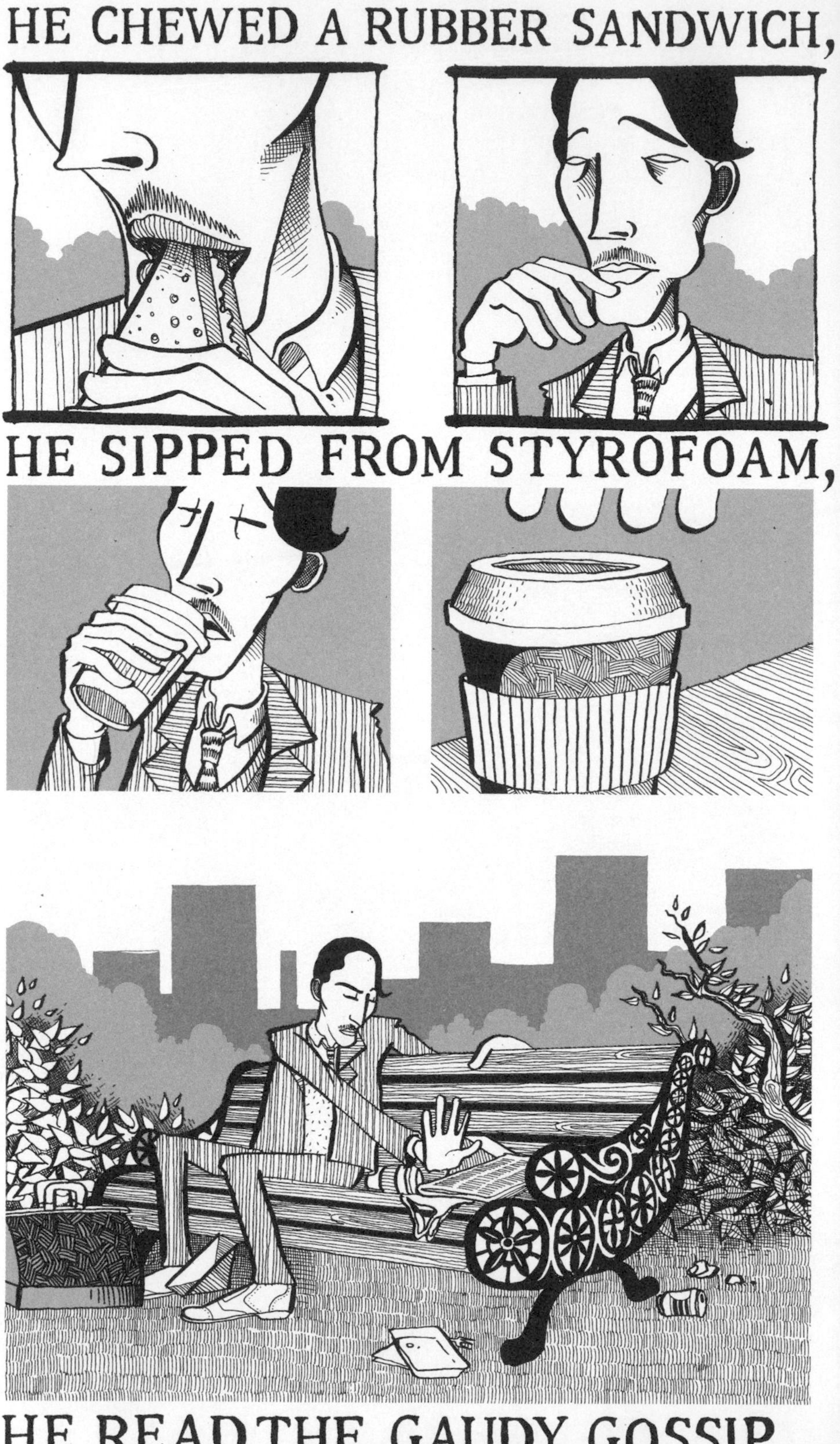
HE CHEWED A RUBBER SANDWICH,
HE SIPPED FROM STYROFOAM,
HE READ THE GAUDY GOSSIP...

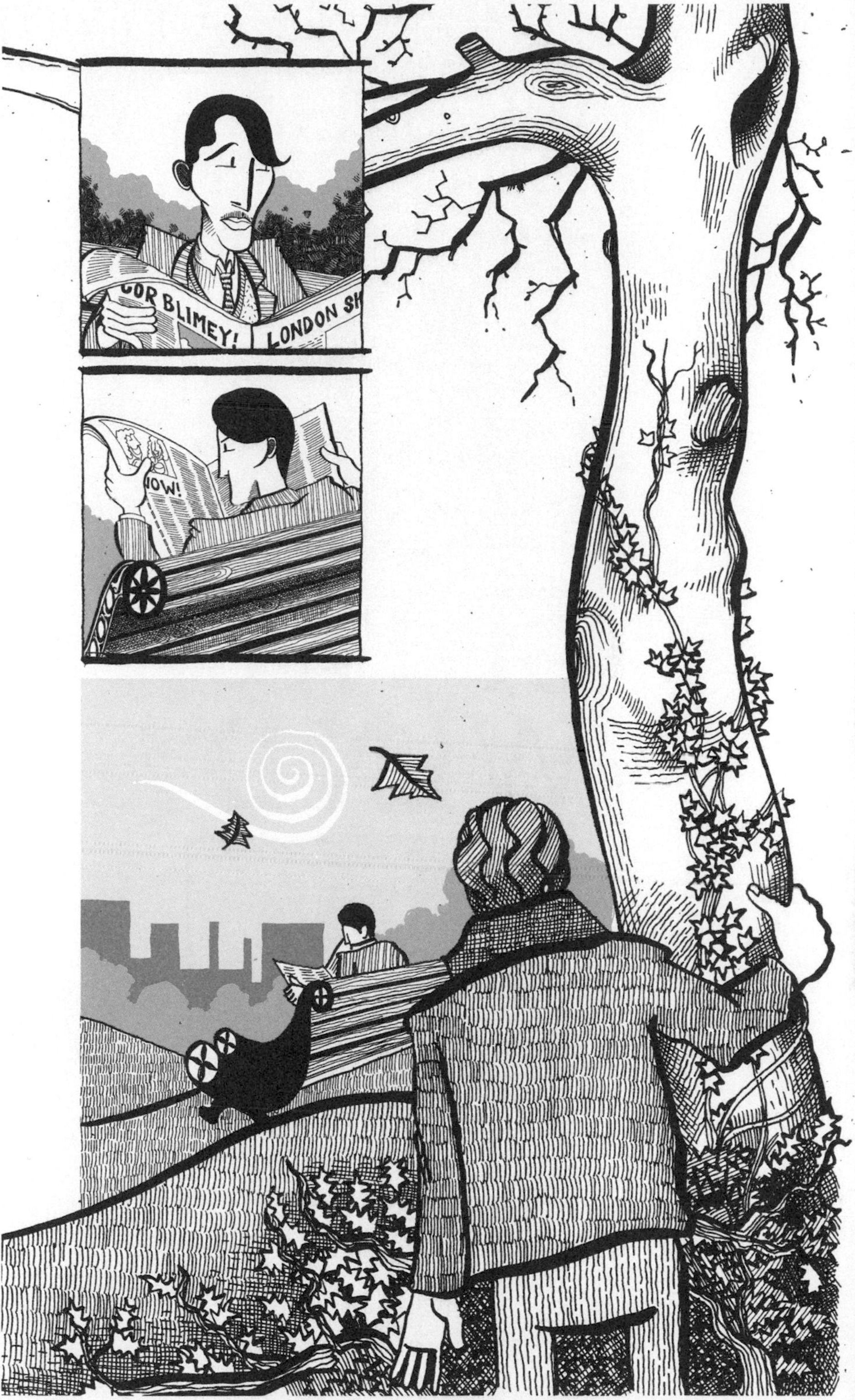
COR BLIMEY!
LONDON SH
NOW!

AND ASSUMED HE WAS ALONE.

HE HEARD THE WHISTLING WHISPER

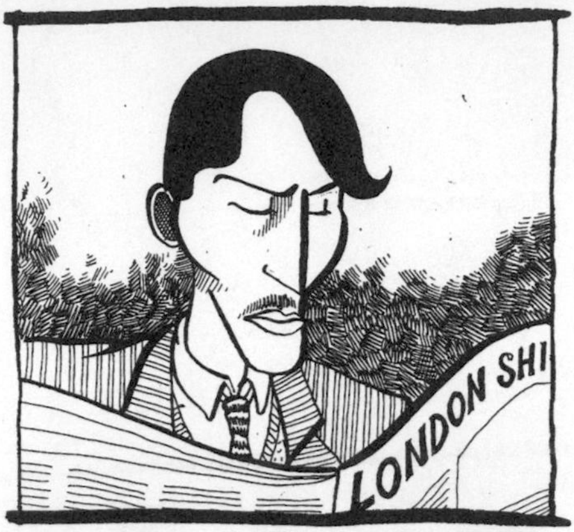
LONDON SHI

OF THE WIND

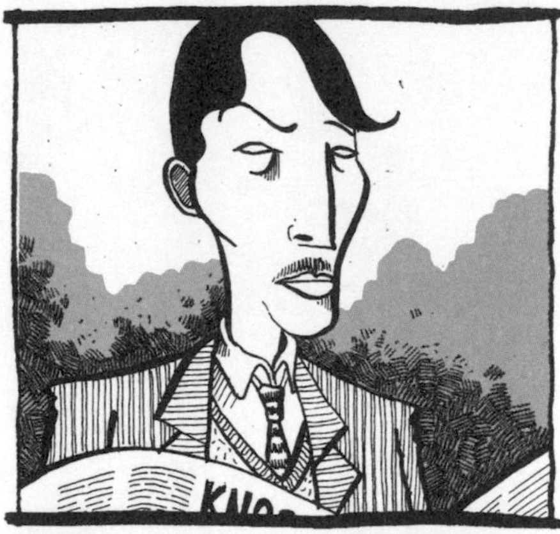

BEGIN TO RISE...

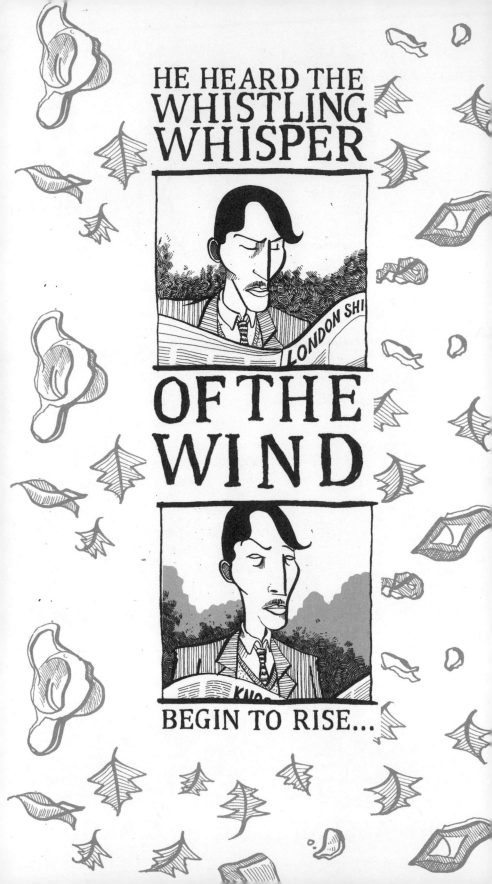

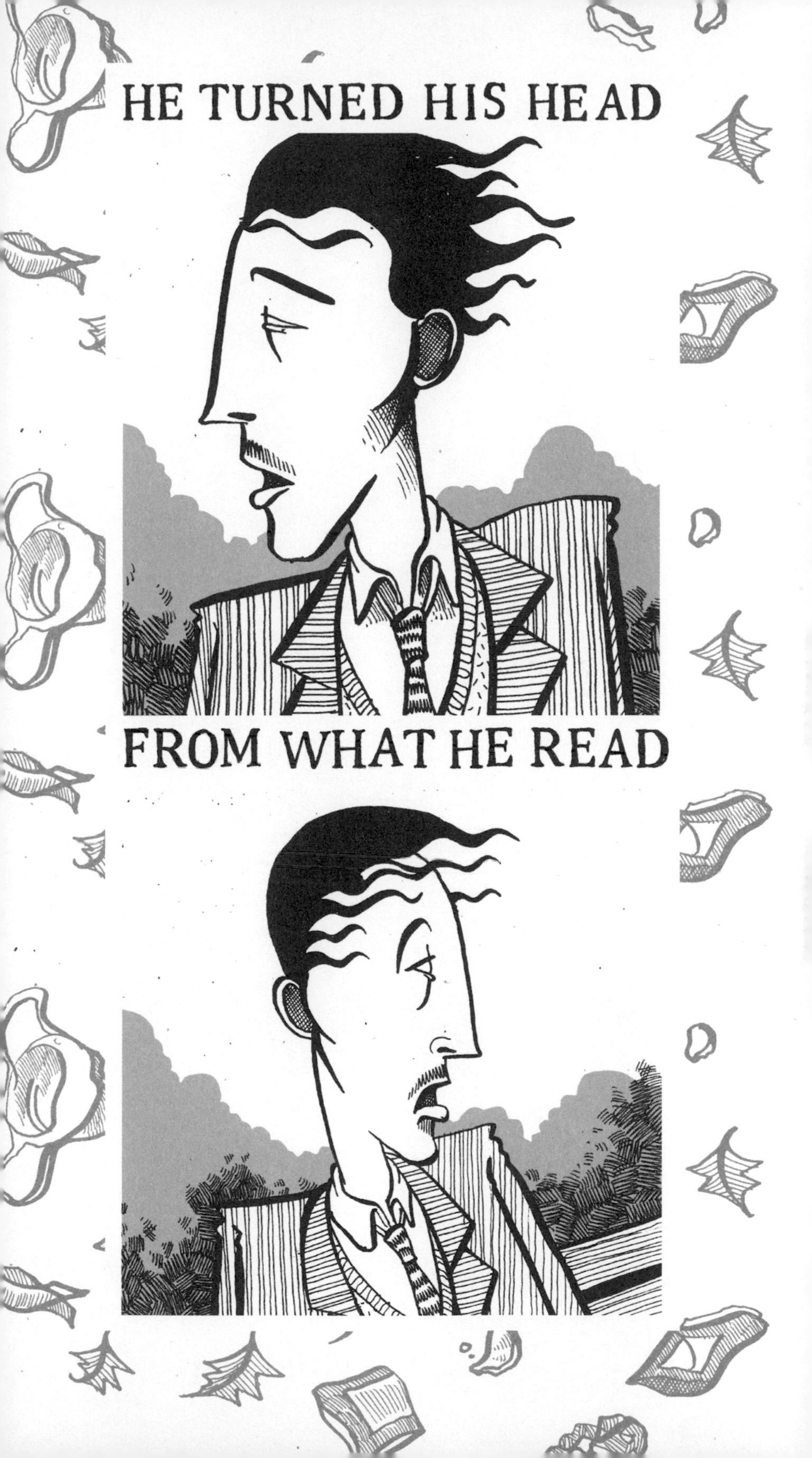
HE TURNED HIS HEAD
FROM WHAT HE READ

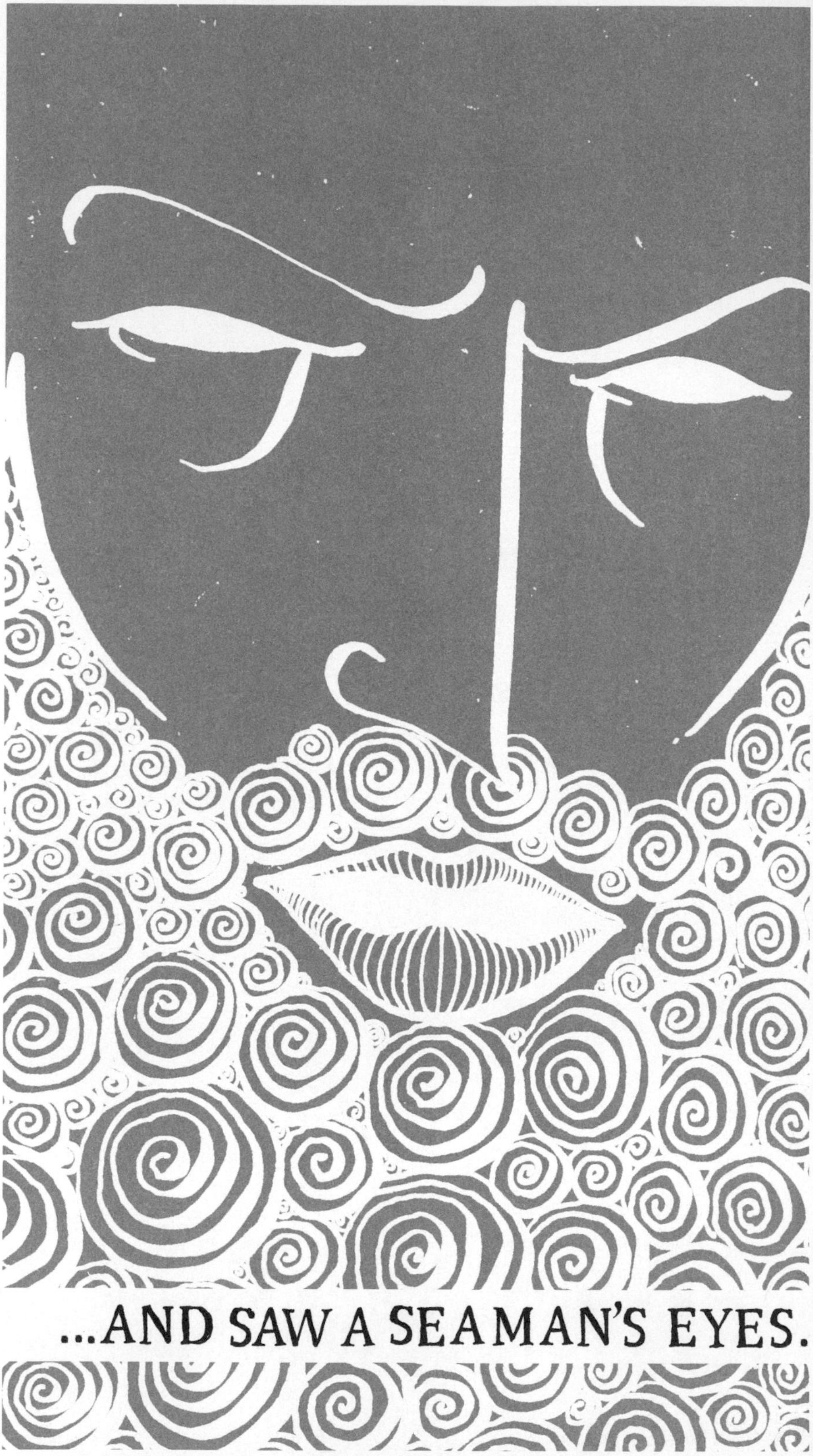
...AND SAW A SEAMAN'S EYES.

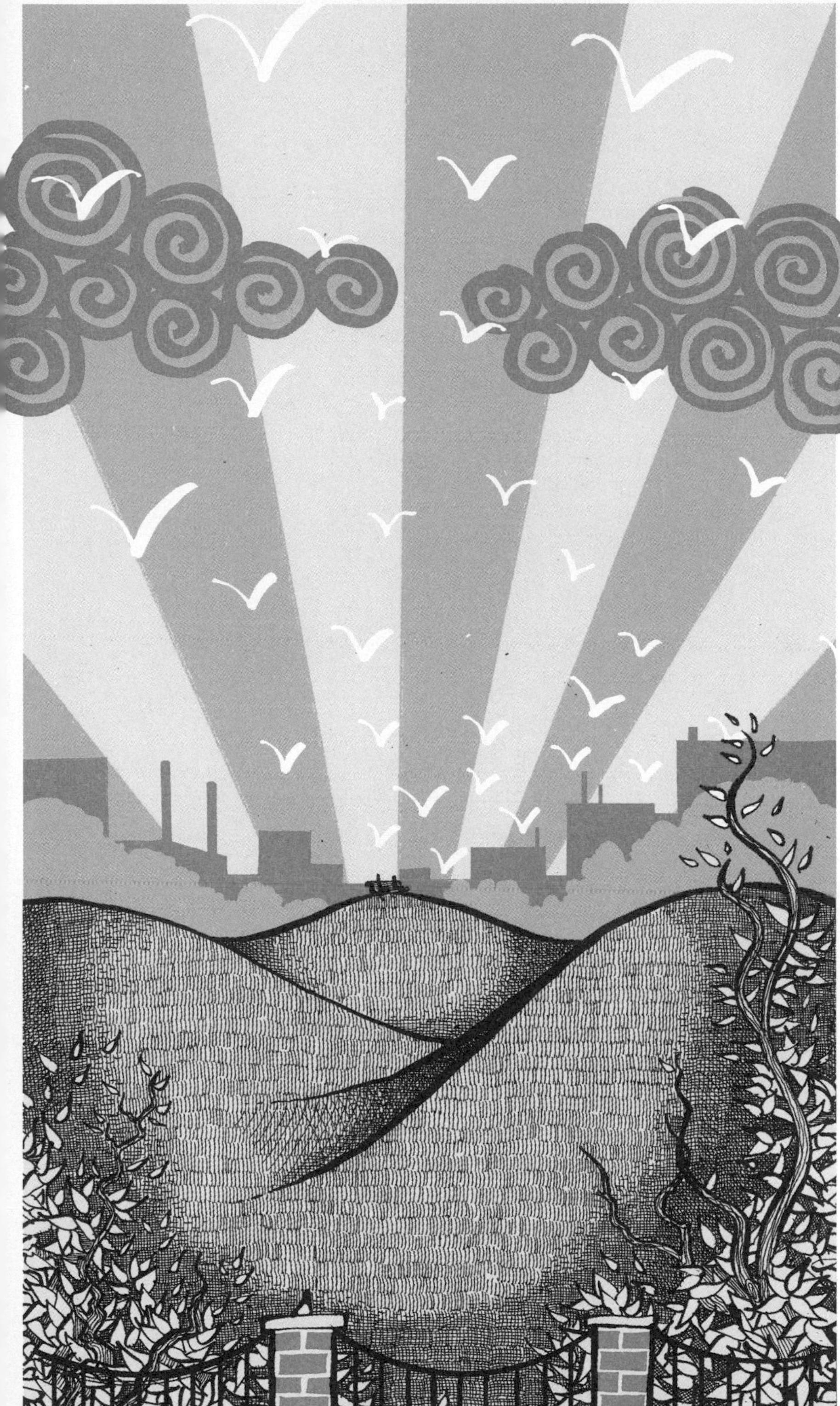

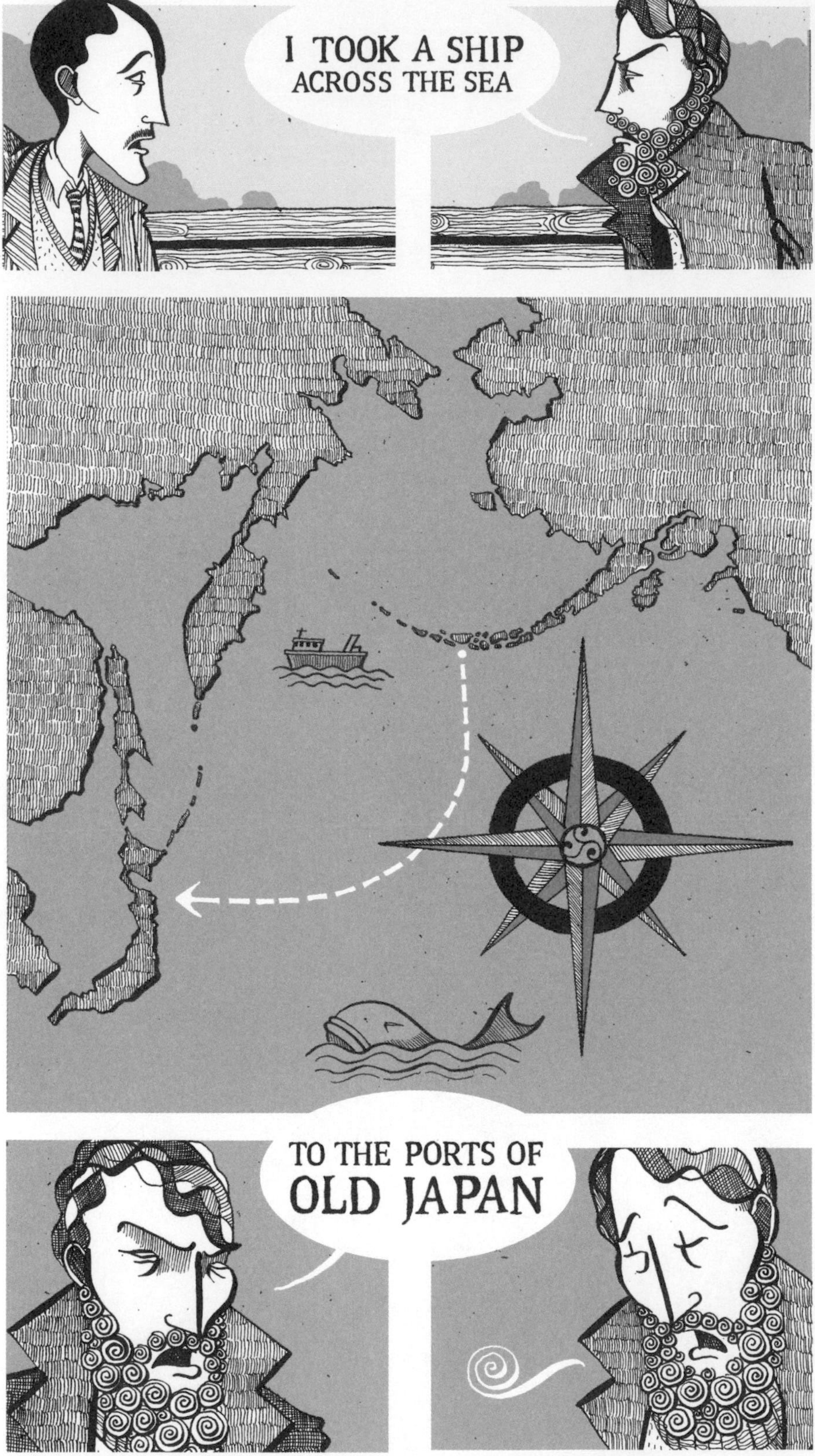
I TOOK A SHIP ACROSS THE SEA
TO THE PORTS OF OLD JAPAN

I BROUGHT MY GUN
AND SCRIMSHAW TOOLS...

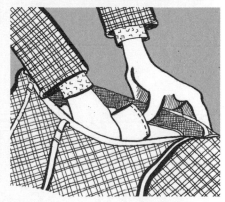

...INTEGRAL
TO MY PLAN.

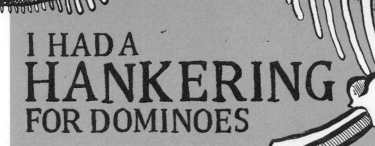

I HAD A
HANKERING
FOR DOMINOES

...MADE OF WHALEBONE

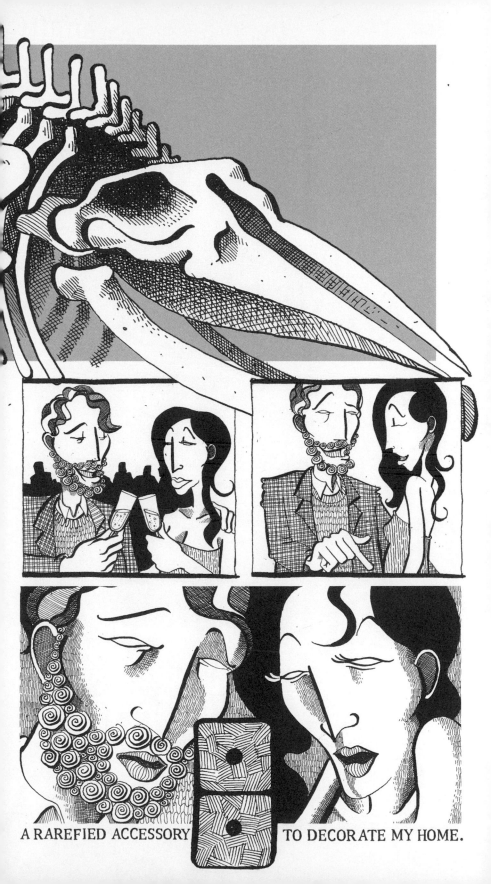

A RAREFIED ACCESSORY TO DECORATE MY HOME.

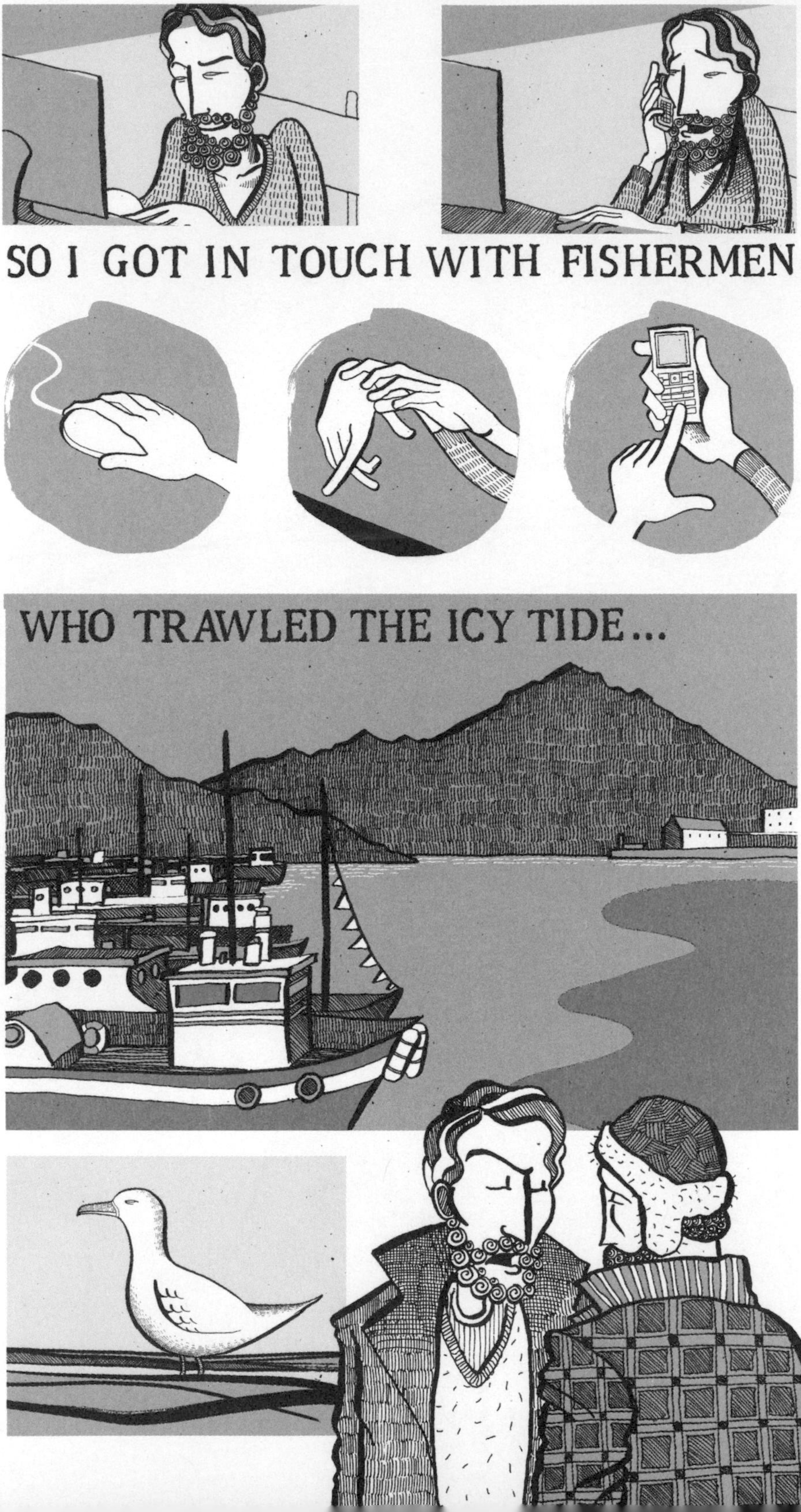
SO I GOT IN TOUCH WITH FISHERMEN
WHO TRAWLED THE ICY TIDE...

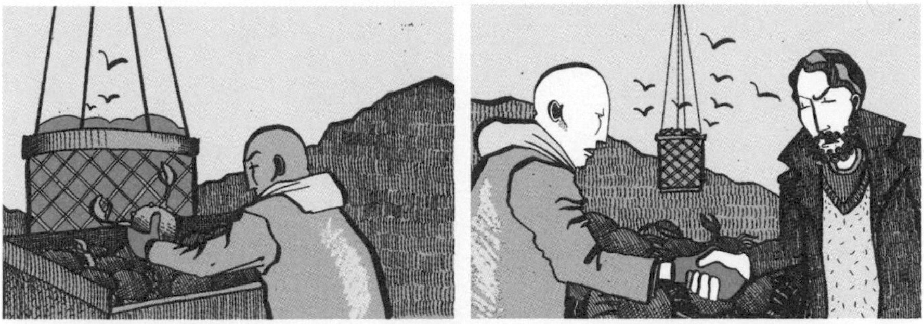

... AND DISCREETLY PROBED THEIR INTEREST

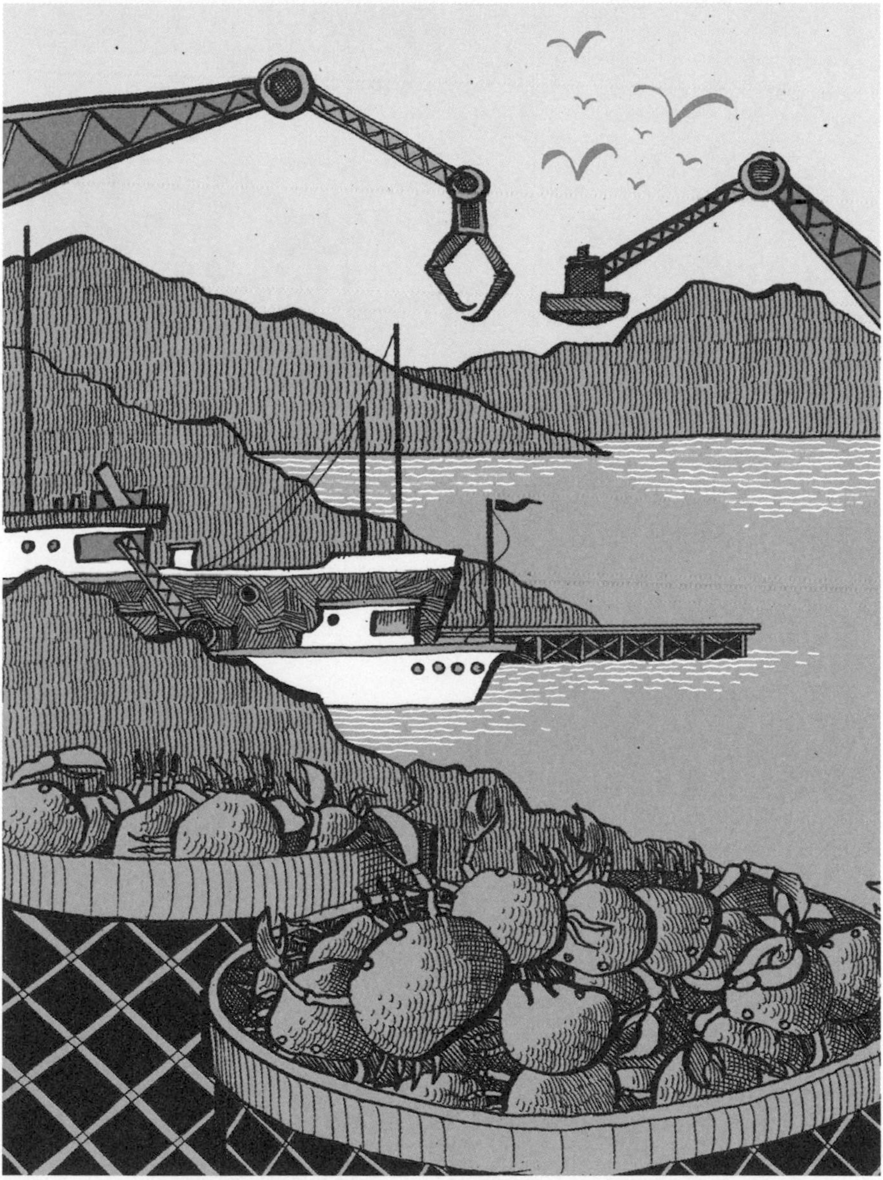

... IN MAKING MONEY ON THE SIDE.

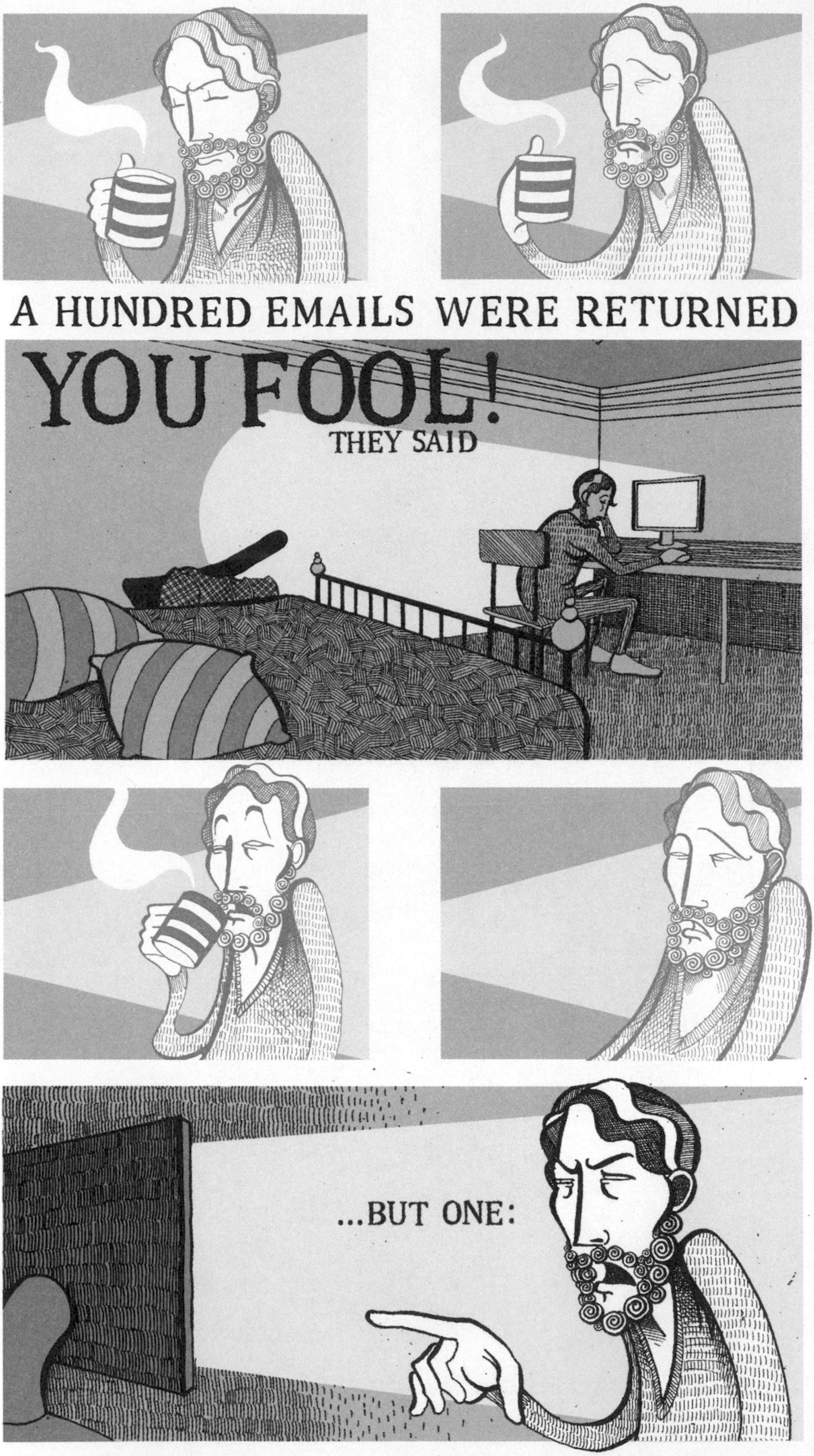
A HUNDRED EMAILS WERE RETURNED
YOU FOOL!
THEY SAID
...BUT ONE:

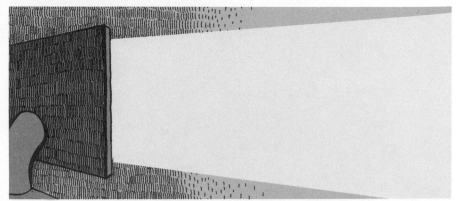

HIS SHIP WAS DUE TO LEAVE THAT DAY...

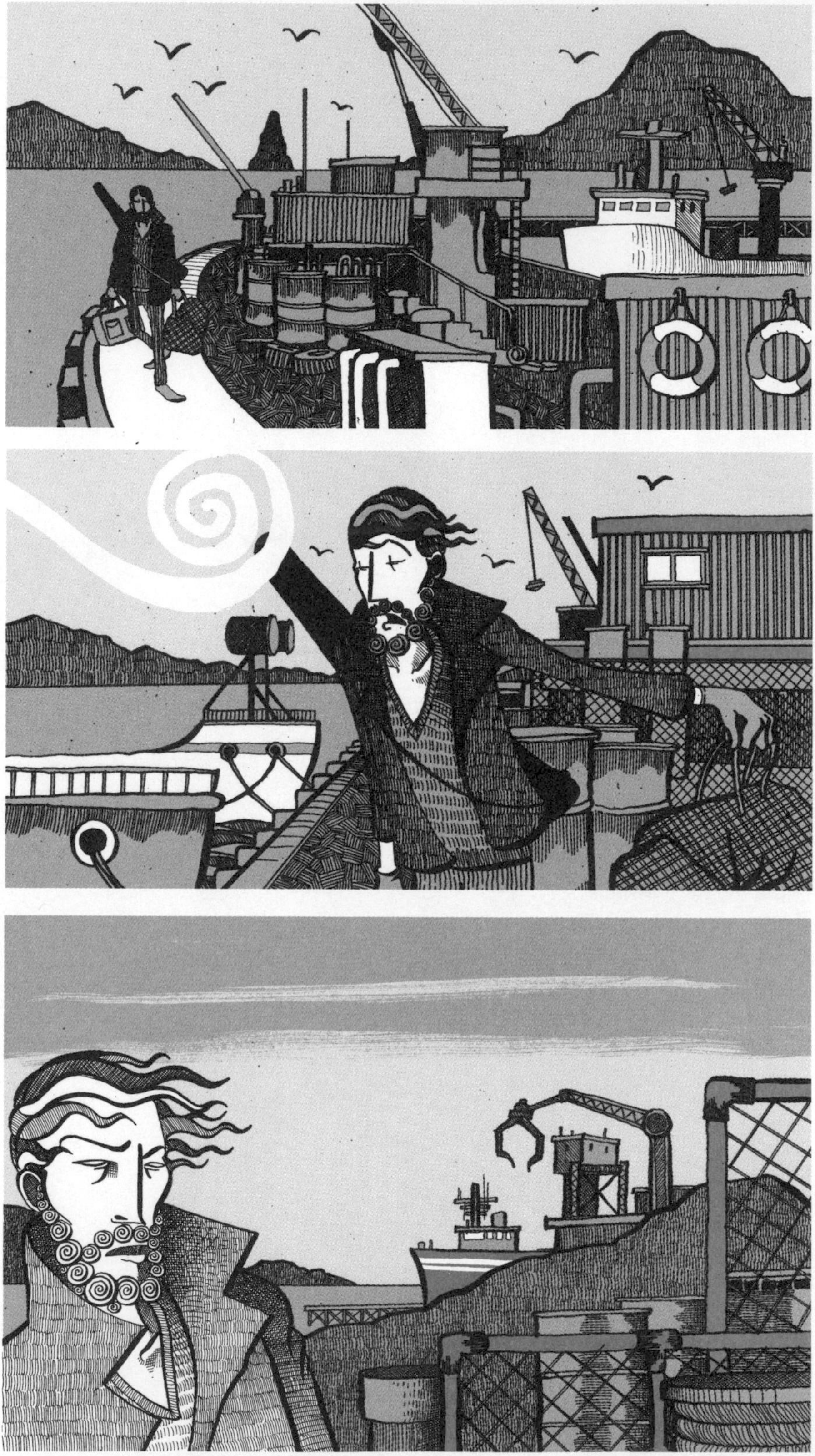

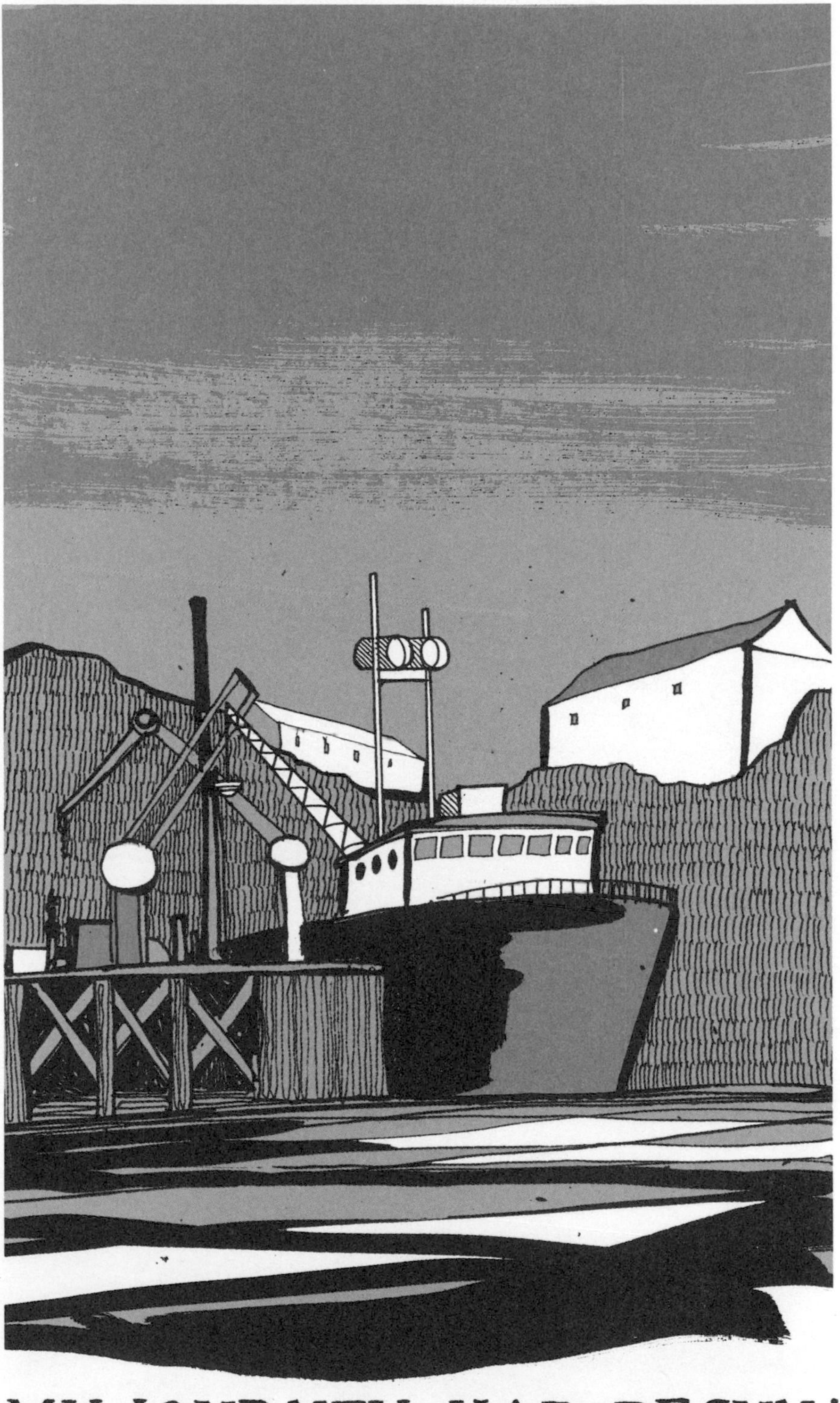

MY JOURNEY HAD BEGUN!

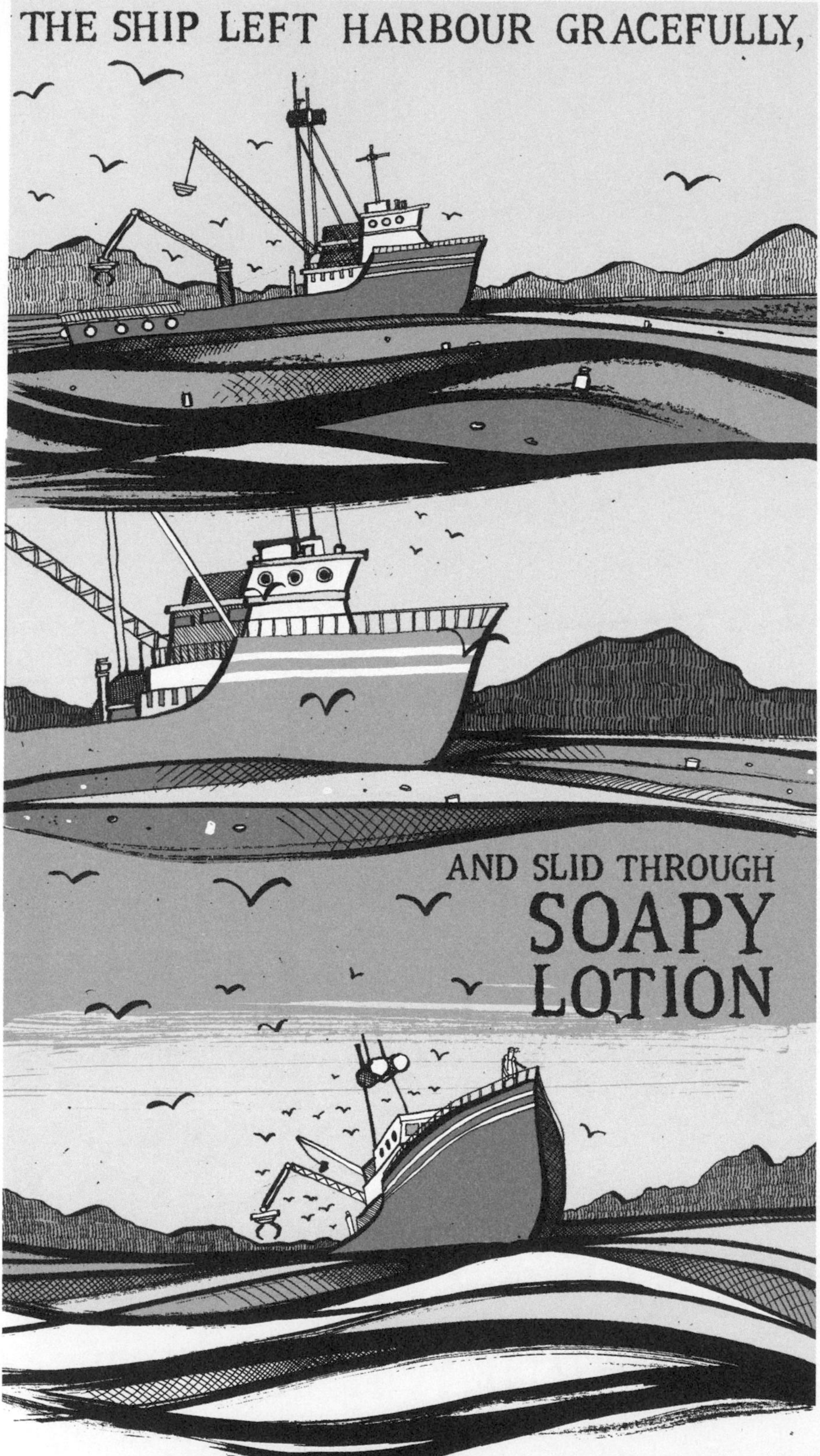
THE SHIP LEFT HARBOUR GRACEFULLY,
AND SLID THROUGH
SOAPY
LOTION

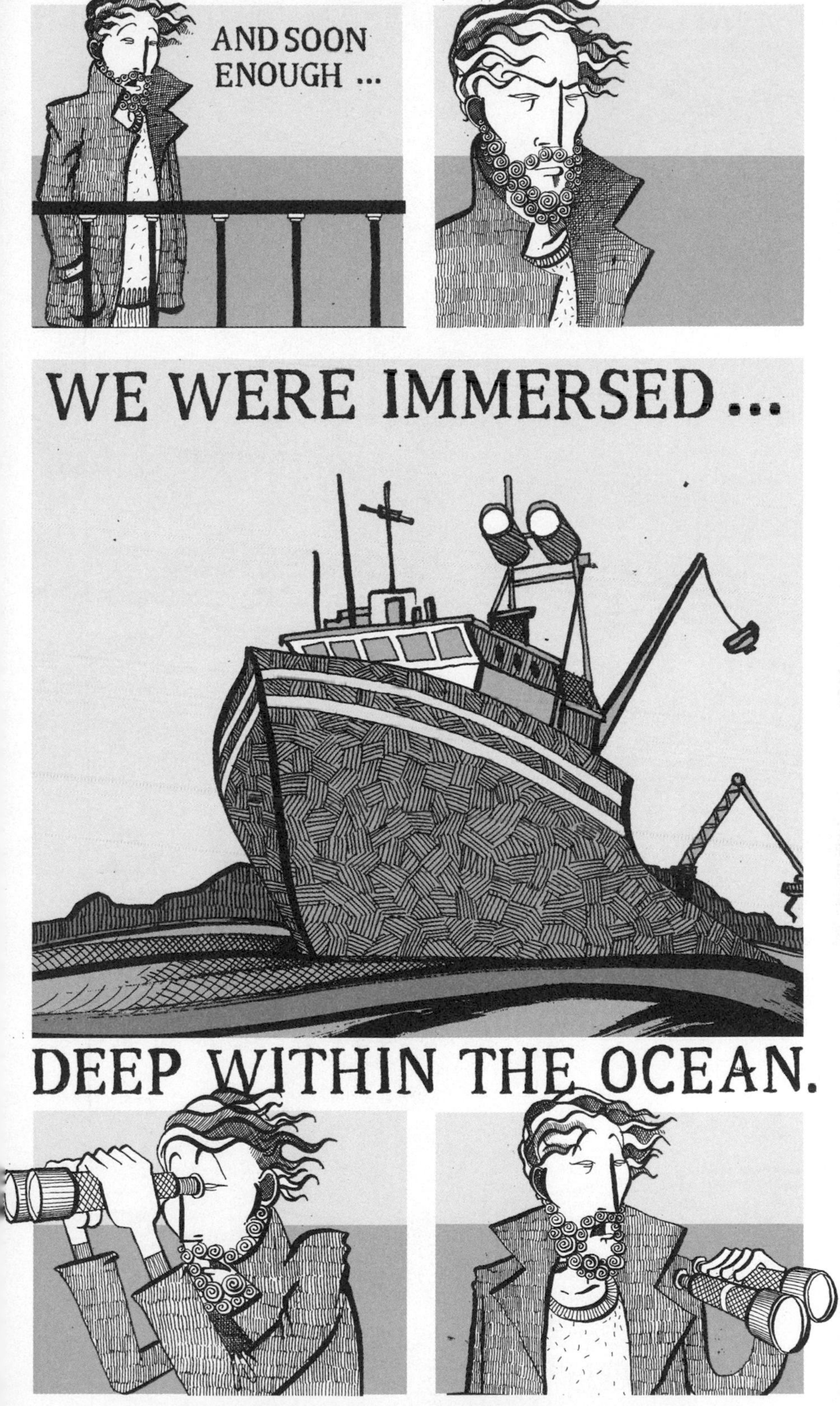
AND SOON ENOUGH ...
WE WERE IMMERSED ...
DEEP WITHIN THE OCEAN.

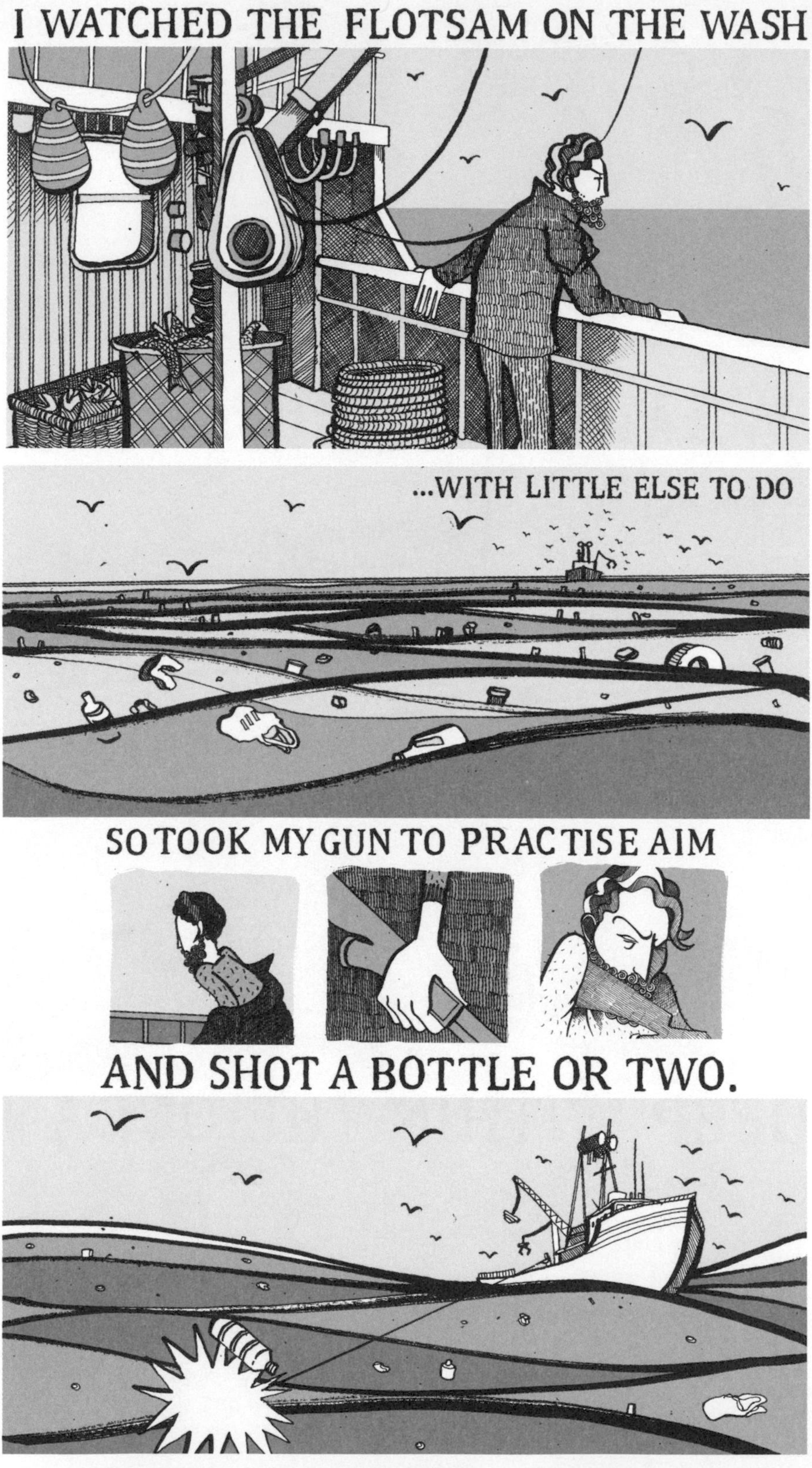
I WATCHED THE FLOTSAM ON THE WASH
...WITH LITTLE ELSE TO DO
SO TOOK MY GUN TO PRACTISE AIM
AND SHOT A BOTTLE OR TWO.

BUT SHOOTING PLASTIC SITTING DUCKS

SOON FAILED TO ENTERTAIN;

I LOWERED MY GUN ...AND SAW A BIRD...

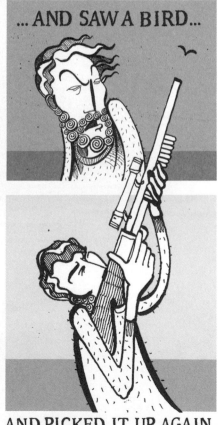

AND PICKED IT UP AGAIN.

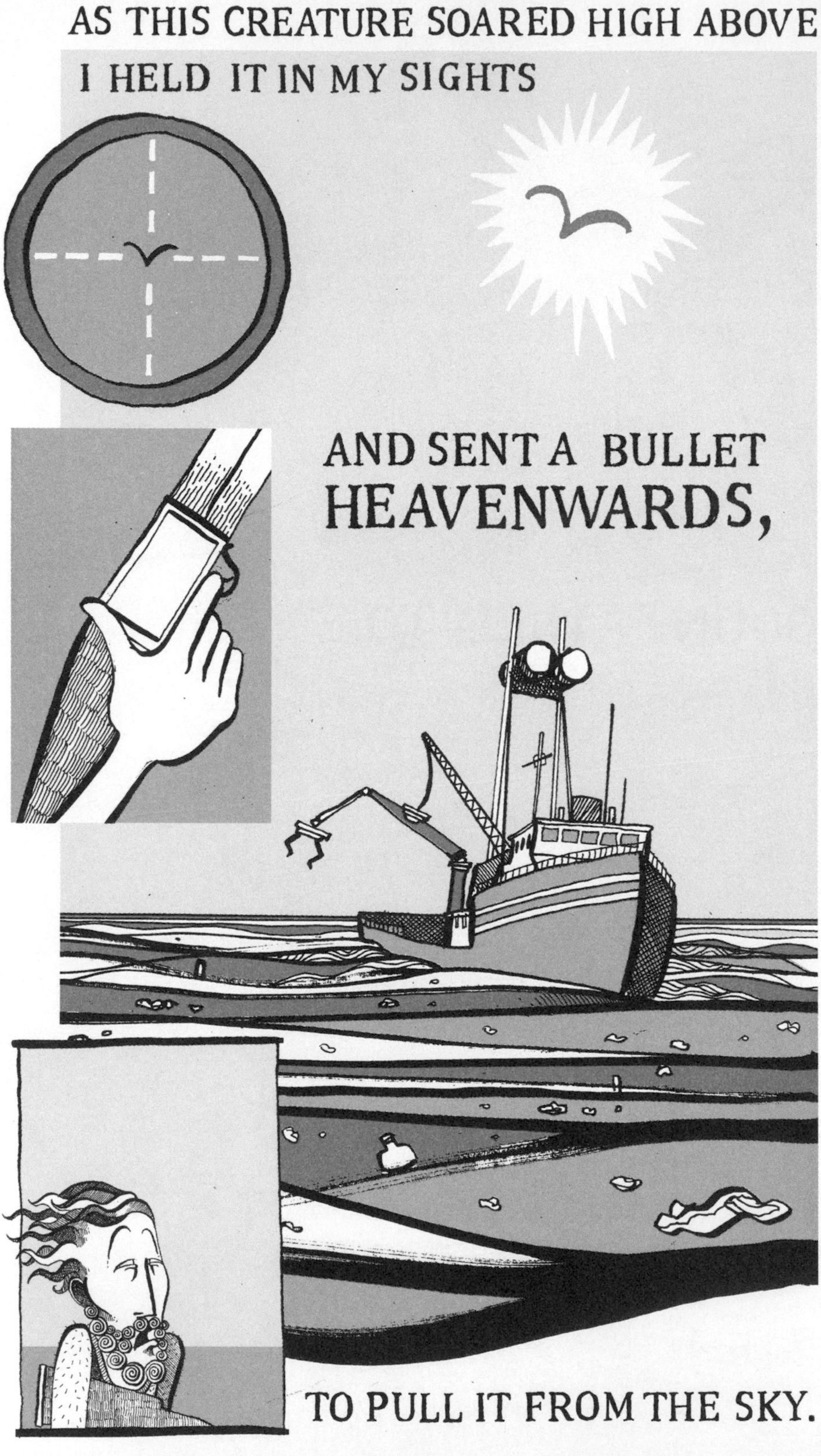
AS THIS CREATURE SOARED HIGH ABOVE
I HELD IT IN MY SIGHTS
AND SENT A BULLET HEAVENWARDS,
TO PULL IT FROM THE SKY.

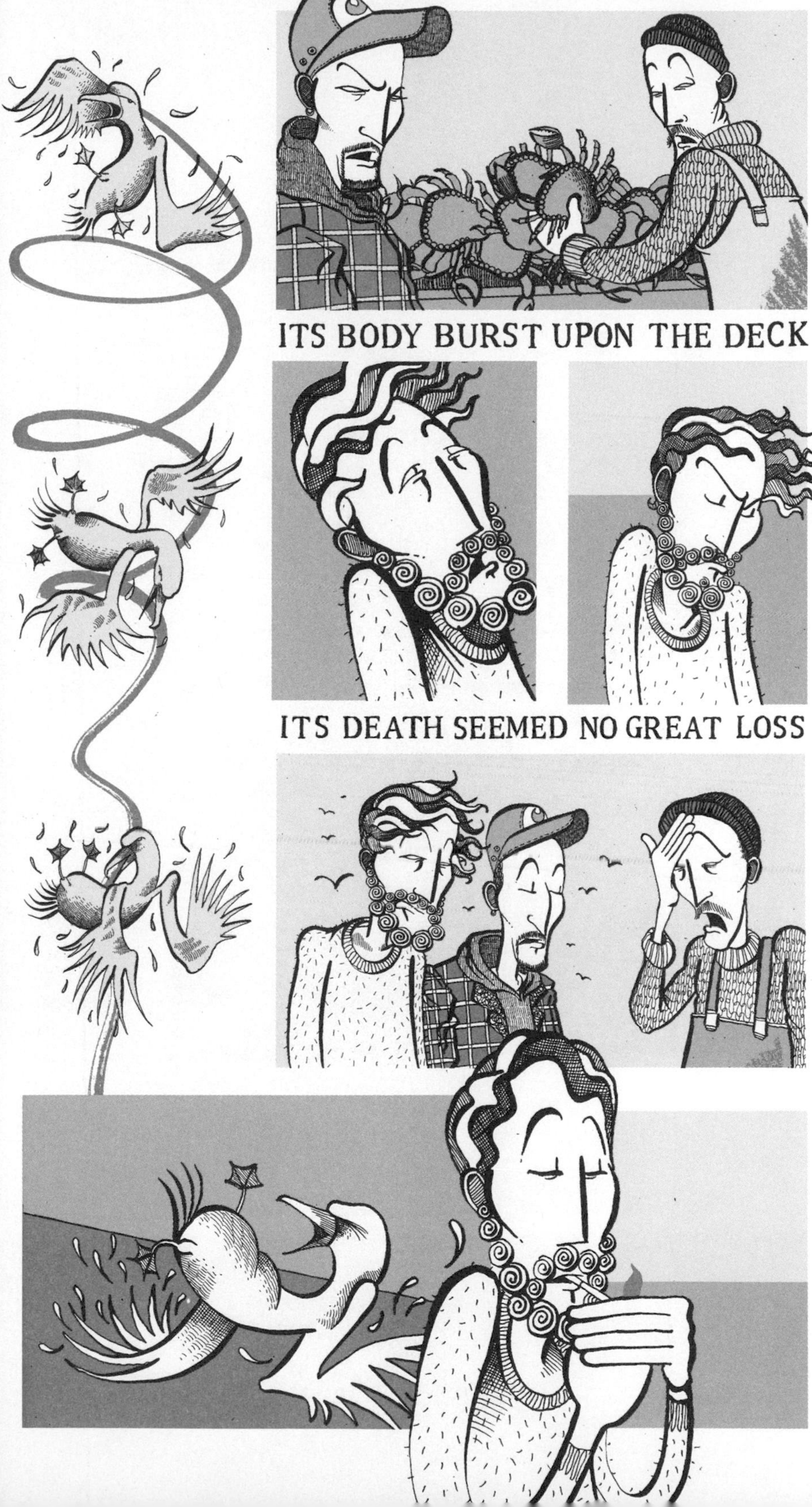
ITS BODY BURST UPON THE DECK
ITS DEATH SEEMED NO GREAT LOSS

IT LOOKED AS OLD AS TIME ITSELF

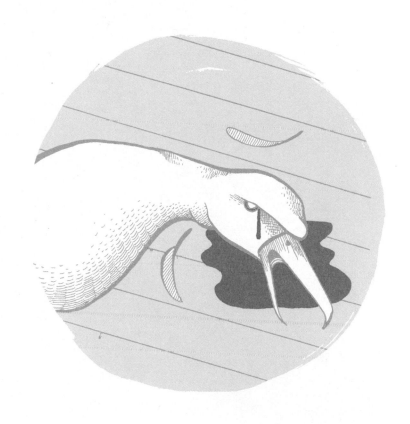

...IT WAS JUST AN ALBATROSS.

PART TWO

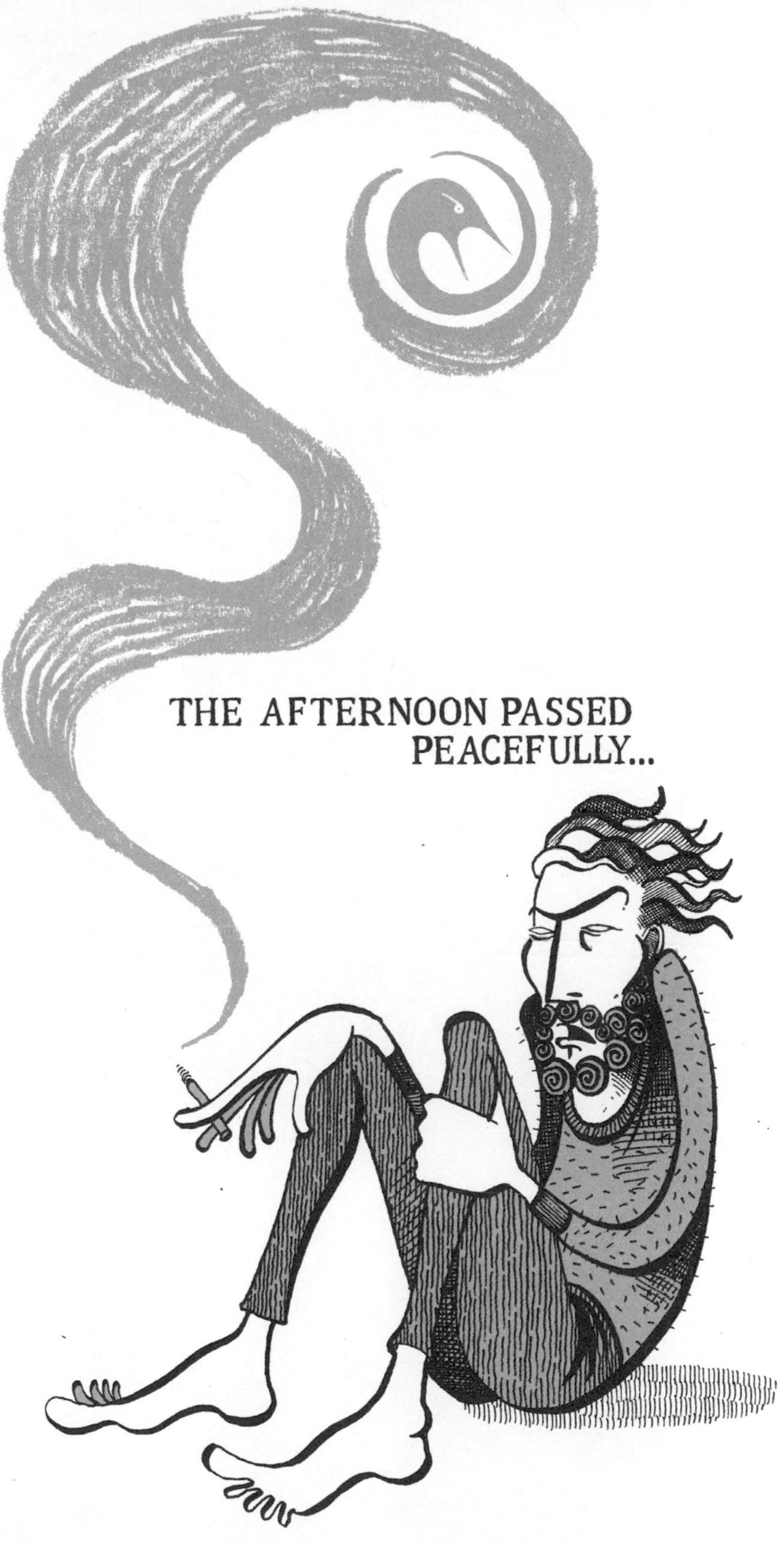
THE AFTERNOON PASSED PEACEFULLY...

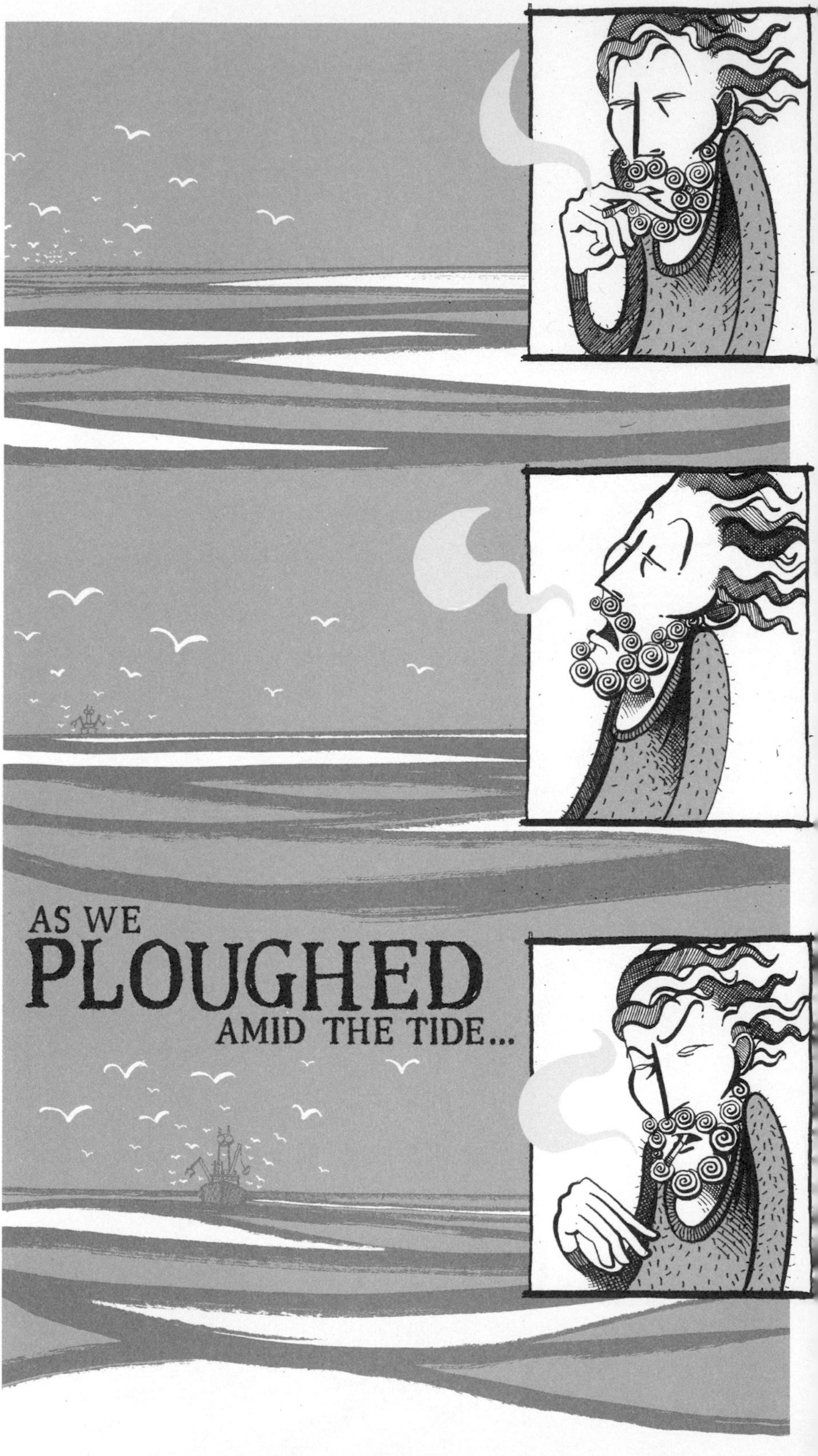
AS WE
PLOUGHED
AMID THE TIDE...

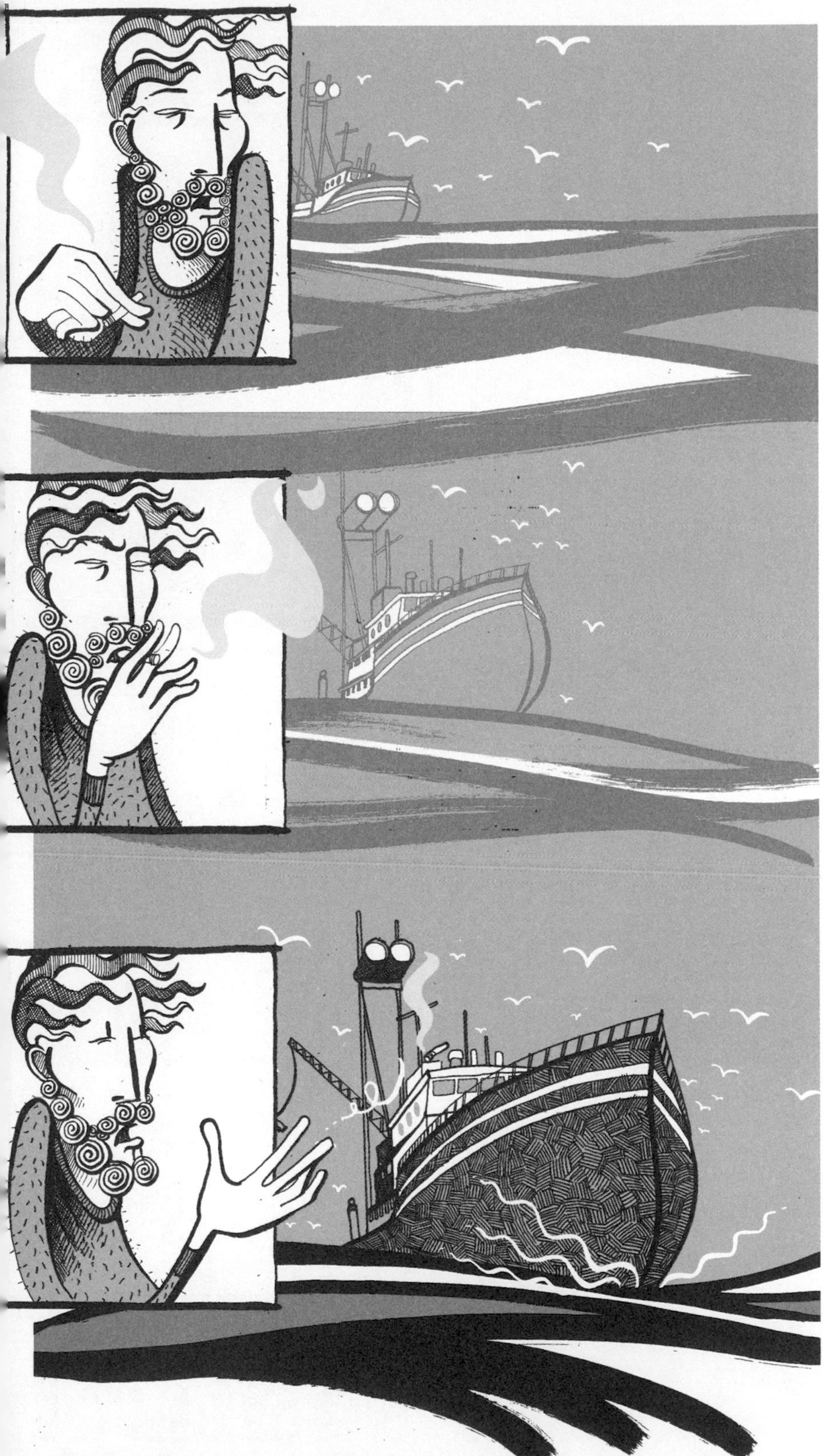

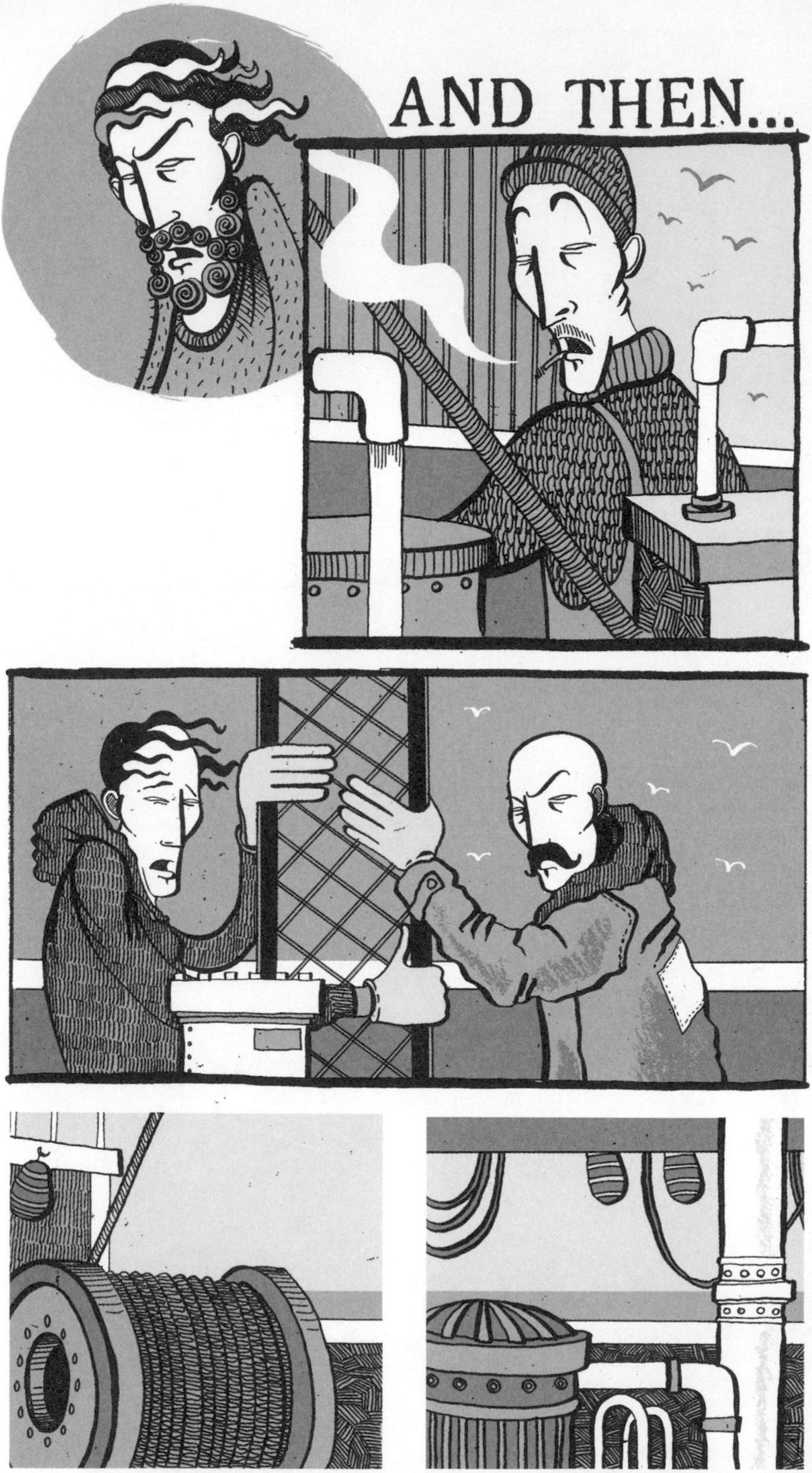
AND THEN...

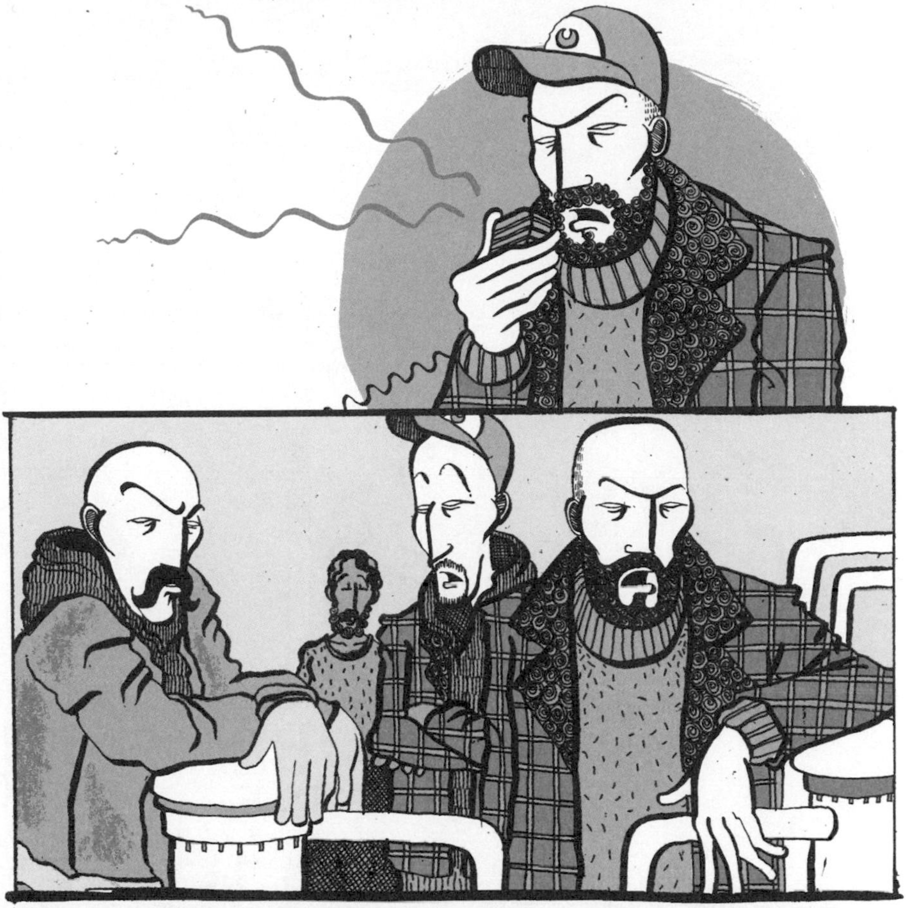

QUITE INEXPLICABLY...

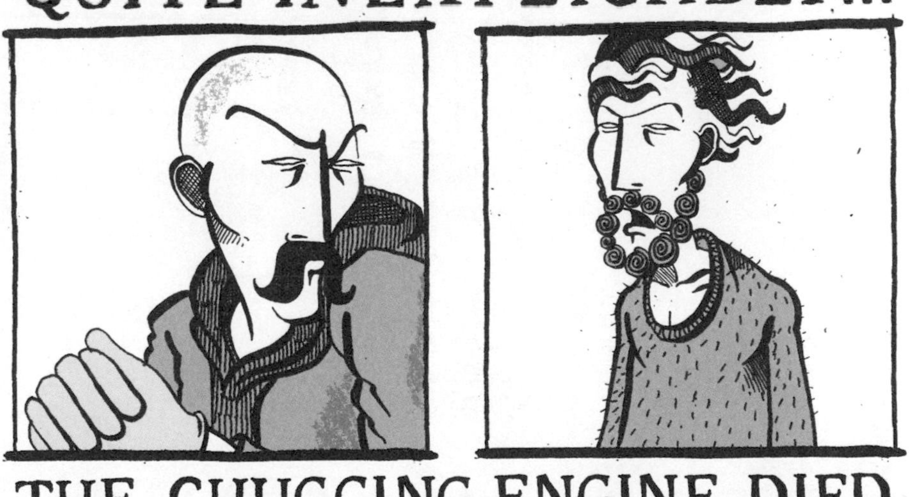

THE CHUGGING ENGINE DIED.

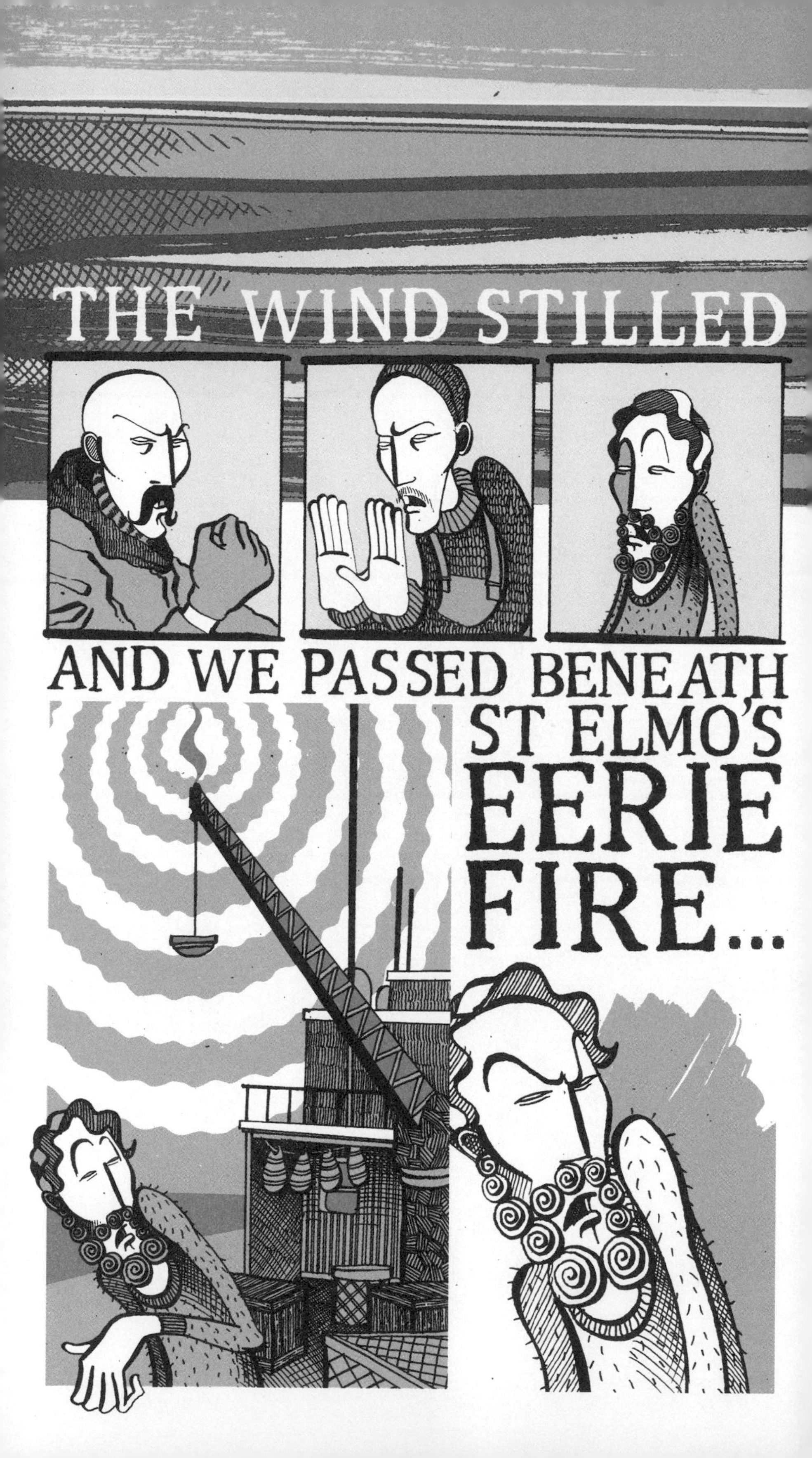
THE WIND STILLED
AND WE PASSED BENEATH
ST ELMO'S
EERIE
FIRE...

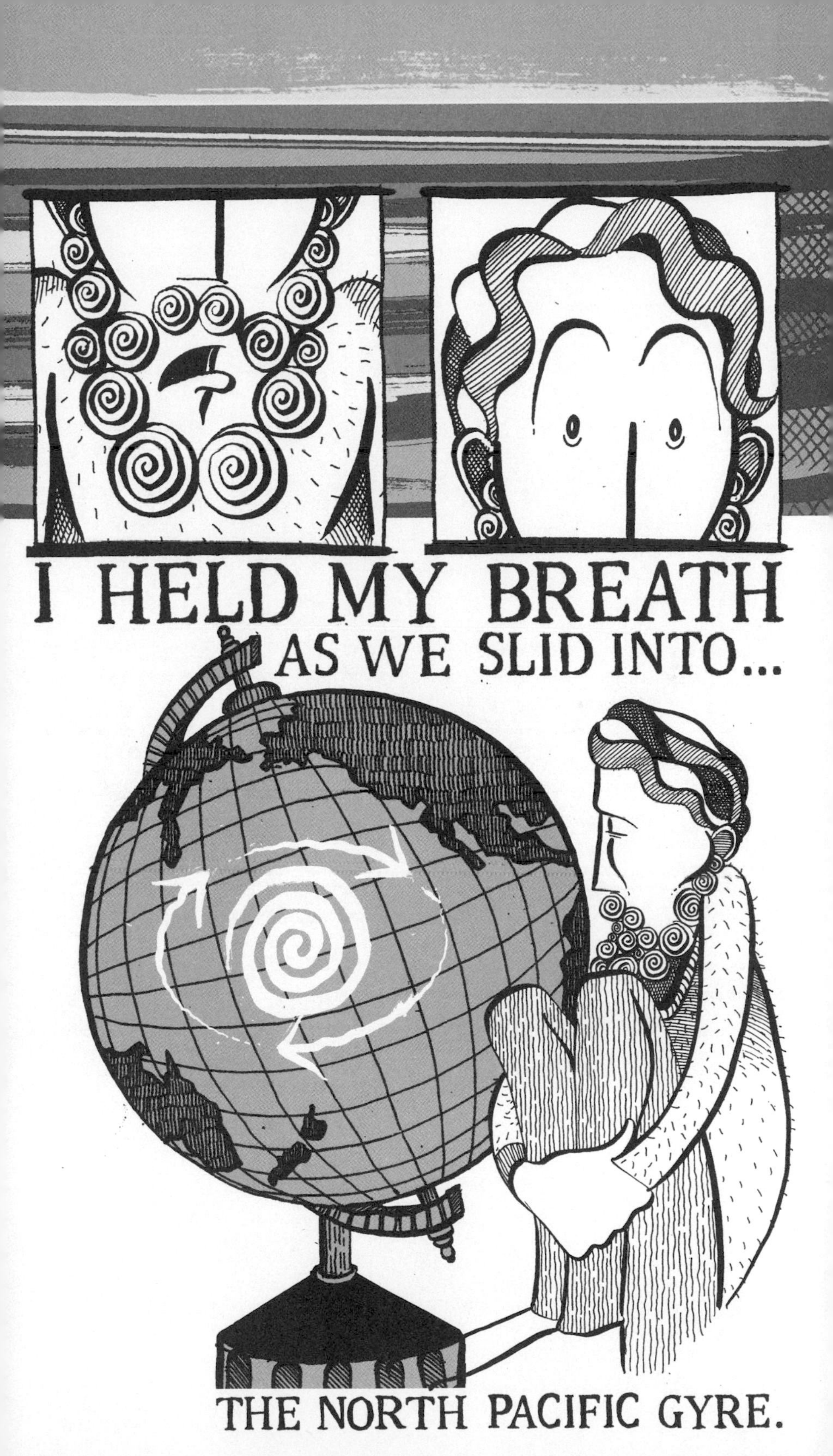
I HELD MY BREATH
AS WE SLID INTO...
THE NORTH PACIFIC GYRE.

A DESERT
OF SUBTROPIC BRINE,

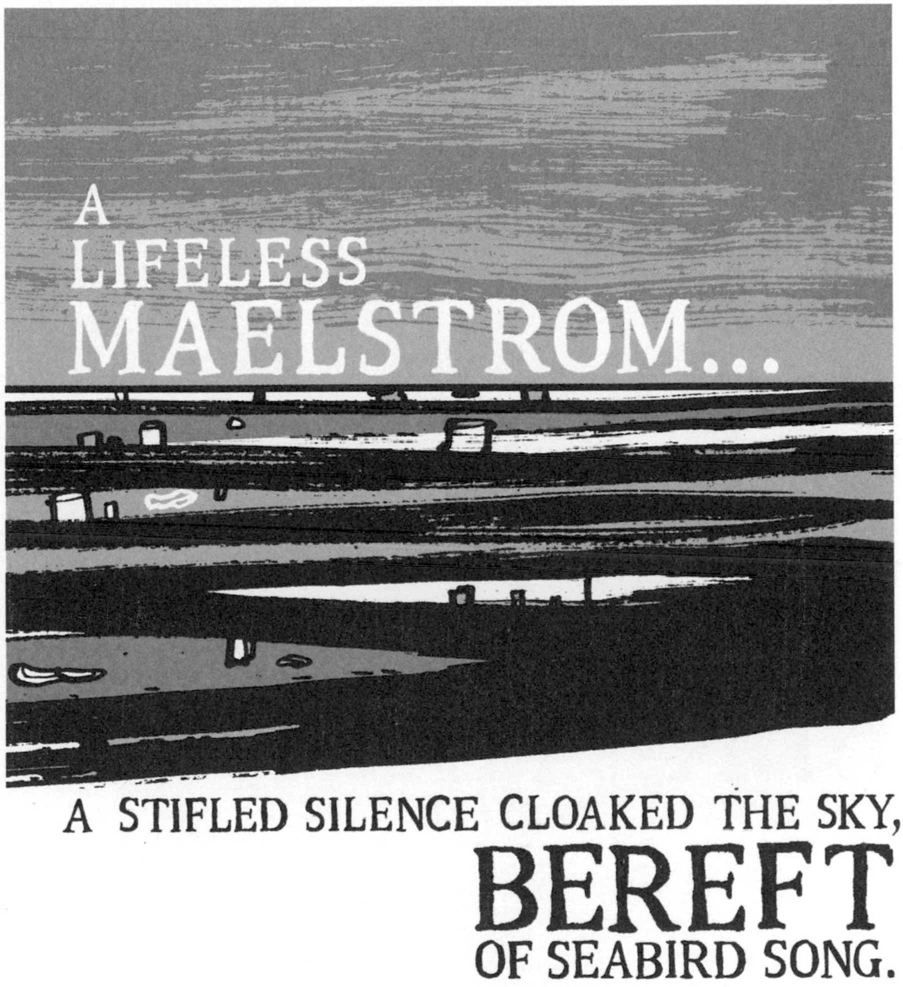
A LIFELESS MAELSTROM...

A STIFLED SILENCE CLOAKED THE SKY,
BEREFT
OF SEABIRD SONG.

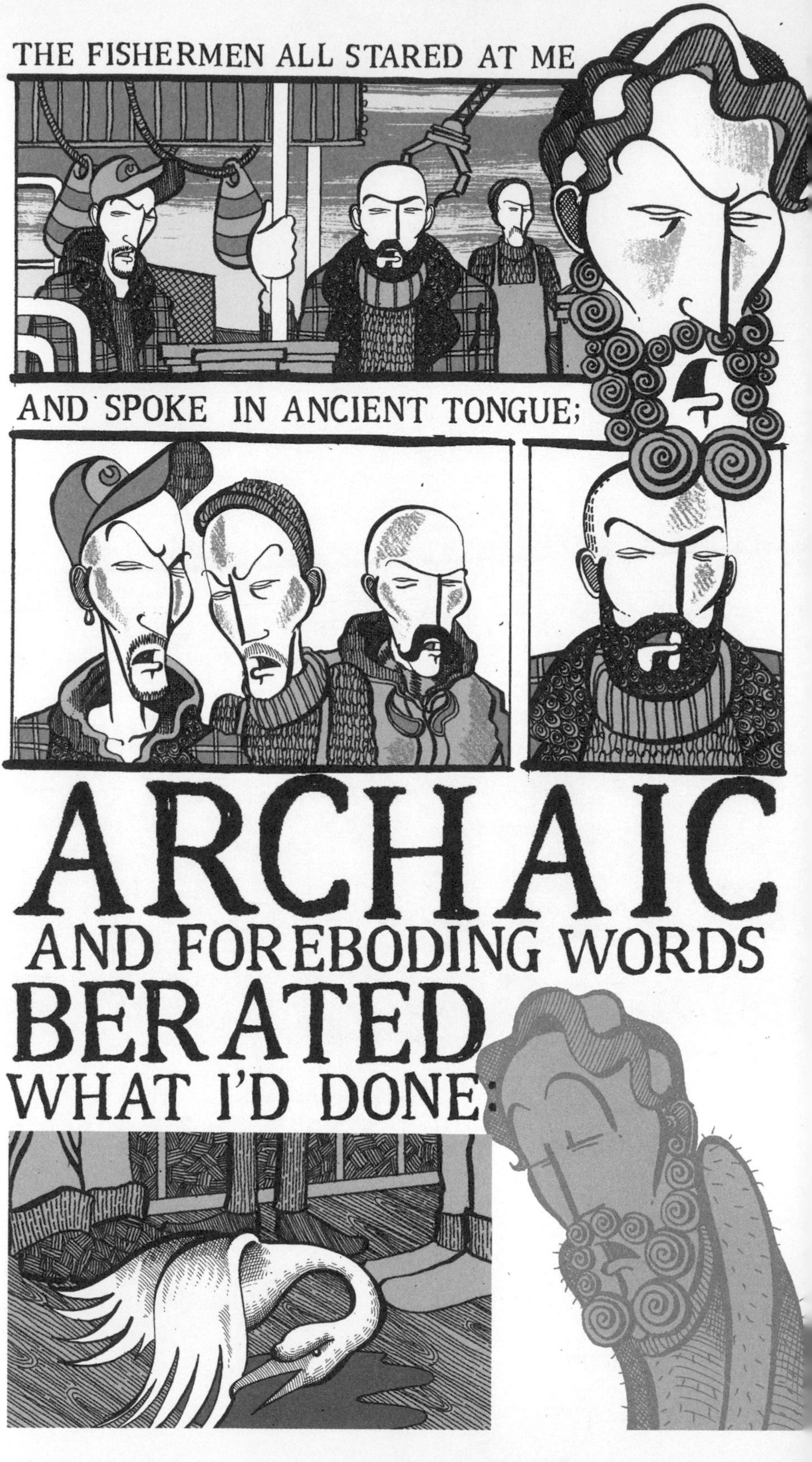
THE FISHERMEN ALL STARED AT ME
AND SPOKE IN ANCIENT TONGUE;
ARCHAIC
AND FOREBODING WORDS
BERATED
WHAT I'D DONE:

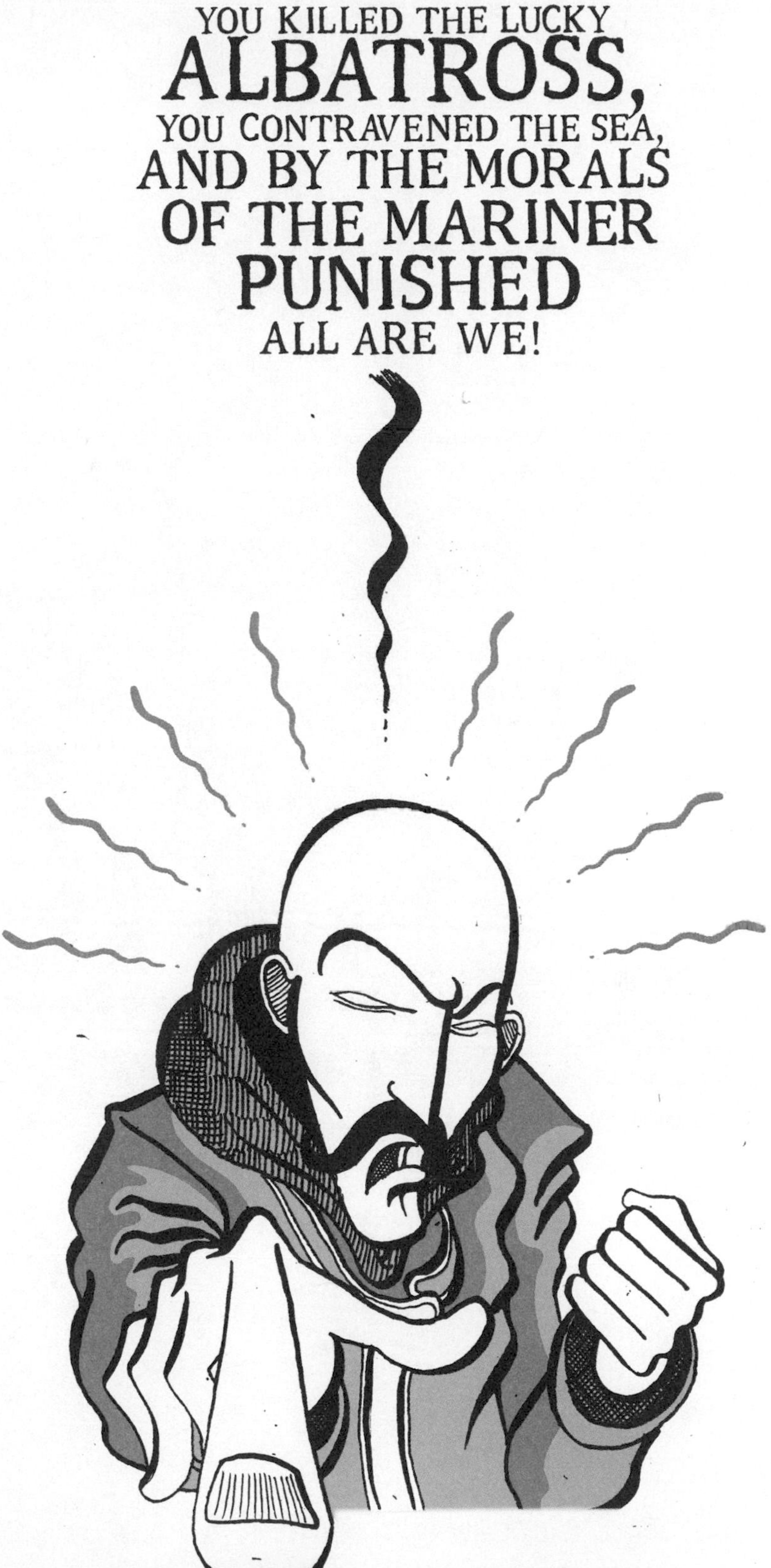
YOU KILLED THE LUCKY
ALBATROSS,
YOU CONTRAVENED THE SEA,
AND BY THE MORALS
OF THE MARINER
PUNISHED
ALL ARE WE!

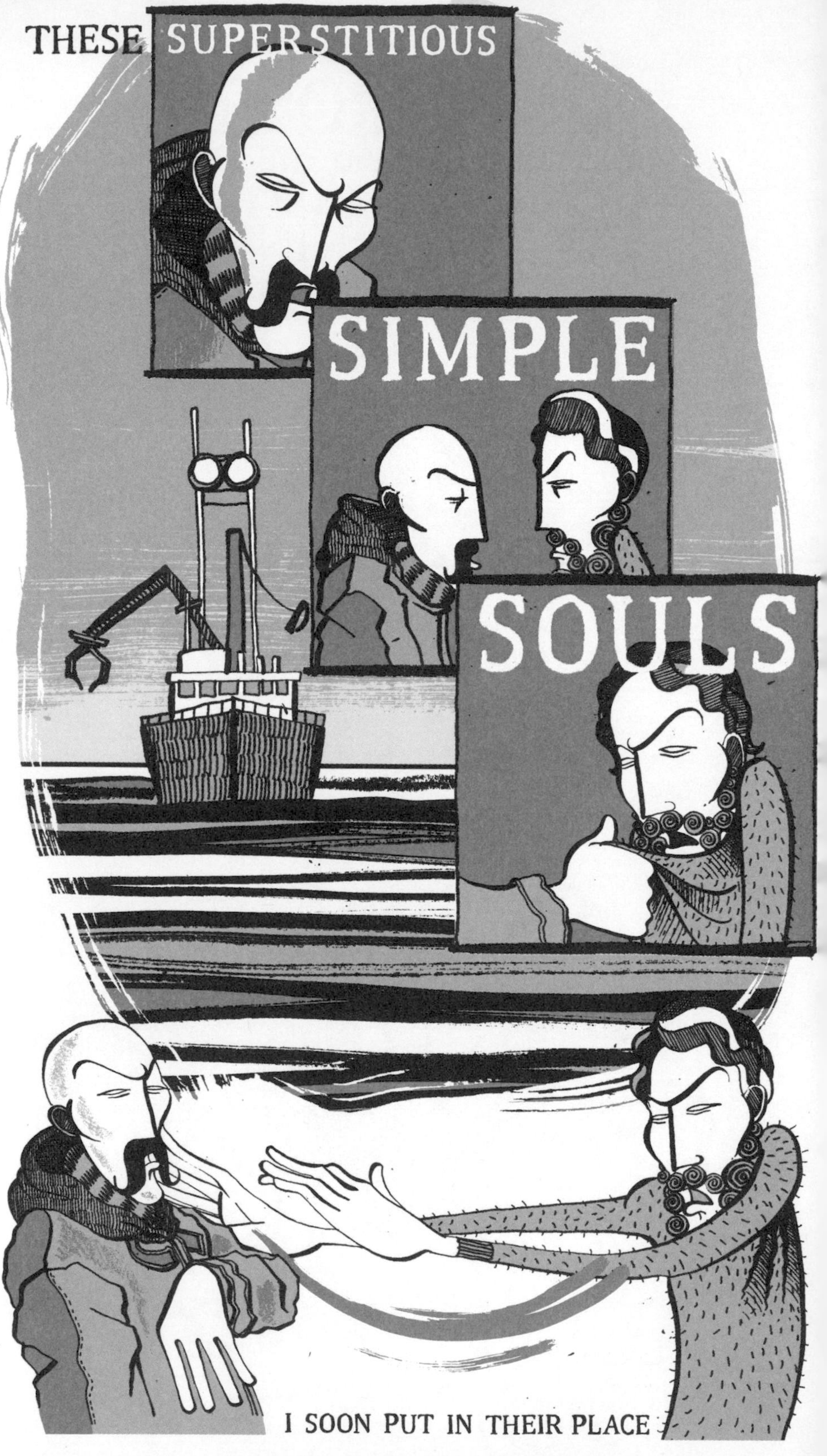
THESE SUPERSTITIOUS
SIMPLE
SOULS
I SOON PUT IN THEIR PLACE

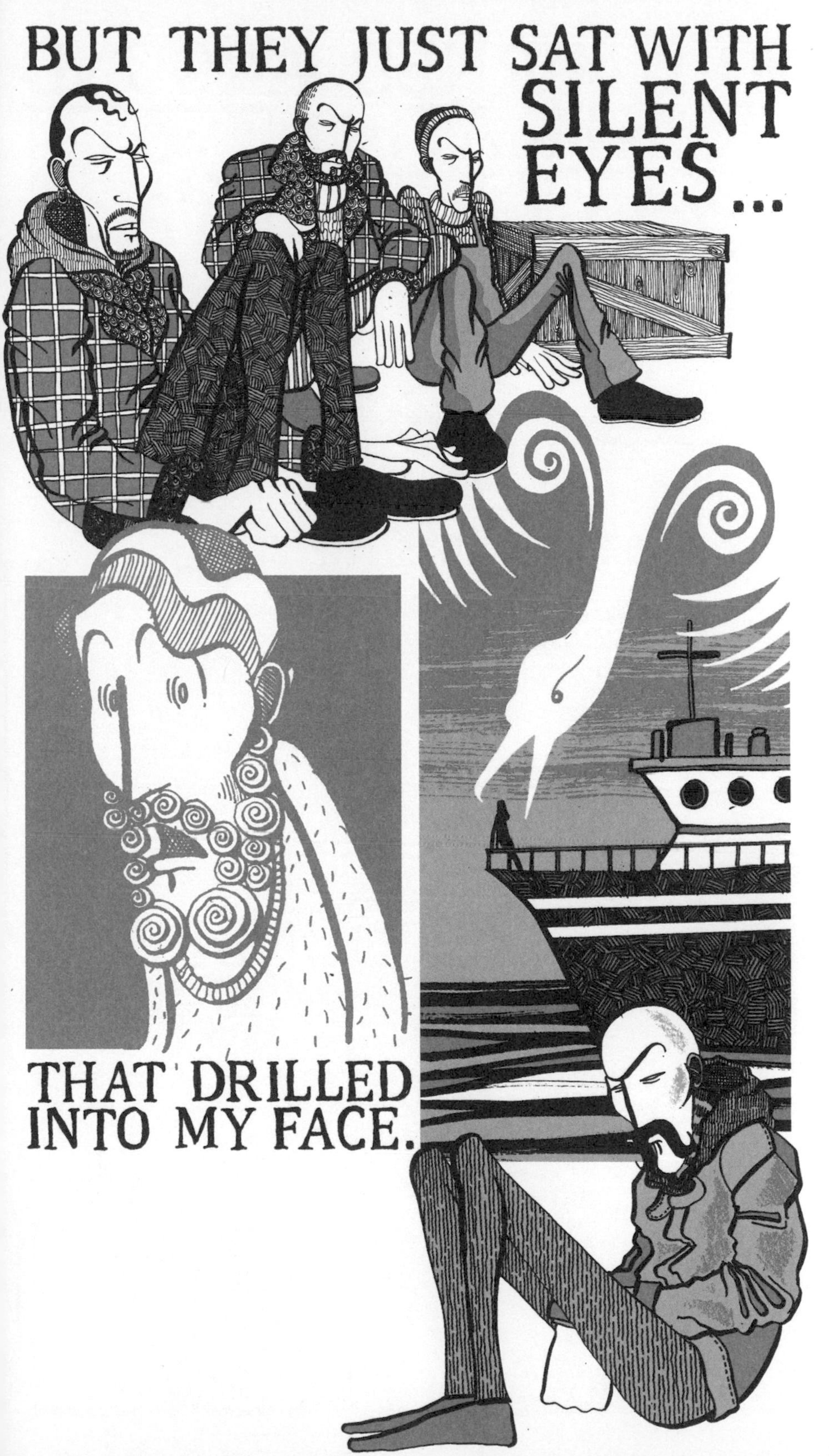
BUT THEY JUST SAT WITH SILENT EYES...
THAT DRILLED INTO MY FACE.

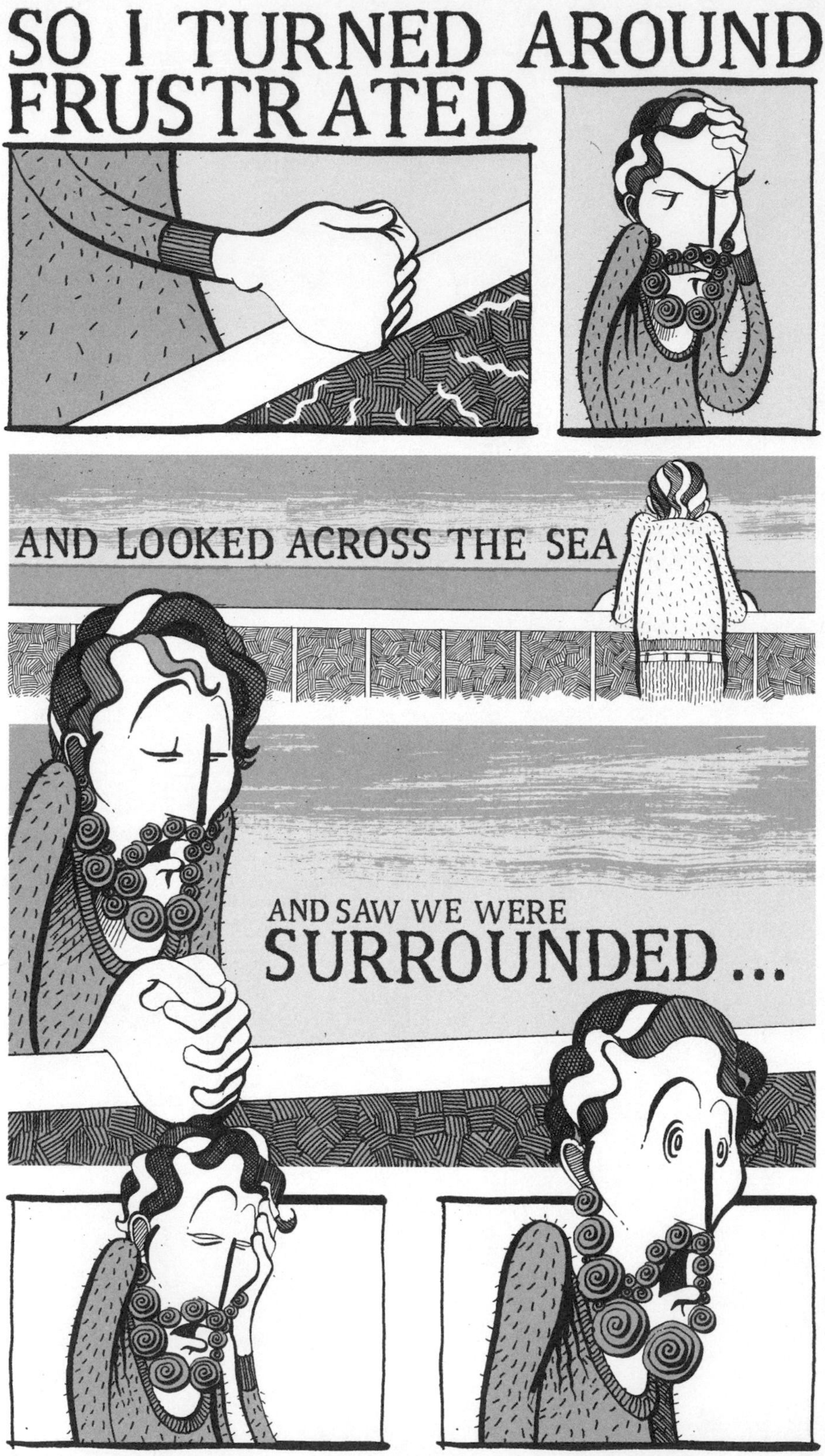
SO I TURNED AROUND FRUSTRATED
AND LOOKED ACROSS THE SEA
AND SAW WE WERE
SURROUNDED...

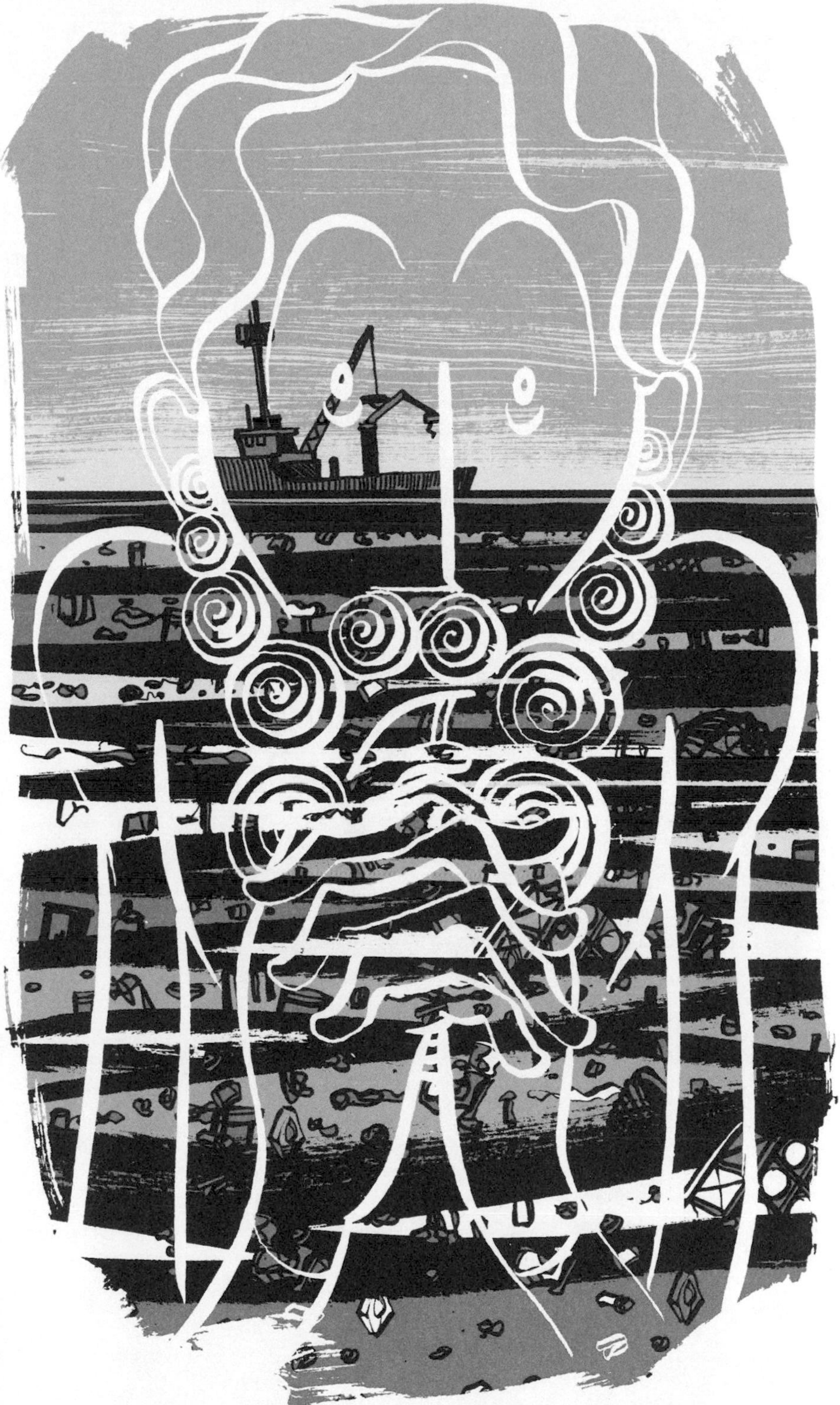

BY A WASH OF POLYTHENE.

SWATHES
OF POLYSTYRENE

BOBBED WITH
TONNES OF

NEOPRENE

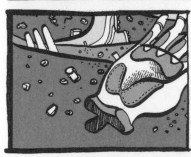

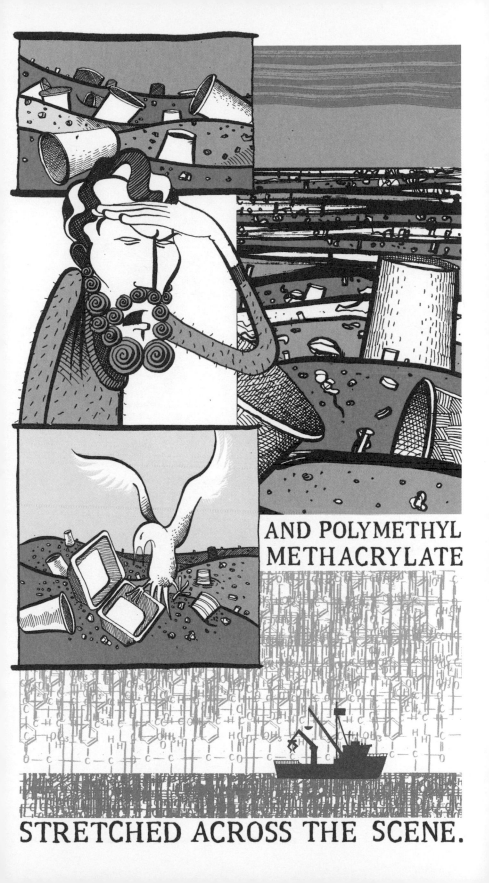

AND POLYMETHYL
METHACRYLATE

STRETCHED ACROSS THE SCENE.

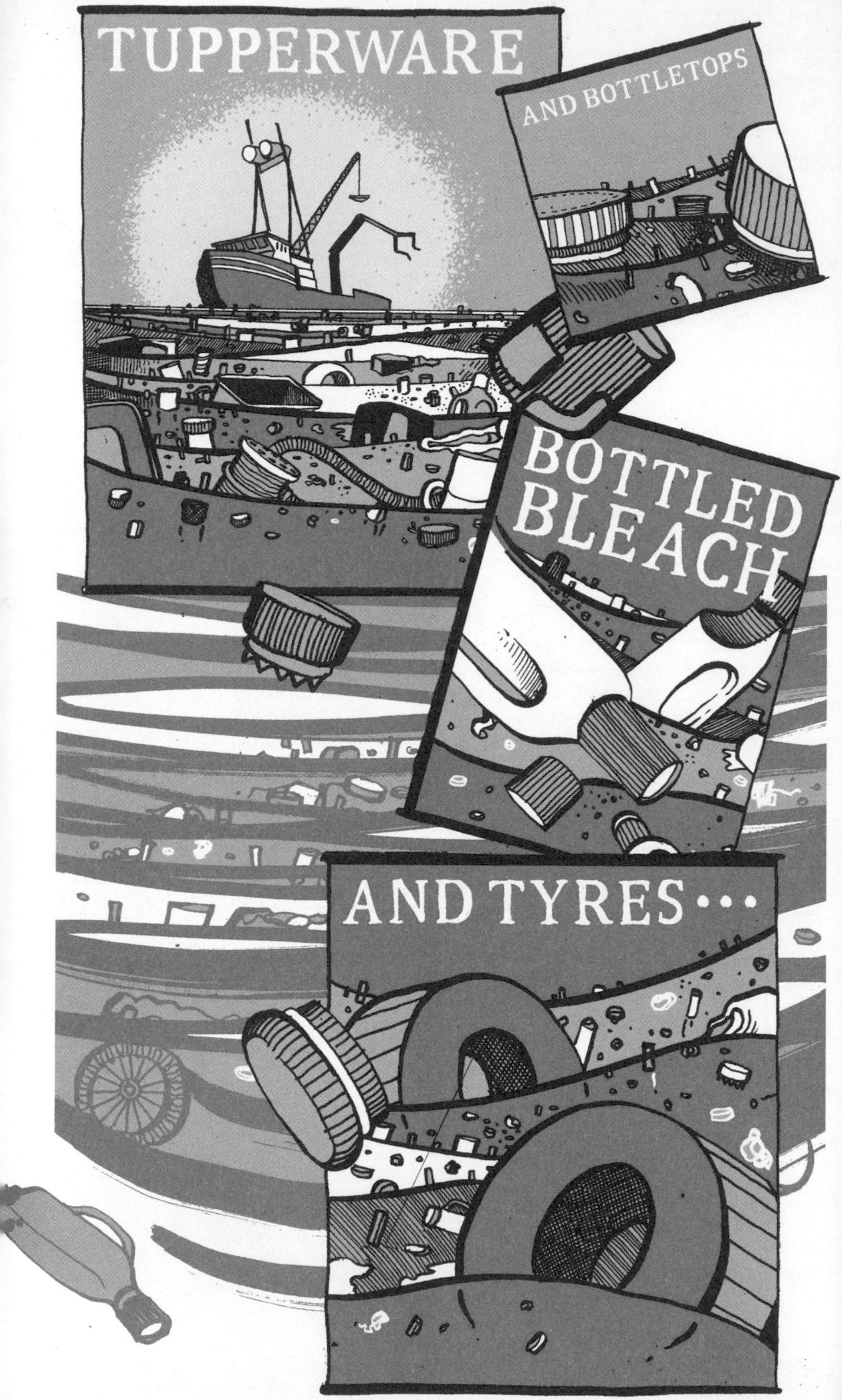
TUPPERWARE
AND BOTTLETOPS
BOTTLED BLEACH
AND TYRES...

THE DETRITUS OF A CARELESS KIND...

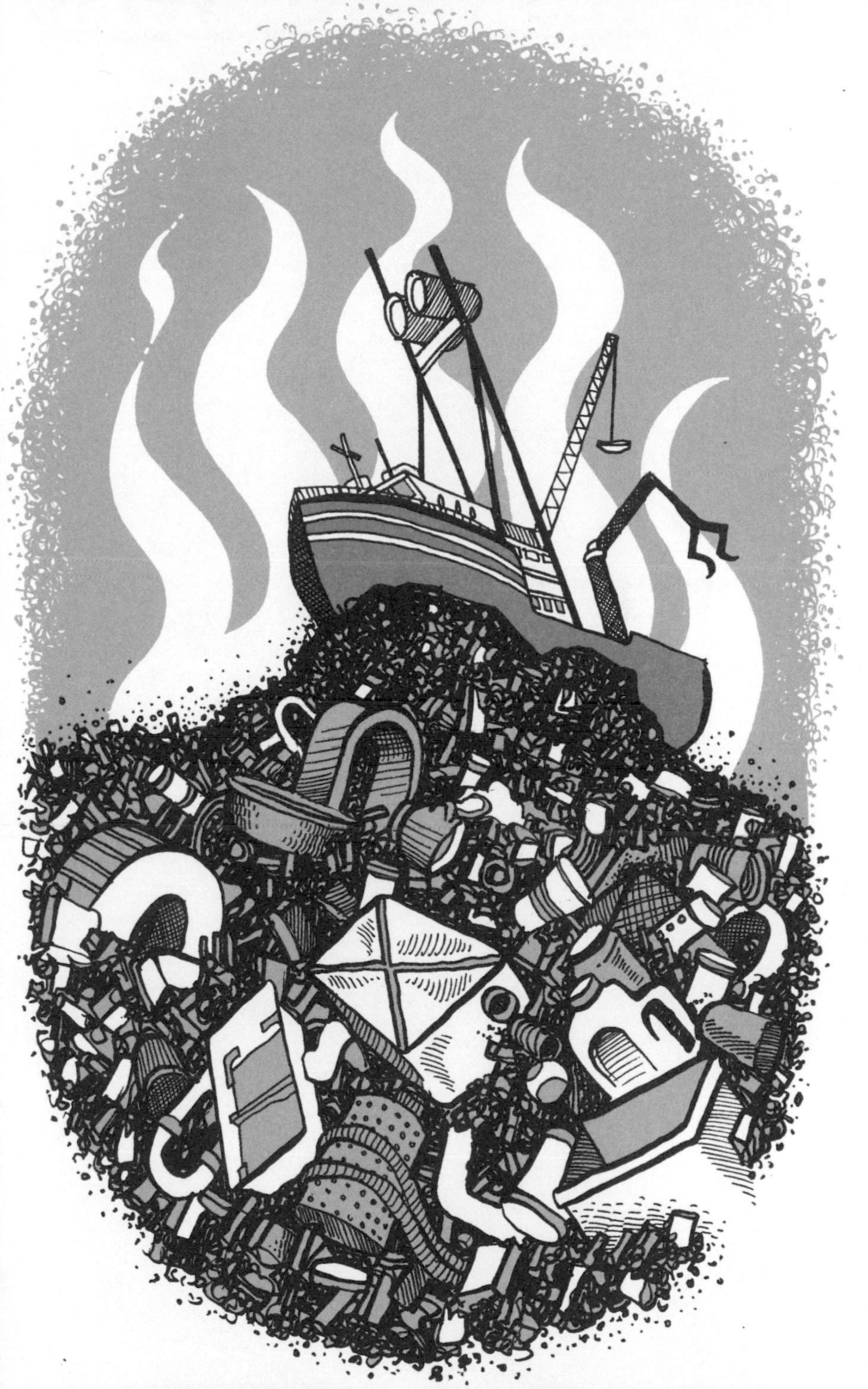

A SCATTERED FUNERAL PYRE.

MY EYES WERE WILD

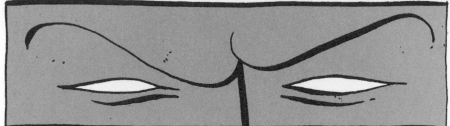

AND WIDE AWAKE

WHILE OTHERS SANK TO SLEEP

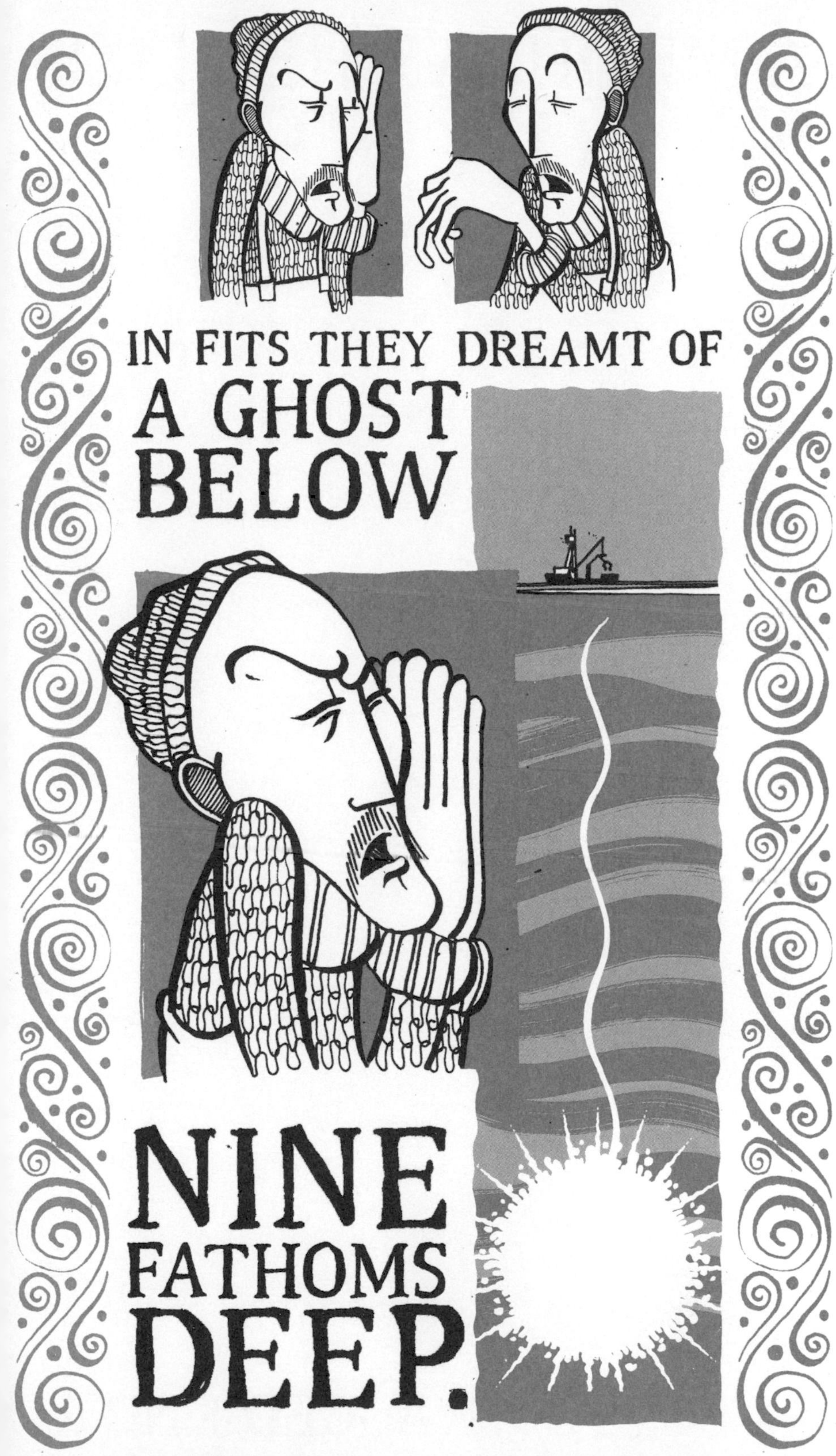
IN FITS THEY DREAMT OF
A GHOST
BELOW
NINE
FATHOMS
DEEP.

A MEDUSA'S HEAD OF NYLON NETS...

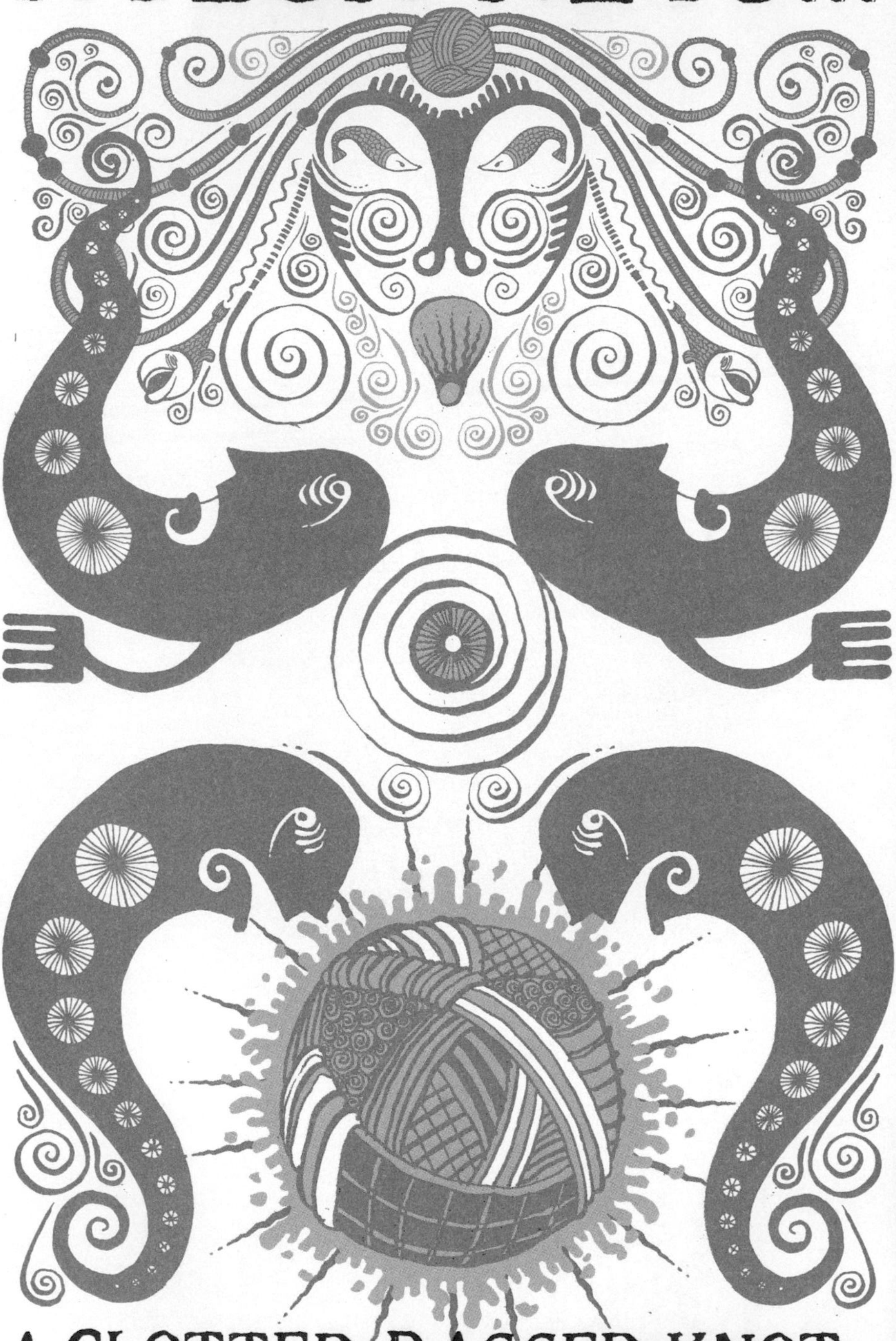

A CLOTTED, RAGGED KNOT...

ACRYLIC, FOAM AND POLYMERS

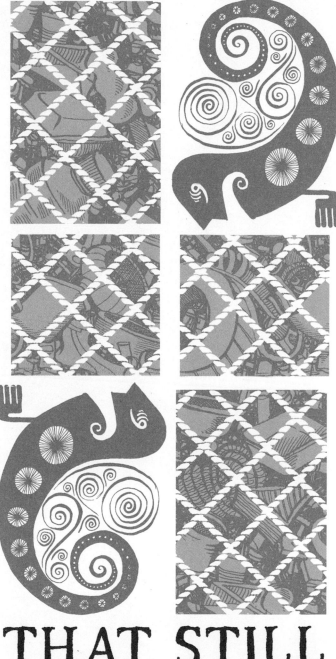

THAT STILL
REFUSE TO ROT.

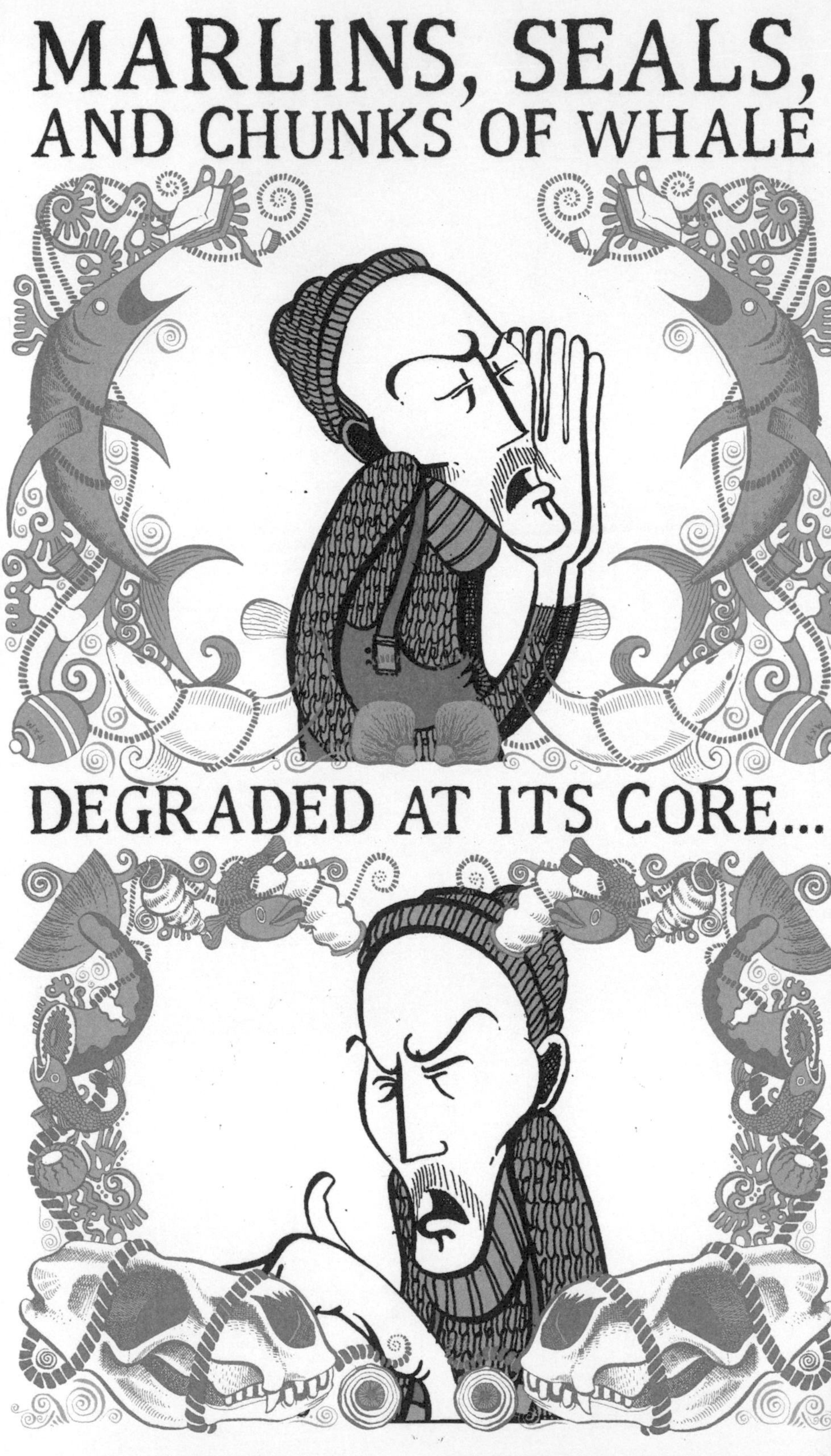
MARLINS, SEALS, AND CHUNKS OF WHALE
DEGRADED AT ITS CORE...

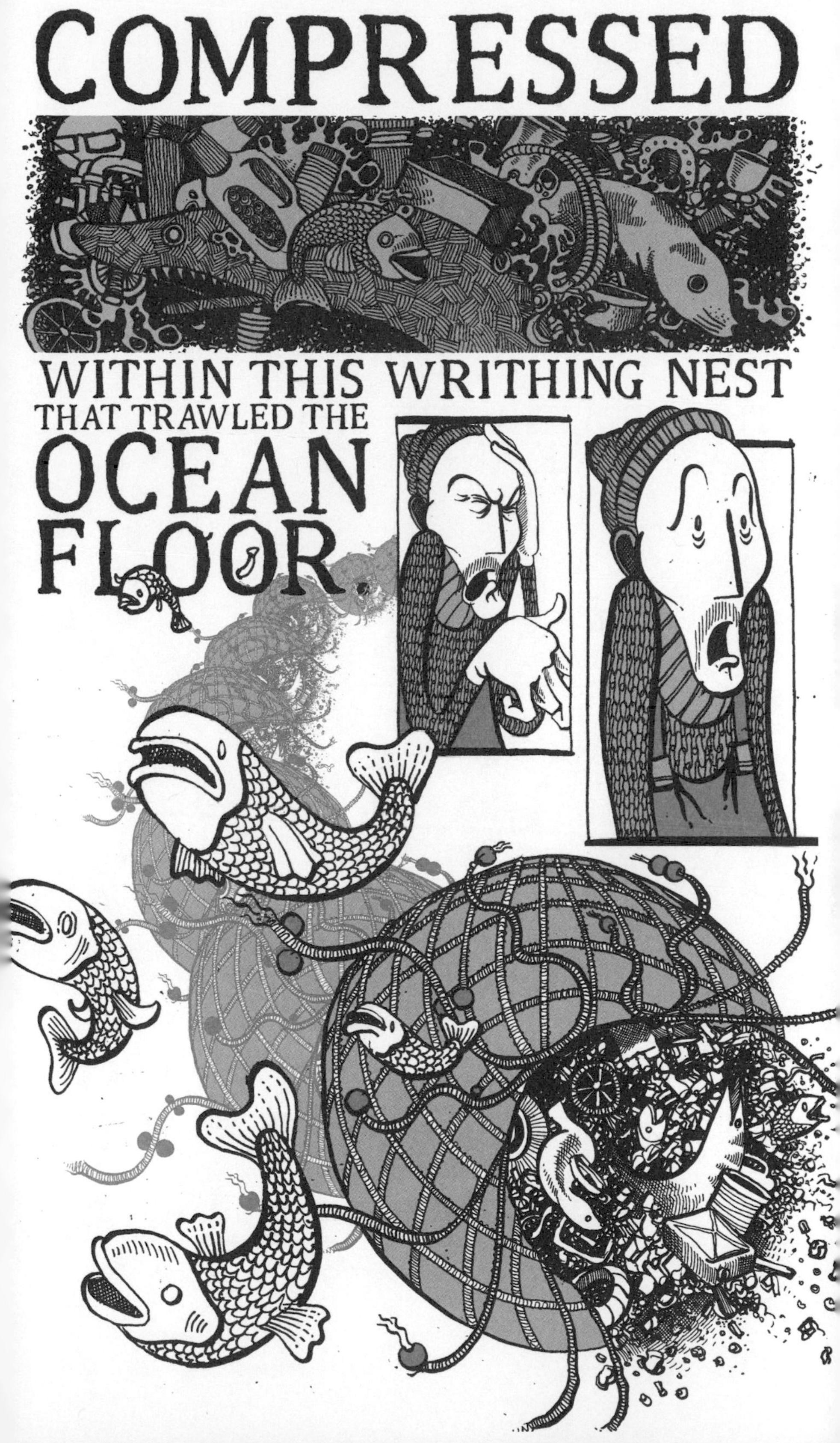
COMPRESSED
WITHIN THIS WRITHING NEST
THAT TRAWLED THE
OCEAN
FLOOR

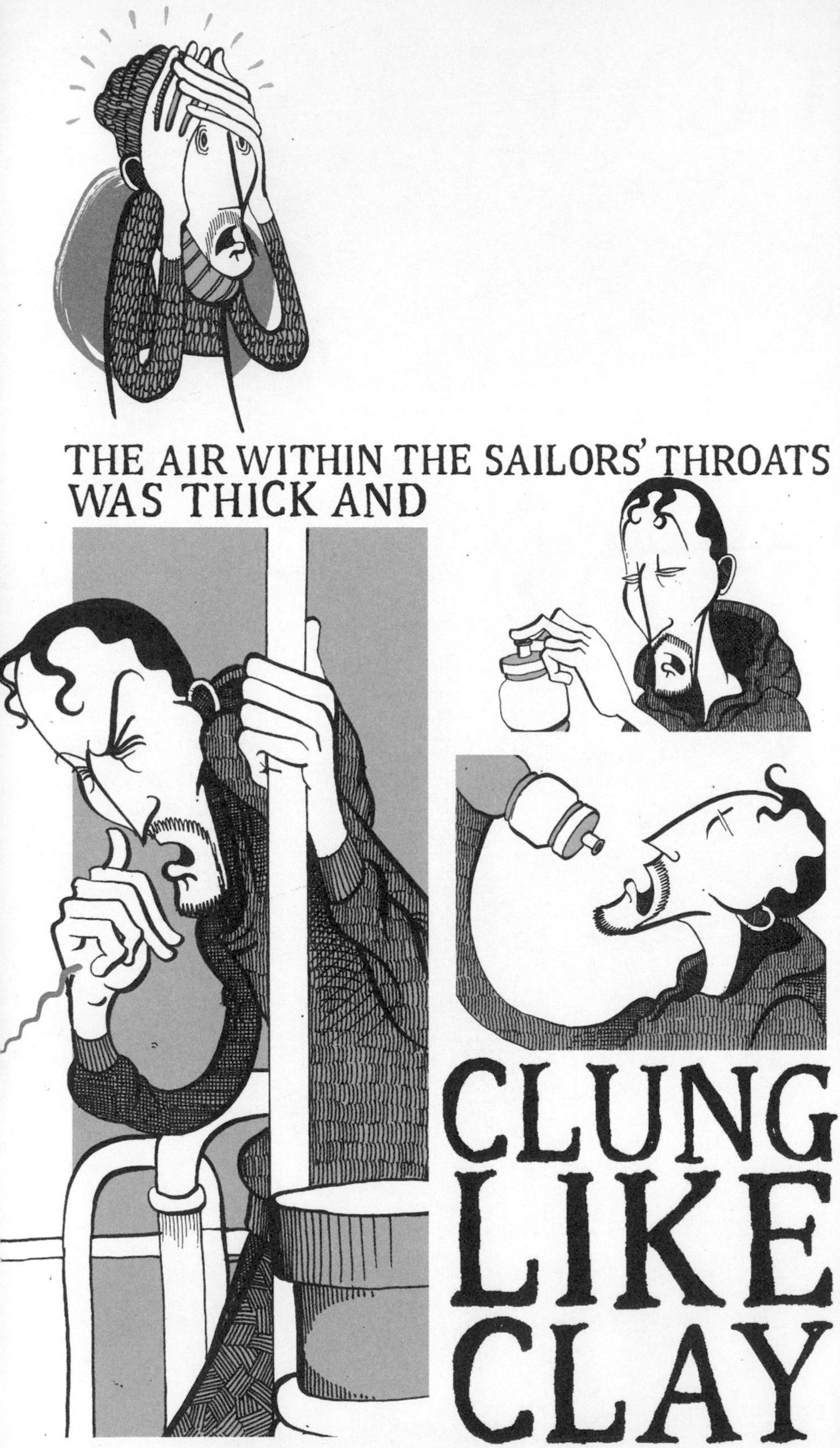
THE AIR WITHIN THE SAILORS' THROATS
WAS THICK AND
CLUNG
LIKE
CLAY

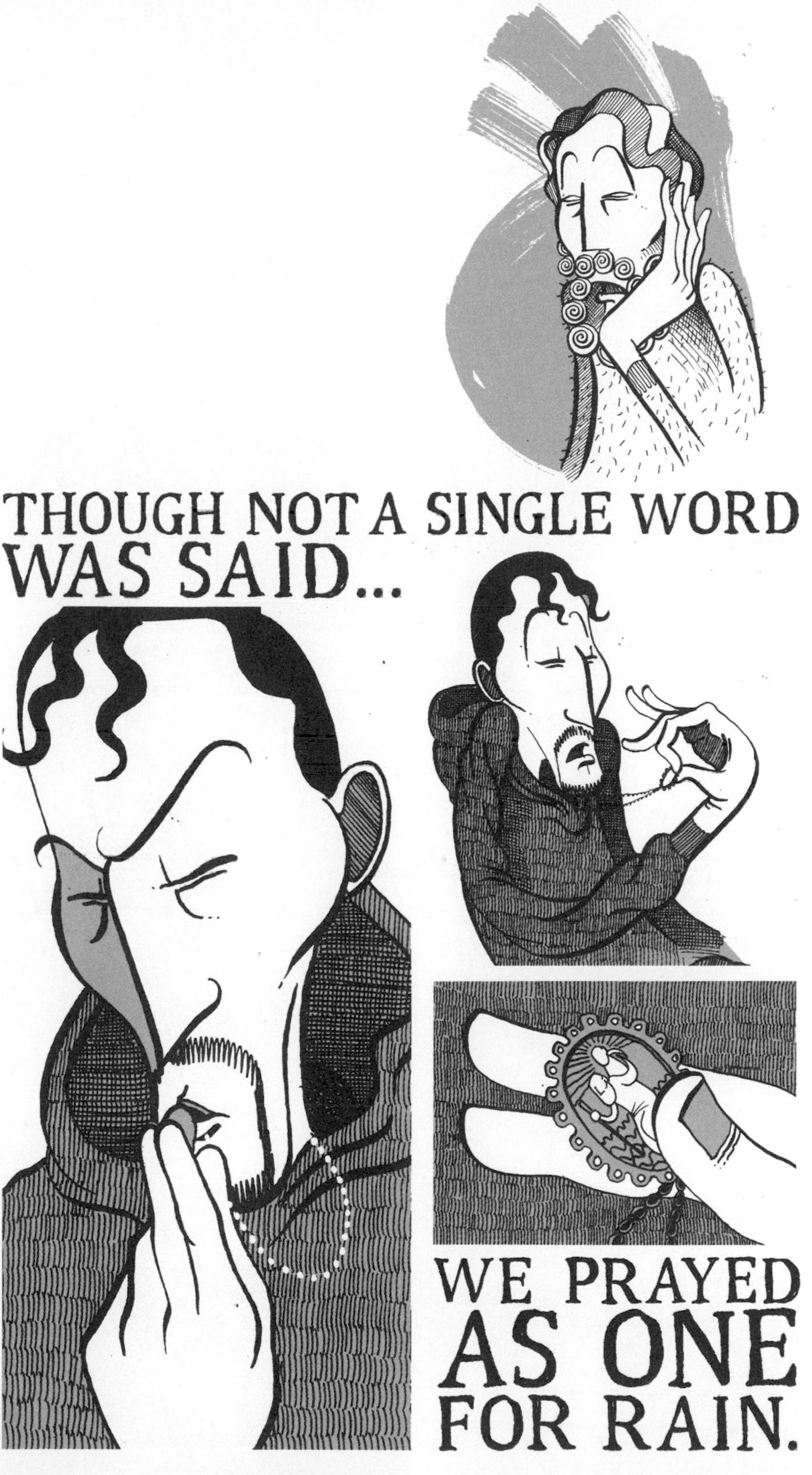
THOUGH NOT A SINGLE WORD WAS SAID...
WE PRAYED AS ONE FOR RAIN.

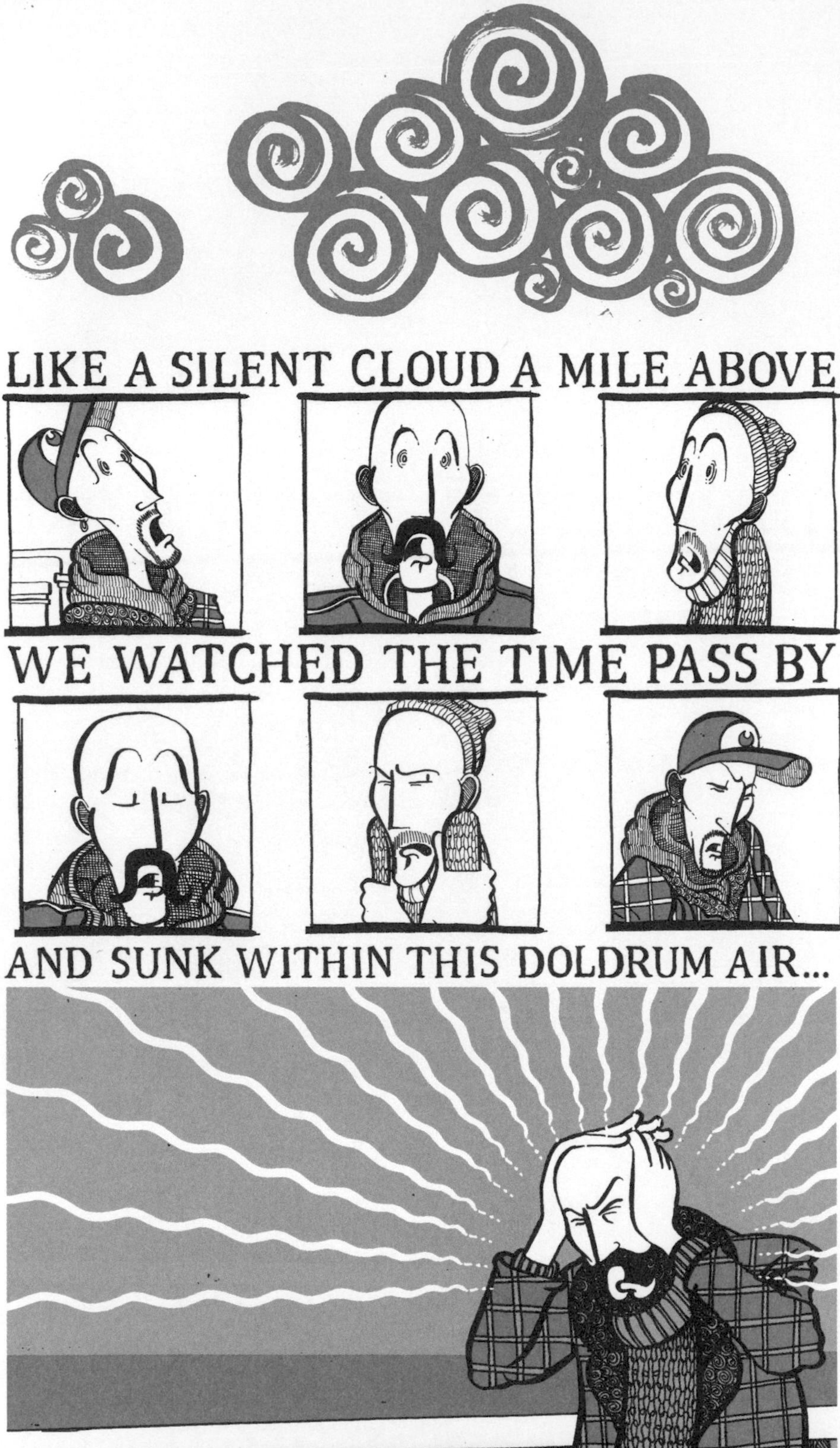
LIKE A SILENT CLOUD A MILE ABOVE
WE WATCHED THE TIME PASS BY
AND SUNK WITHIN THIS DOLDRUM AIR...

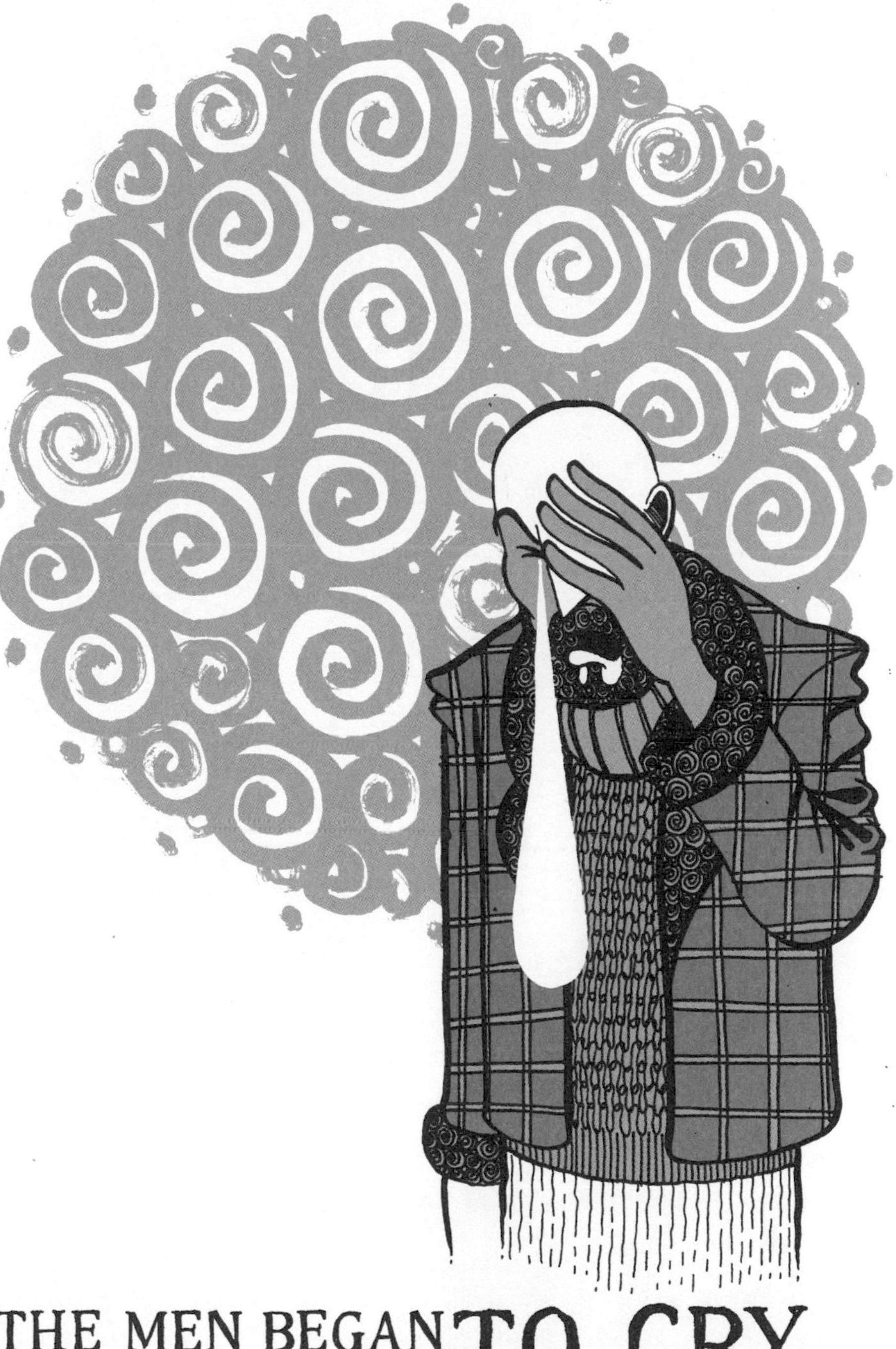

THE MEN BEGAN TO CRY.

DESPAIRING THUS THEY GATHERED ROUND

AND TOOK THE **ALBATROSS;**

THEY HUNG ITS CARCASS
ROUND MY NECK:

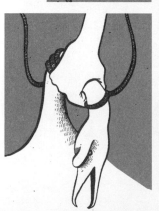

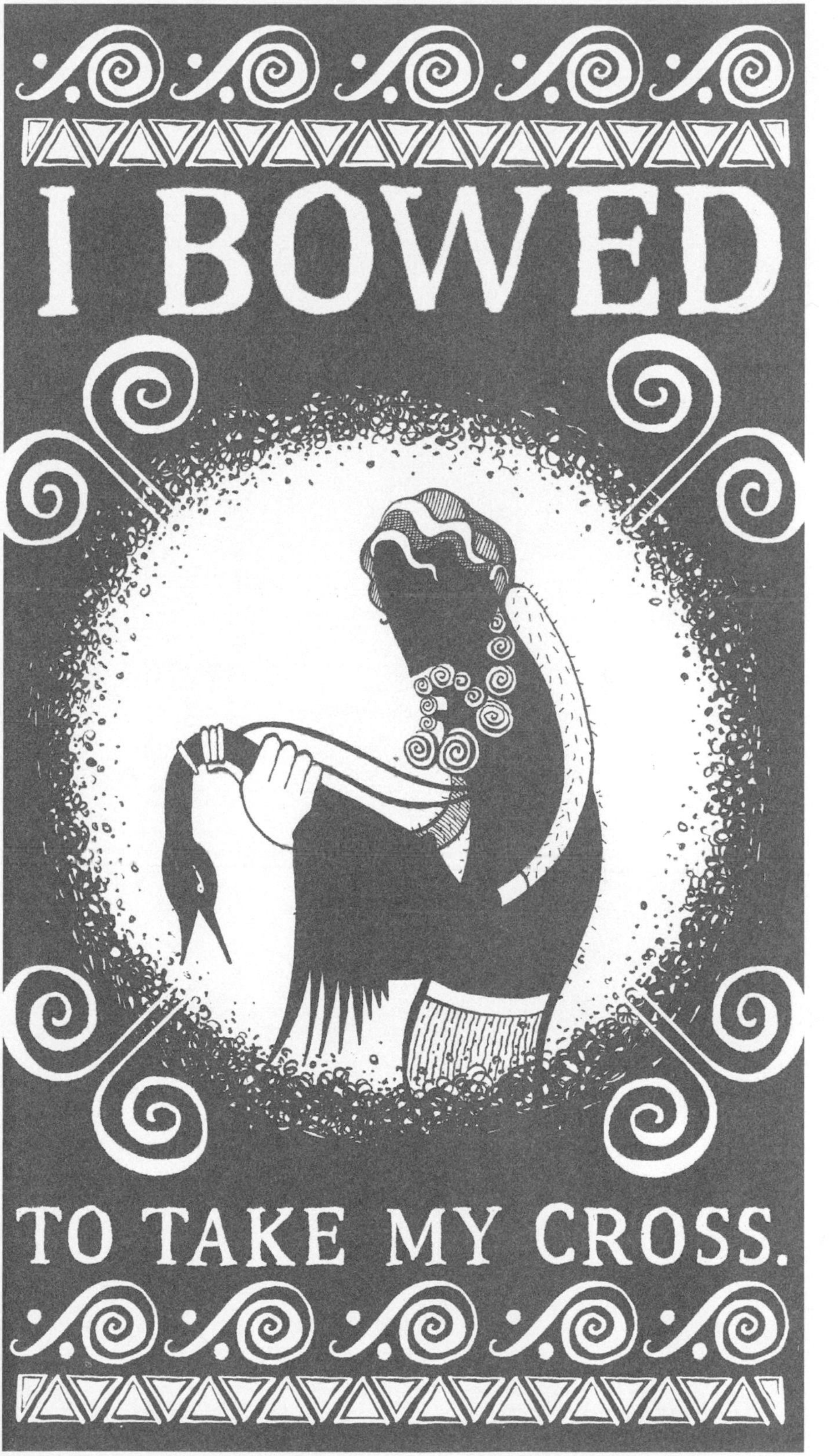
I BOWED
TO TAKE MY CROSS.

PART THREE

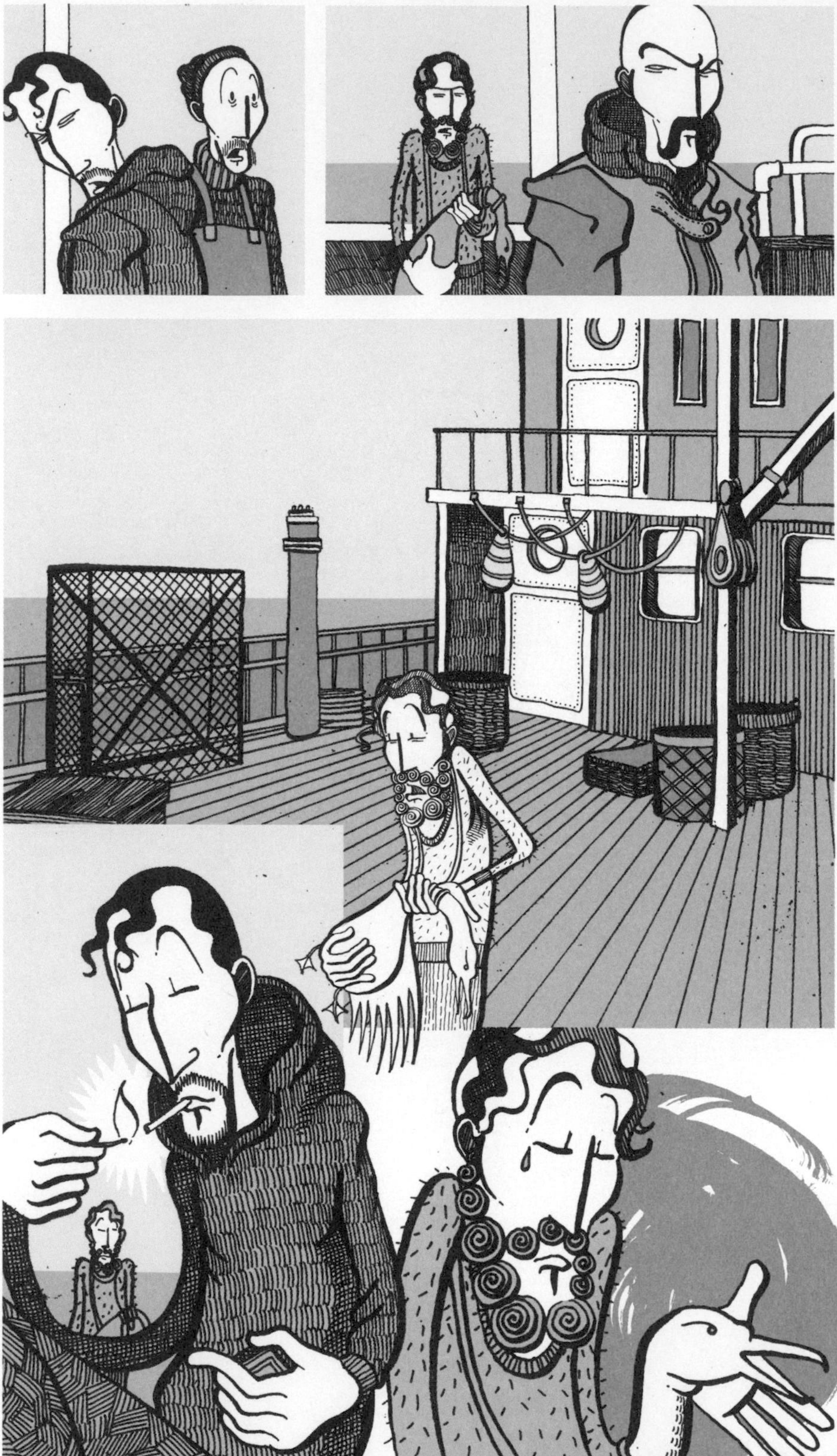

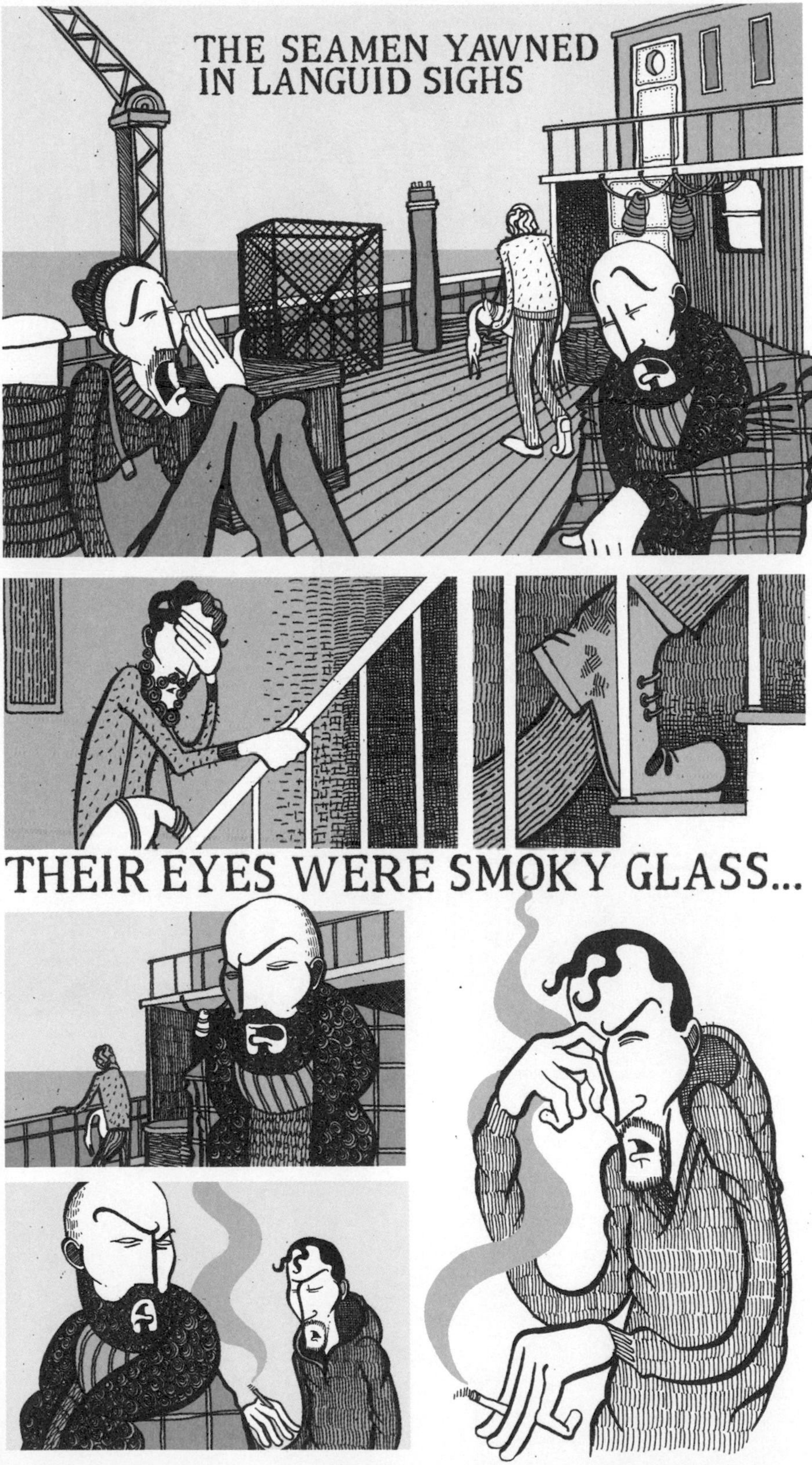
THE SEAMEN YAWNED
IN LANGUID SIGHS
THEIR EYES WERE SMOKY GLASS...

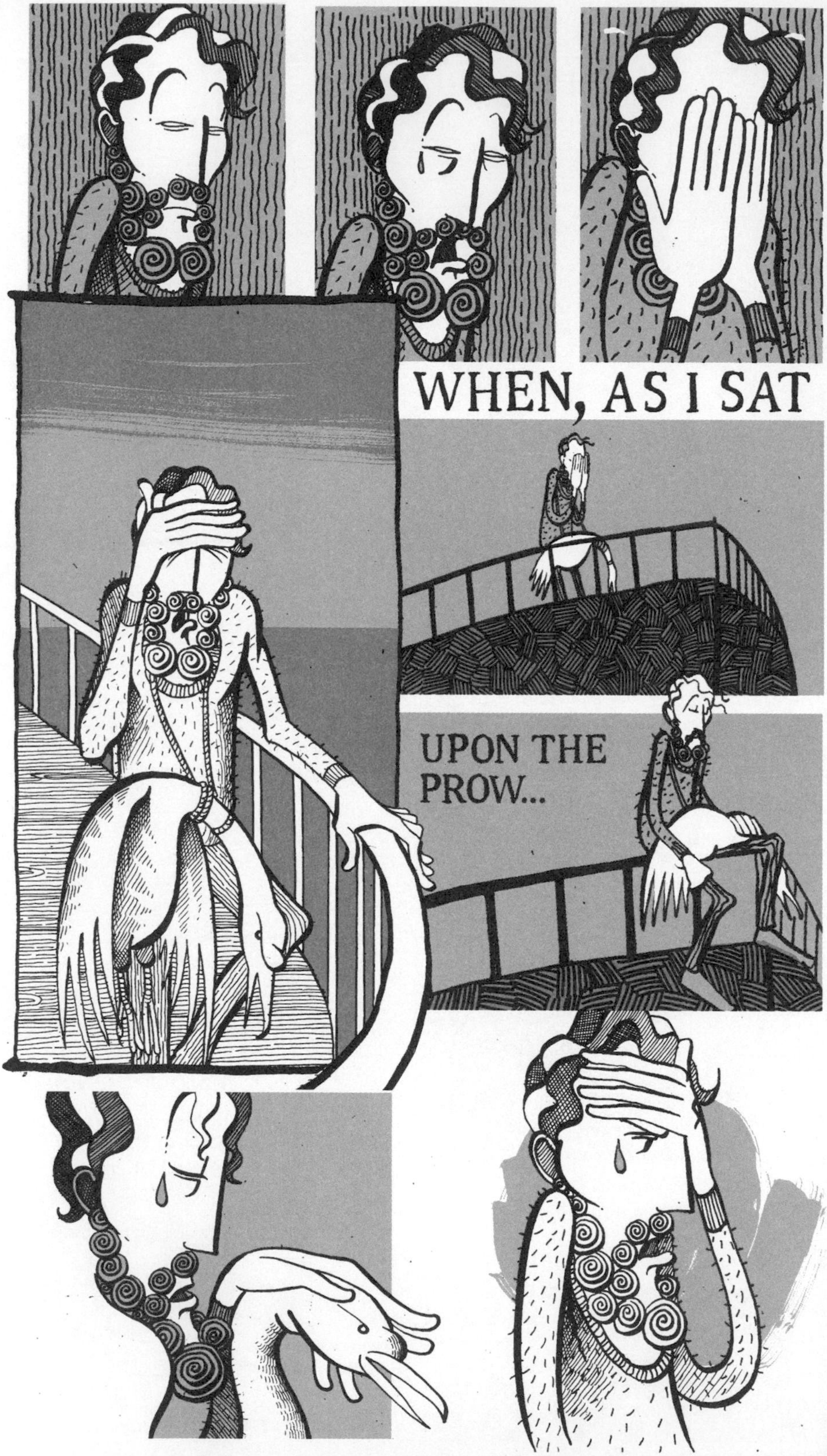
WHEN, AS I SAT
UPON THE PROW...

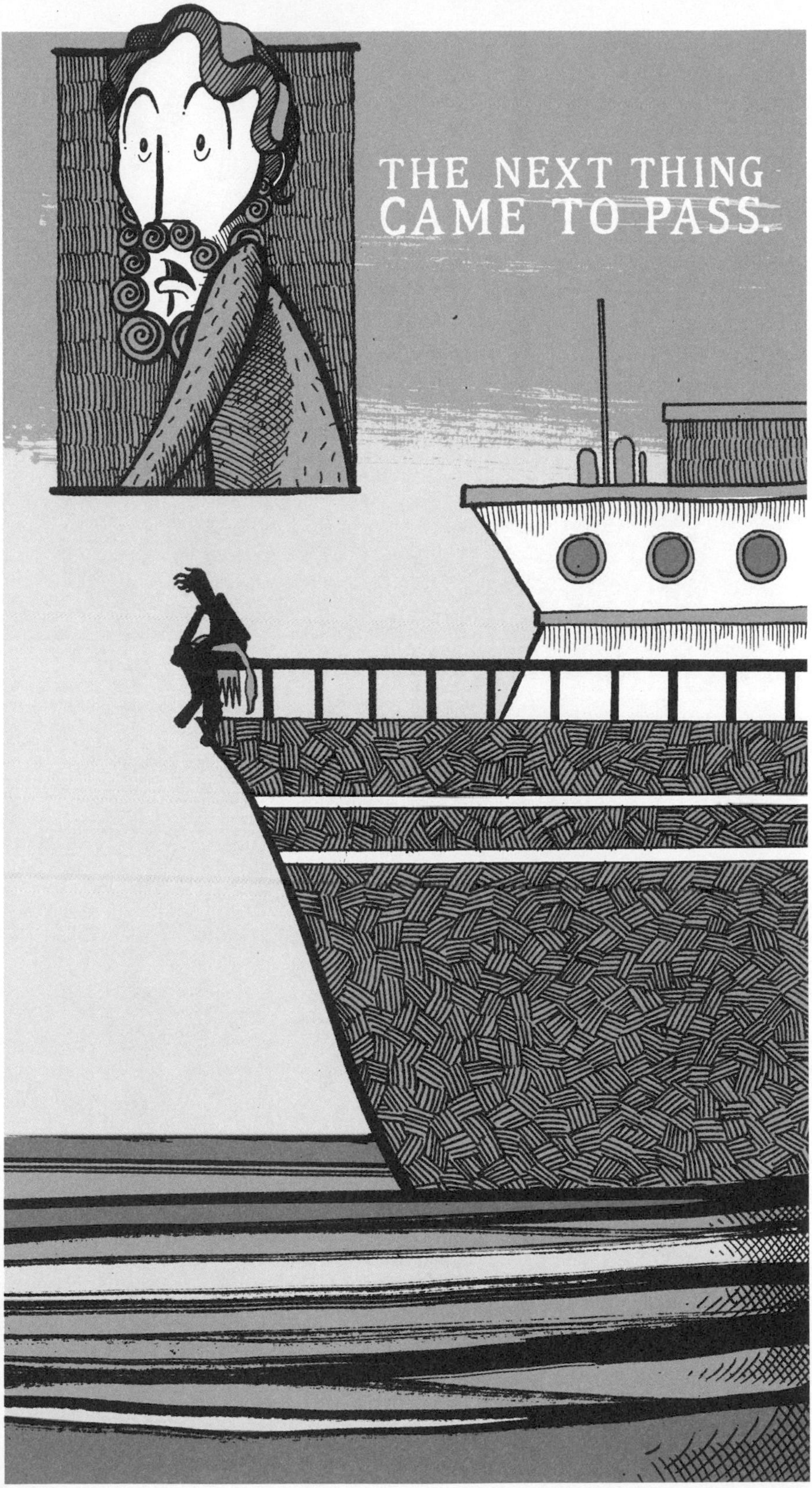
THE NEXT THING CAME TO PASS.

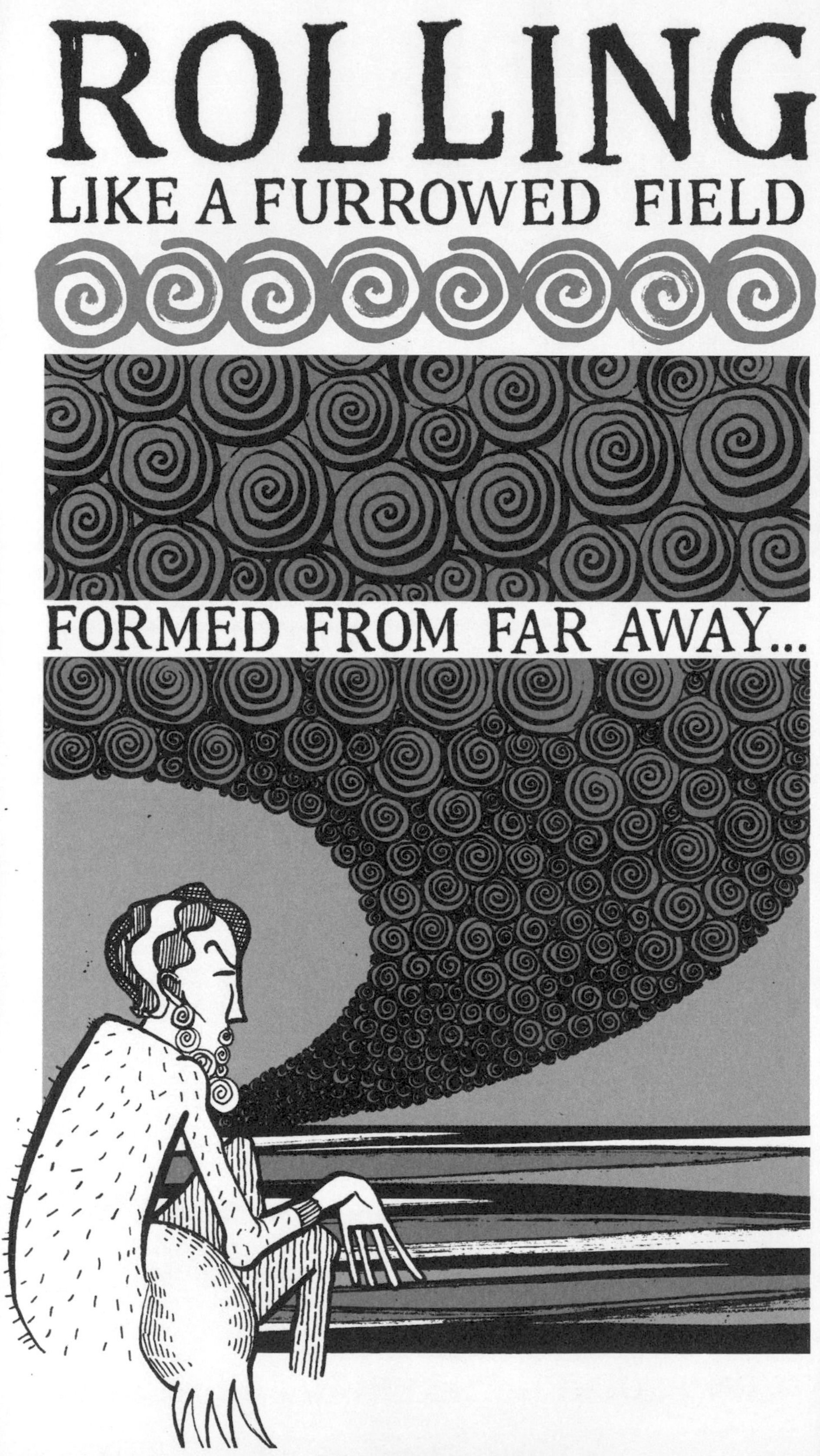
ROLLING
LIKE A FURROWED FIELD
FORMED FROM FAR AWAY...

A CUMULONIMBUS DARKENING CLOUD

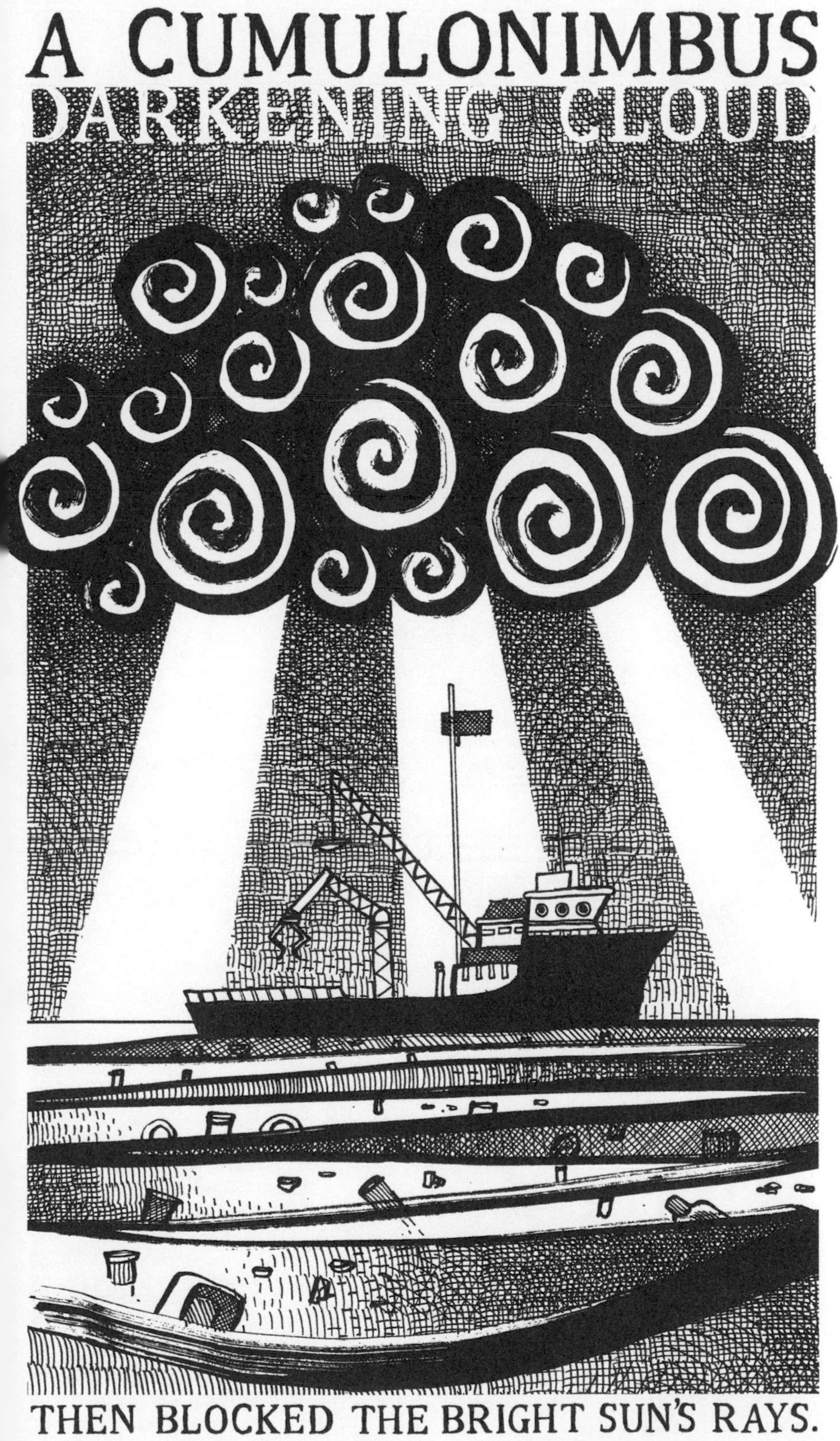

THEN BLOCKED THE BRIGHT SUN'S RAYS.

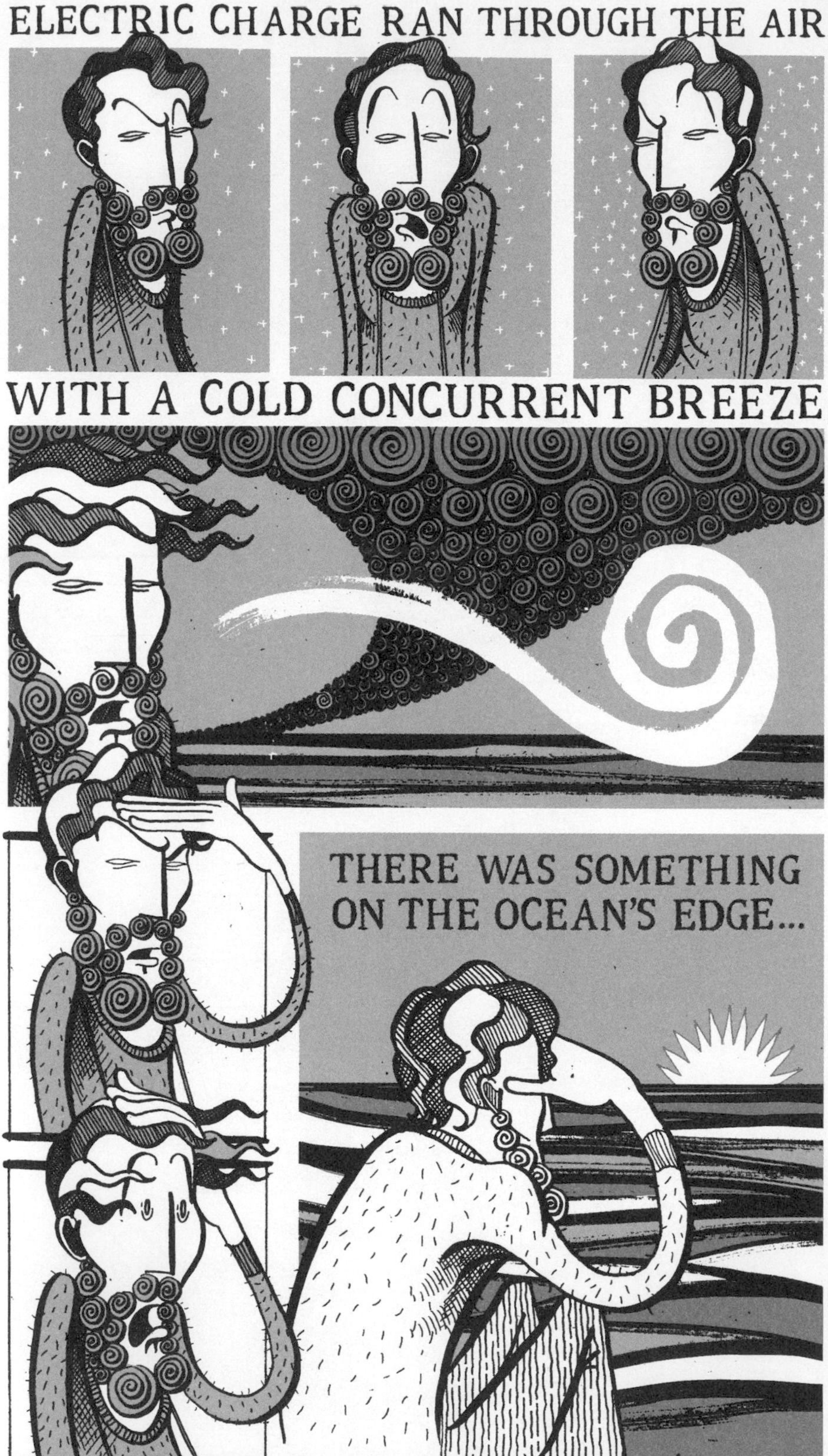
ELECTRIC CHARGE RAN THROUGH THE AIR
WITH A COLD CONCURRENT BREEZE;
THERE WAS SOMETHING ON THE OCEAN'S EDGE...

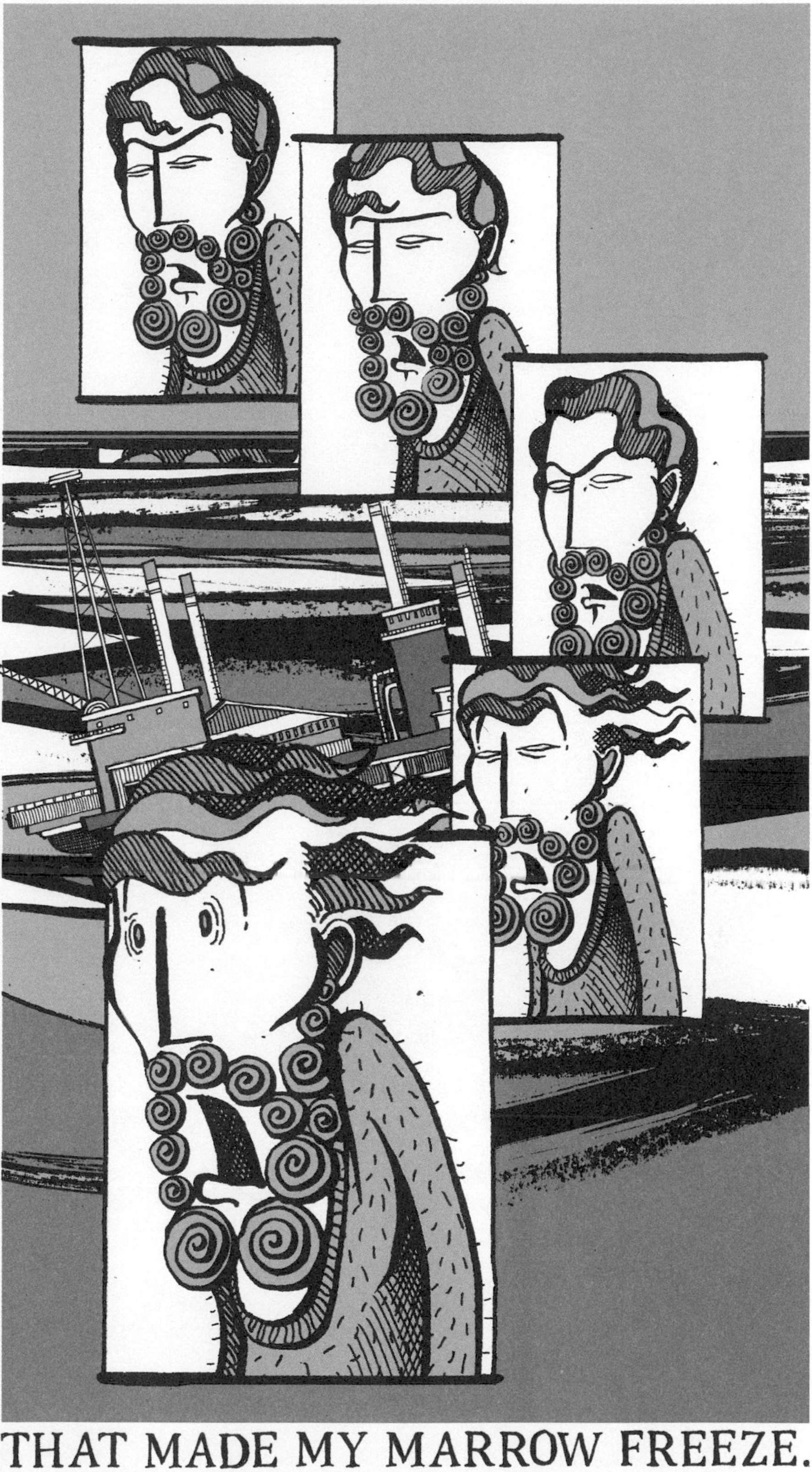

THAT MADE MY MARROW FREEZE.

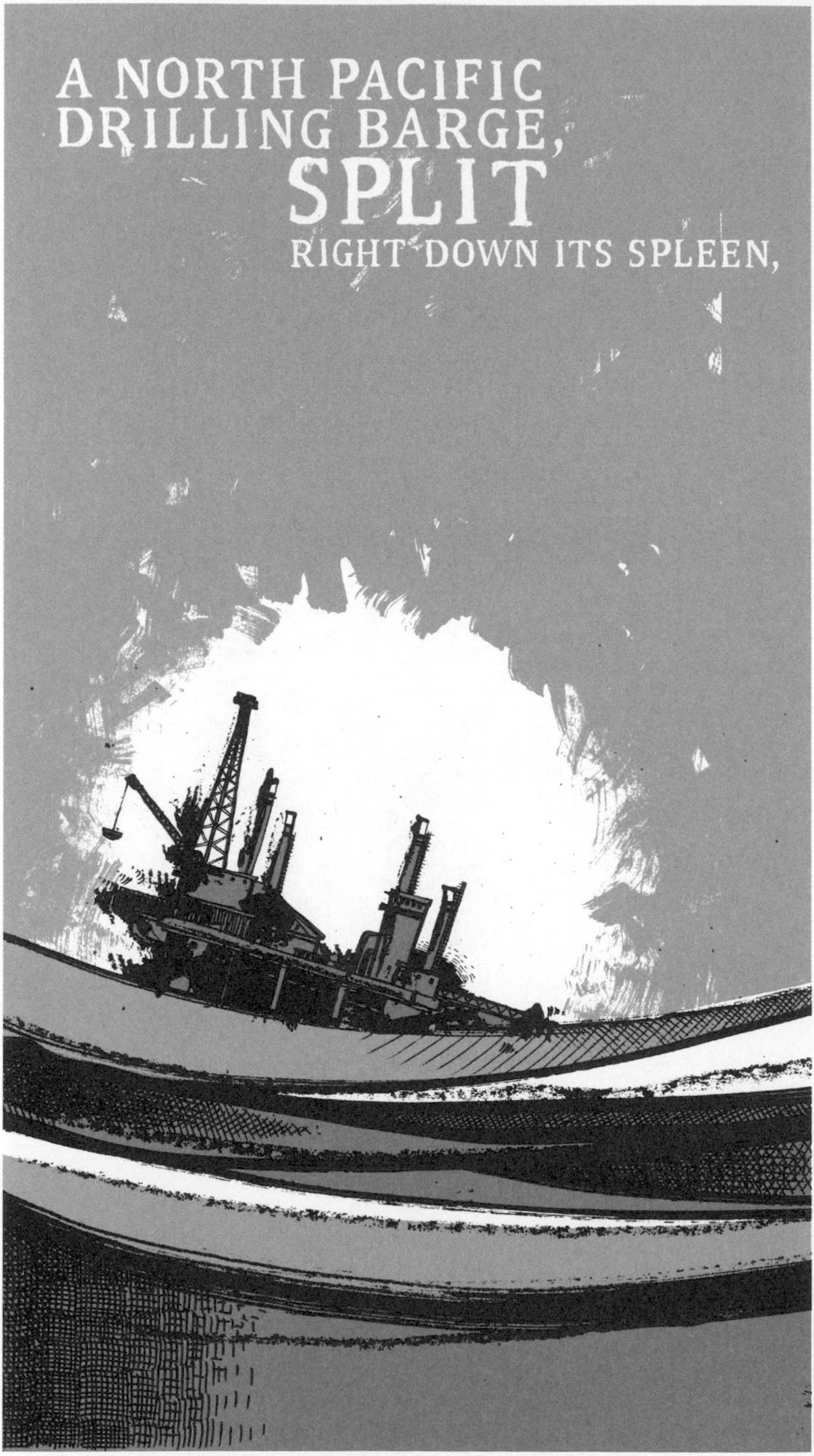
A NORTH PACIFIC
DRILLING BARGE,
SPLIT
RIGHT DOWN ITS SPLEEN,

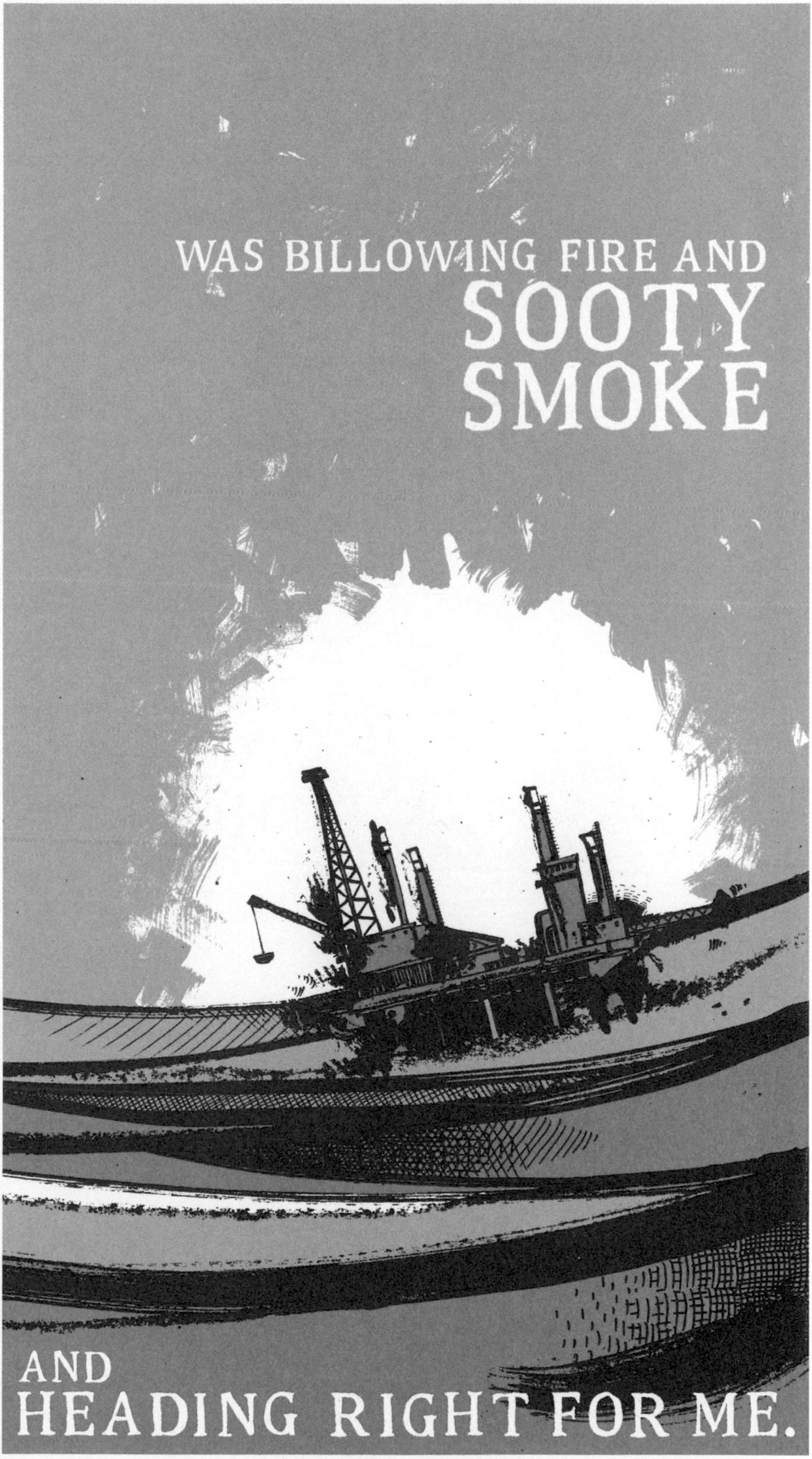
WAS BILLOWING FIRE AND
SOOTY
SMOKE
AND
HEADING RIGHT FOR ME.

AND LIKE A NEGATIVE

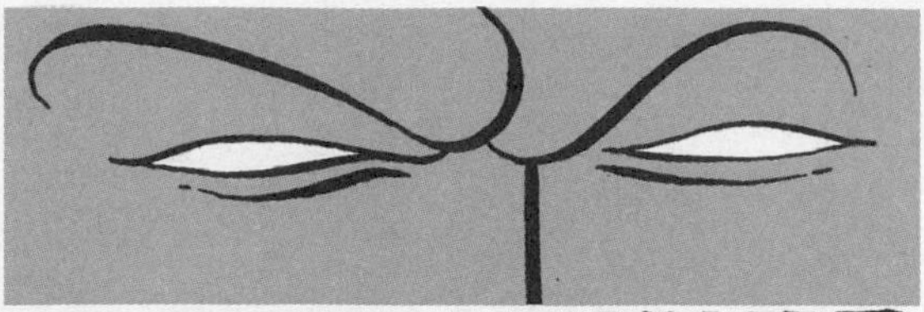

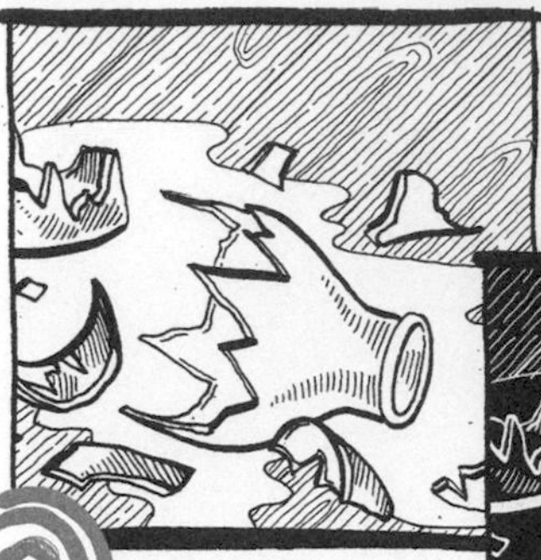

OF PURE WHITE MILK

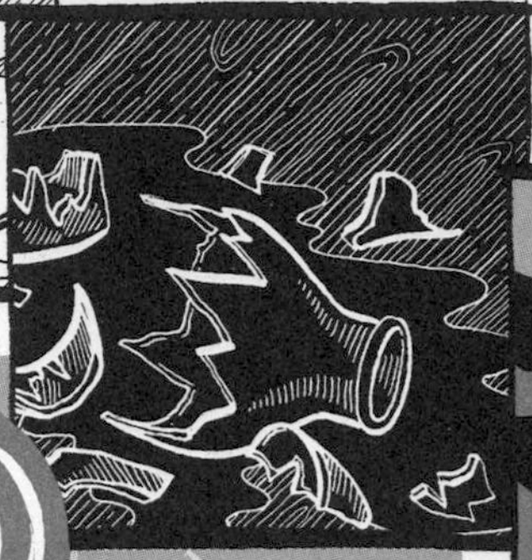

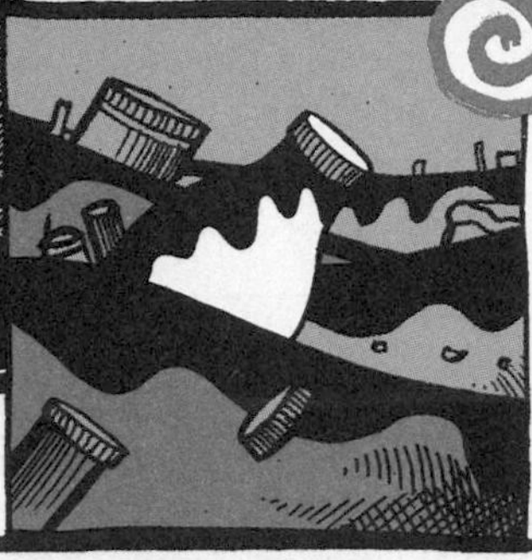

SPILT ACROSS THE FLOOR,

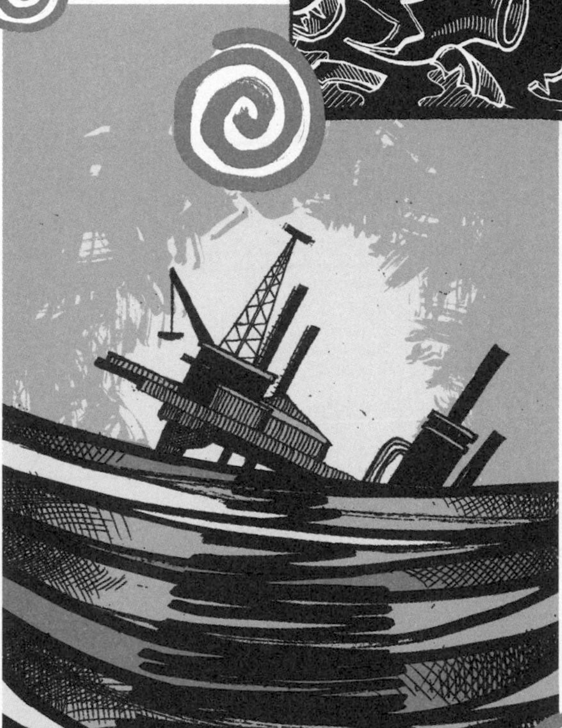

A GLOSSY THICK PETROLEUM SLICK DROWNED THIS WATERY MOOR.

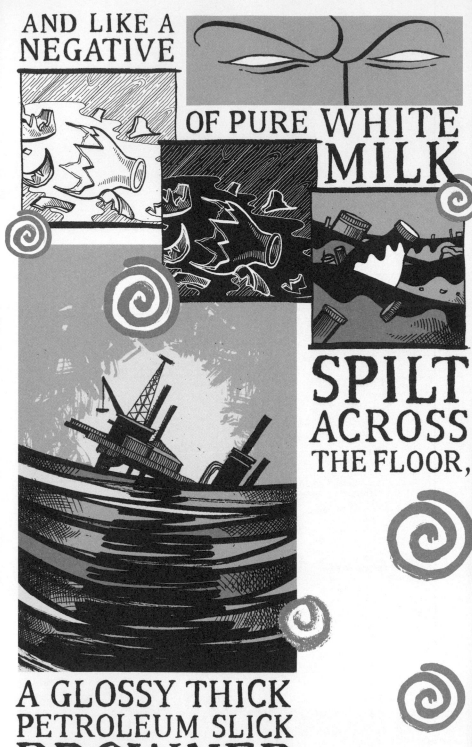

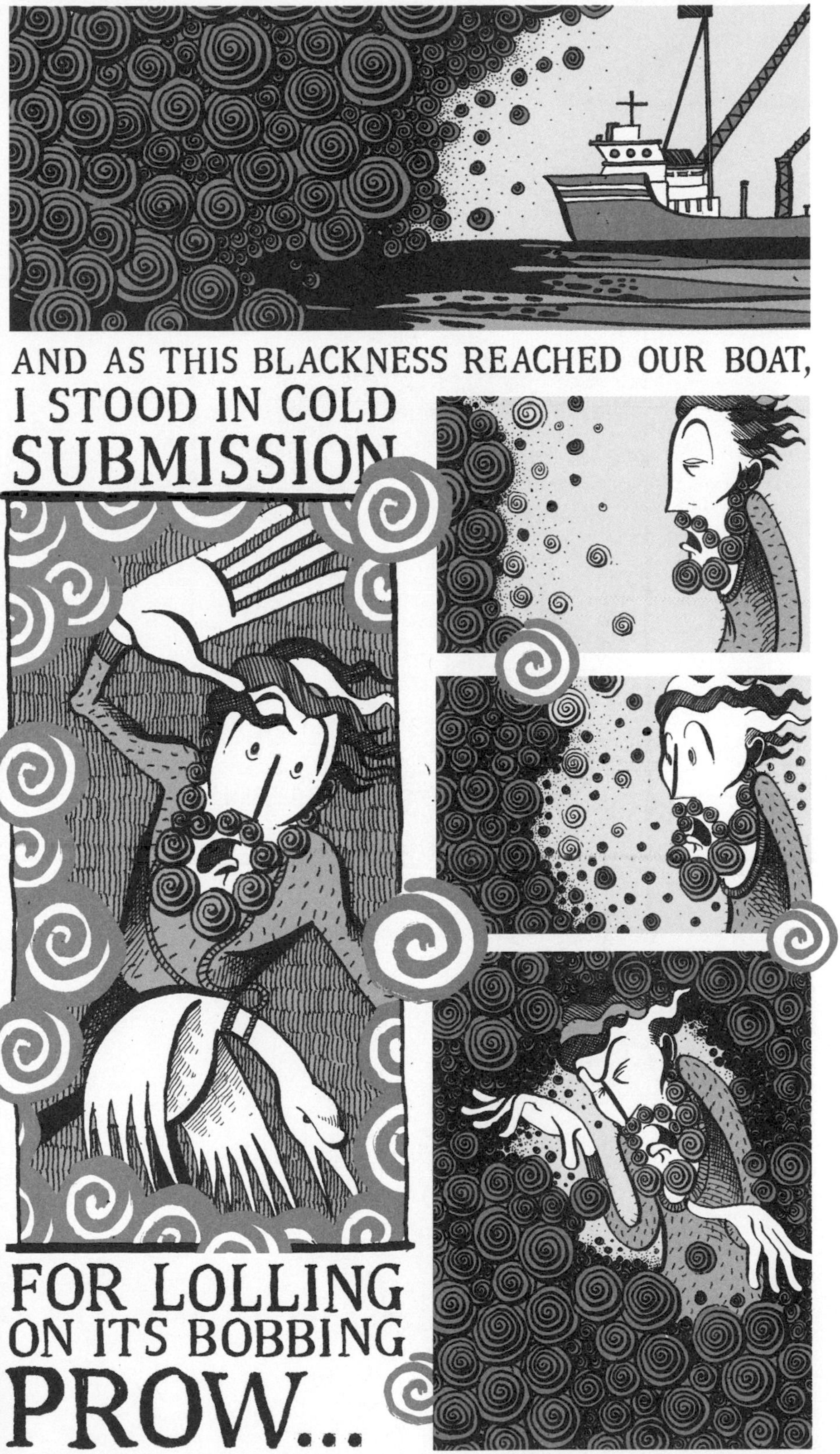
AND AS THIS BLACKNESS REACHED OUR BOAT,
I STOOD IN COLD
SUBMISSION
FOR LOLLING
ON ITS BOBBING
PROW...

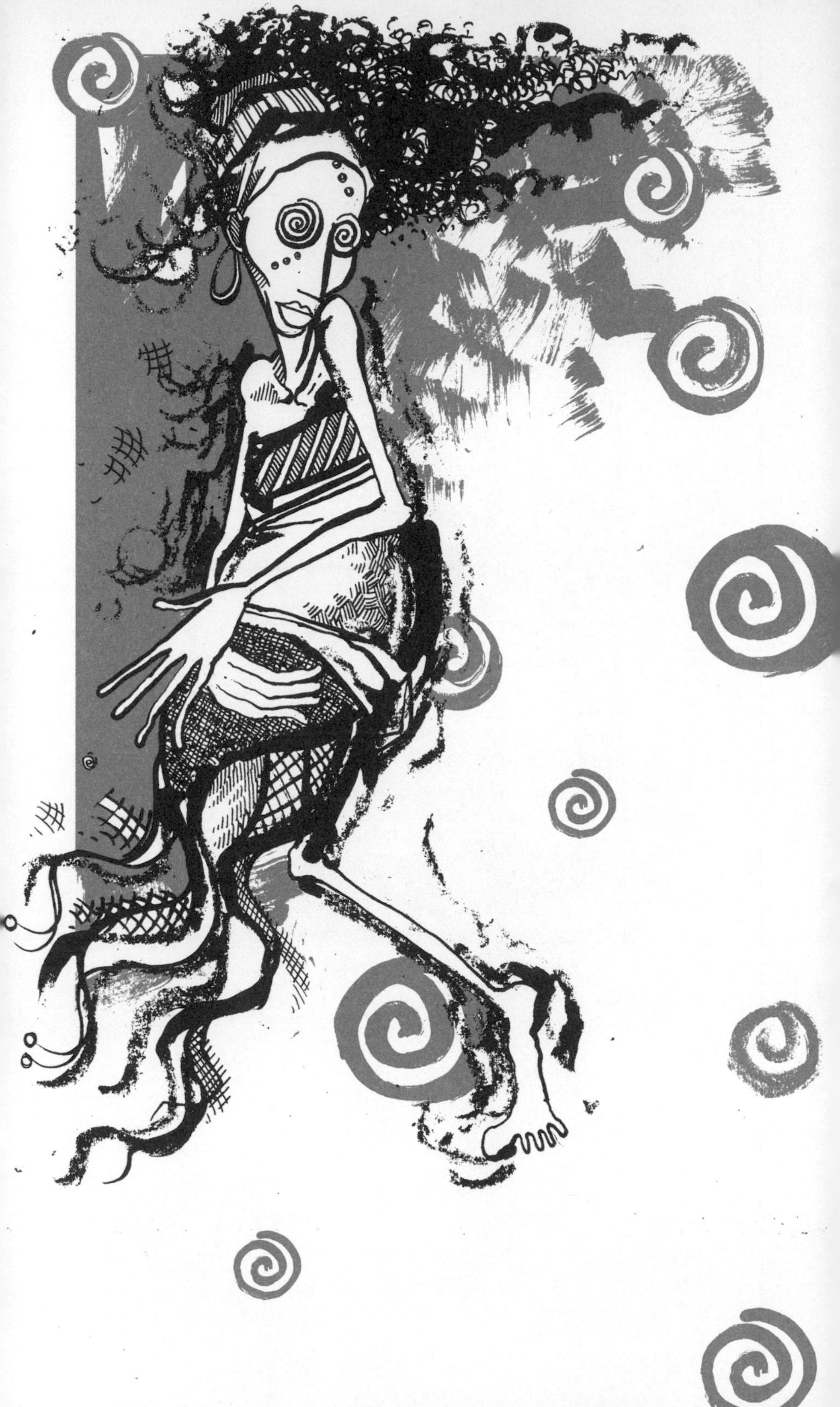

WAS A
GHOULISH
APPARITION.

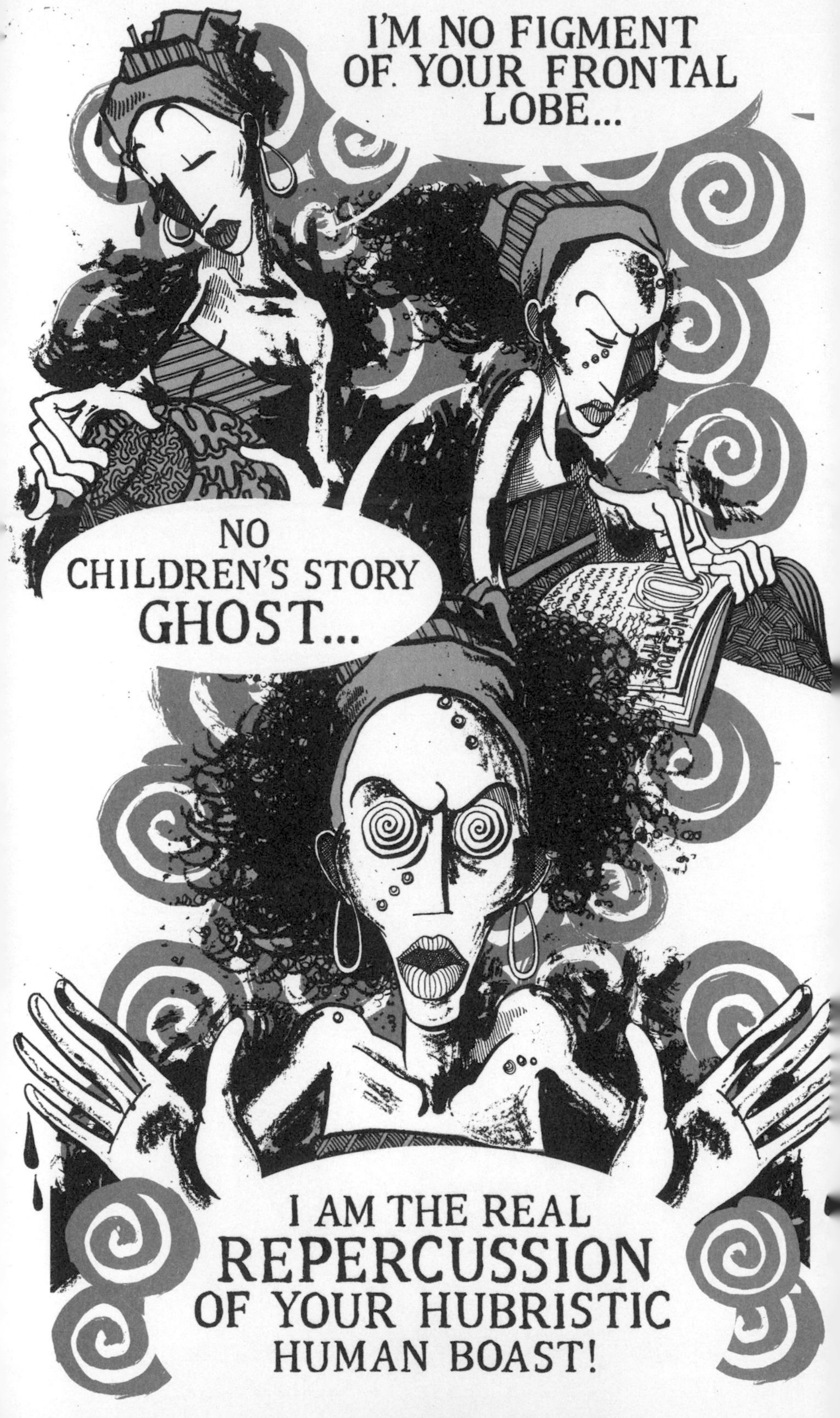
I'M NO FIGMENT OF. YO.UR FRONTAL LOBE...
NO CHILDREN'S STORY GHOST...
I AM THE REAL REPERCUSSION OF YOUR HUBRISTIC HUMAN BOAST!

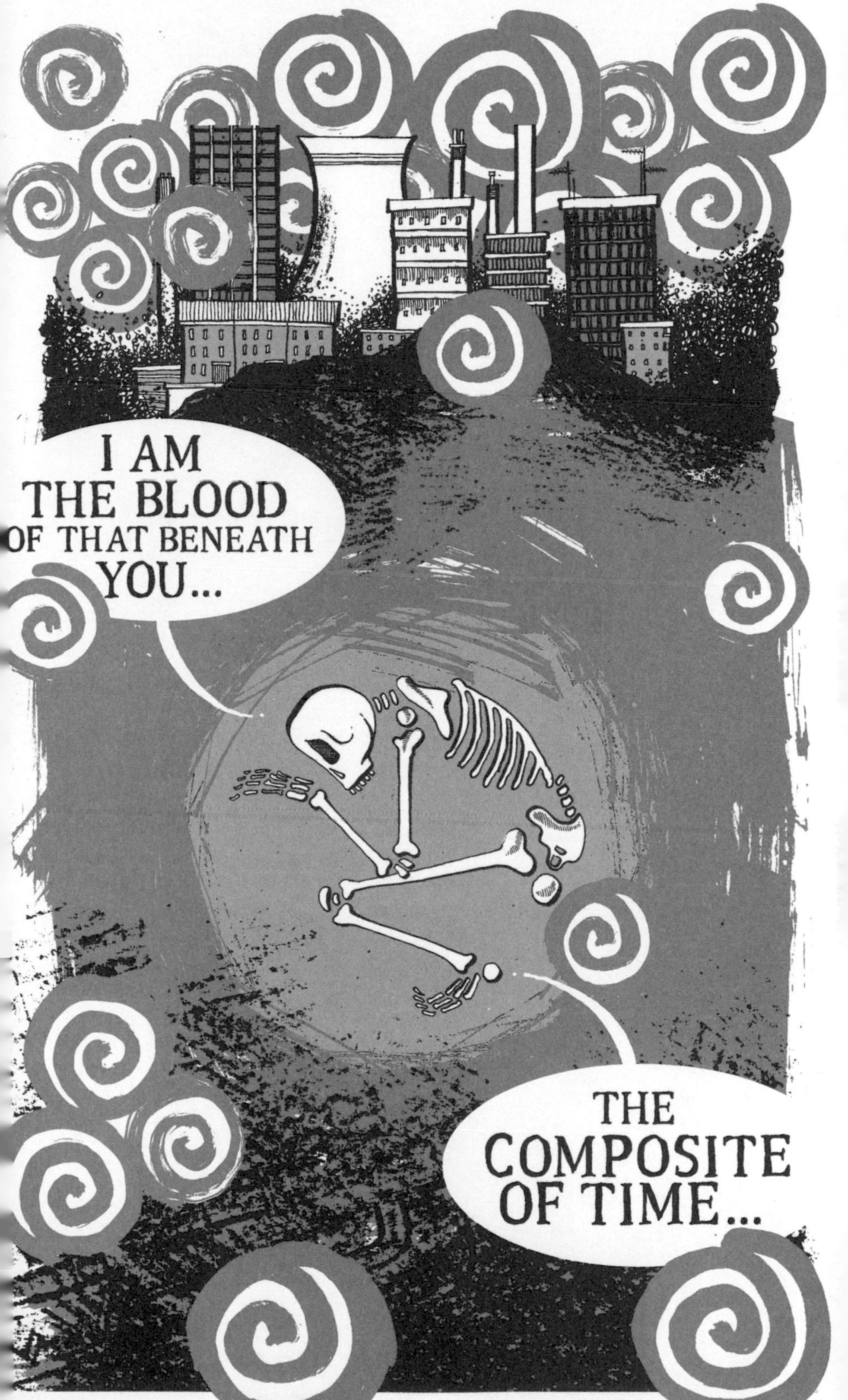
I AM THE BLOOD OF THAT BENEATH YOU...
THE COMPOSITE OF TIME...

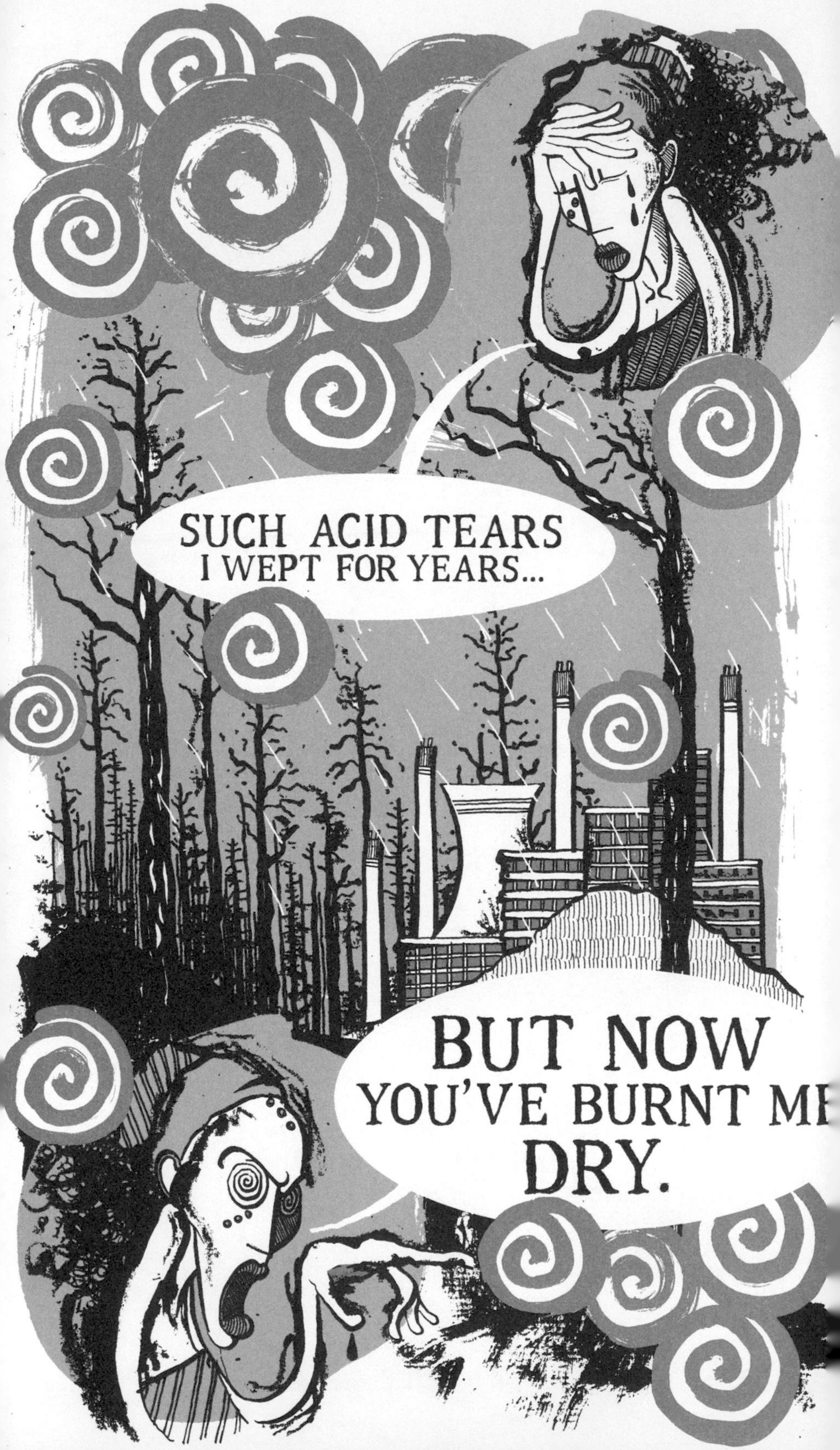
SUCH ACID TEARS I WEPT FOR YEARS...
BUT NOW YOU'VE BURNT ME DRY.

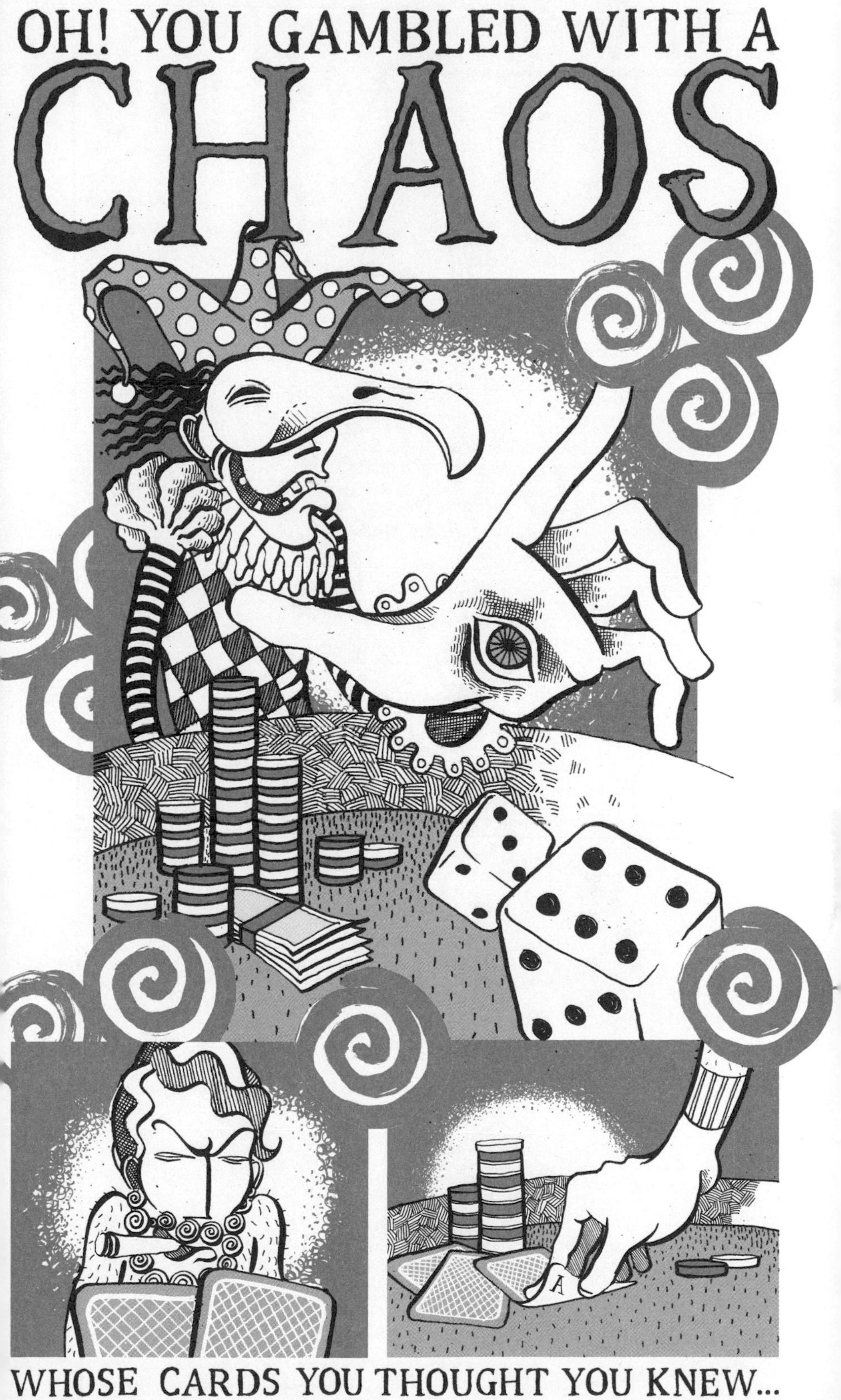
OH! YOU GAMBLED WITH A
CHAOS
A
WHOSE CARDS YOU THOUGHT YOU KNEW...

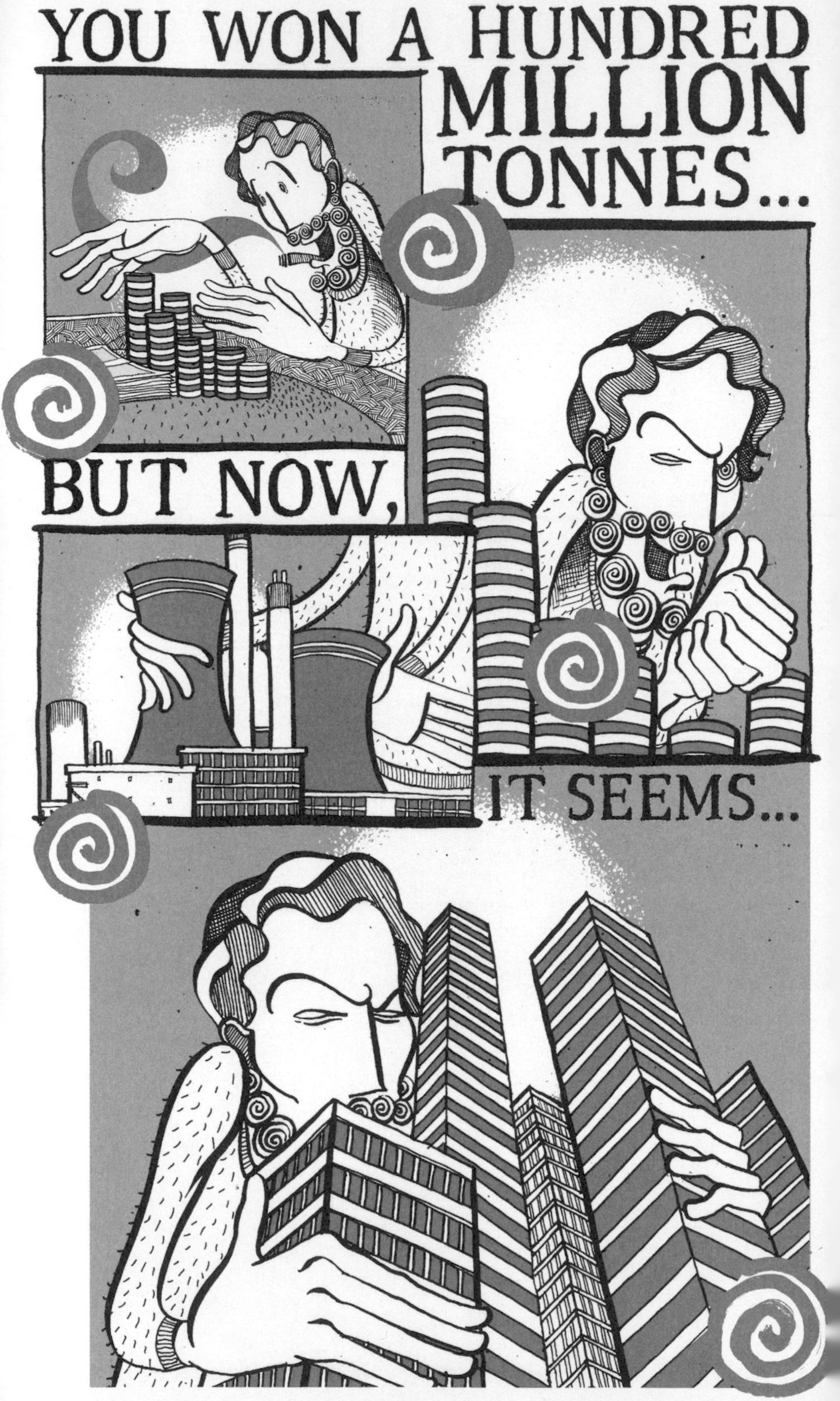
YOU WON A HUNDRED MILLION TONNES...
BUT NOW,
IT SEEMS...

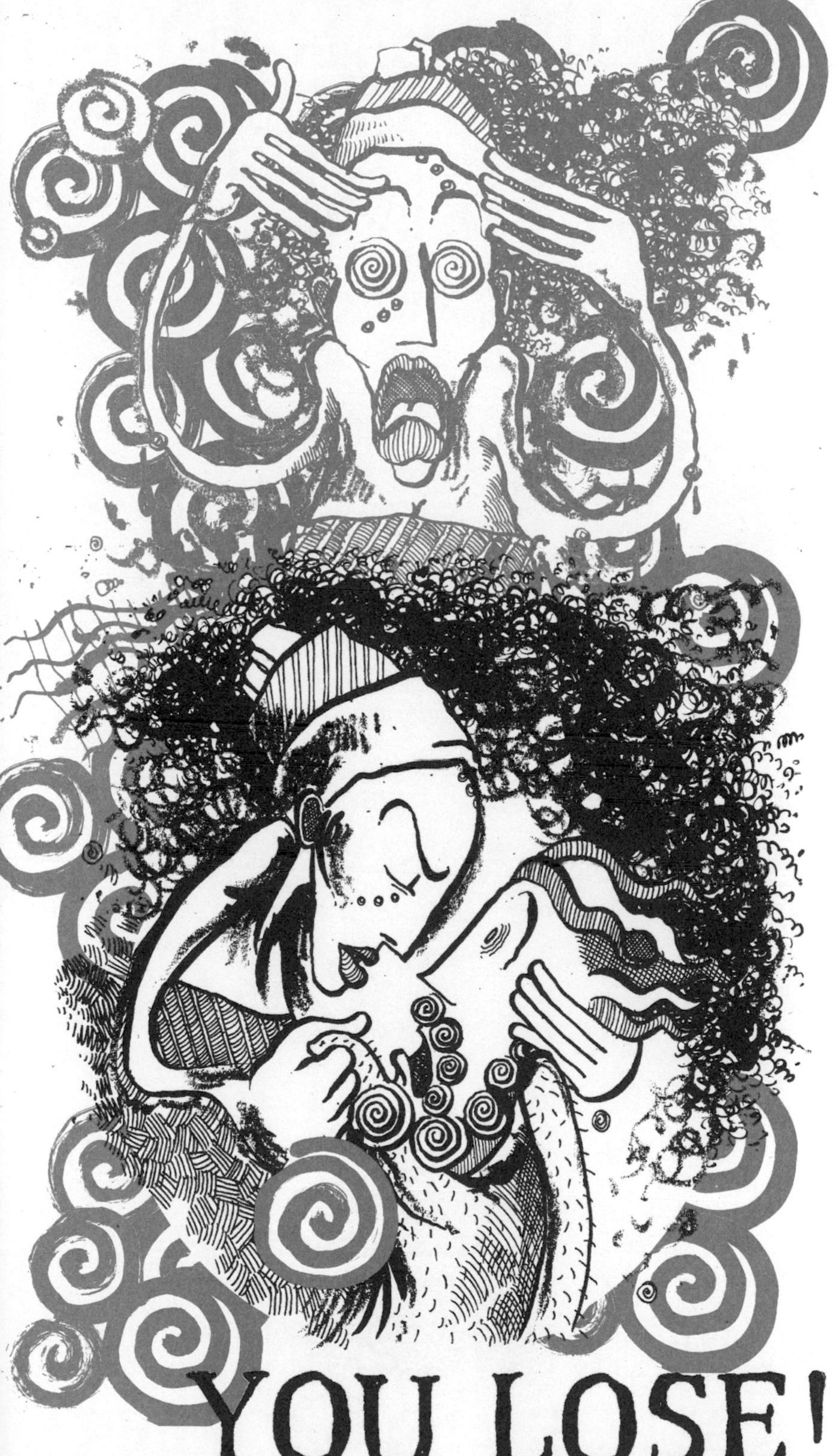
YOU LOSE!

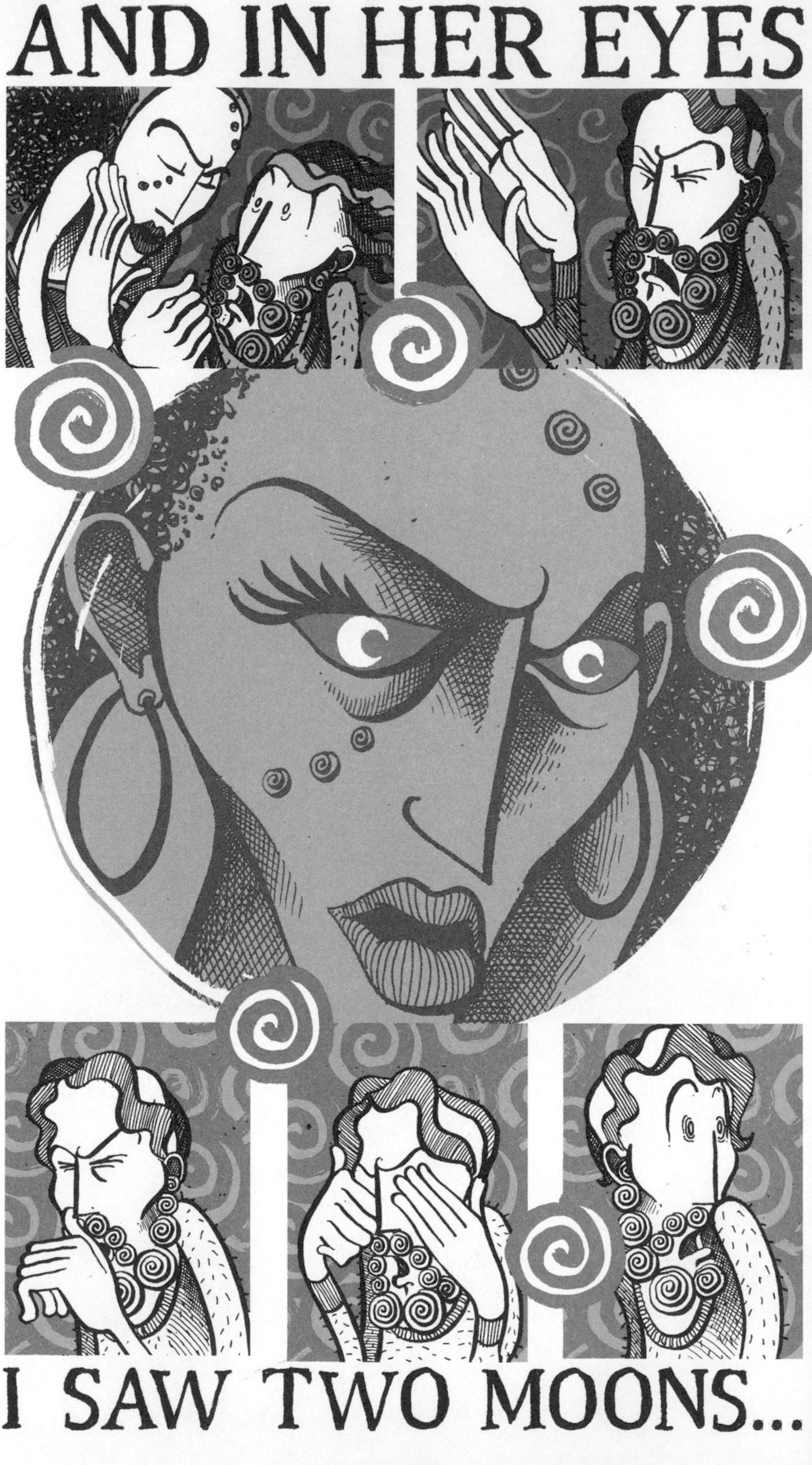
AND IN HER EYES
I SAW TWO MOONS...

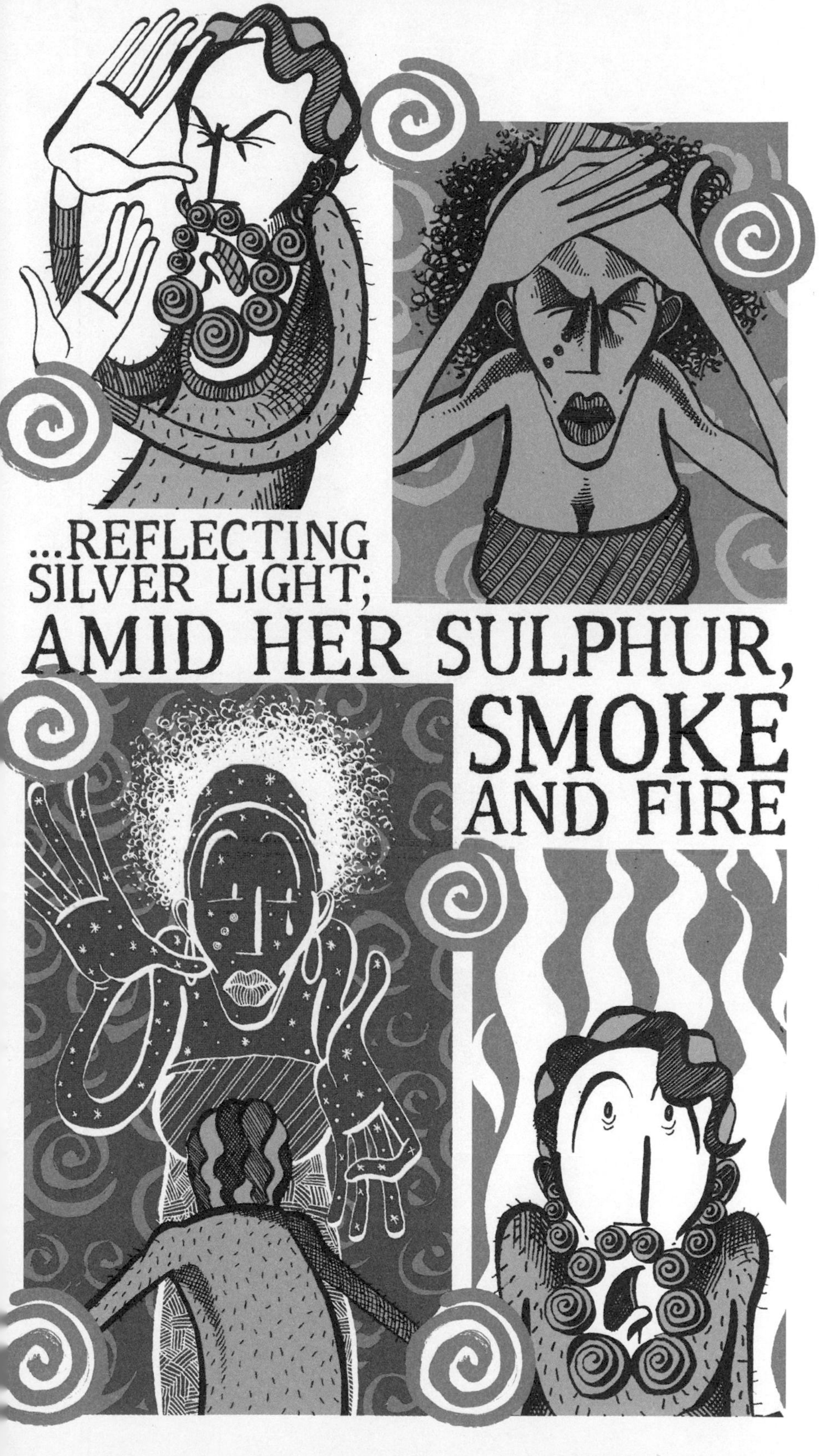
...REFLECTING SILVER LIGHT;
AMID HER SULPHUR, SMOKE AND FIRE

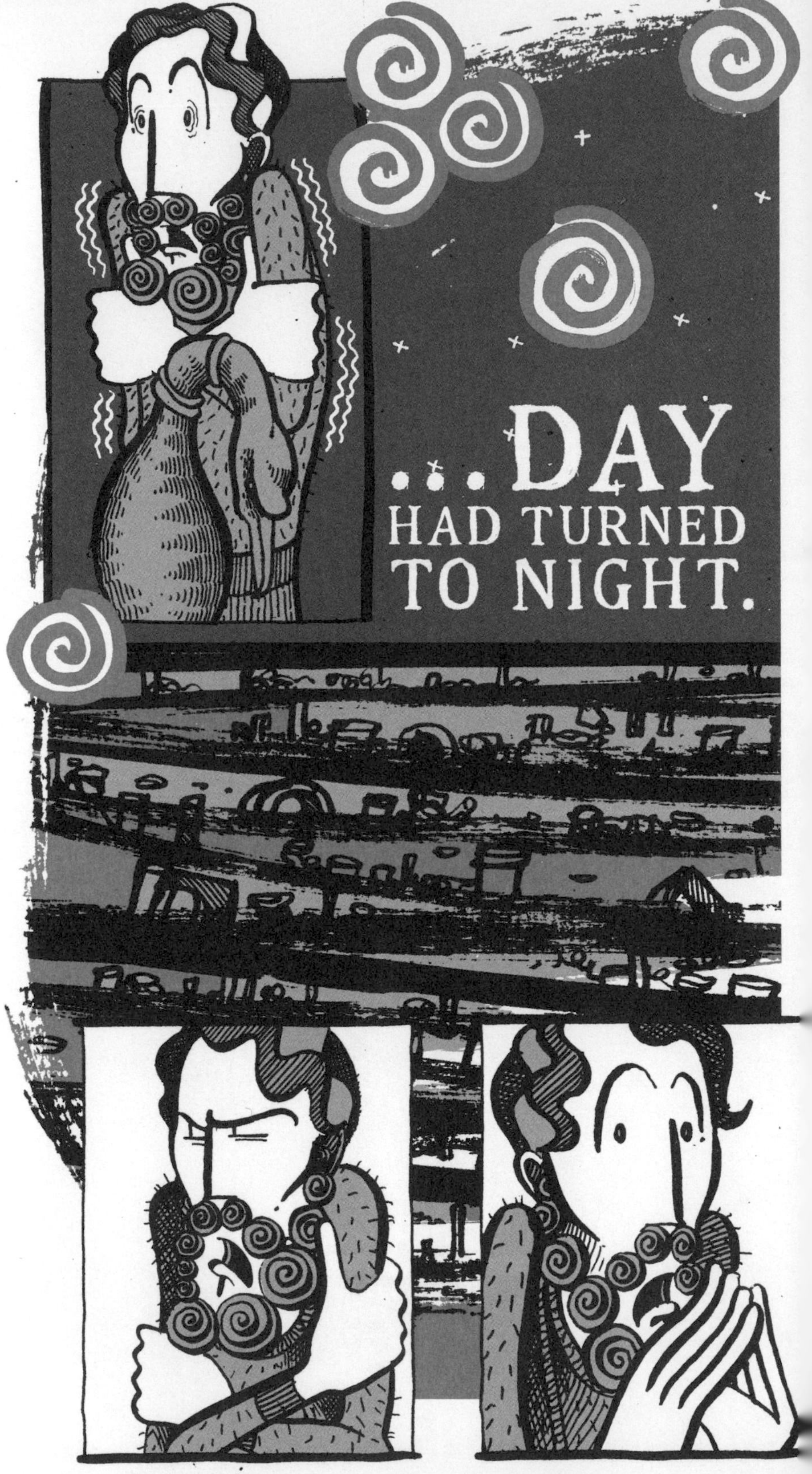
...DAY
HAD TURNED
TO NIGHT.

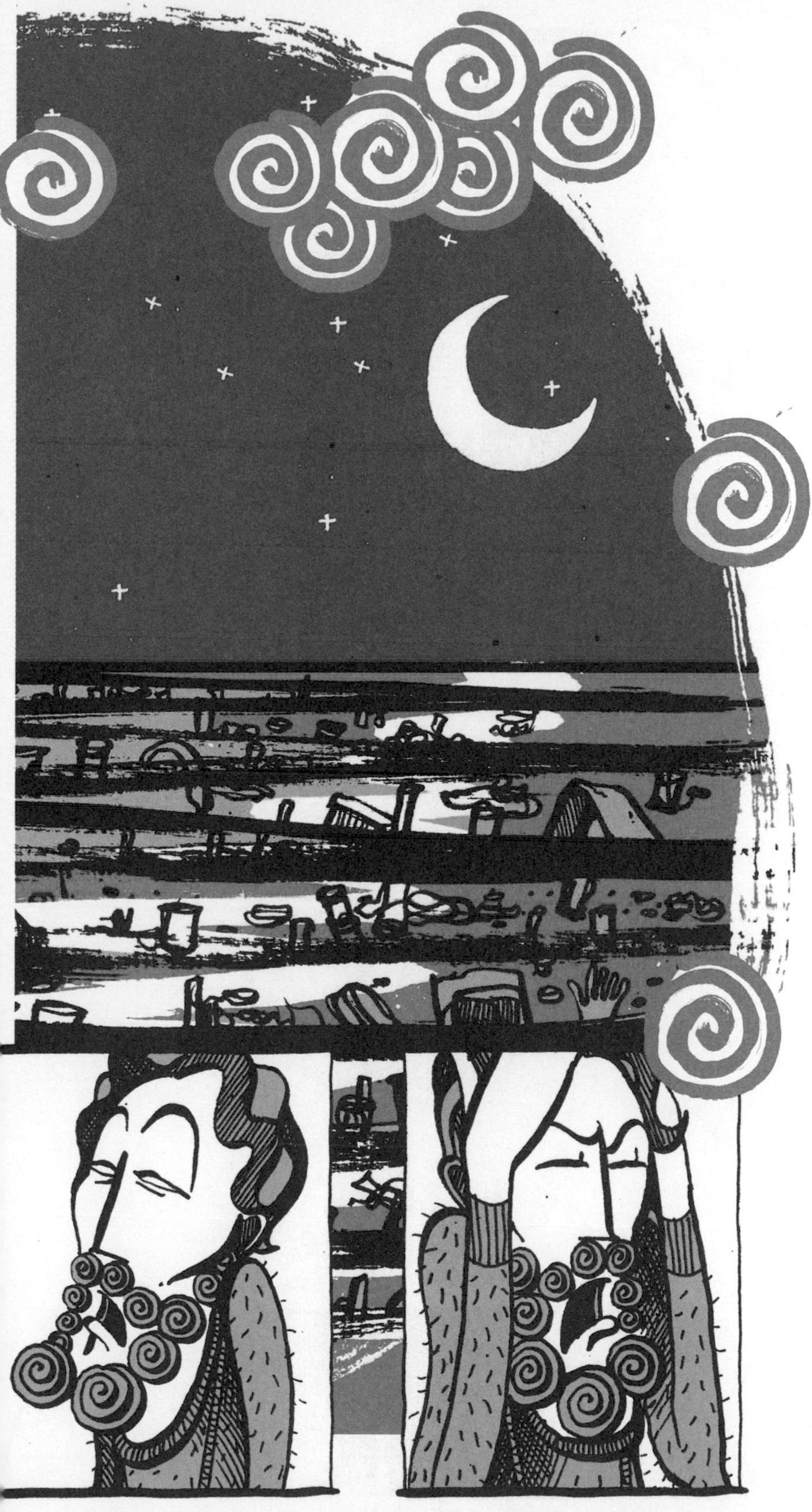

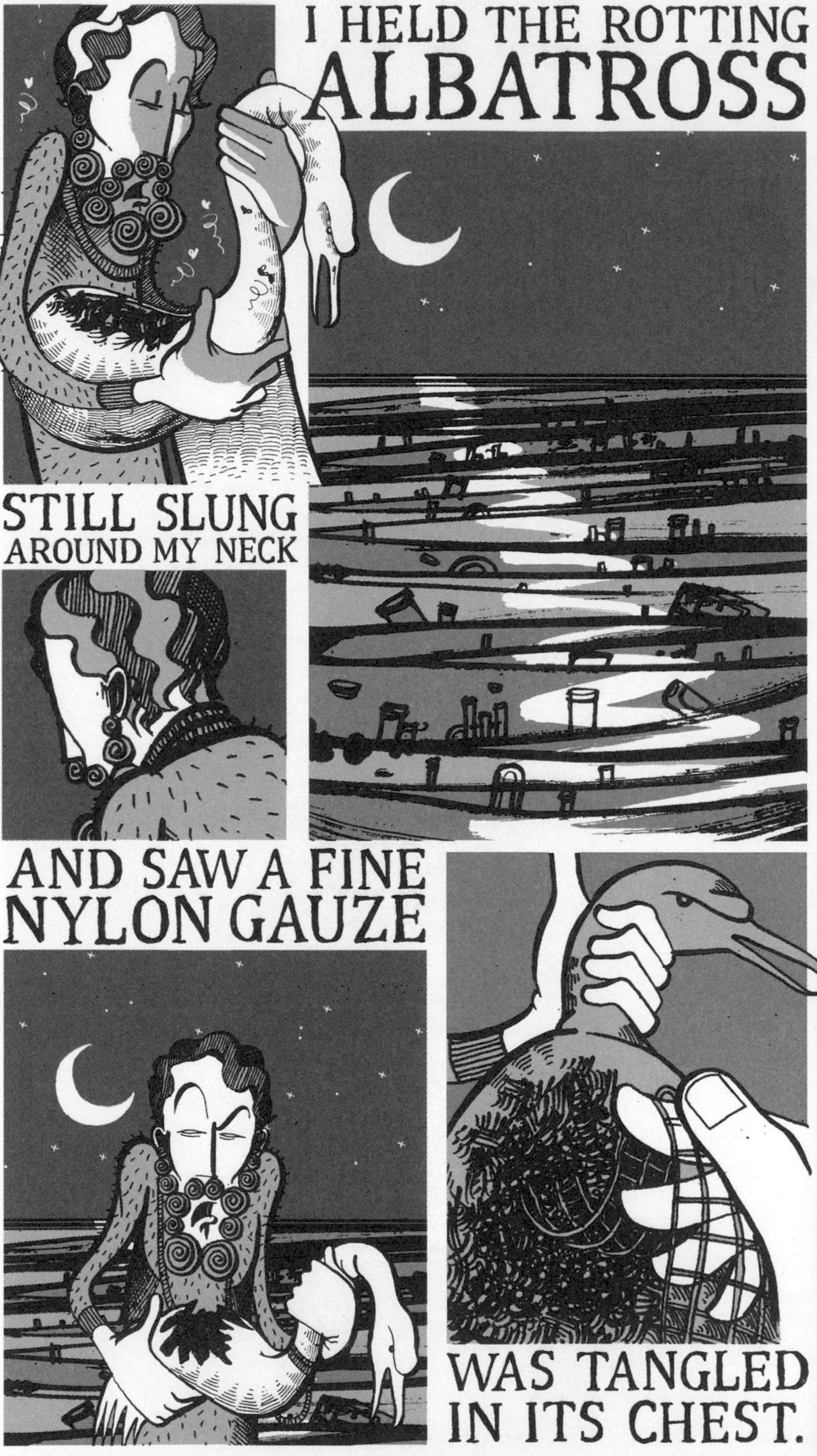
I HELD THE ROTTING ALBATROSS
STILL SLUNG AROUND MY NECK
AND SAW A FINE NYLON GAUZE
WAS TANGLED IN ITS CHEST.

ITS KIDNEYS,
WITHERED BY THE SUN,

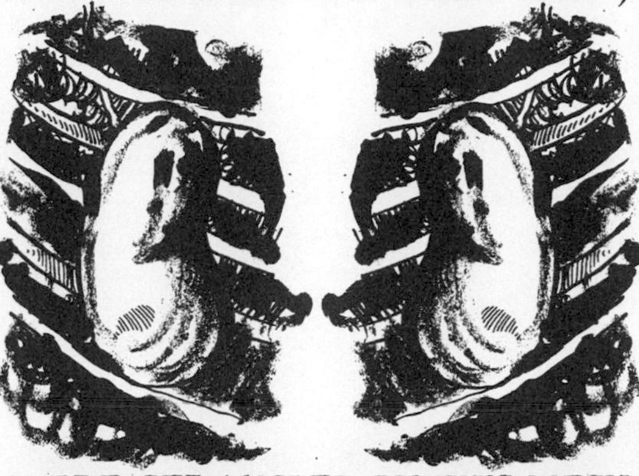

WERE STRANGLED BY THIS MESH;

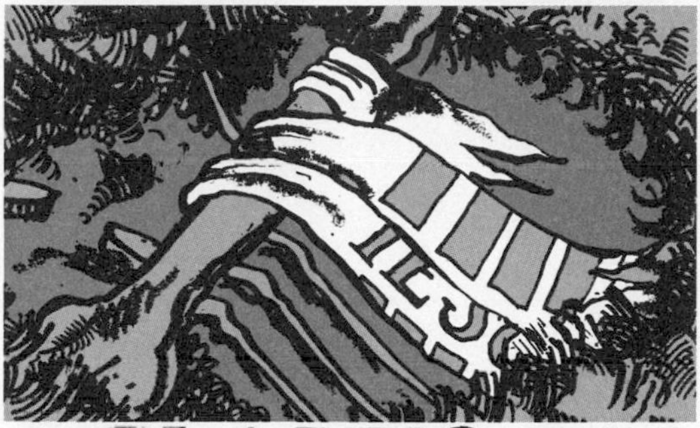

A PLASTIC BAG
HUNG ROUND ITS BONES

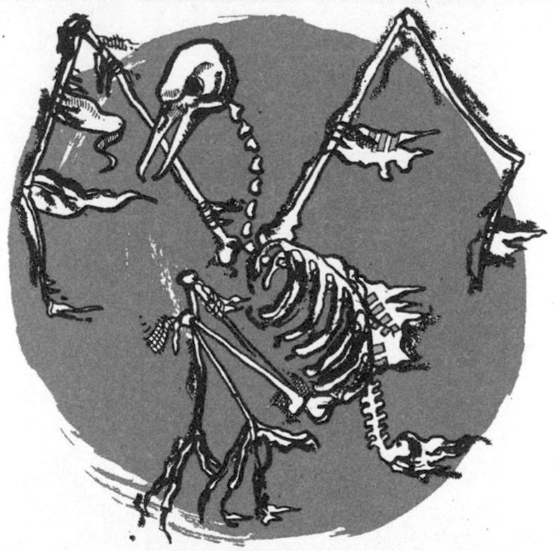

AND DECOMPOSED
LIKE FLESH.

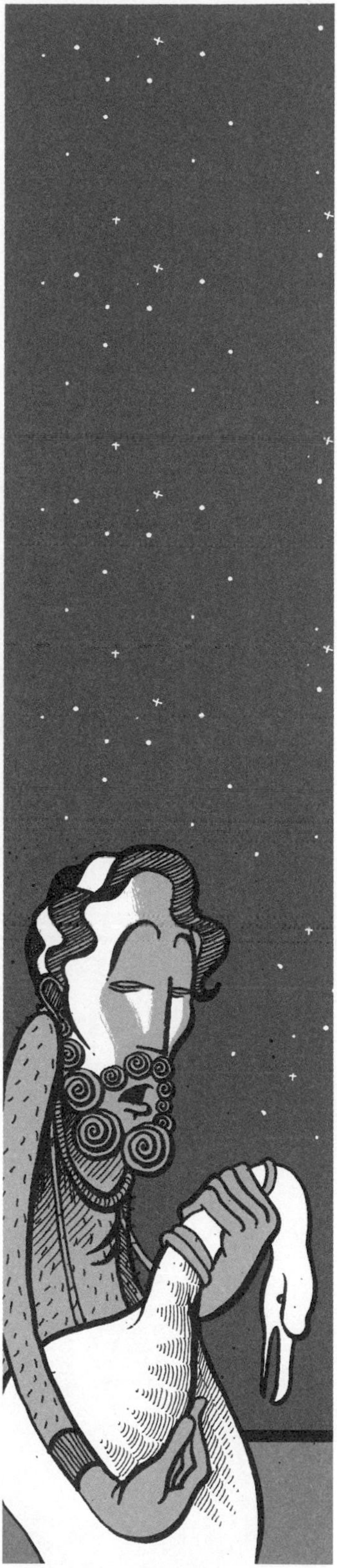

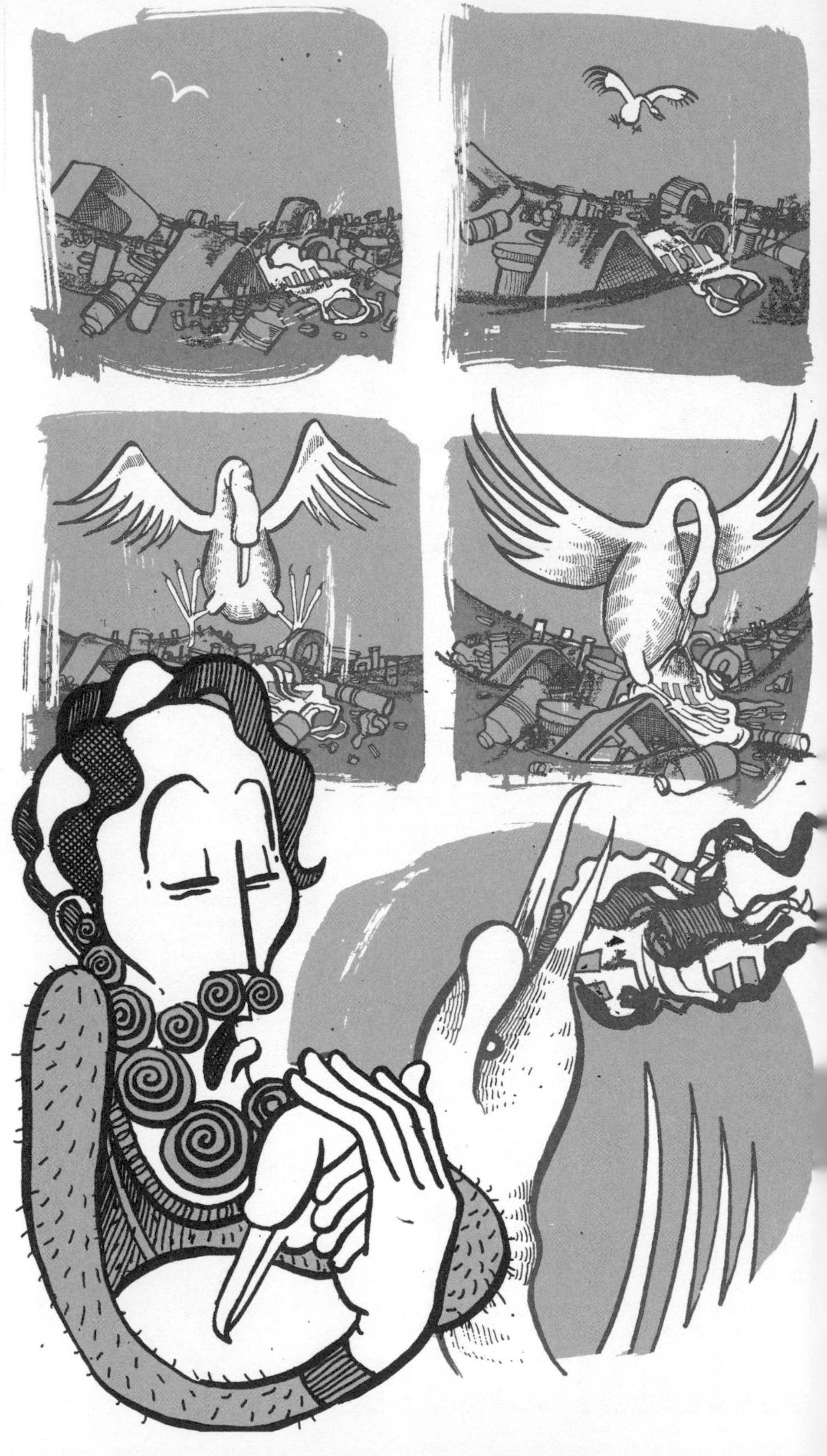

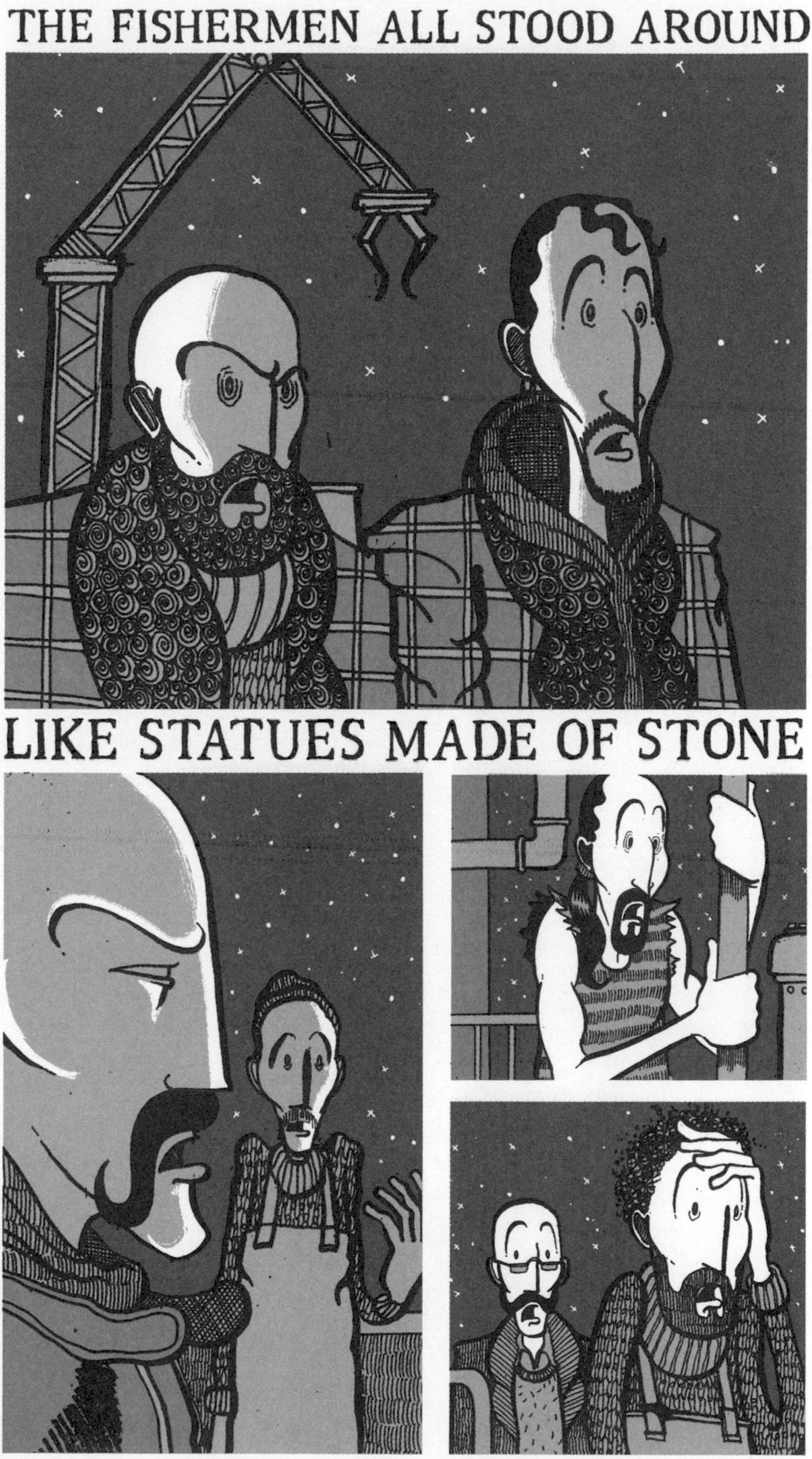
THE FISHERMEN ALL STOOD AROUND
LIKE STATUES MADE OF STONE

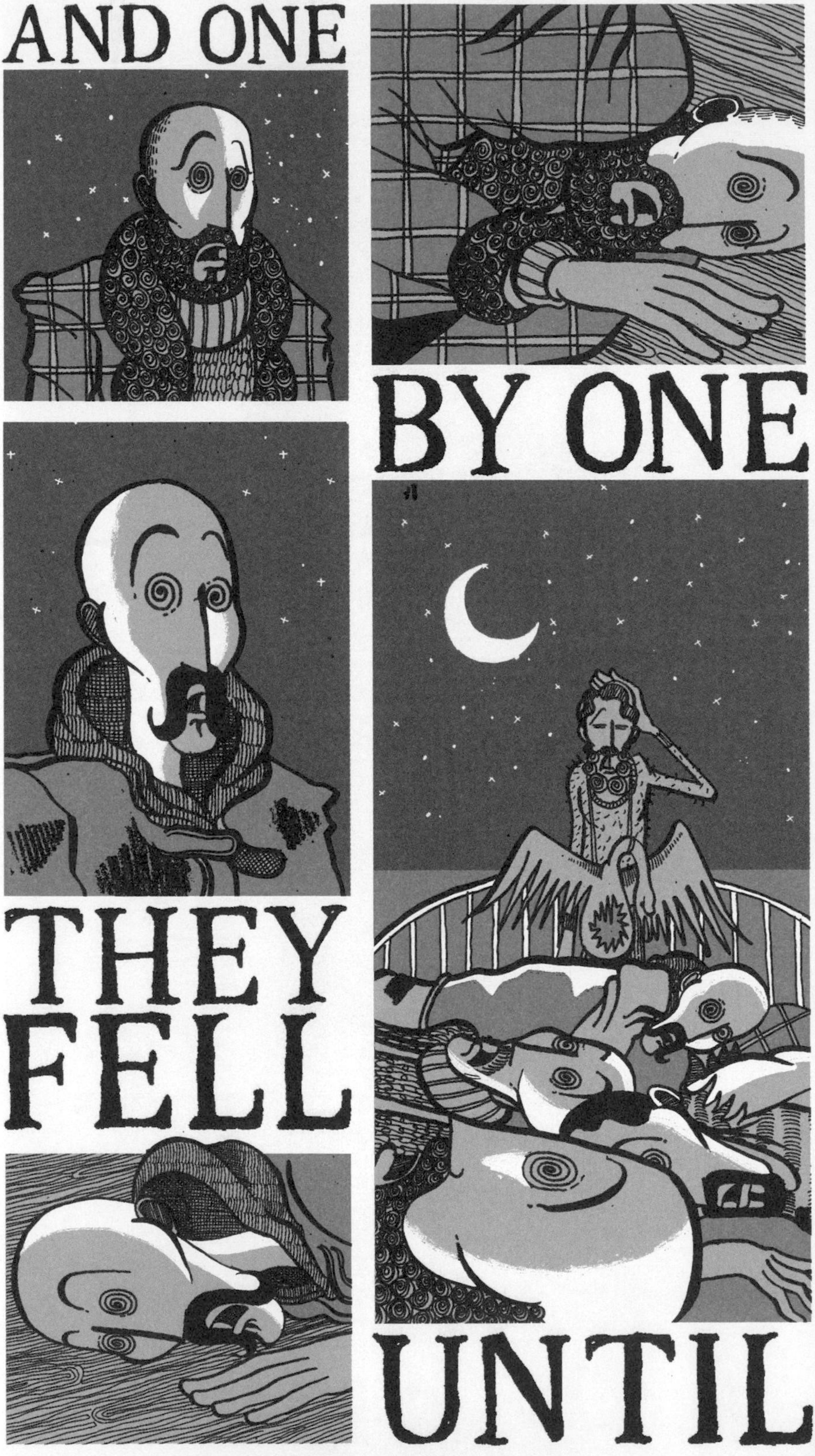
AND ONE
BY ONE
THEY
FELL
UNTIL

AT LAST
I WAS
ALONE.

PART FOUR

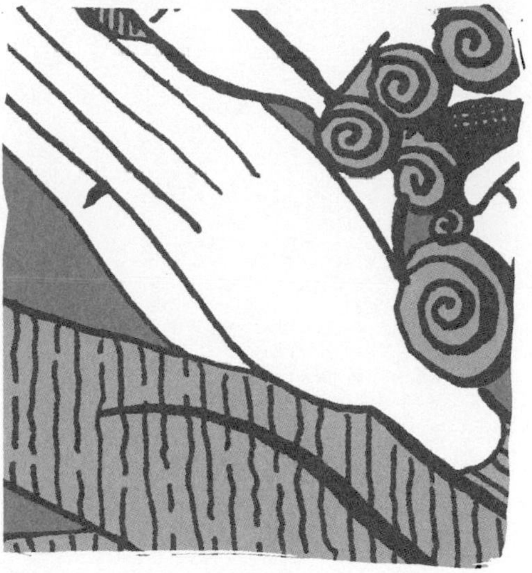

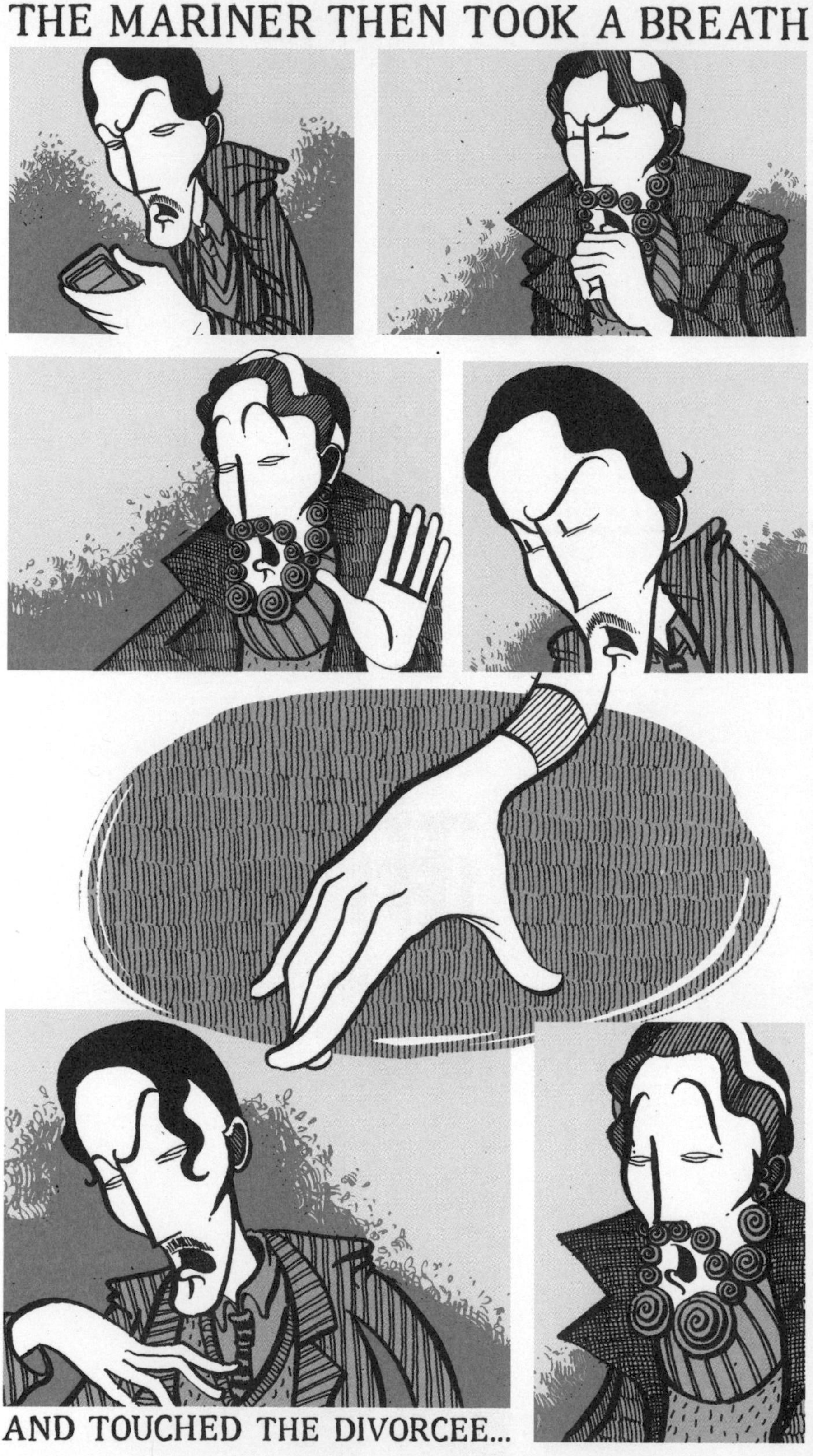
THE MARINER THEN TOOK A BREATH
AND TOUCHED THE DIVORCEE...

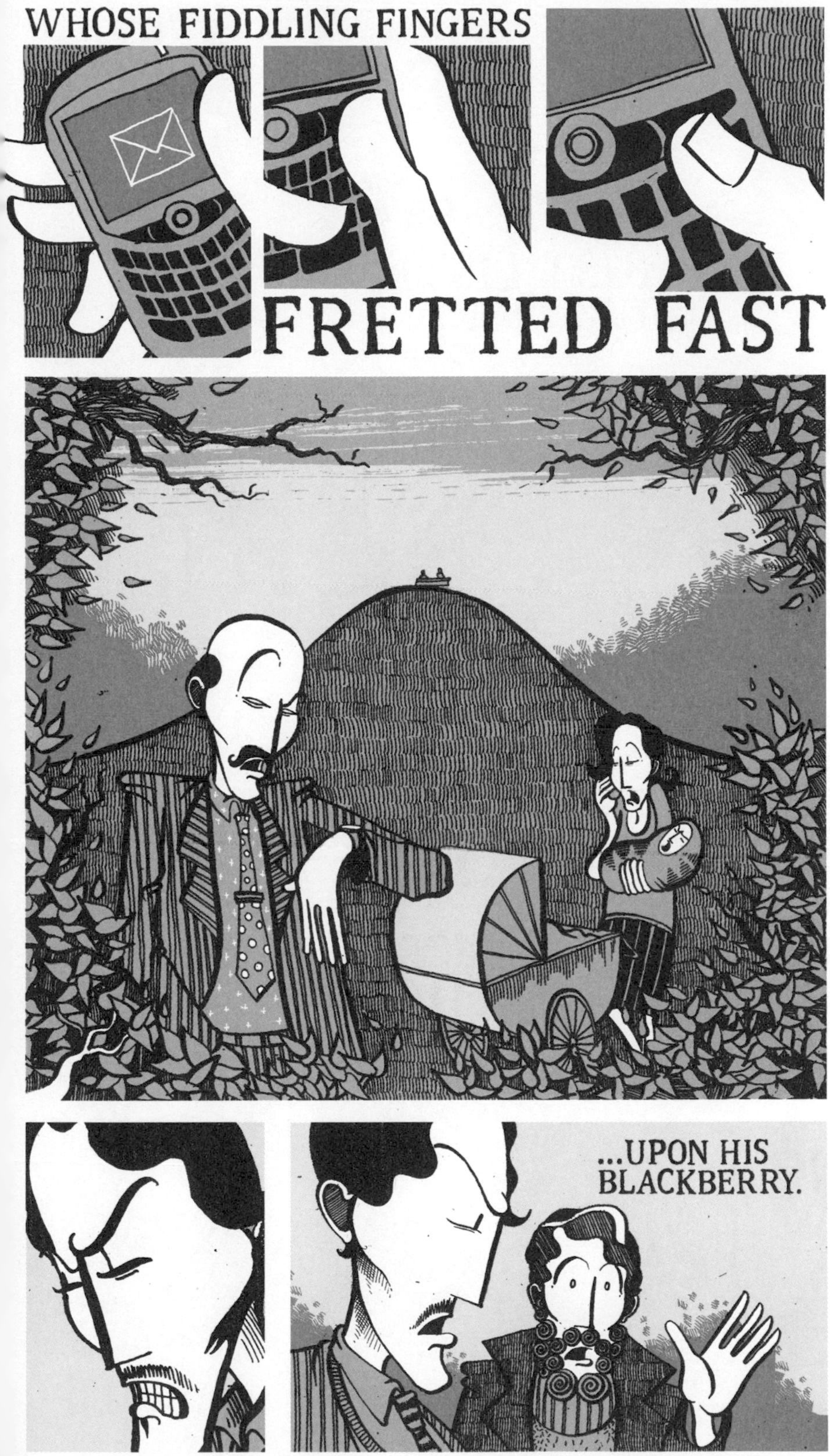
WHOSE FIDDLING FINGERS
FRETTED FAST
...UPON HIS BLACKBERRY.

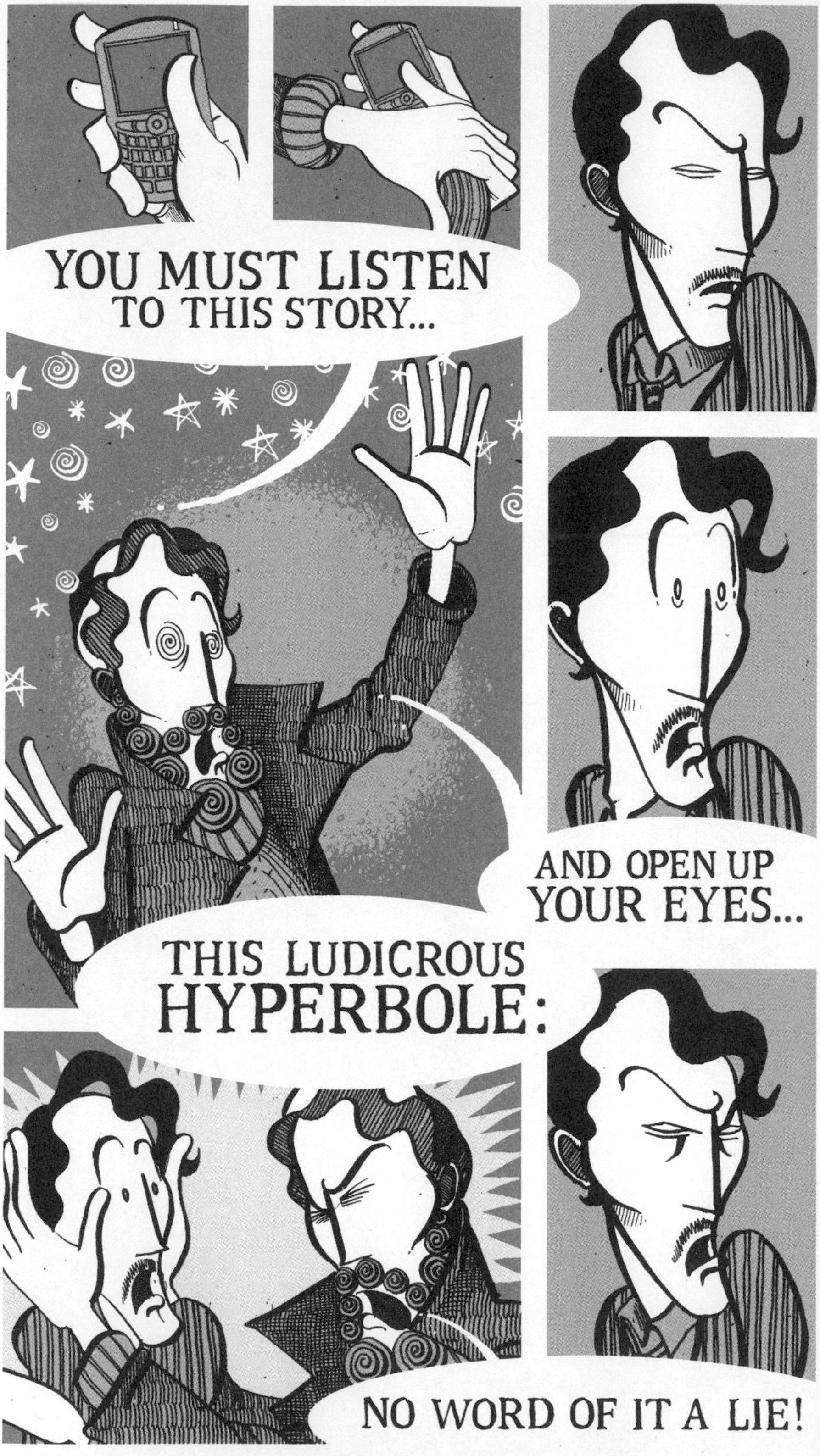
YOU MUST LISTEN TO THIS STORY...
AND OPEN UP YOUR EYES...
THIS LUDICROUS HYPERBOLE:
NO WORD OF IT A LIE!

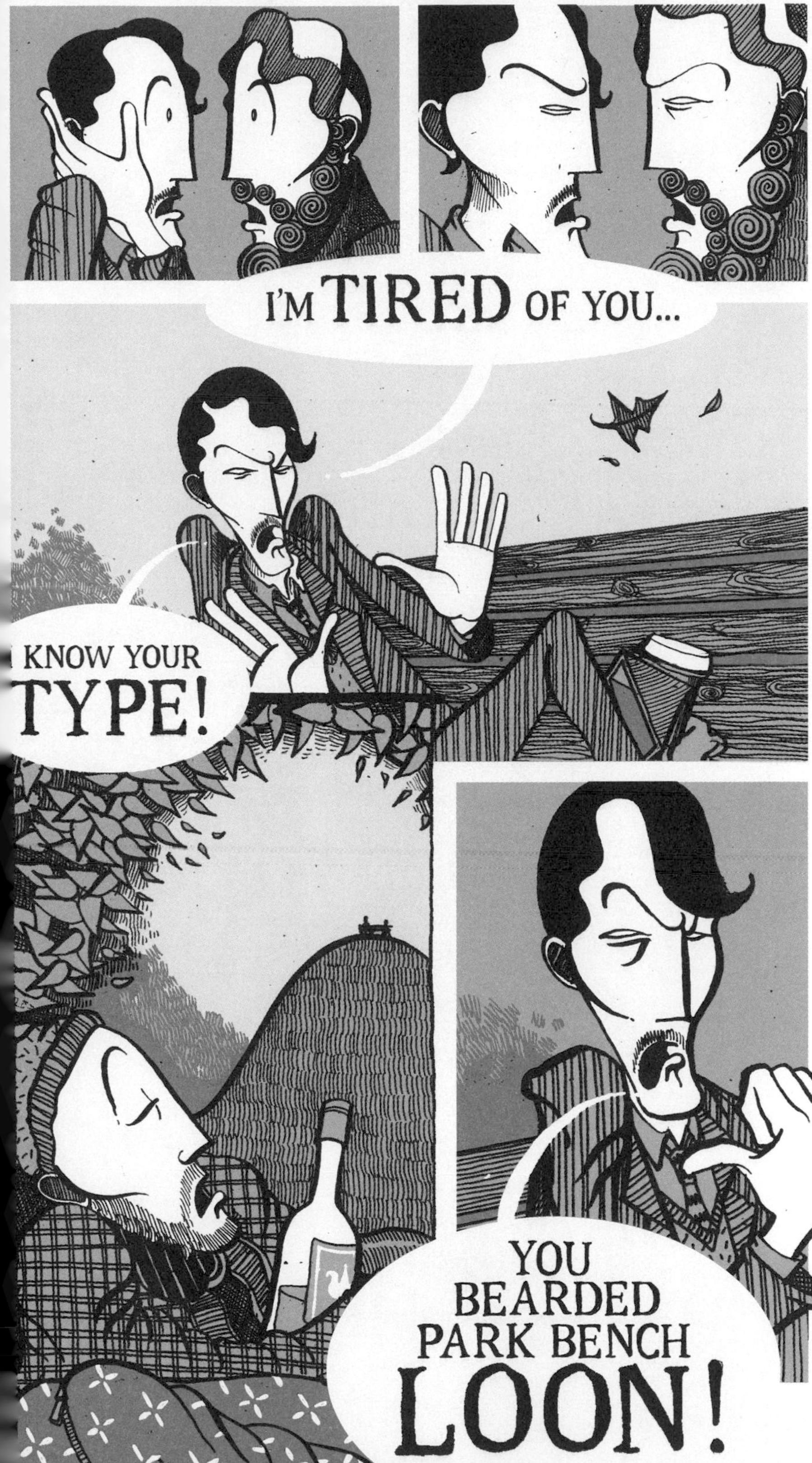

I'M TIRED OF YOU...
I KNOW YOUR TYPE!
YOU BEARDED PARK BENCH LOON!

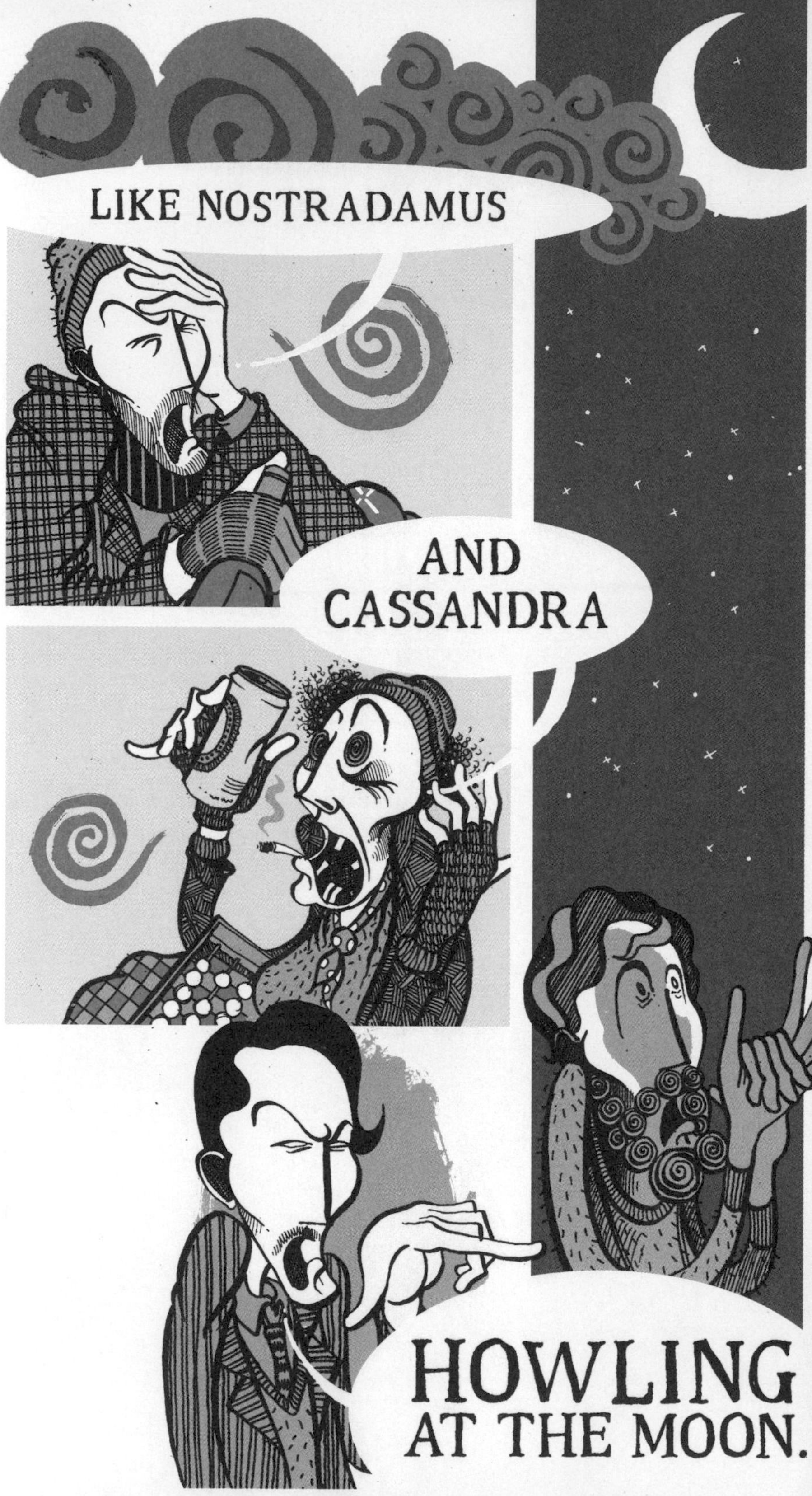
LIKE NOSTRADAMUS
AND CASSANDRA
HOWLING AT THE MOON.

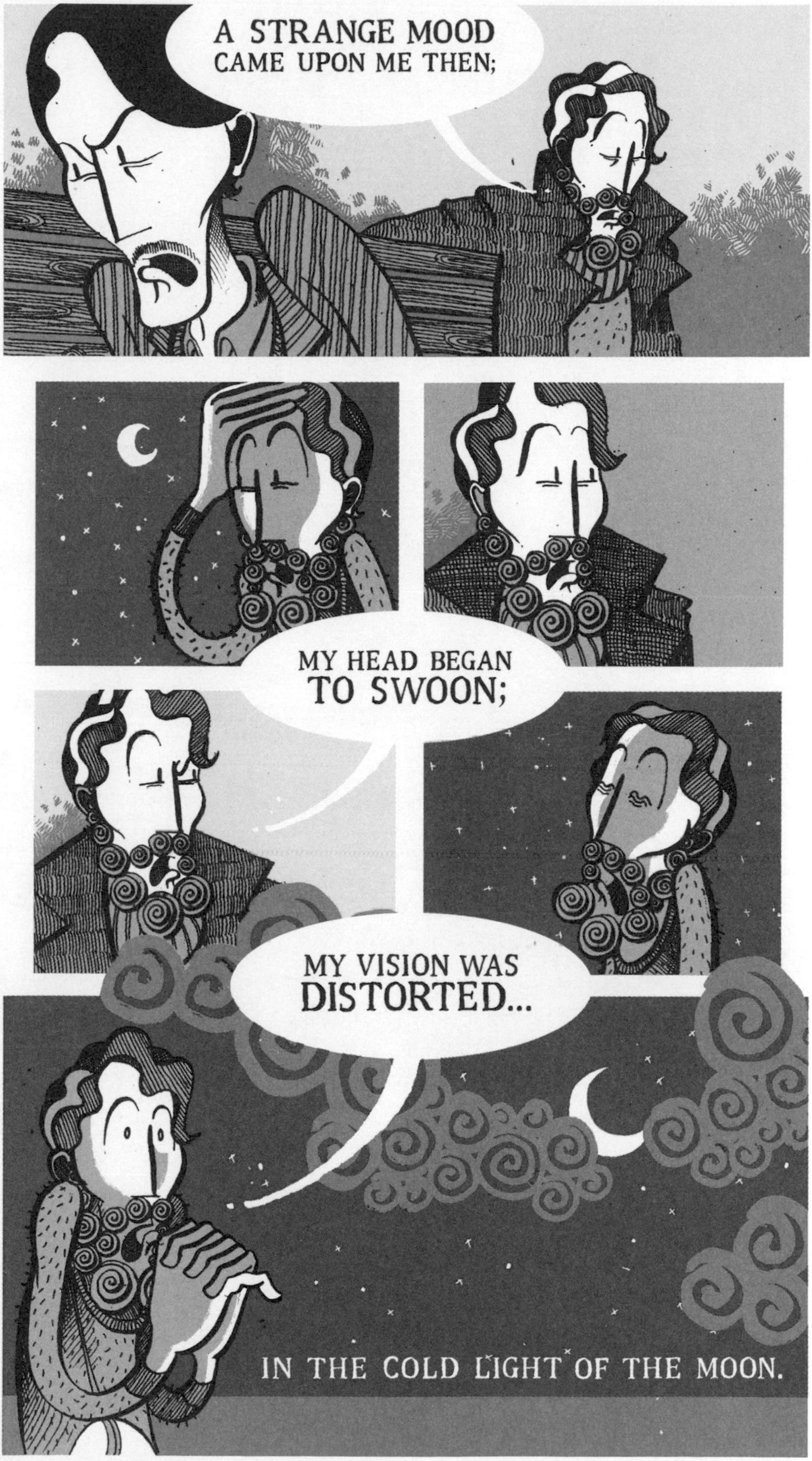
A STRANGE MOOD CAME UPON ME THEN;
MY HEAD BEGAN TO SWOON;
MY VISION WAS DISTORTED...
IN THE COLD LIGHT OF THE MOON.

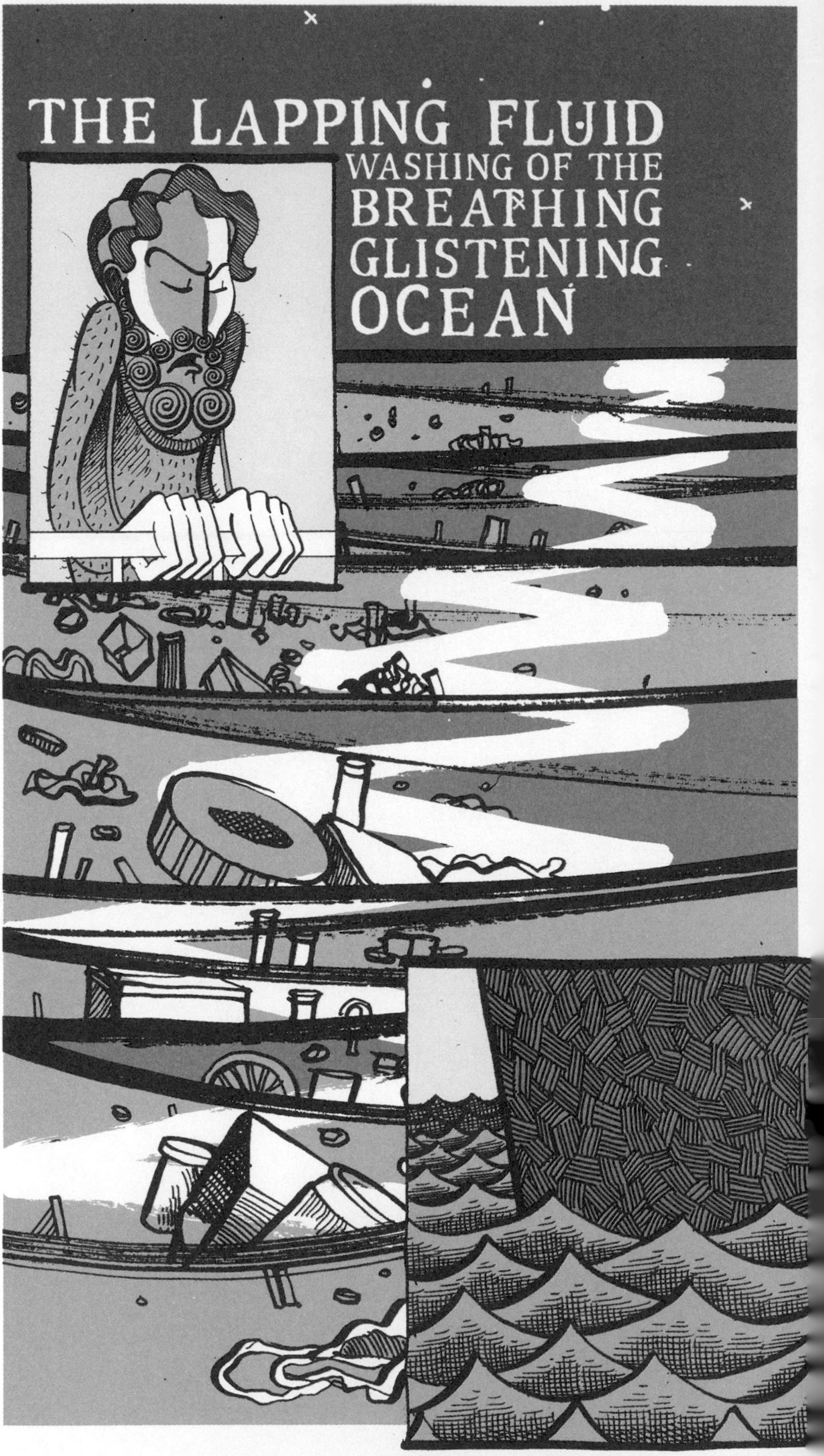
THE LAPPING FLUID
WASHING OF THE
BREATHING
GLISTENING
OCEAN

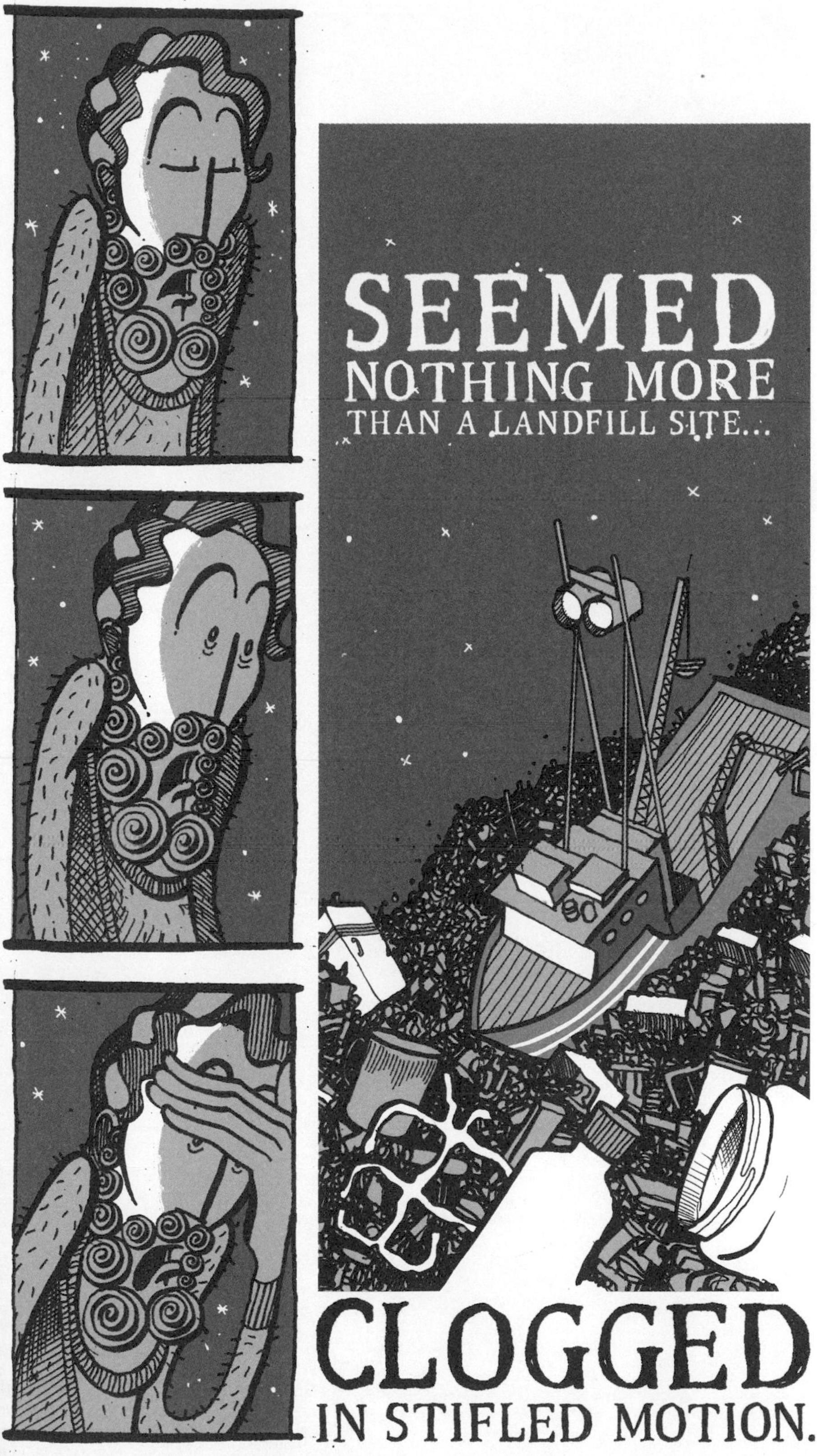
SEEMED NOTHING MORE THAN A LANDFILL SITE...
CLOGGED IN STIFLED MOTION.

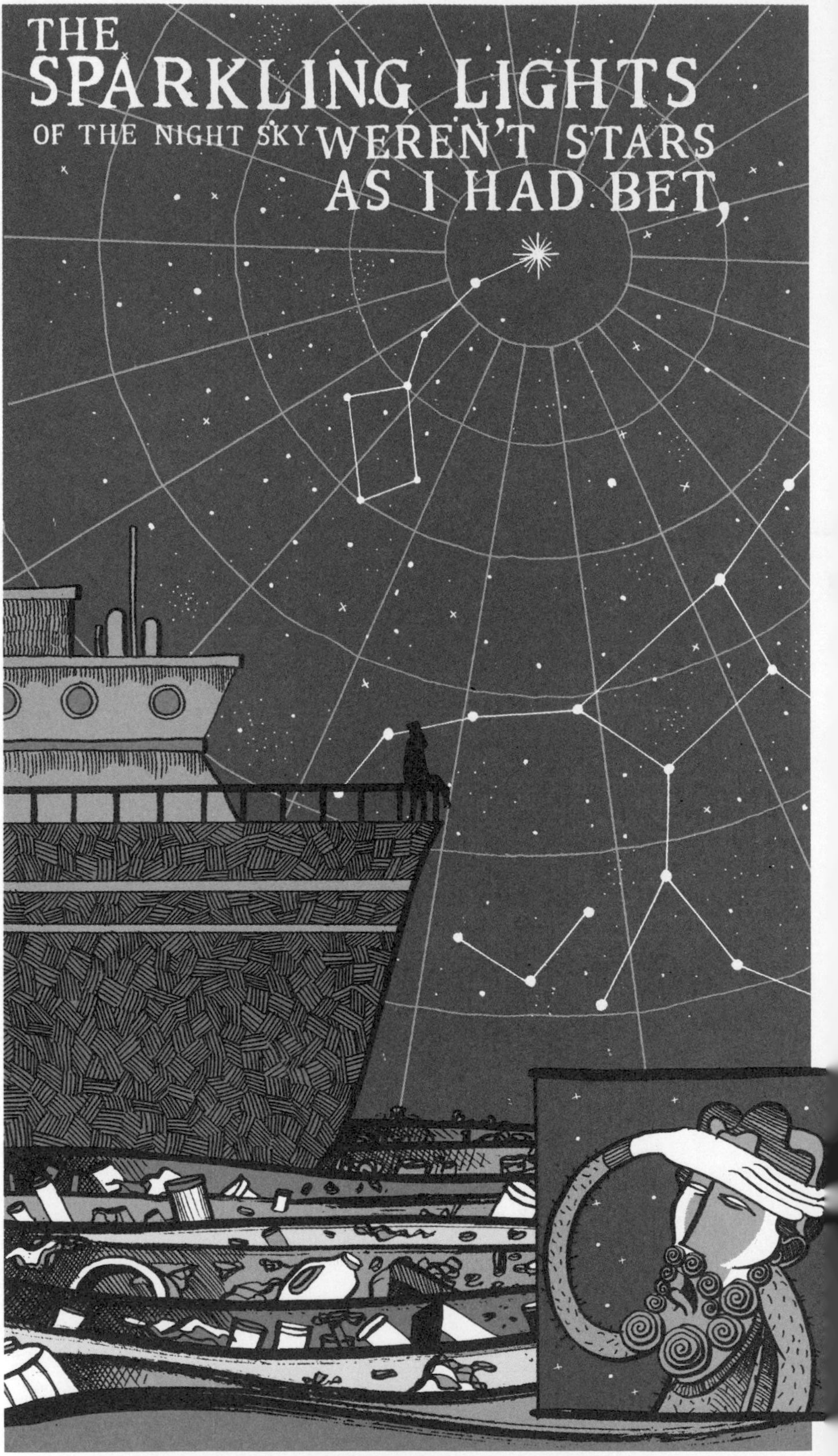

THE SPARKLING LIGHTS OF THE NIGHT SKY WEREN'T STARS AS I HAD BET,

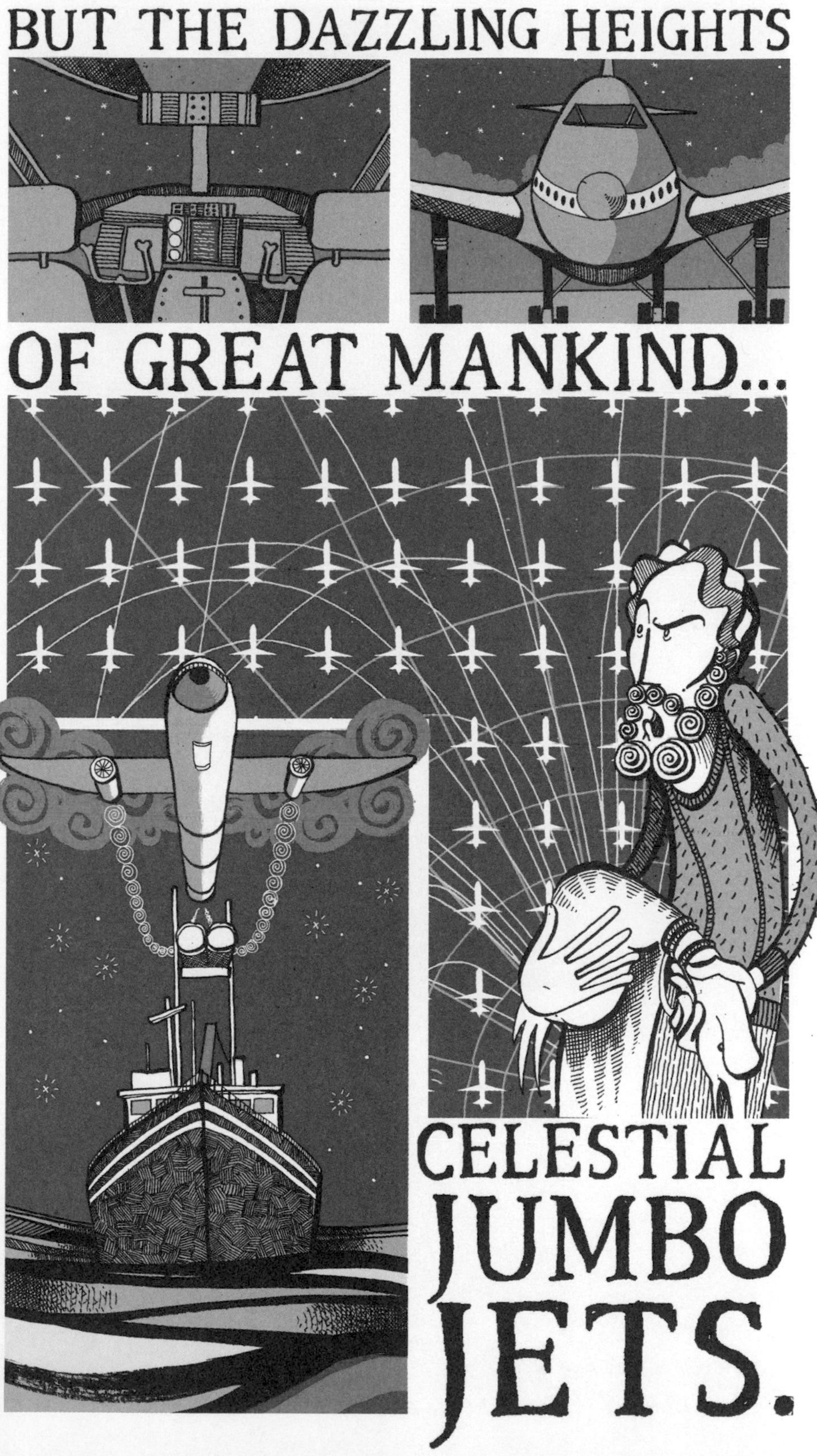
BUT THE DAZZLING HEIGHTS
OF GREAT MANKIND...
CELESTIAL JUMBO JETS.

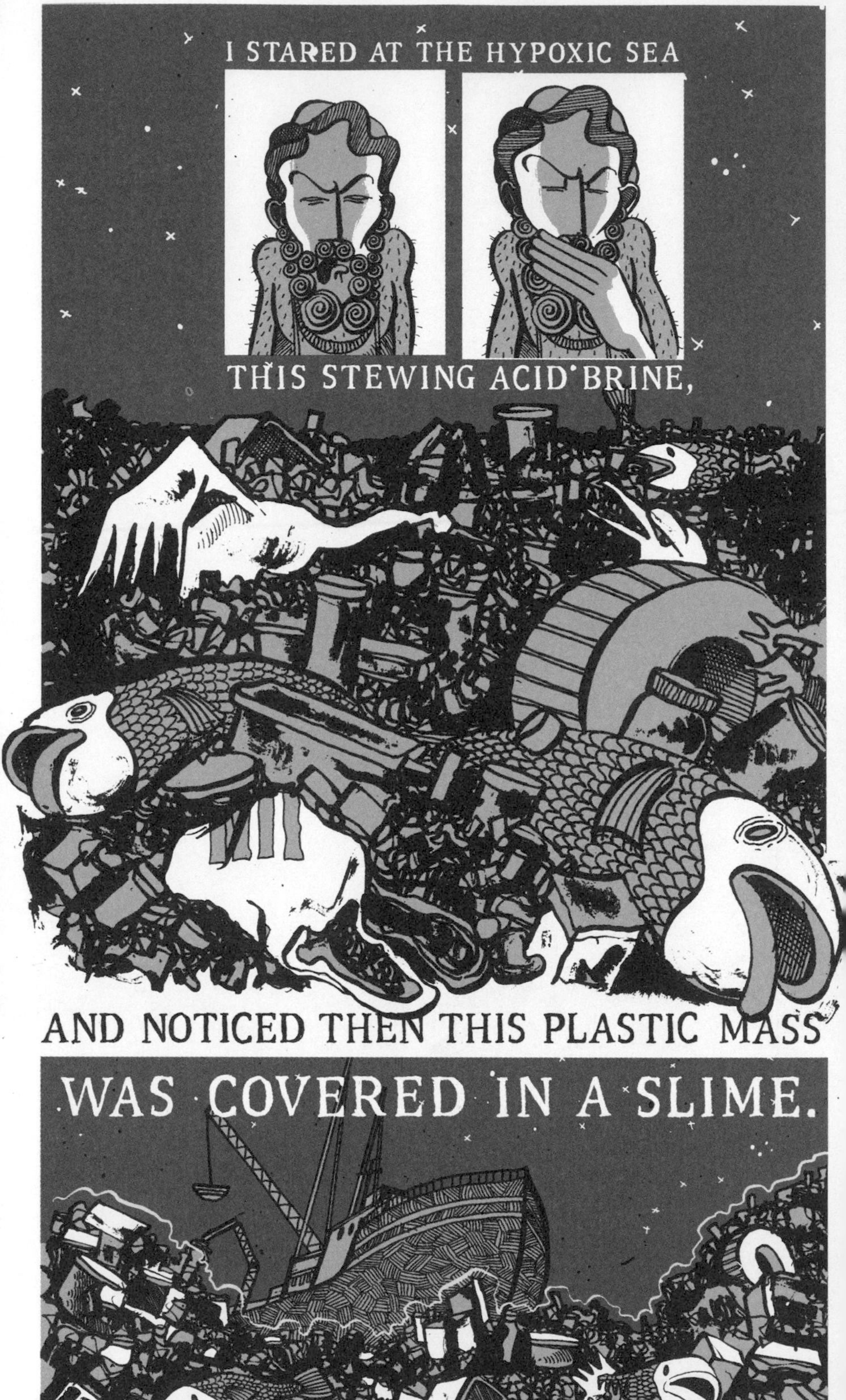
I STARED AT THE HYPOXIC SEA
THIS STEWING ACID BRINE,
AND NOTICED THEN THIS PLASTIC MASS
WAS COVERED IN A SLIME.

I LOOKED A LITTLE CLOSER,

AND FELT MY EYES DILATE:

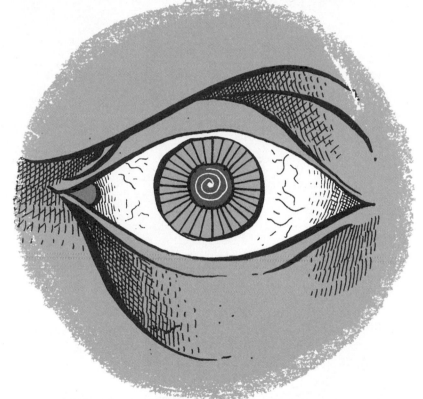

FOR SLOPPED ACROSS THE BOBBING DROSS...

WAS A FILM OF TUNICATES.

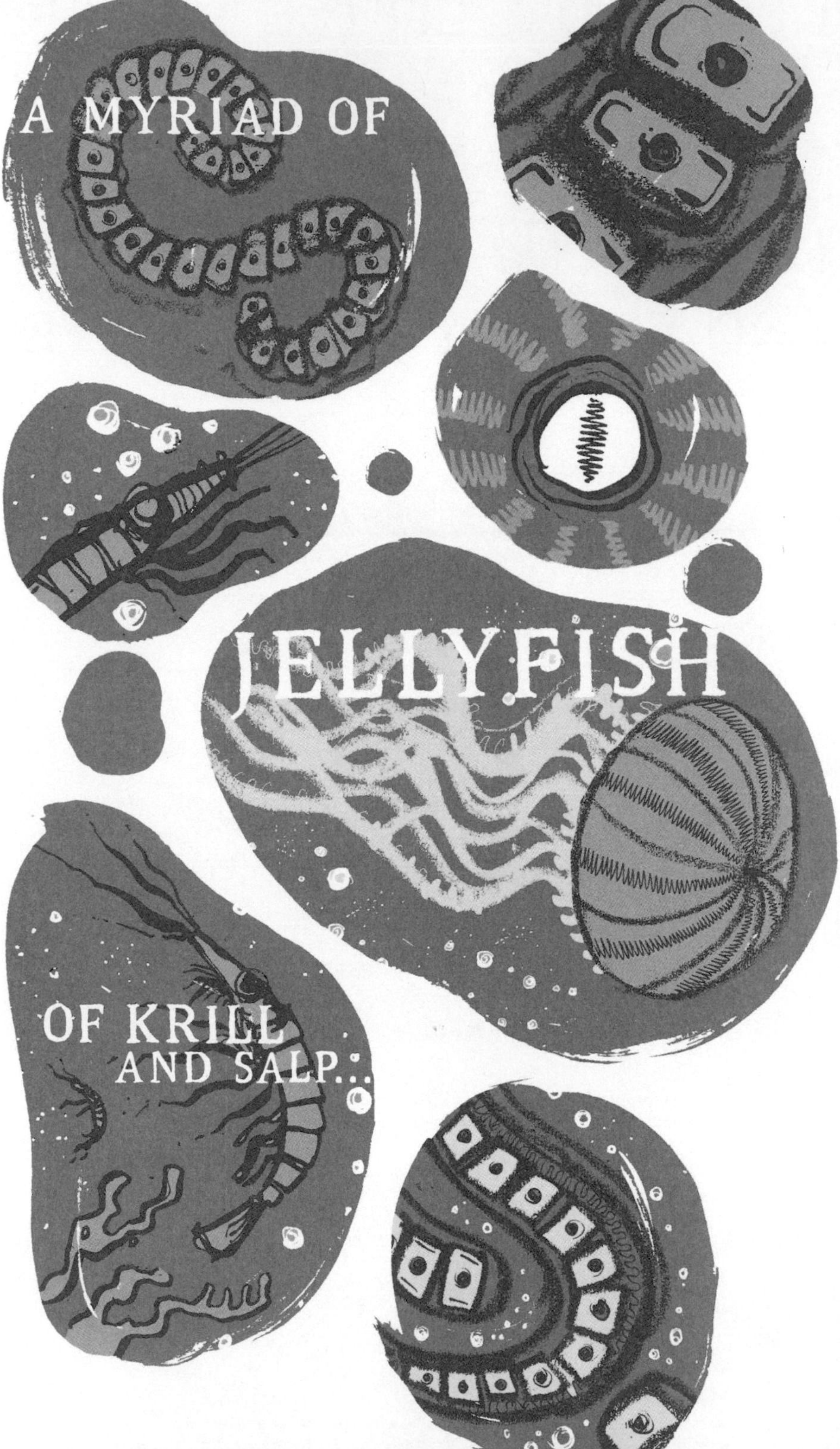
A MYRIAD OF
JELLYFISH
OF KRILL
AND SALP...

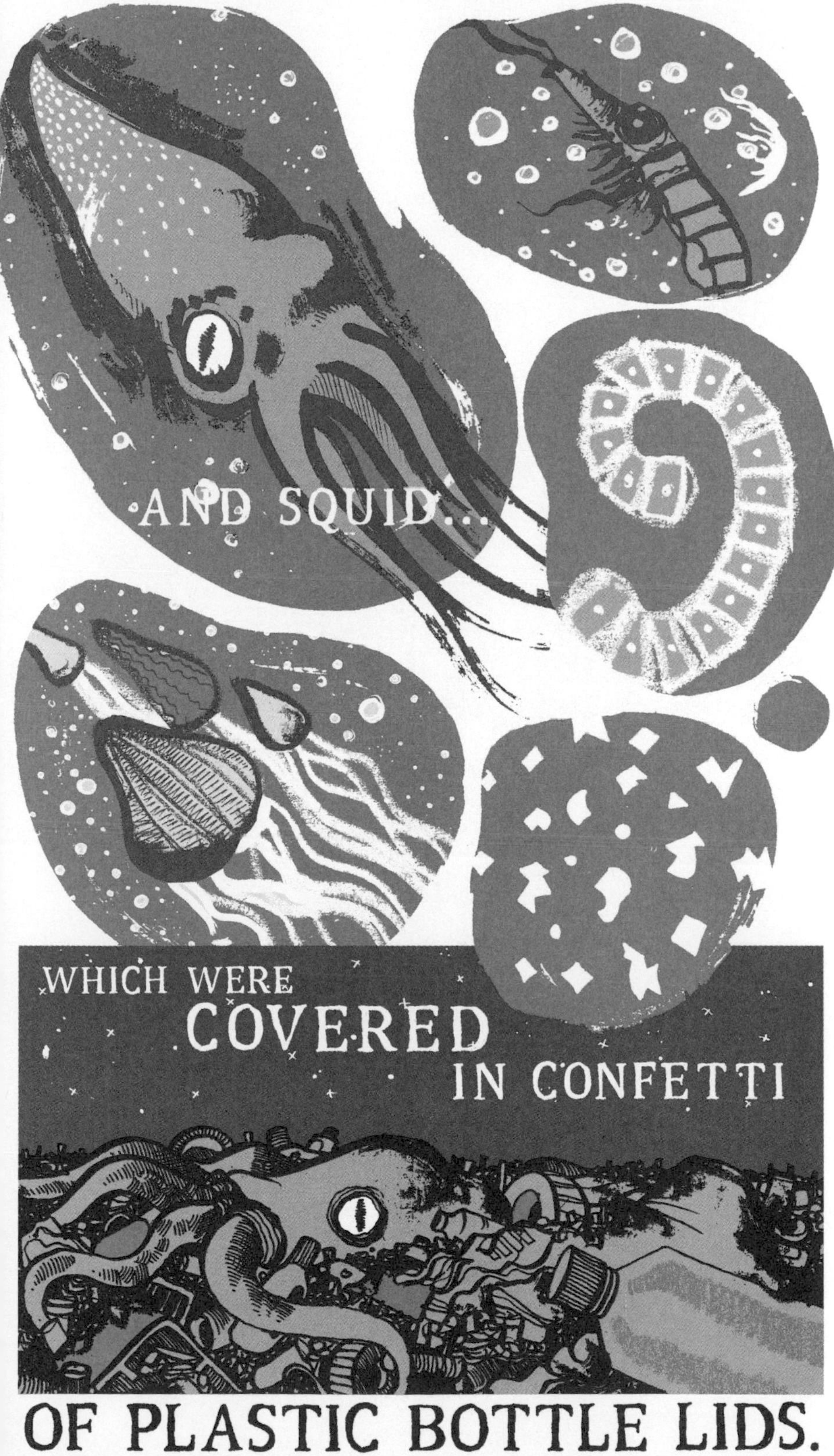
AND SQUID...
WHICH WERE
COVERED
IN CONFETTI

OF PLASTIC BOTTLE LIDS.

I LOOKED A LITTLE CLOSER,

I STARED AT THEM AFRESH...

THE BITS
WEREN'T STREWN UPON THEM,

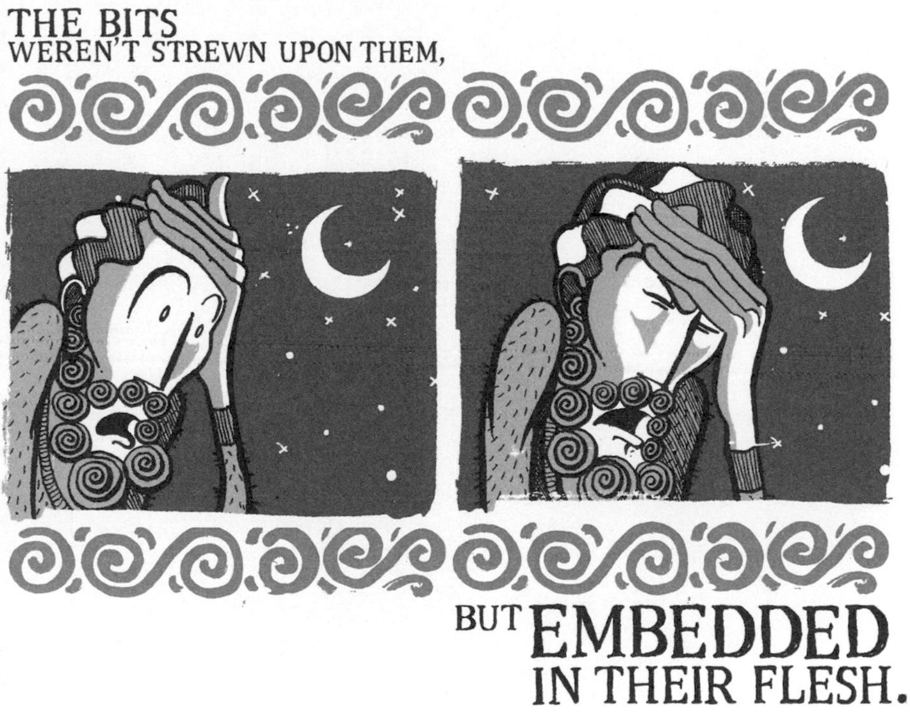

BUT EMBEDDED
IN THEIR FLESH.

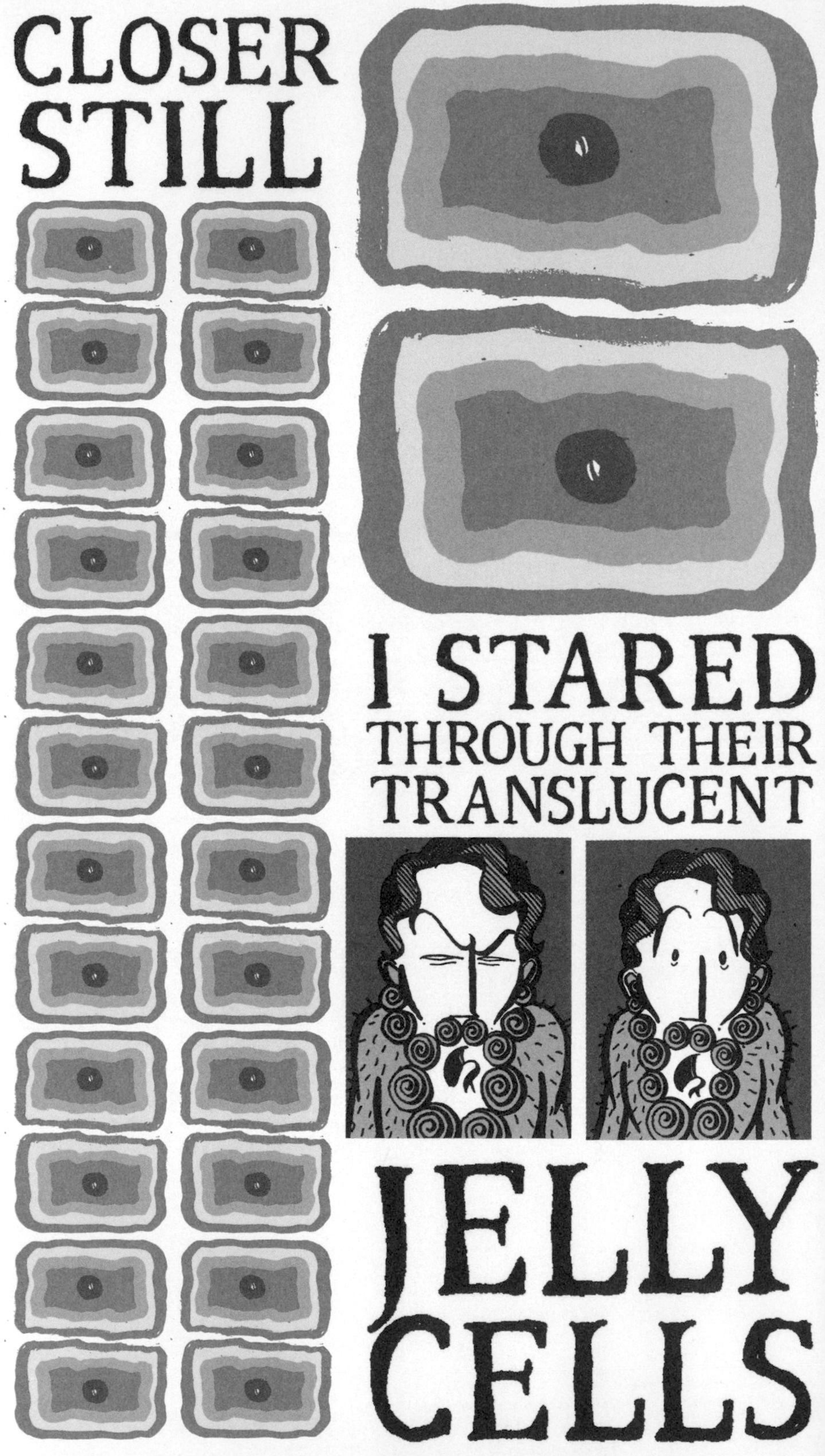
CLOSER STILL
I STARED THROUGH THEIR TRANSLUCENT
JELLY CELLS

AND SAW THE HEART

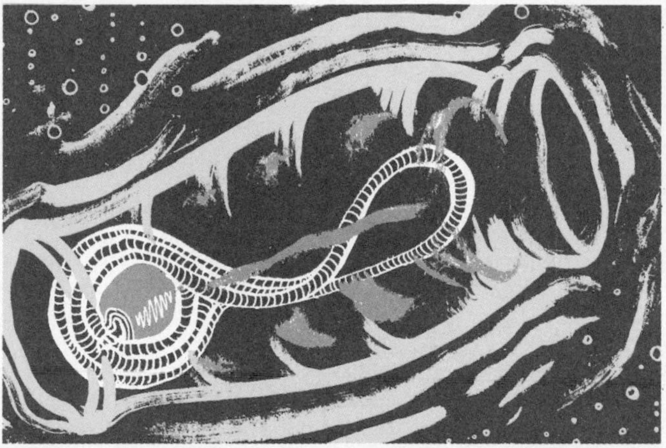

OF A TWO INCH SALP

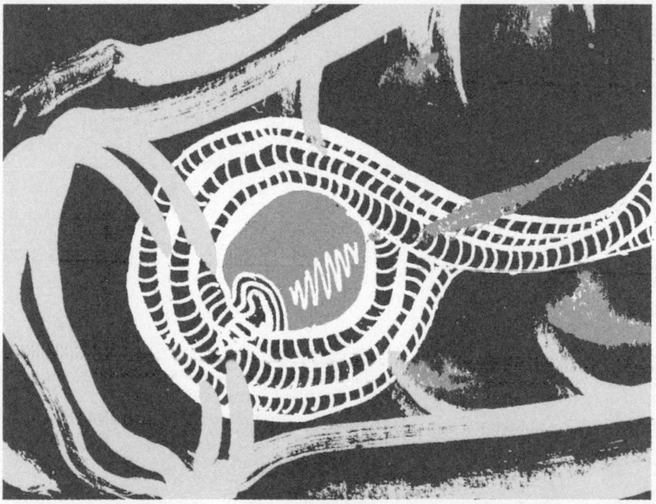

BEATING

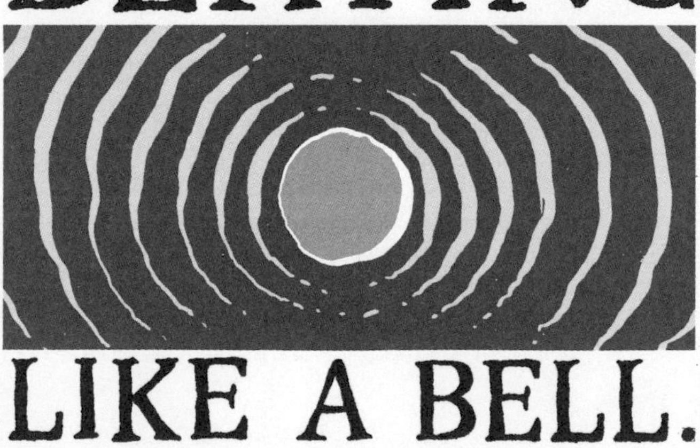

LIKE A BELL.

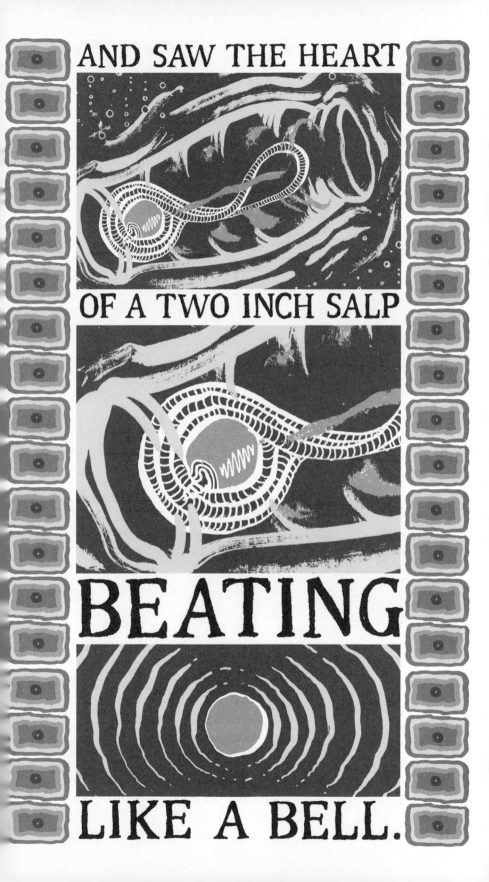

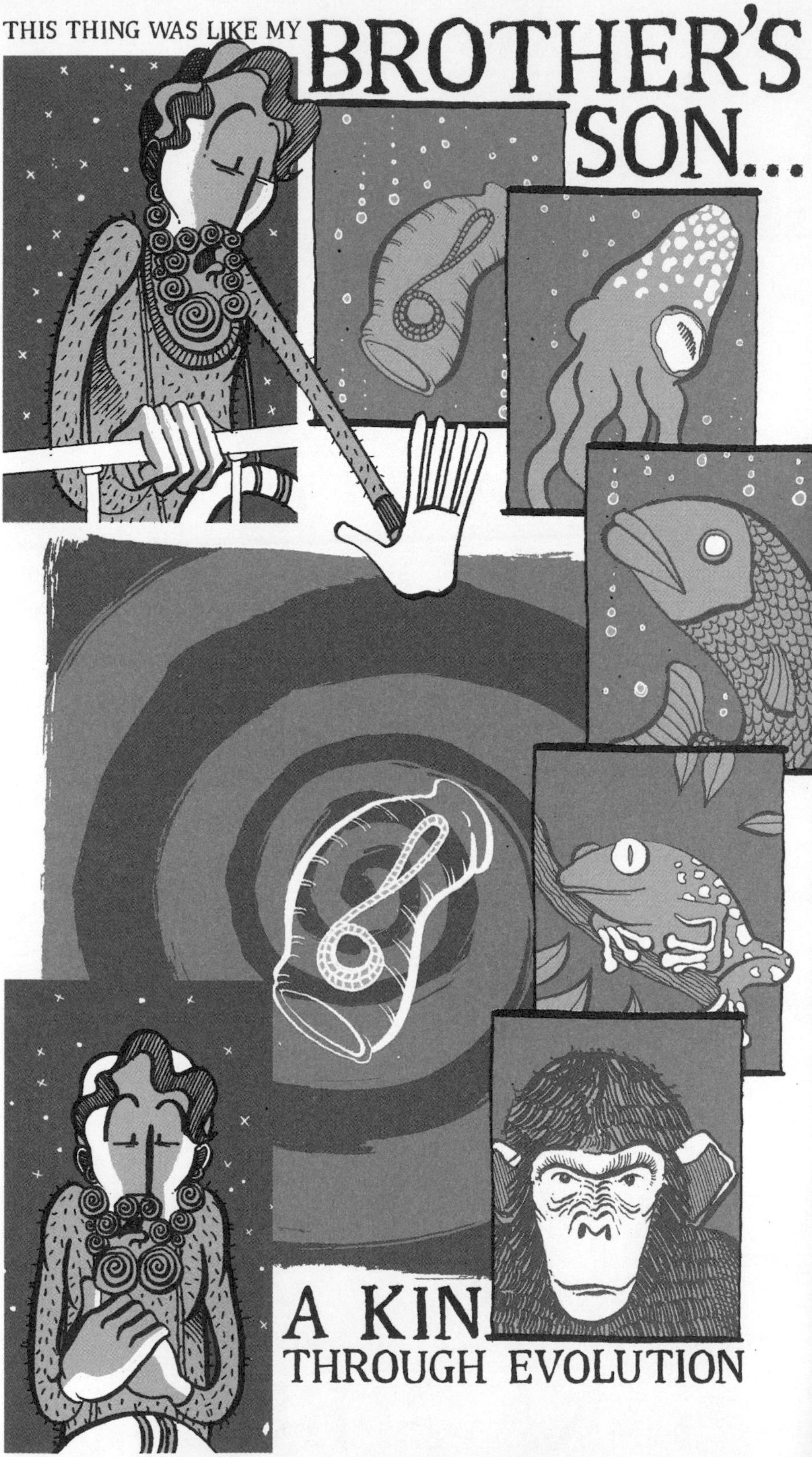
THIS THING WAS LIKE MY BROTHER'S SON...
A KIN THROUGH EVOLUTION

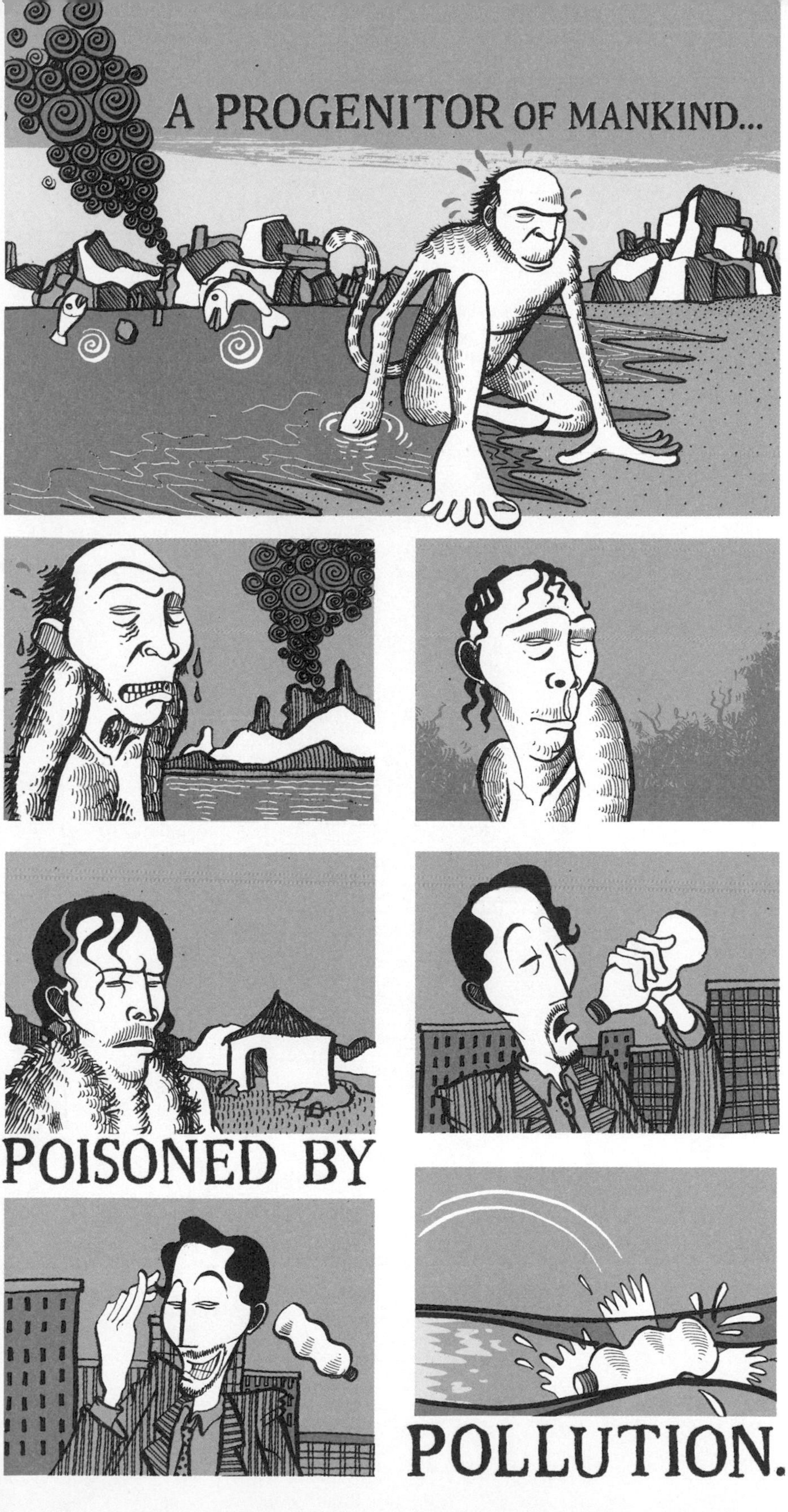
A PROGENITOR OF MANKIND...
POISONED BY
POLLUTION.

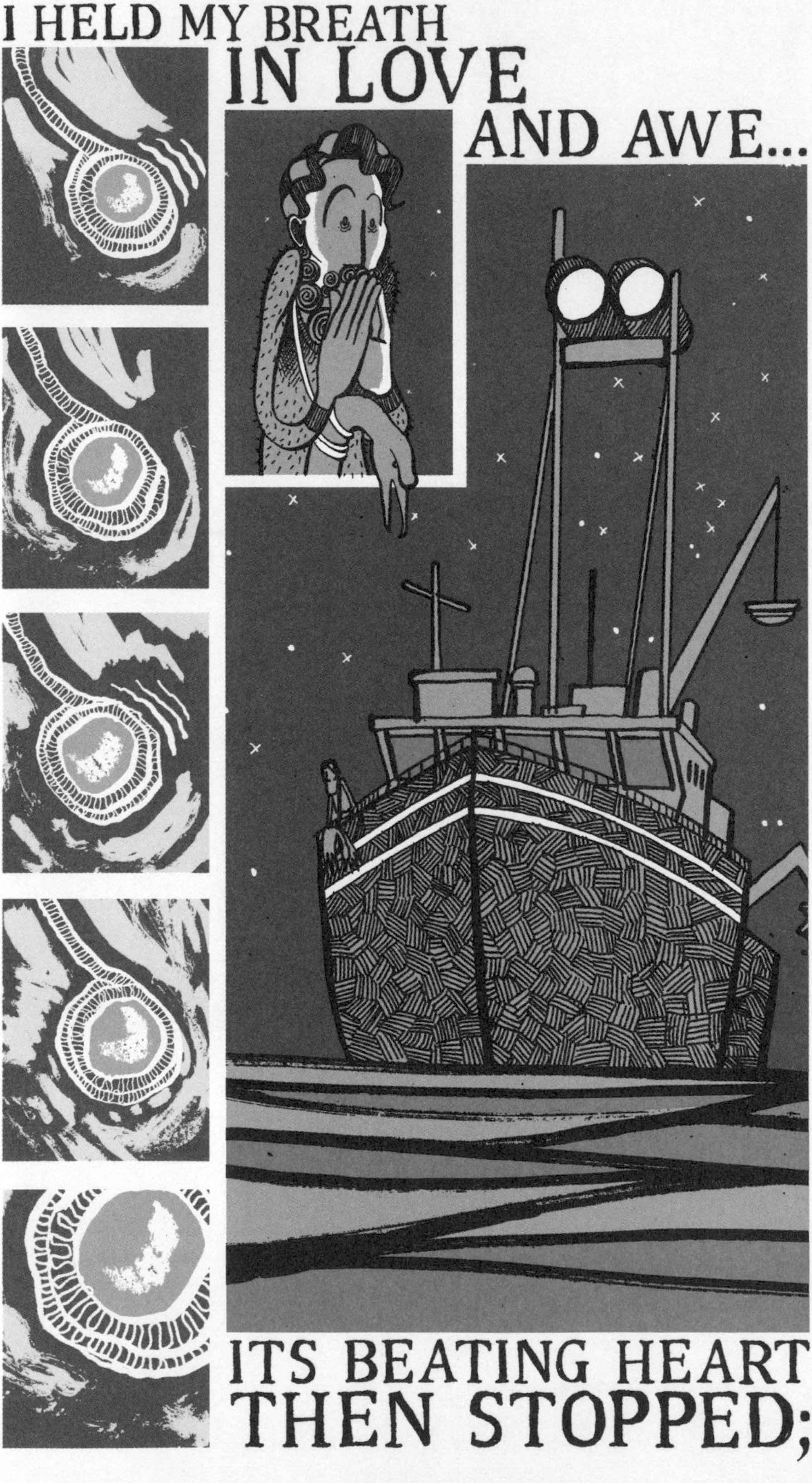
I HELD MY BREATH
IN LOVE
AND AWE...
ITS BEATING HEART
THEN STOPPED;

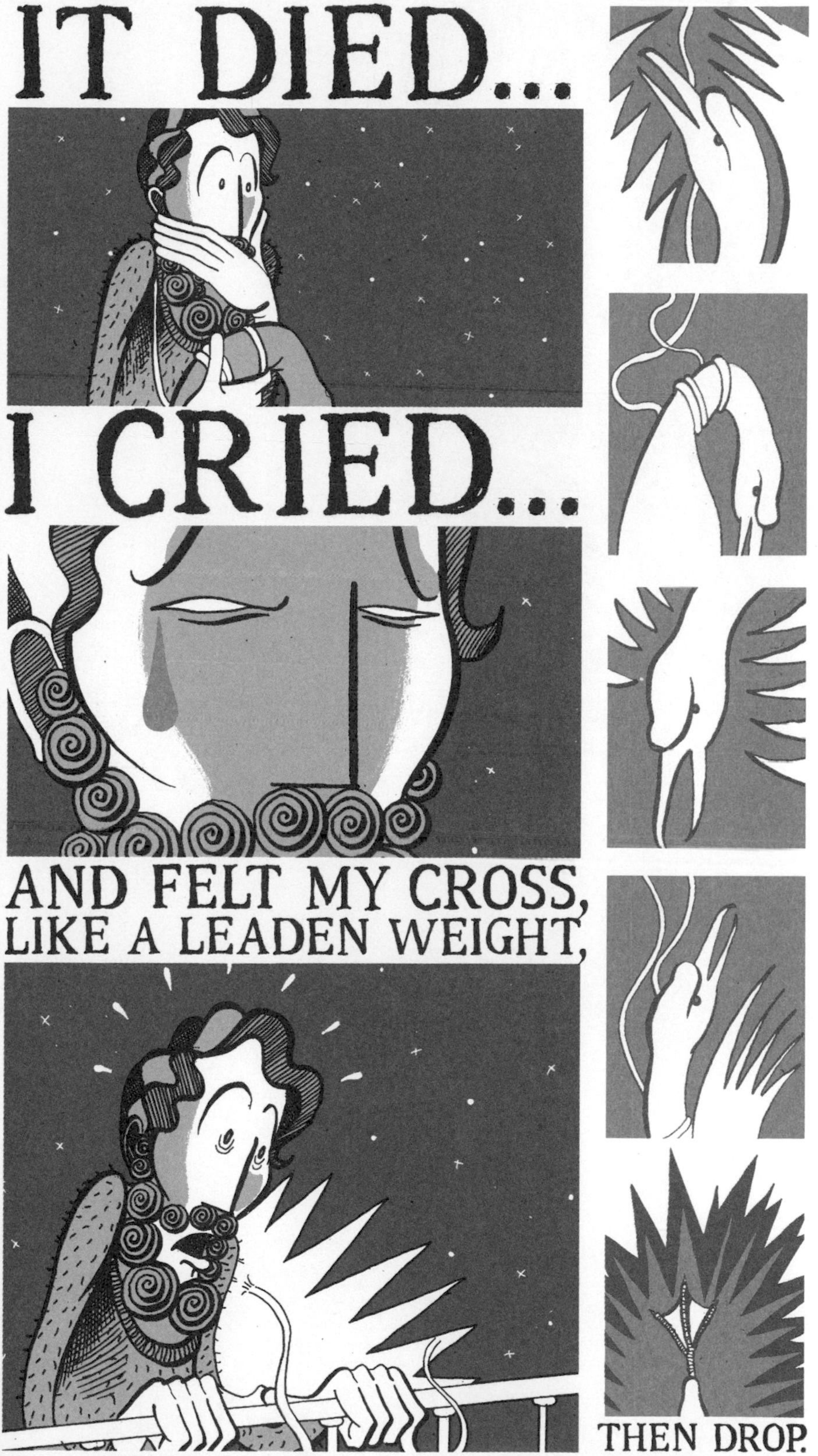
IT DIED...
I CRIED...
AND FELT MY CROSS,
LIKE A LEADEN WEIGHT,
THEN DROP.

AND WITH THIS WEIGHT
CUT FREE FROM ME

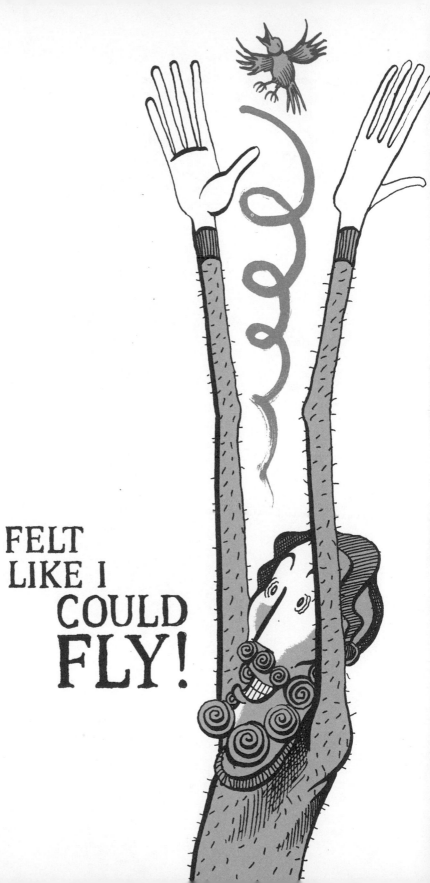

I FELT
LIKE I
COULD
FLY!

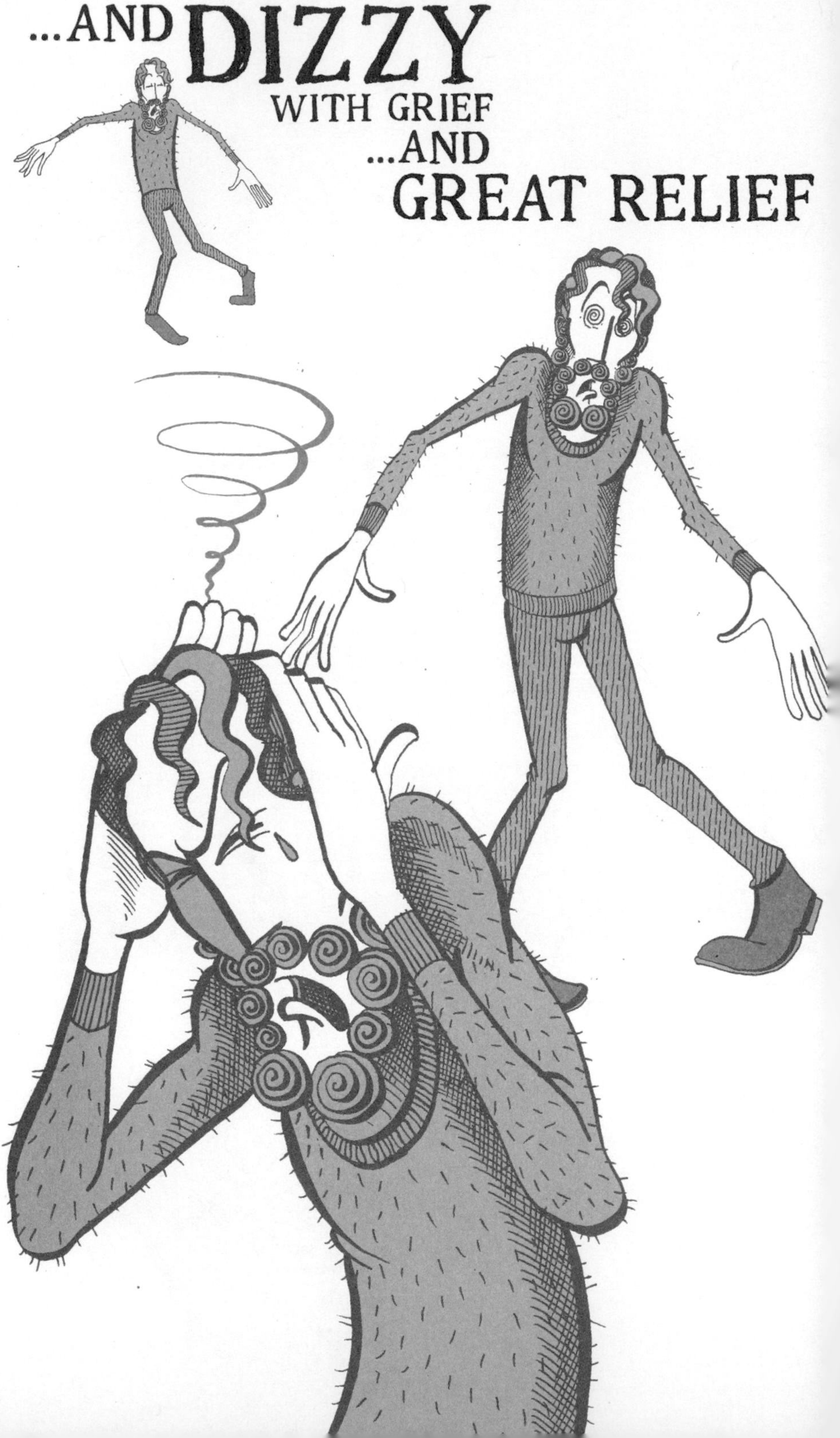
...AND DIZZY
WITH GRIEF
...AND
GREAT RELIEF

AT LAST
I CLOSED
MY EYES.

PART FIVE

IN
SLUMBER
THEN

I SLOWLY
SLUMPED...

A FOG

SUBMERGED
MY BRAIN;

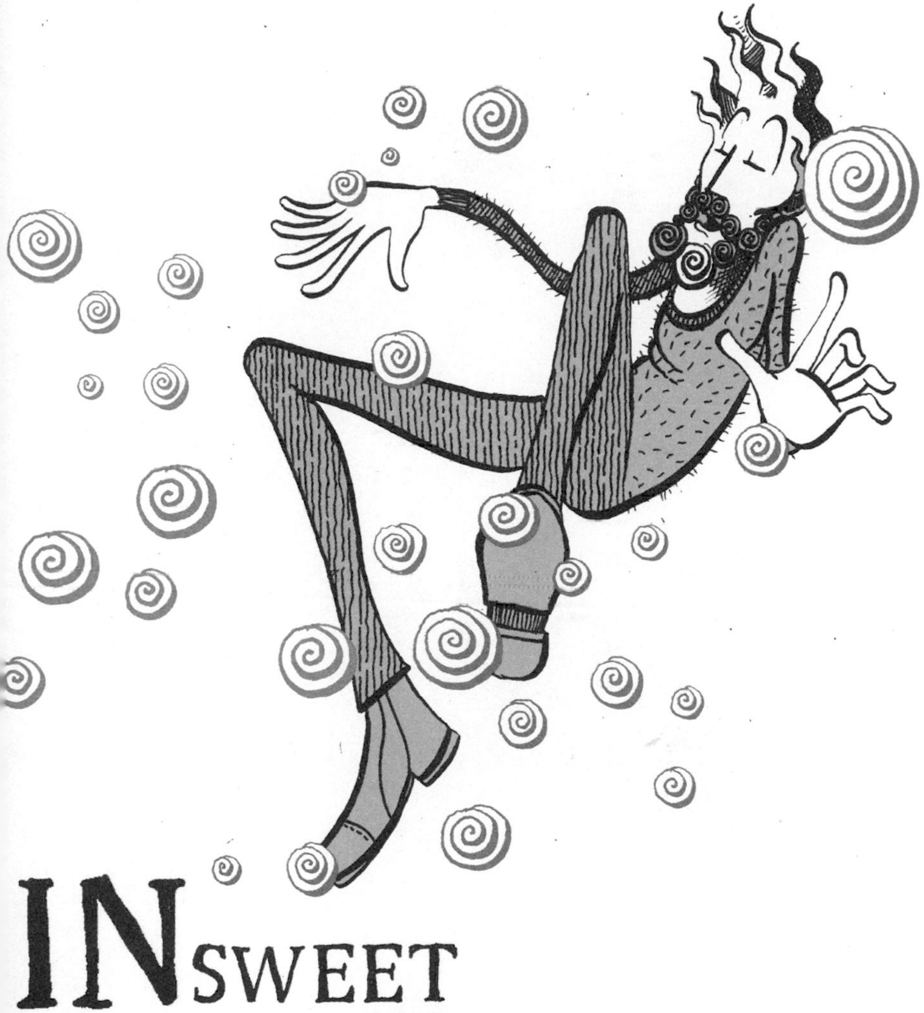

IN SWEET AND SOFT OBLIVION…

I SLEPT AND DREAMT OF RAIN.

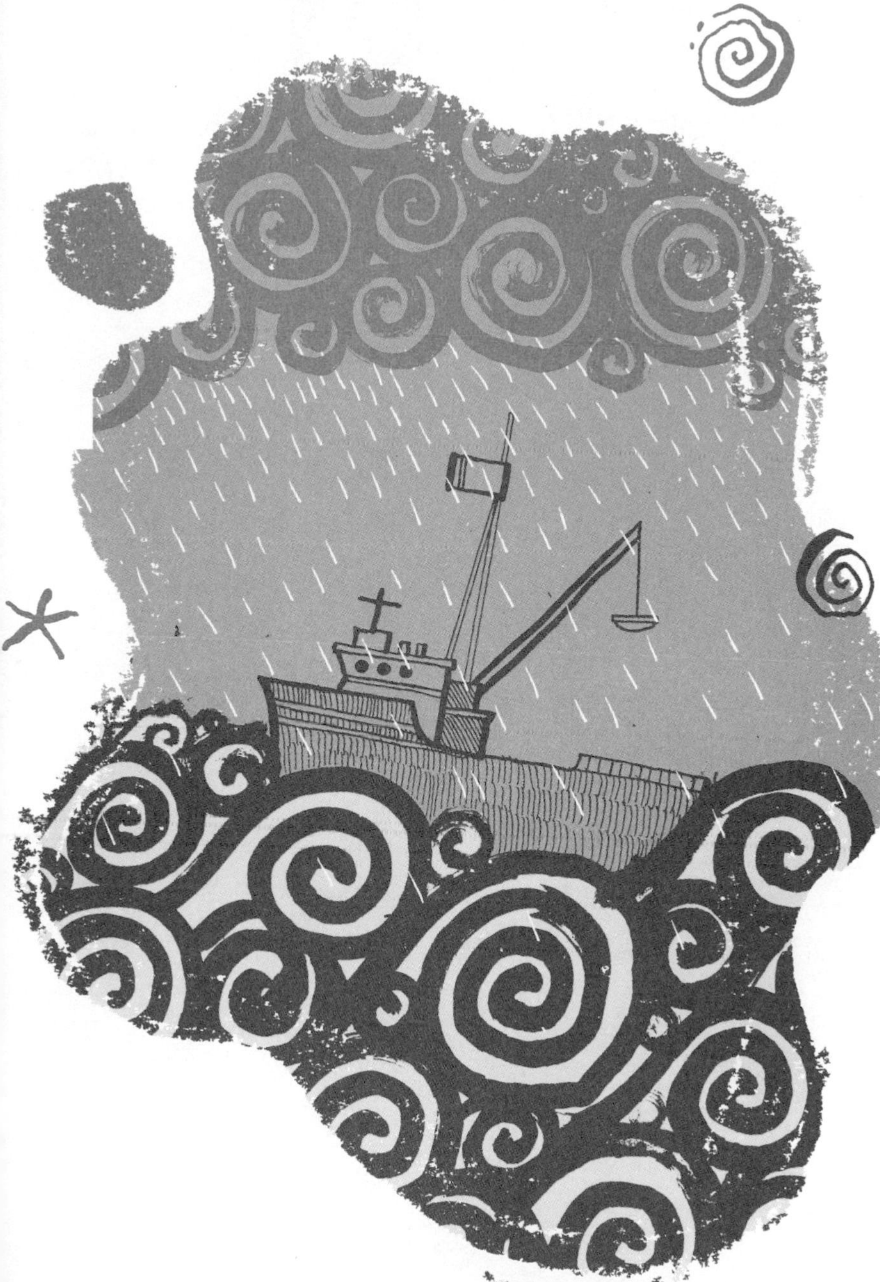

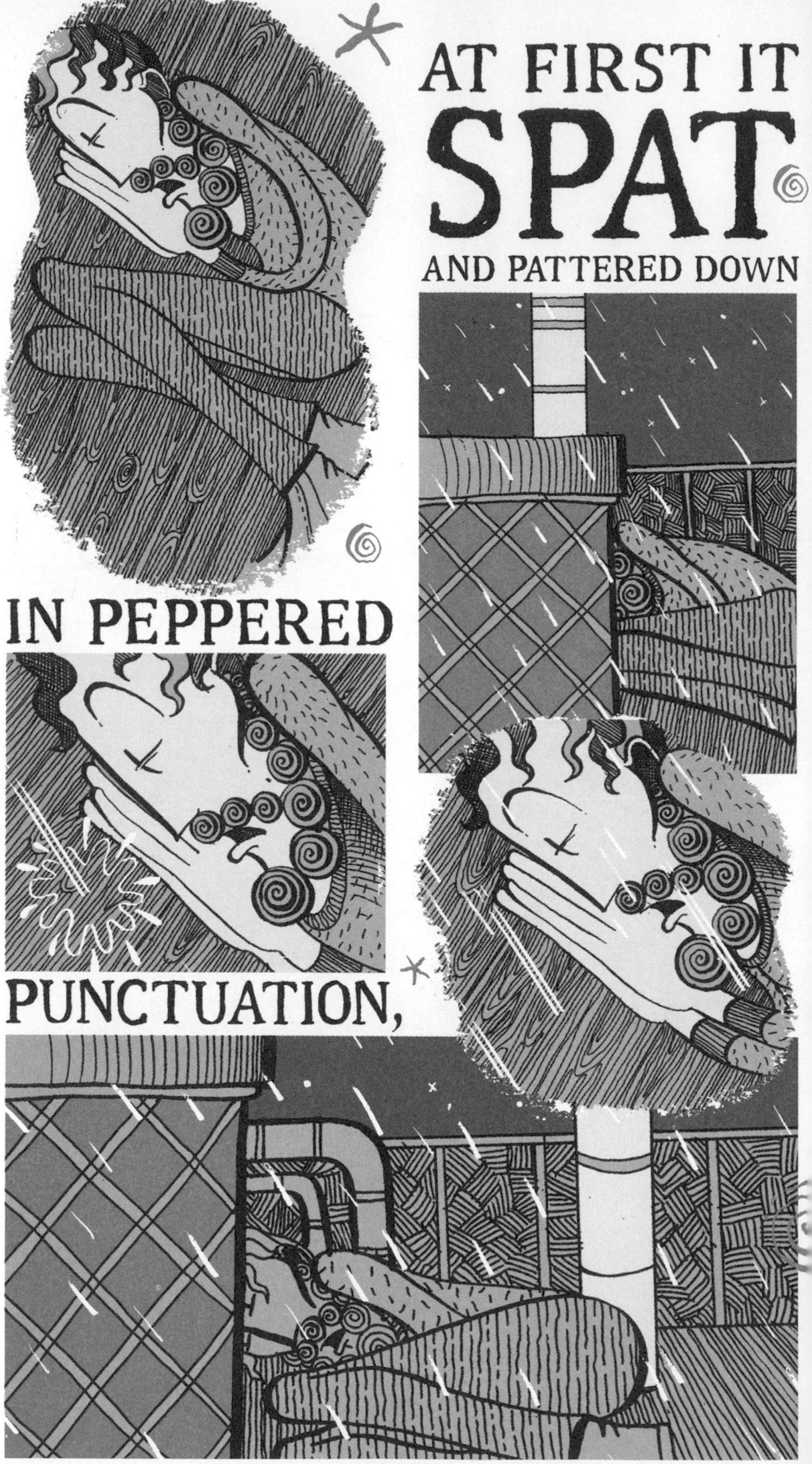
AT FIRST IT
SPAT
AND PATTERED DOWN
IN PEPPERED
PUNCTUATION,

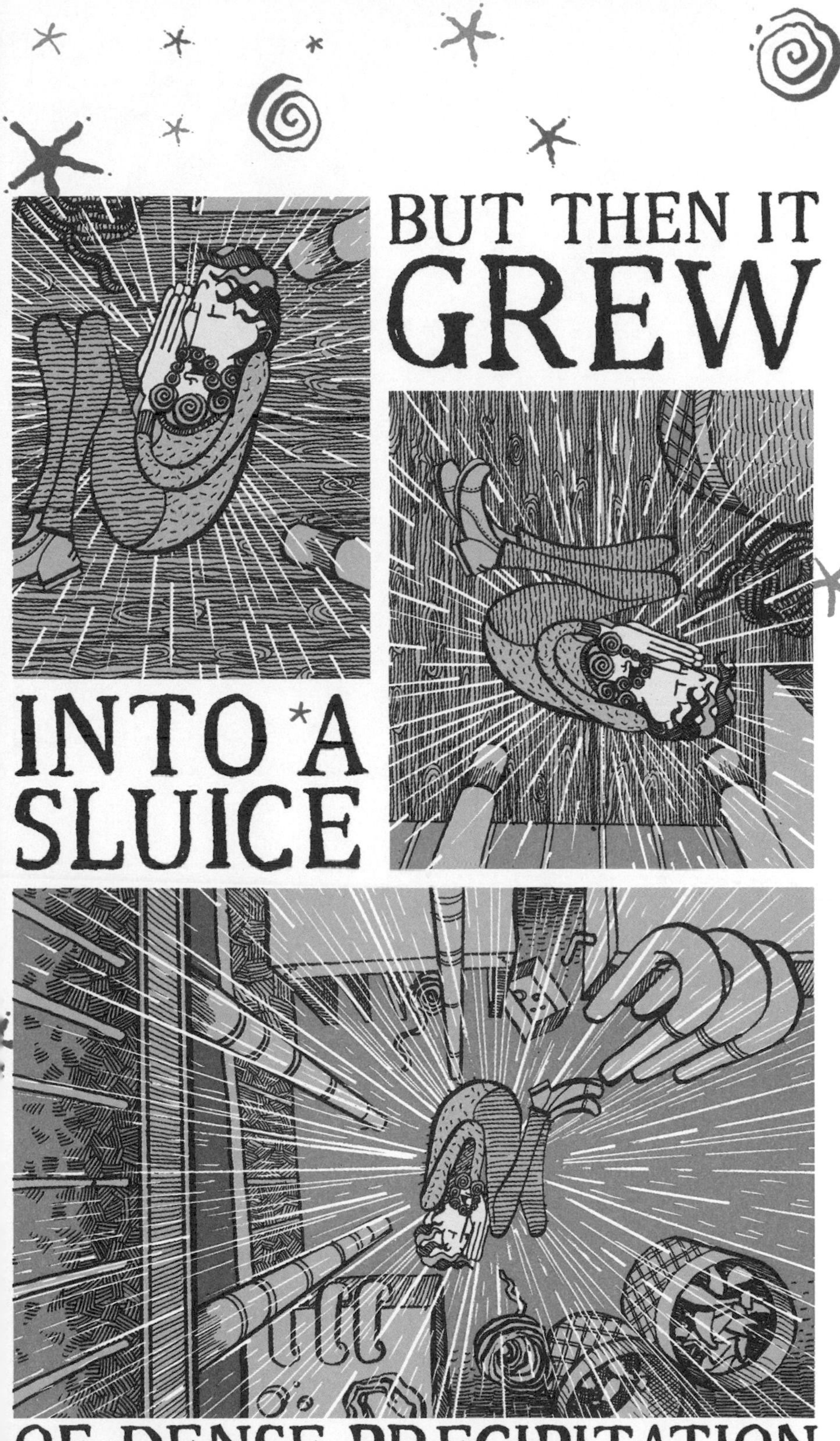
BUT THEN IT
GREW
INTO A
SLUICE
OF DENSE PRECIPITATION.

THOUGH MY BODY

LAY

COMATOSE

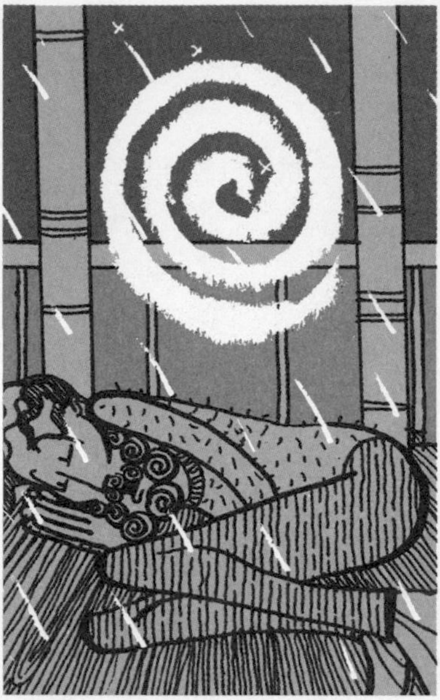

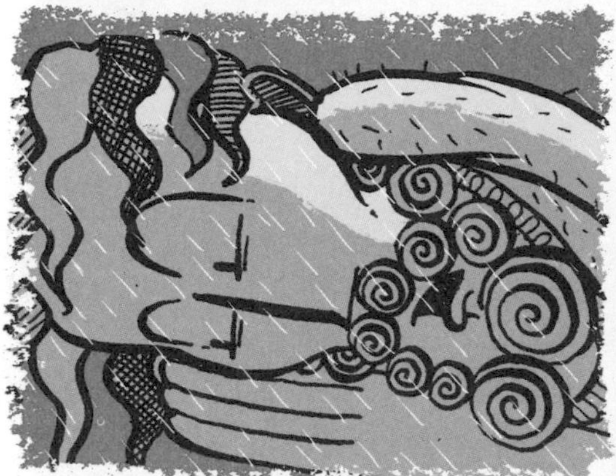

MY EARS AND EYES

AWOKE

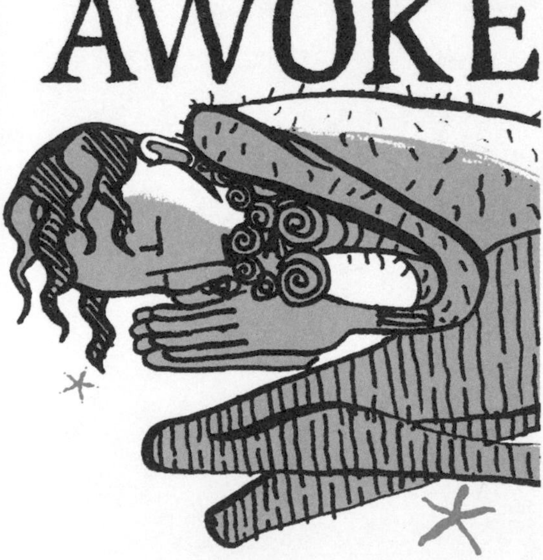

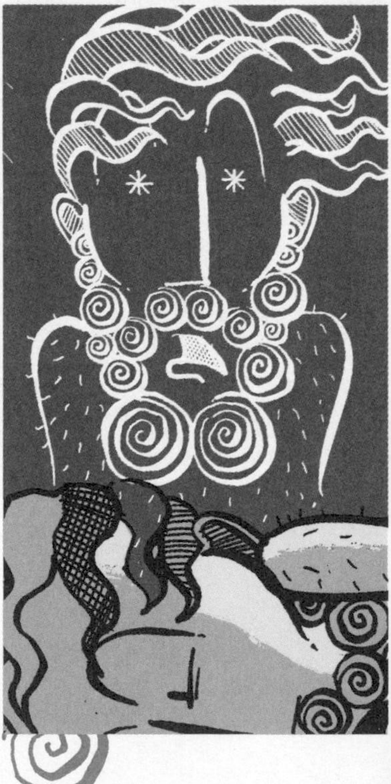

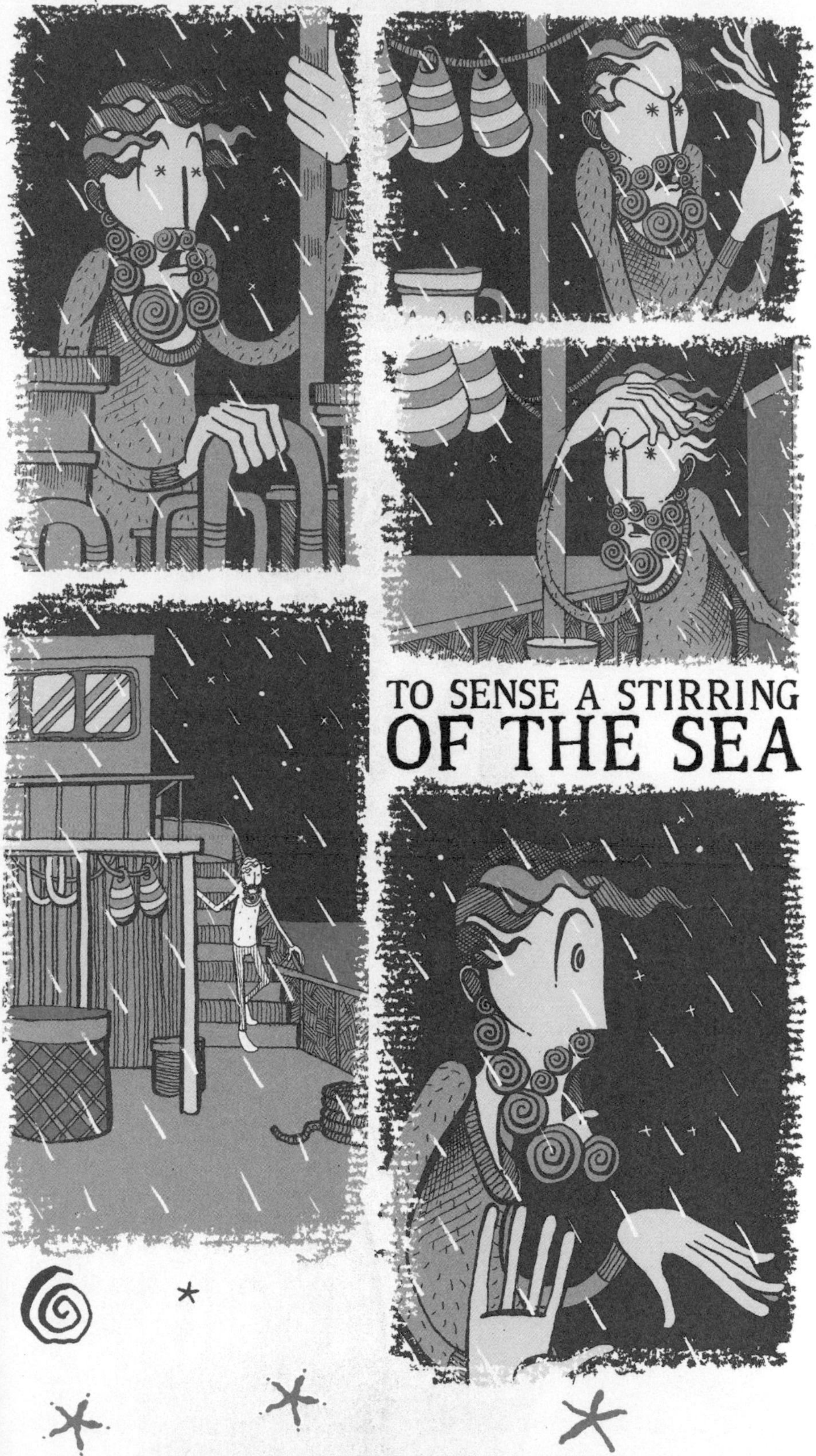
TO SENSE A STIRRING
OF THE SEA

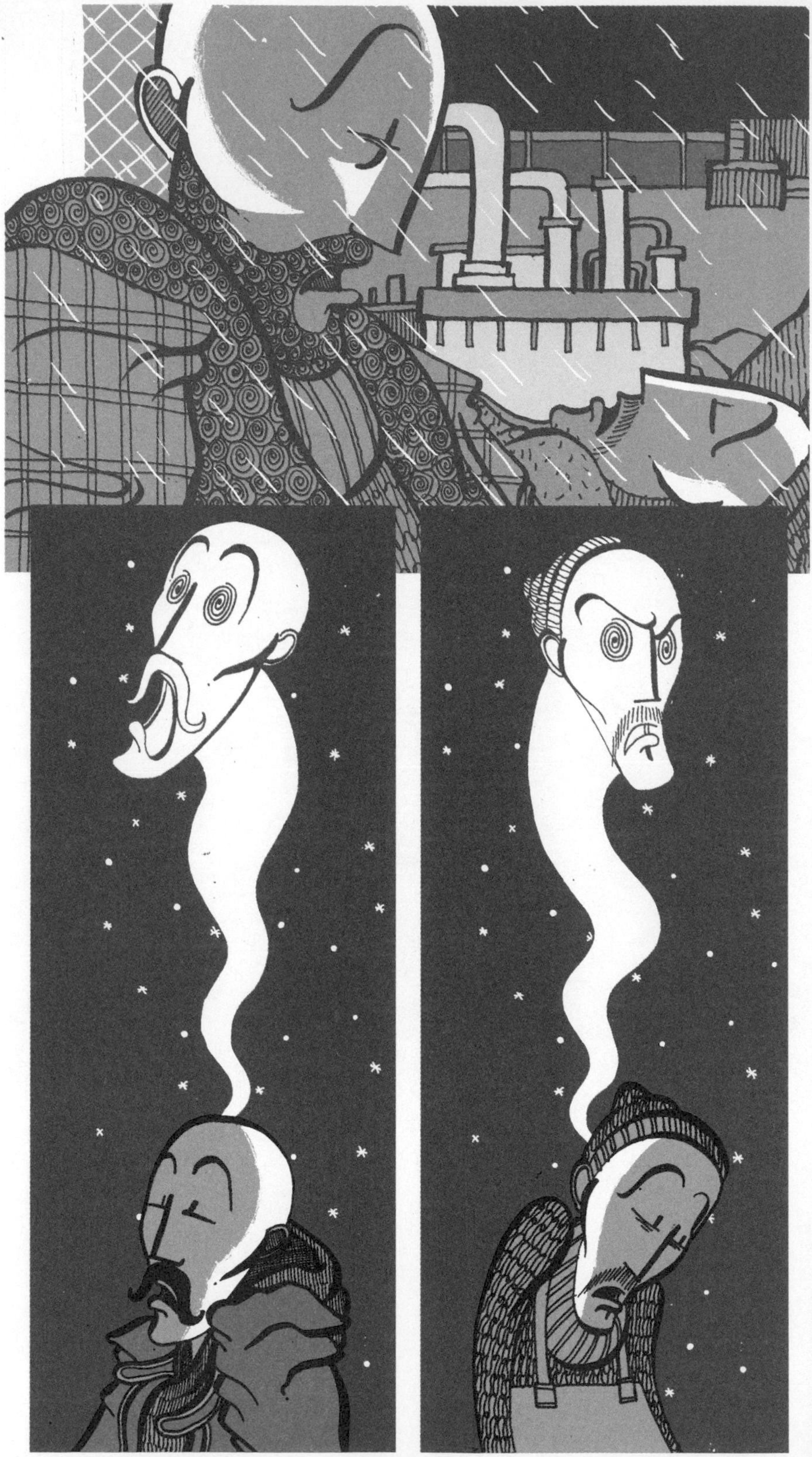

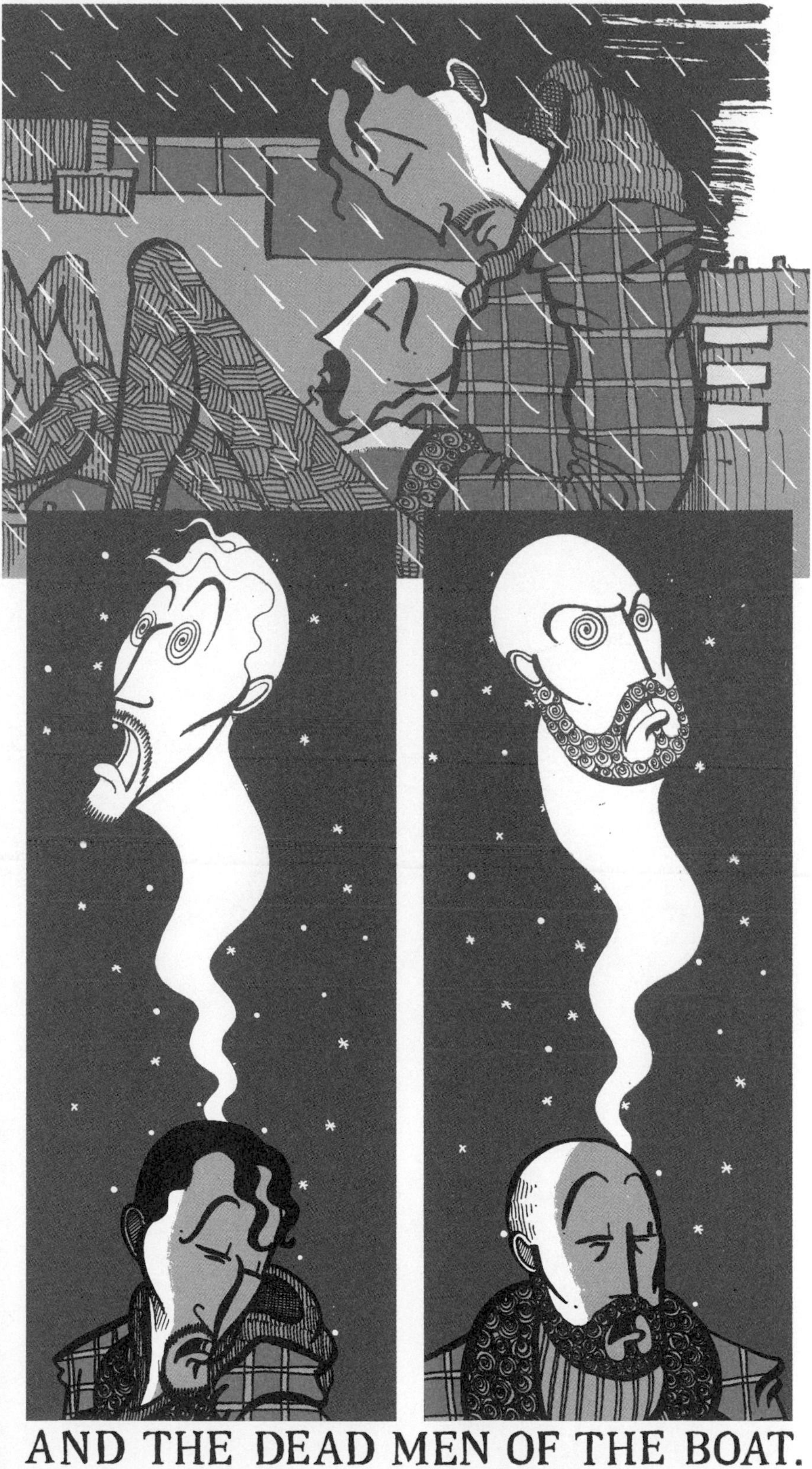

AND THE DEAD MEN OF THE BOAT.

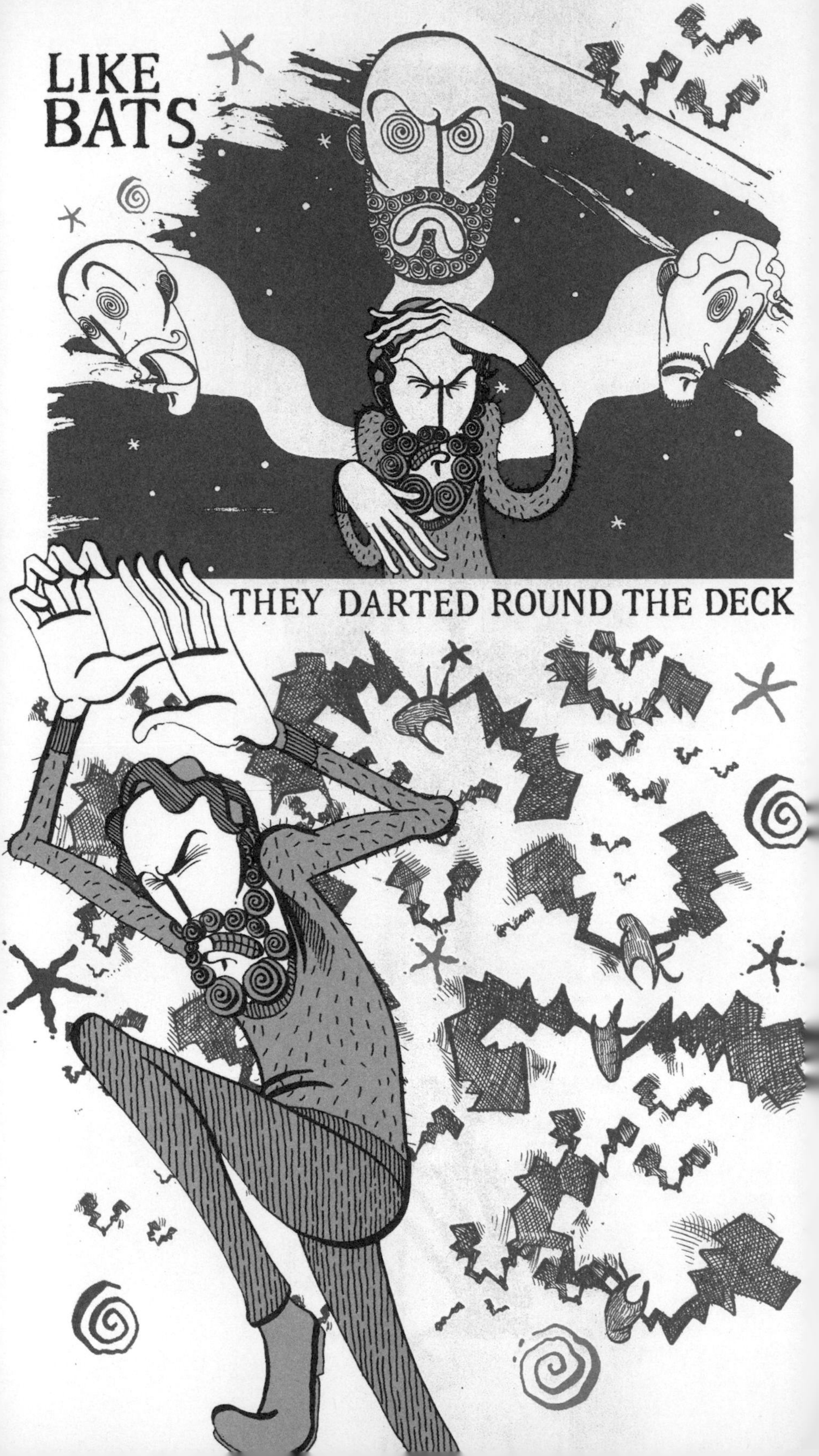
LIKE BATS
THEY DARTED ROUND THE DECK

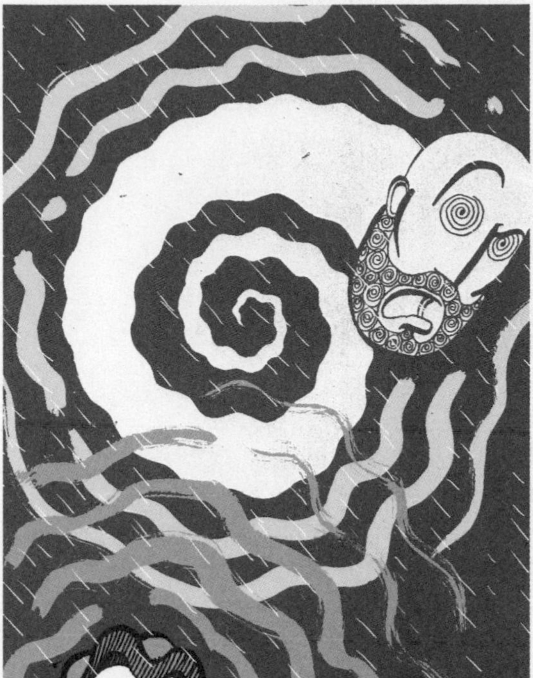

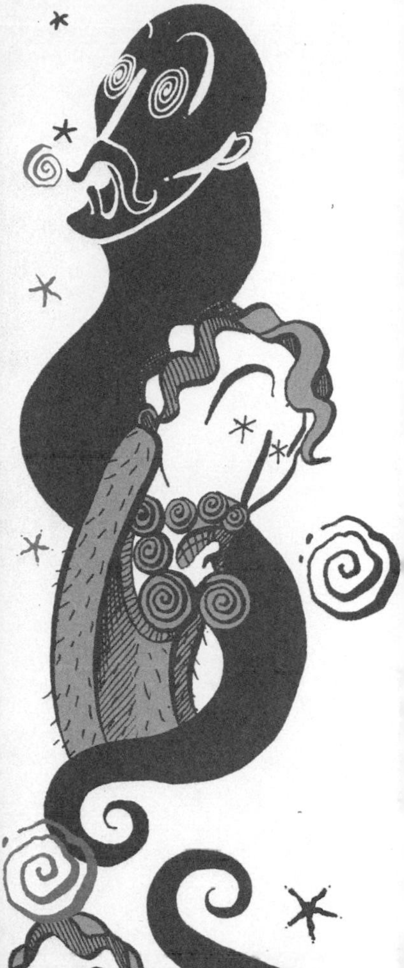

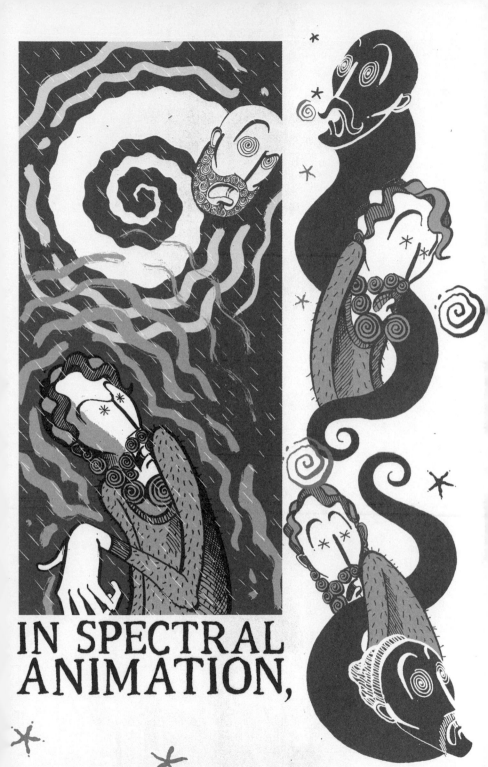

IN SPECTRAL ANIMATION,

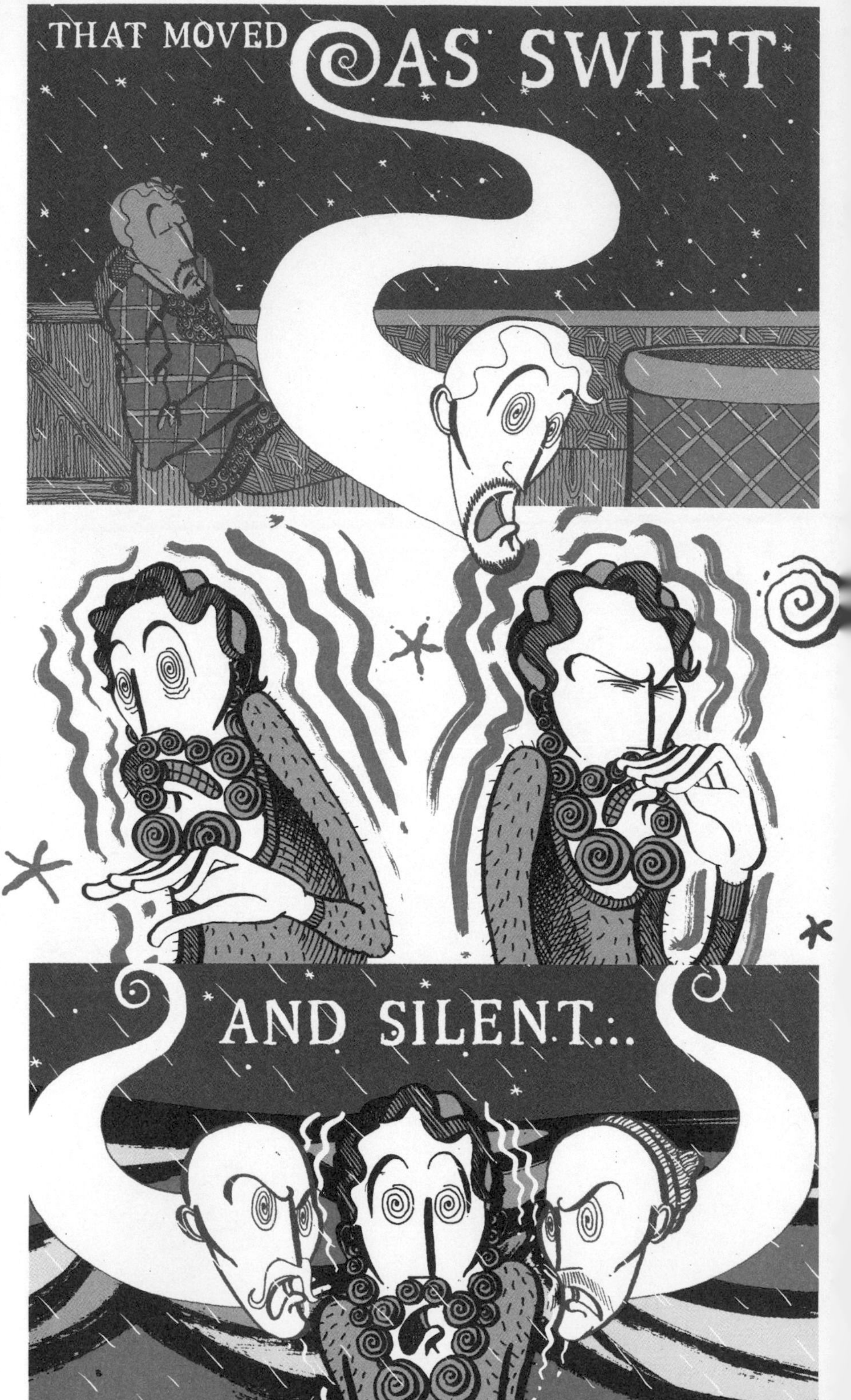
THAT MOVED AS SWIFT
AND SILENT...

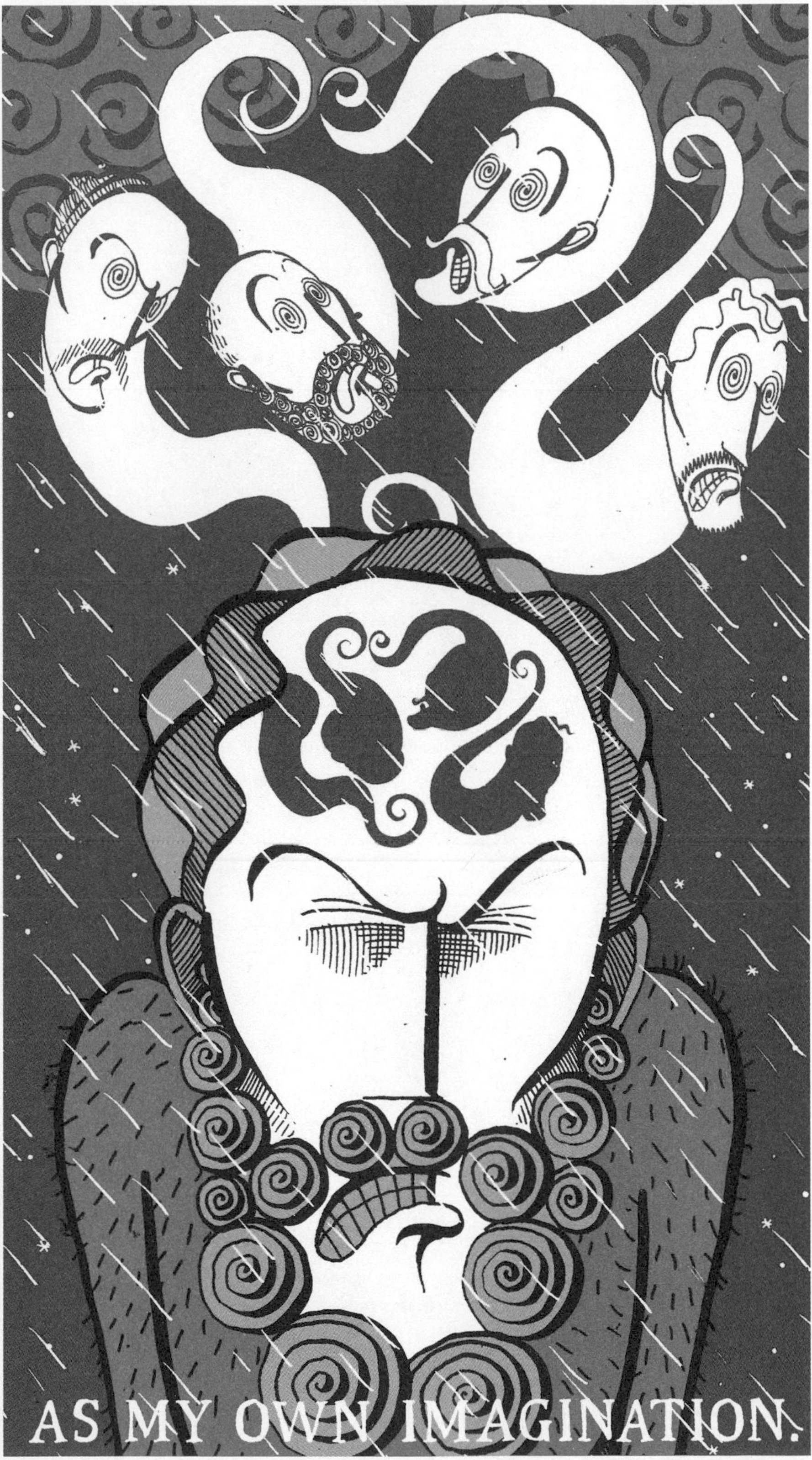
AS MY OWN IMAGINATION.

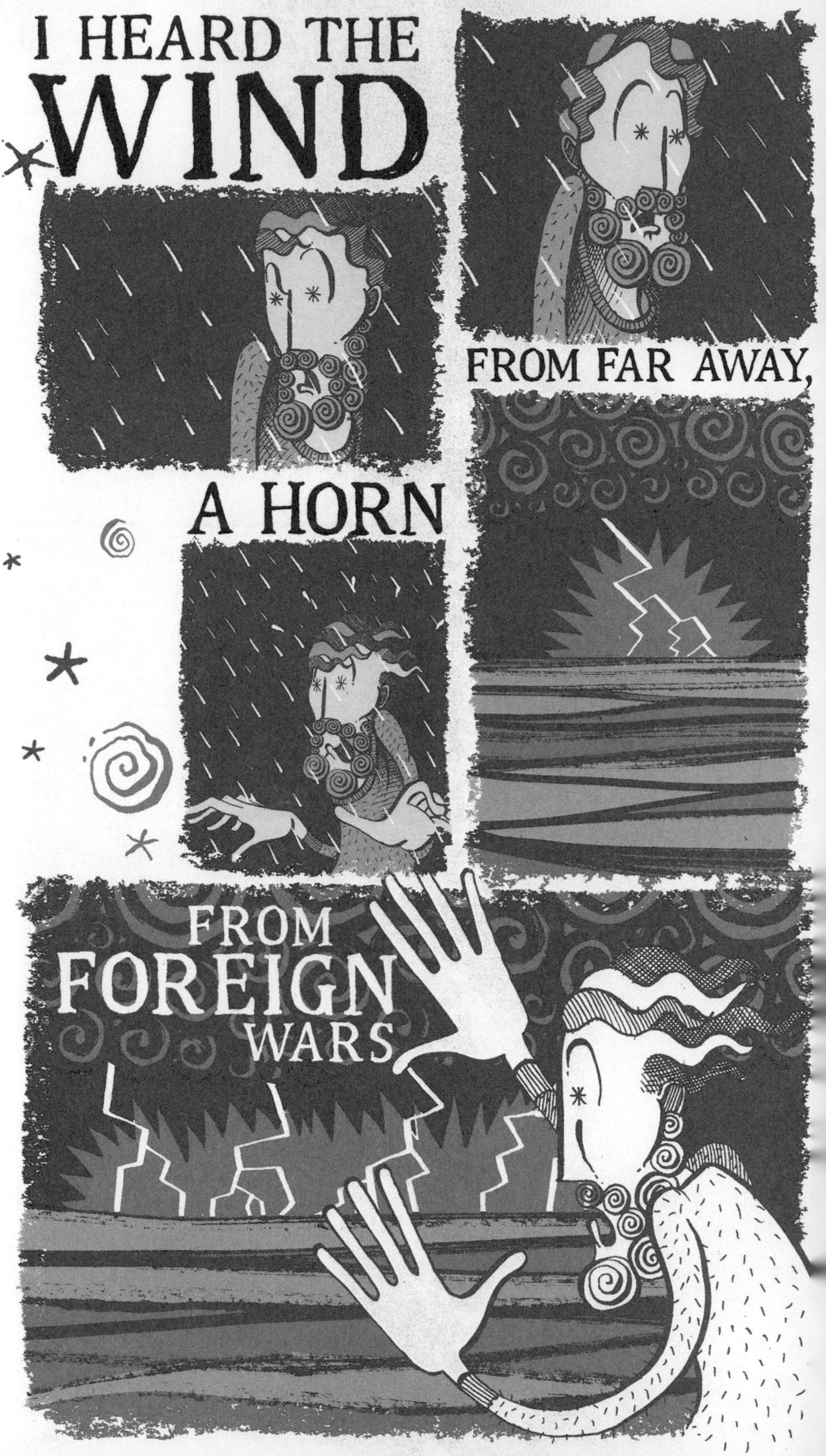
I HEARD THE WIND
FROM FAR AWAY,
A HORN
FROM FOREIGN WARS

AND LIKE A WRATHFUL GOD

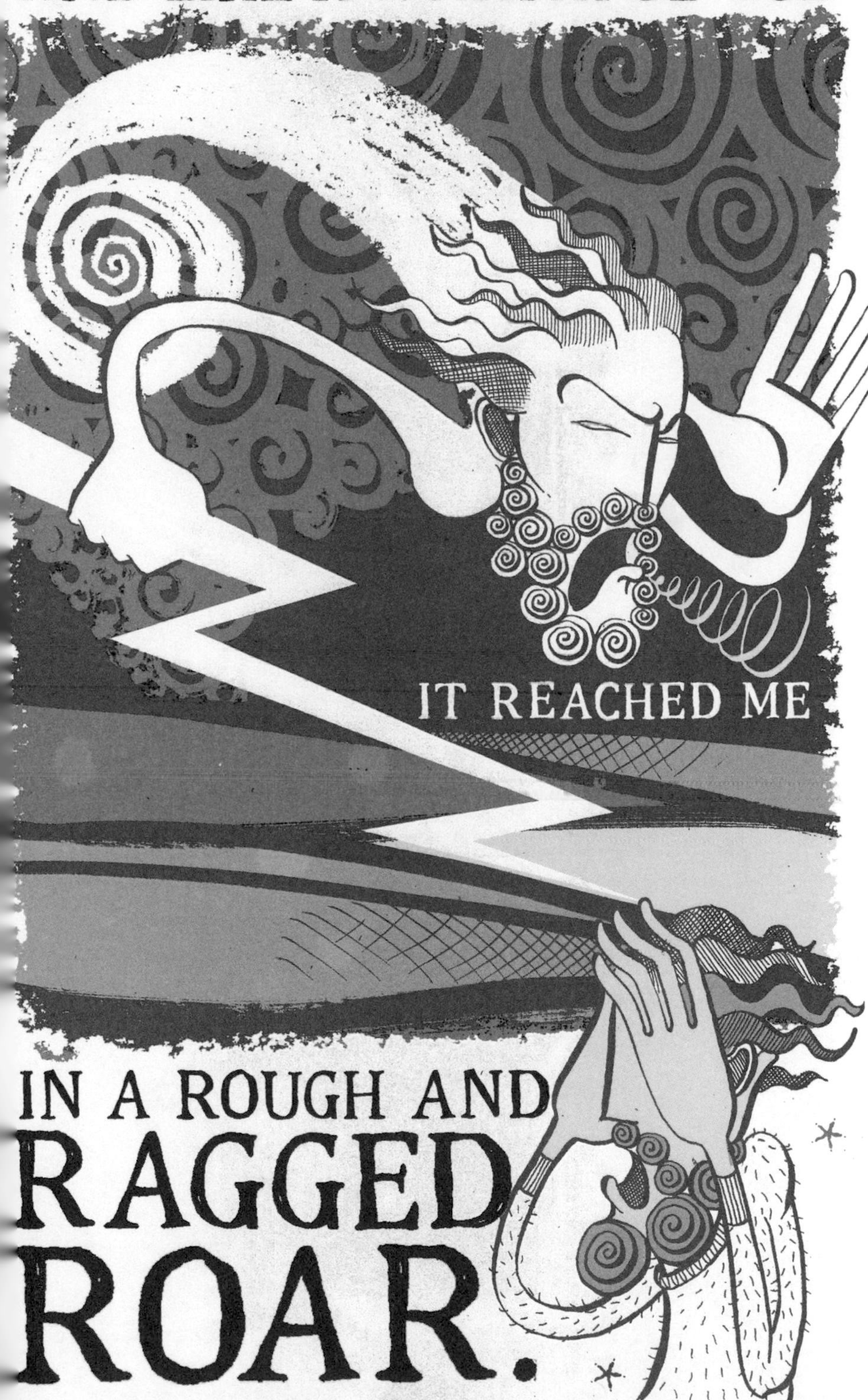
IT REACHED ME

IN A ROUGH AND RAGGED ROAR.

THE OCEAN ROUSED INSURGENT STRENGTH

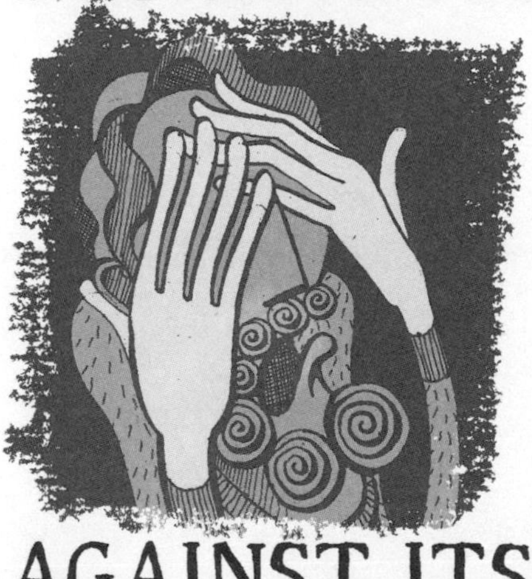

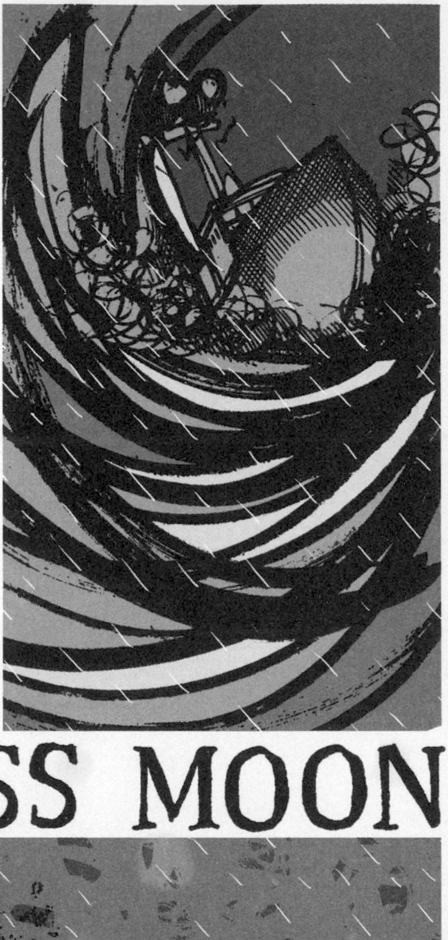

AGAINST ITS MISTRESS MOON

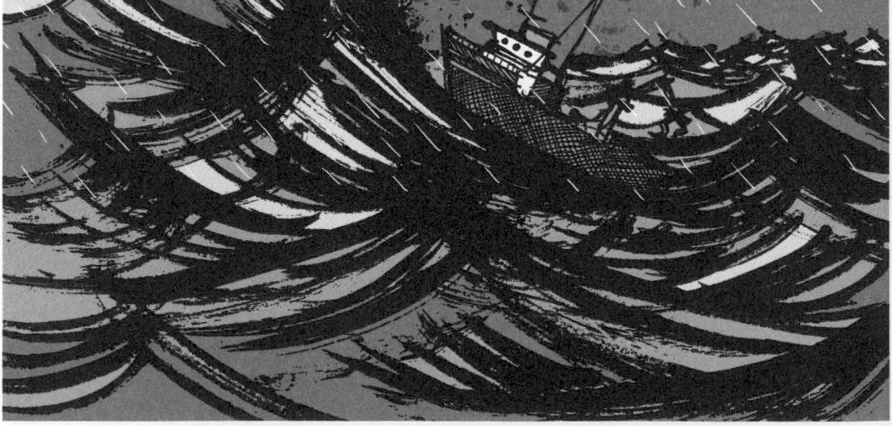

THE SKY CRIED OUT A

SYMPHONY

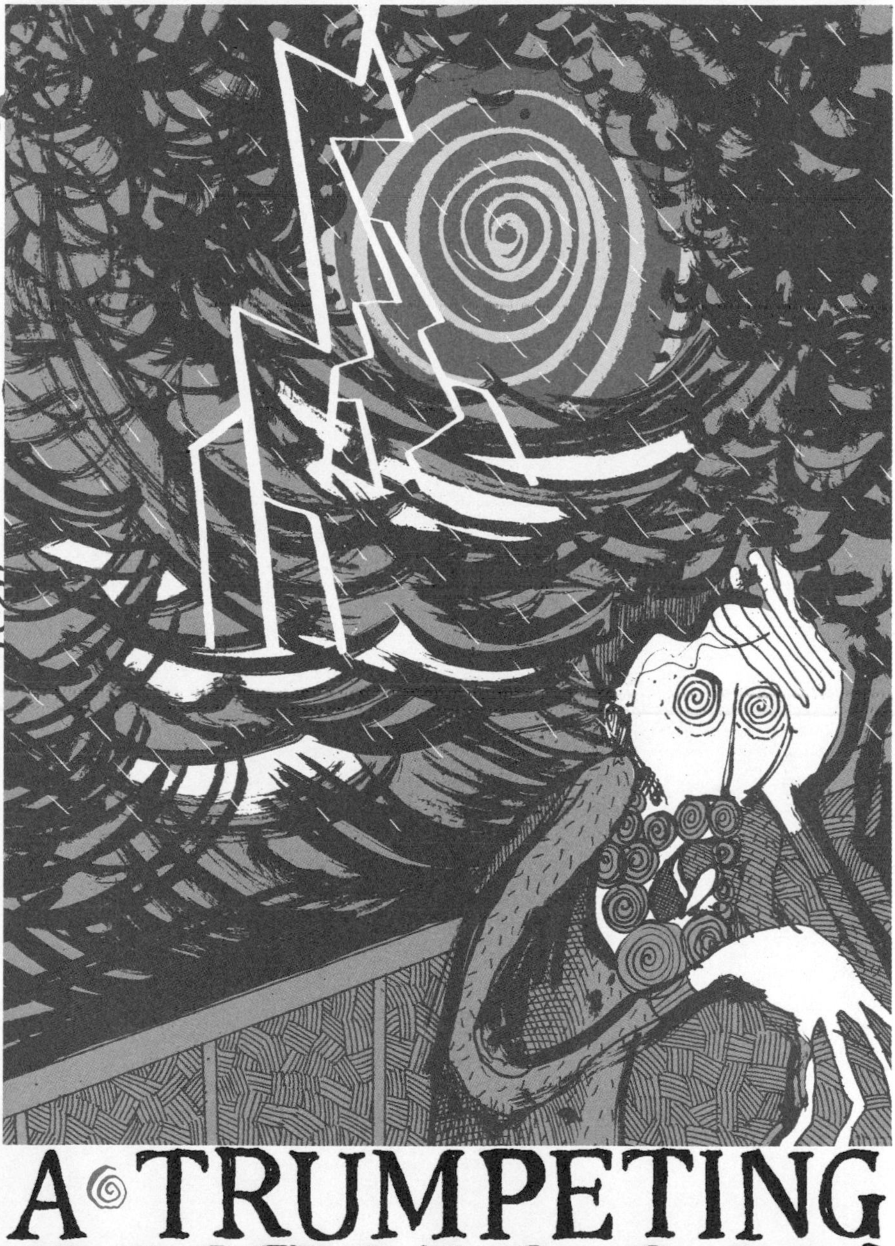

A TRUMPETING

TYPHOON!

SCREAMING FISTS OF HAIL AND ICE

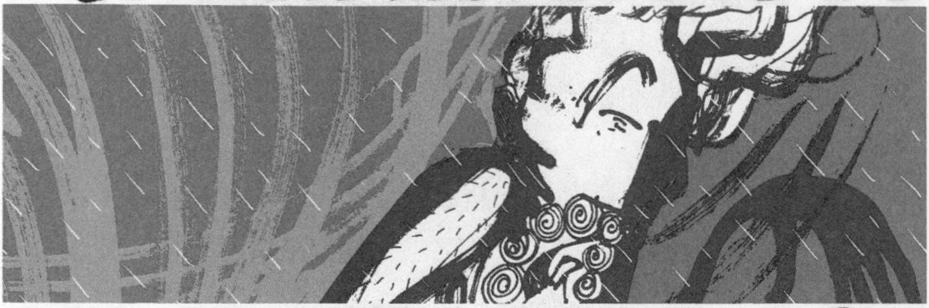

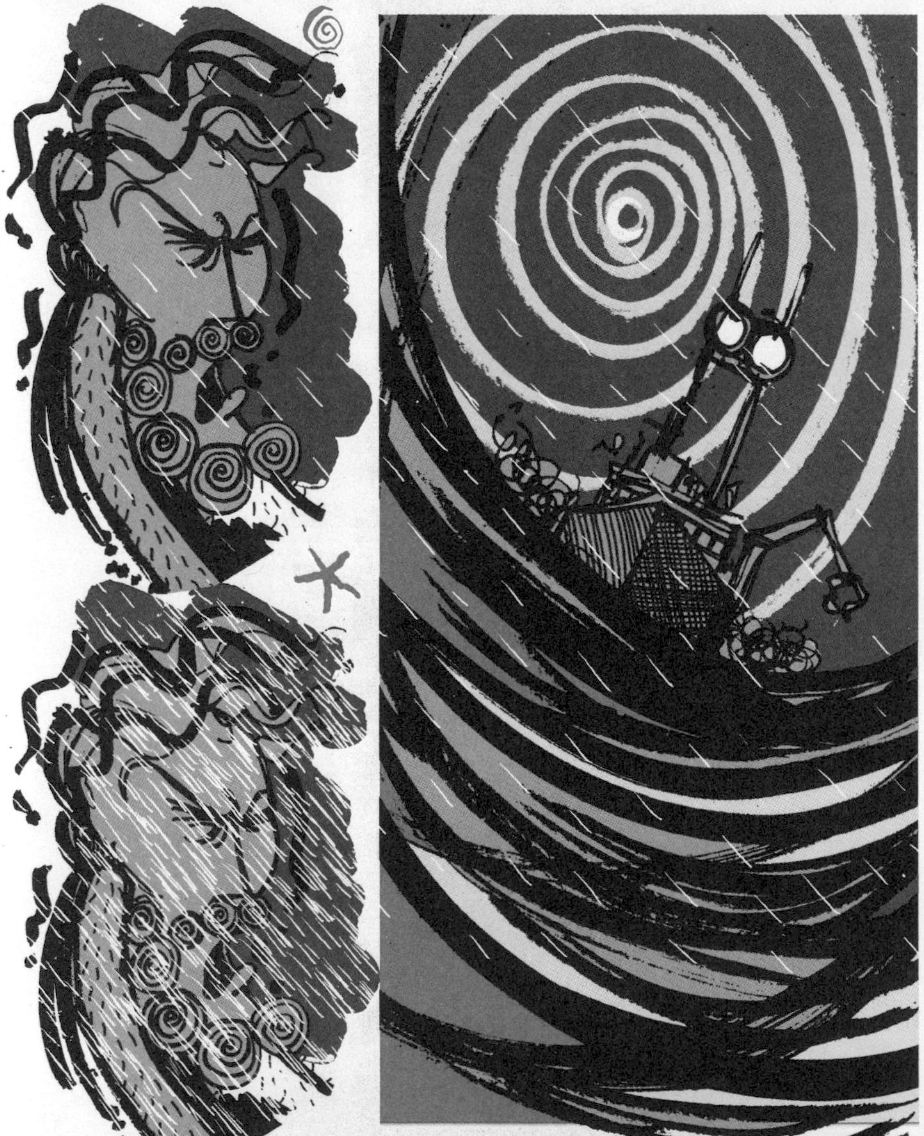

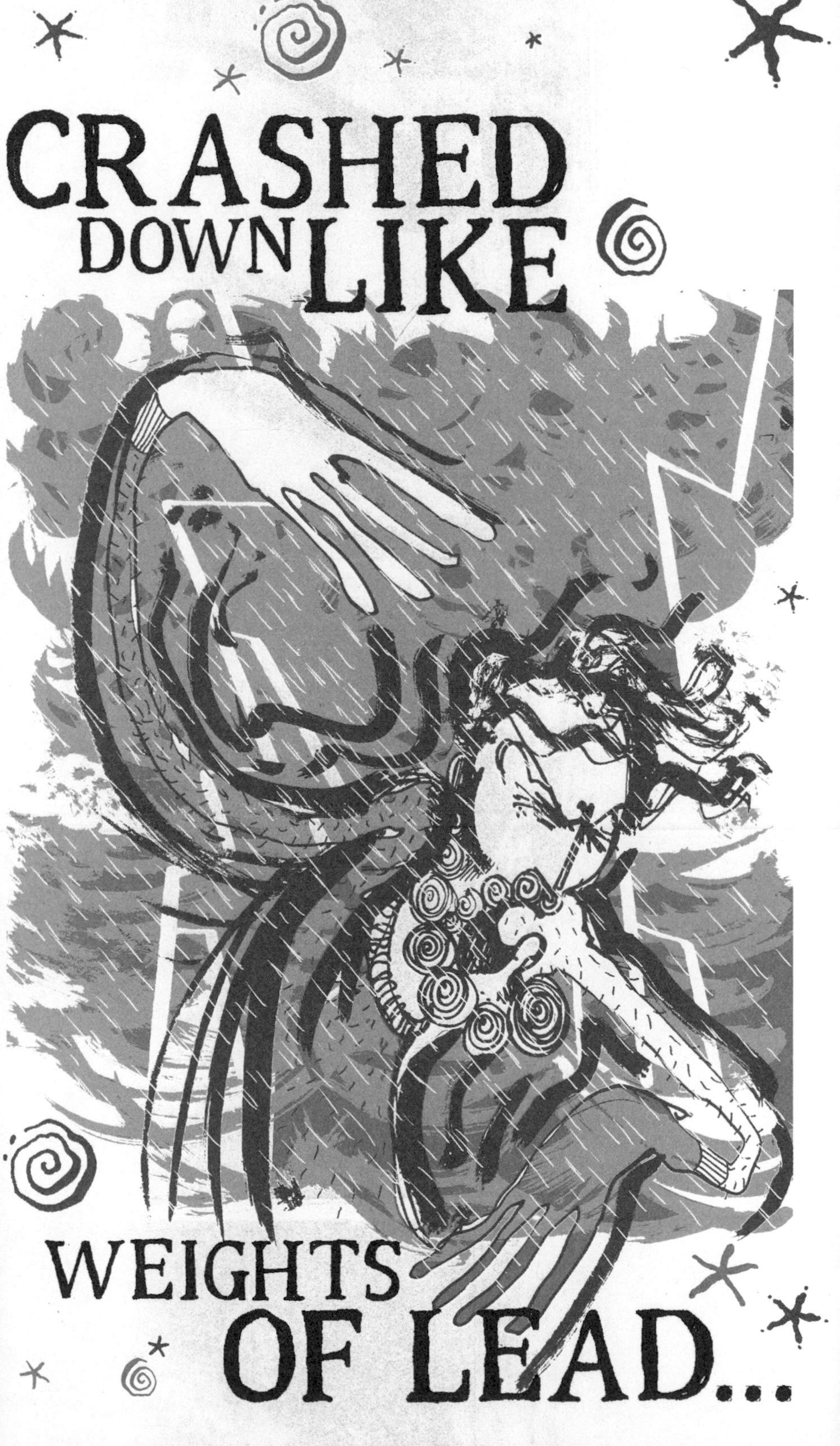
CRASHED DOWN LIKE
WEIGHTS OF LEAD...

...AND ANCIENT THOR

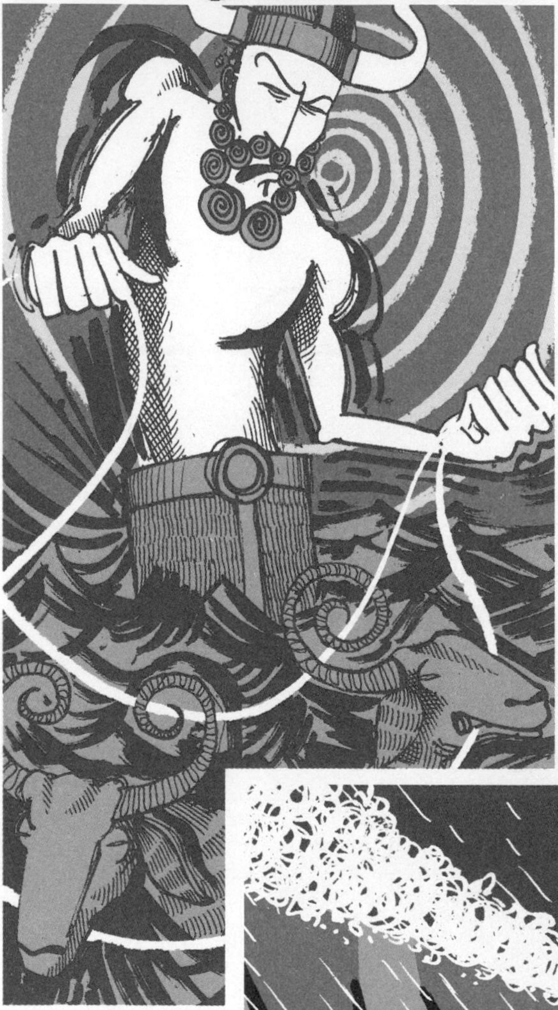

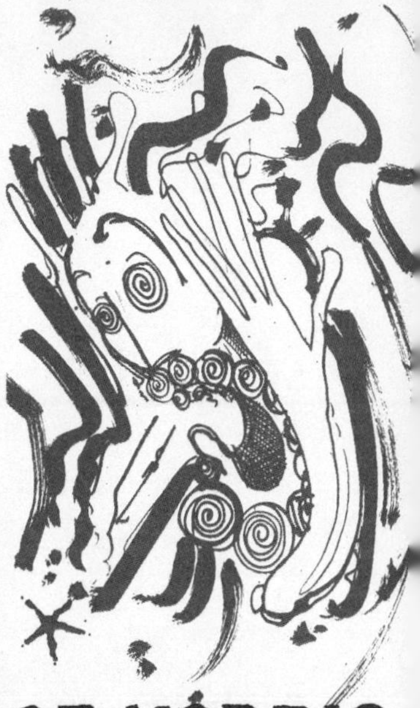

OF NORDIC LORE

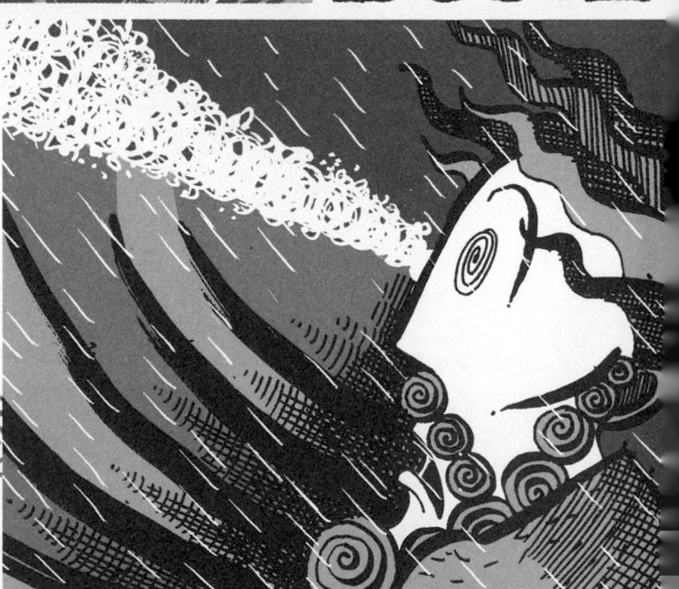

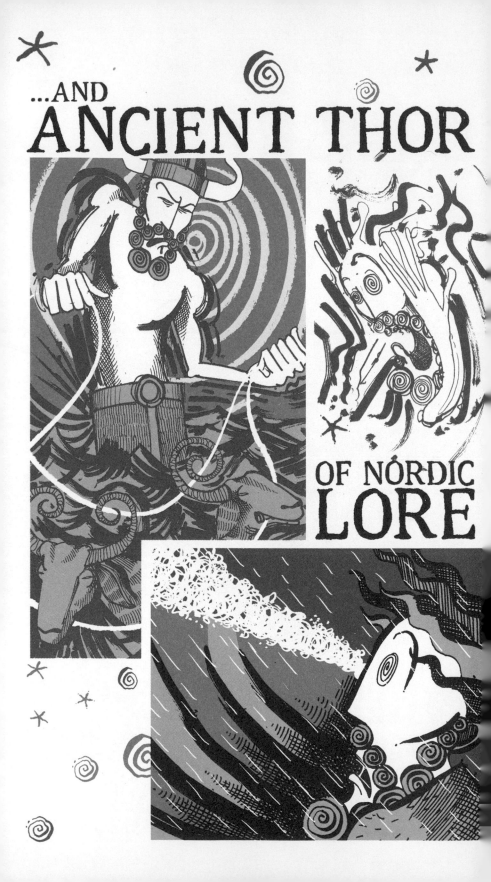

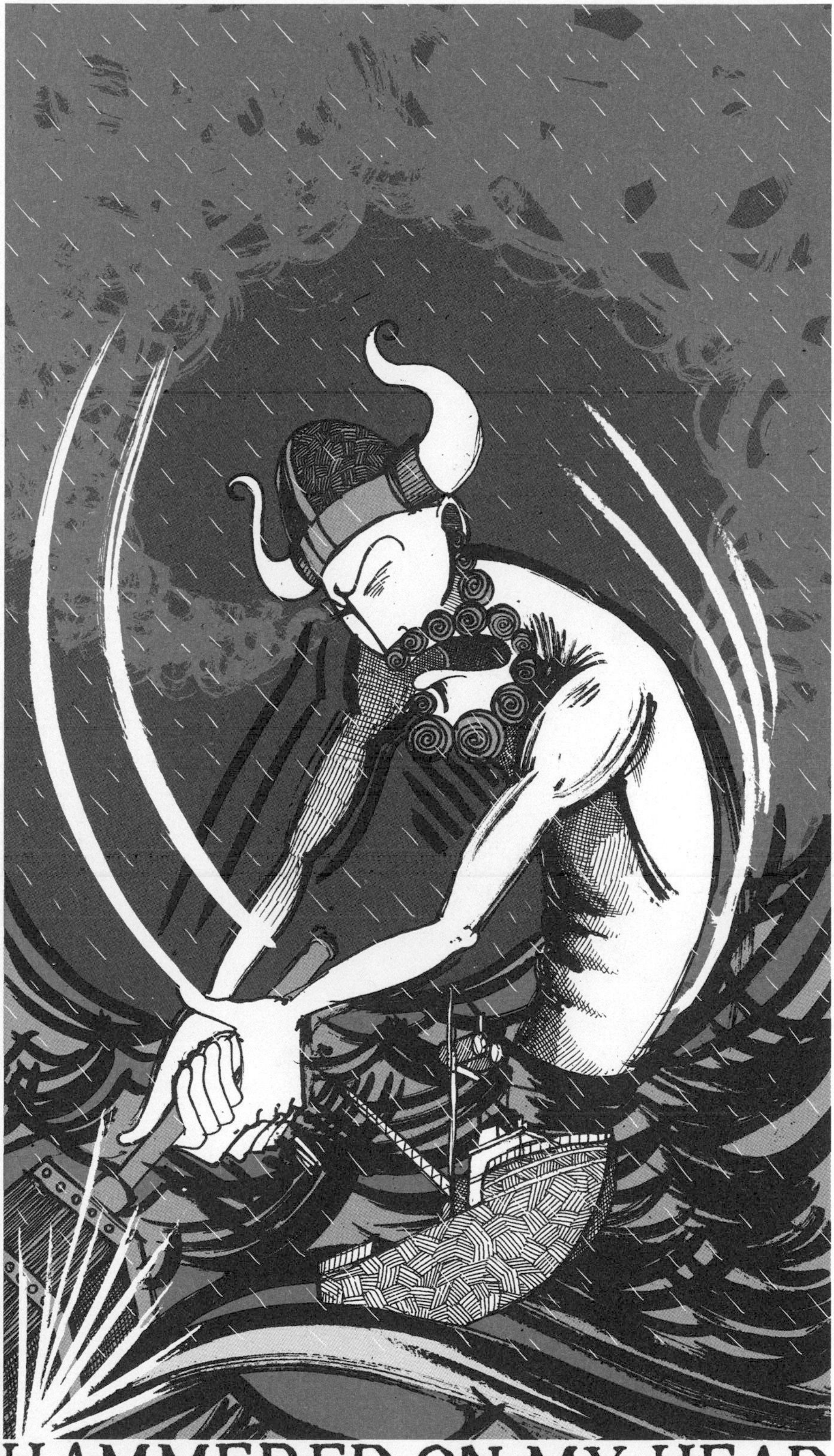

HAMMERED ON MY HEAD.

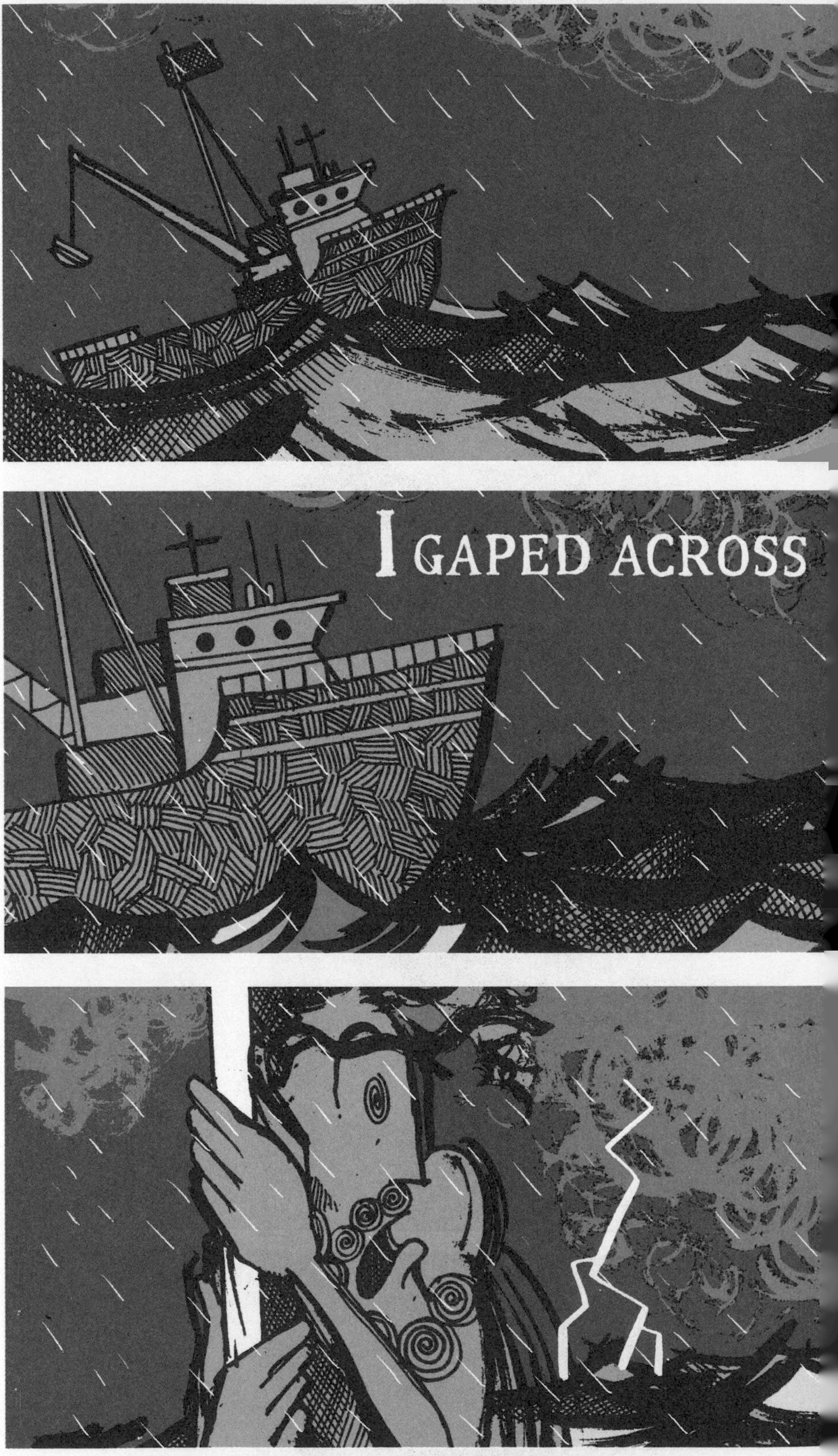
I GAPED ACROSS

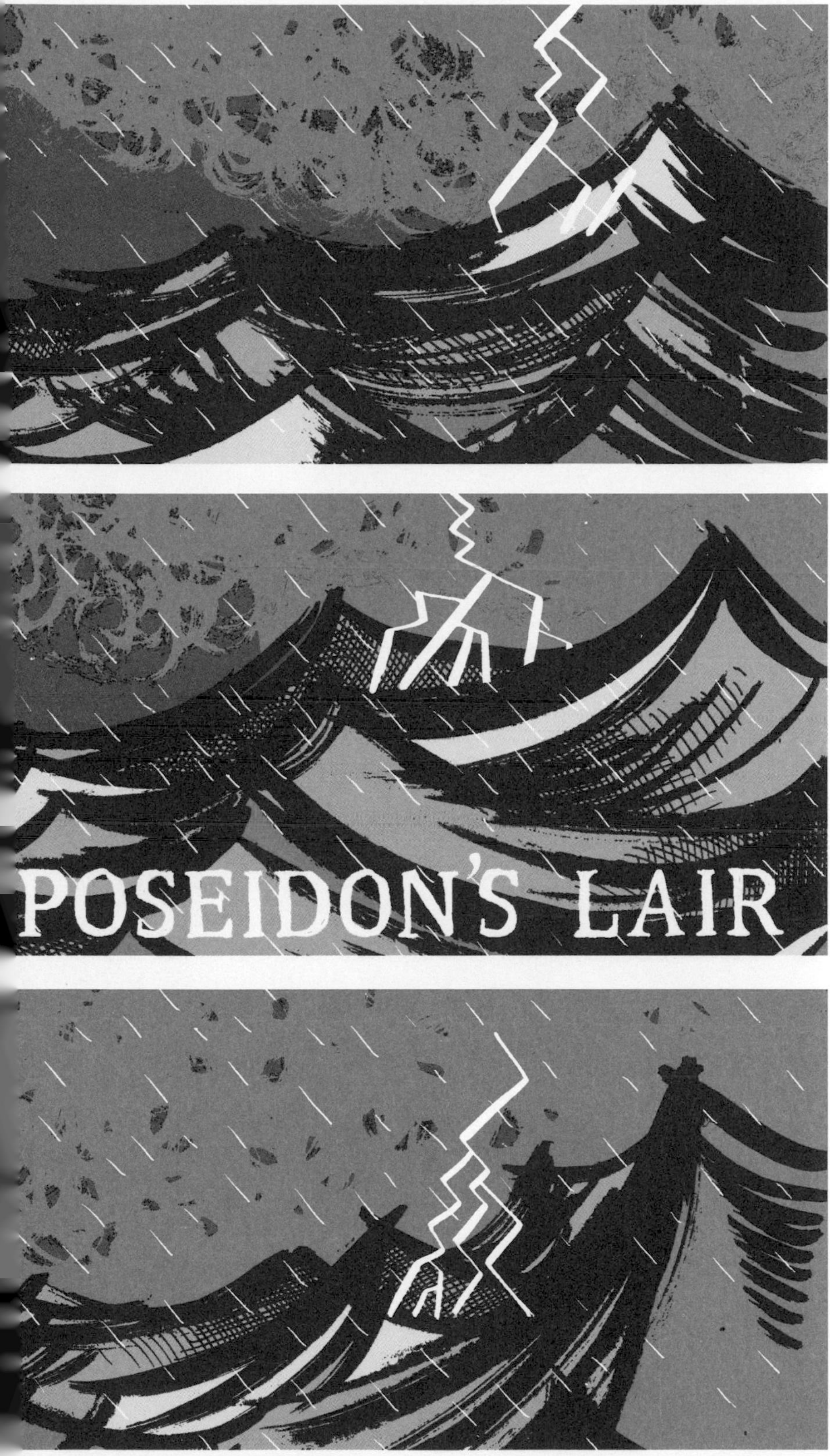
POSEIDON'S LAIR

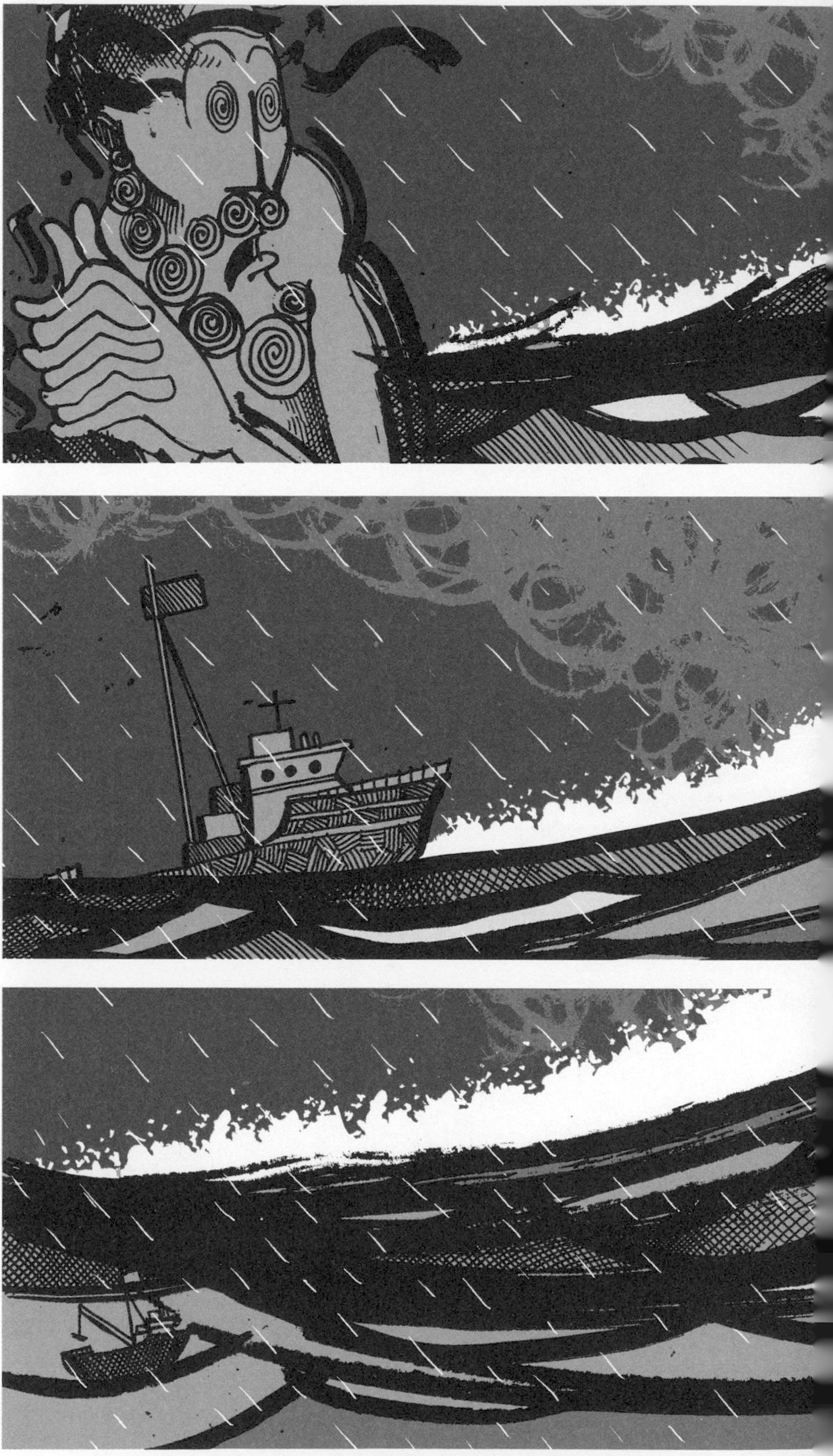

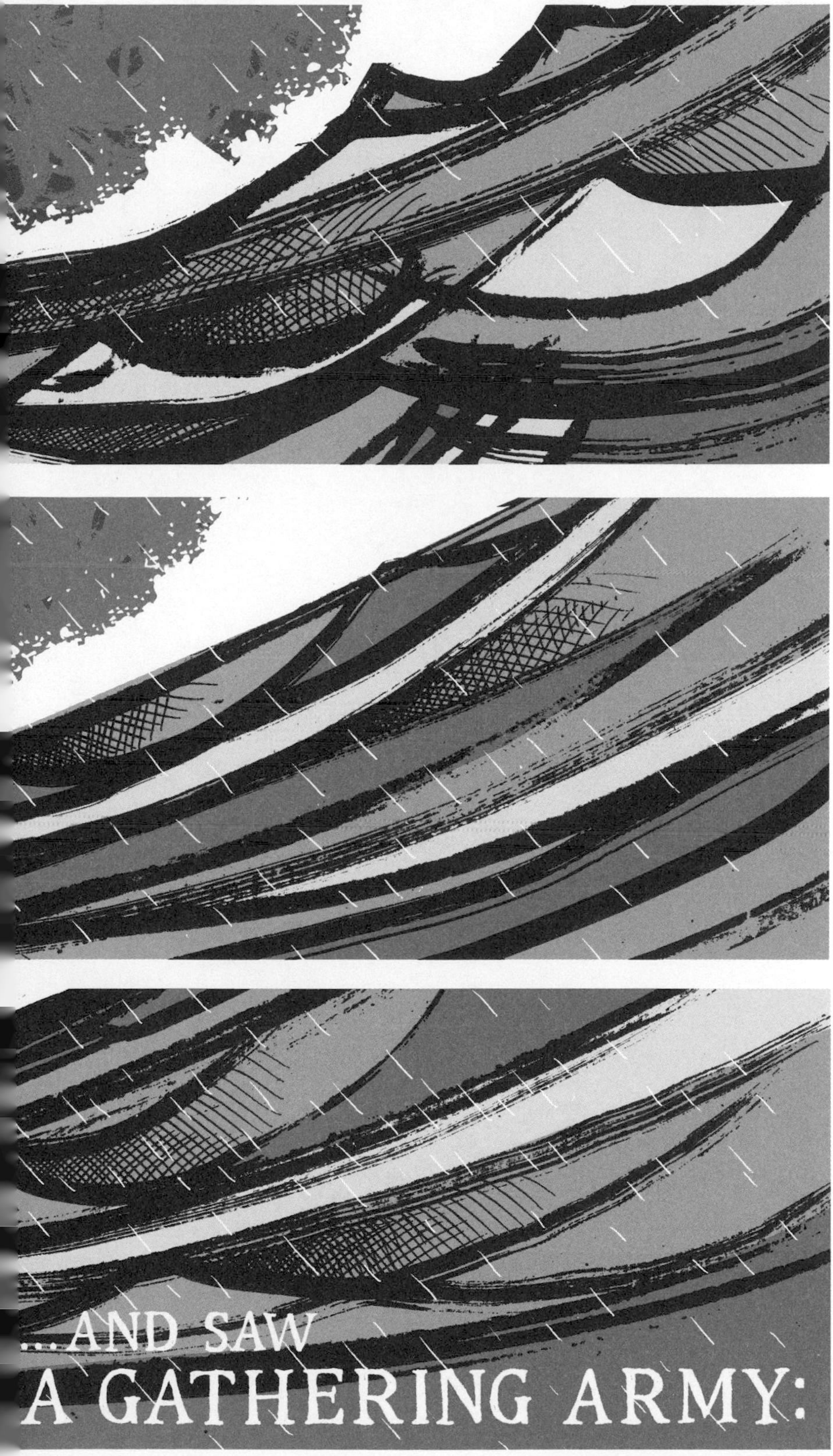
...AND SAW
A GATHERING ARMY:

WAVES OF WAILING

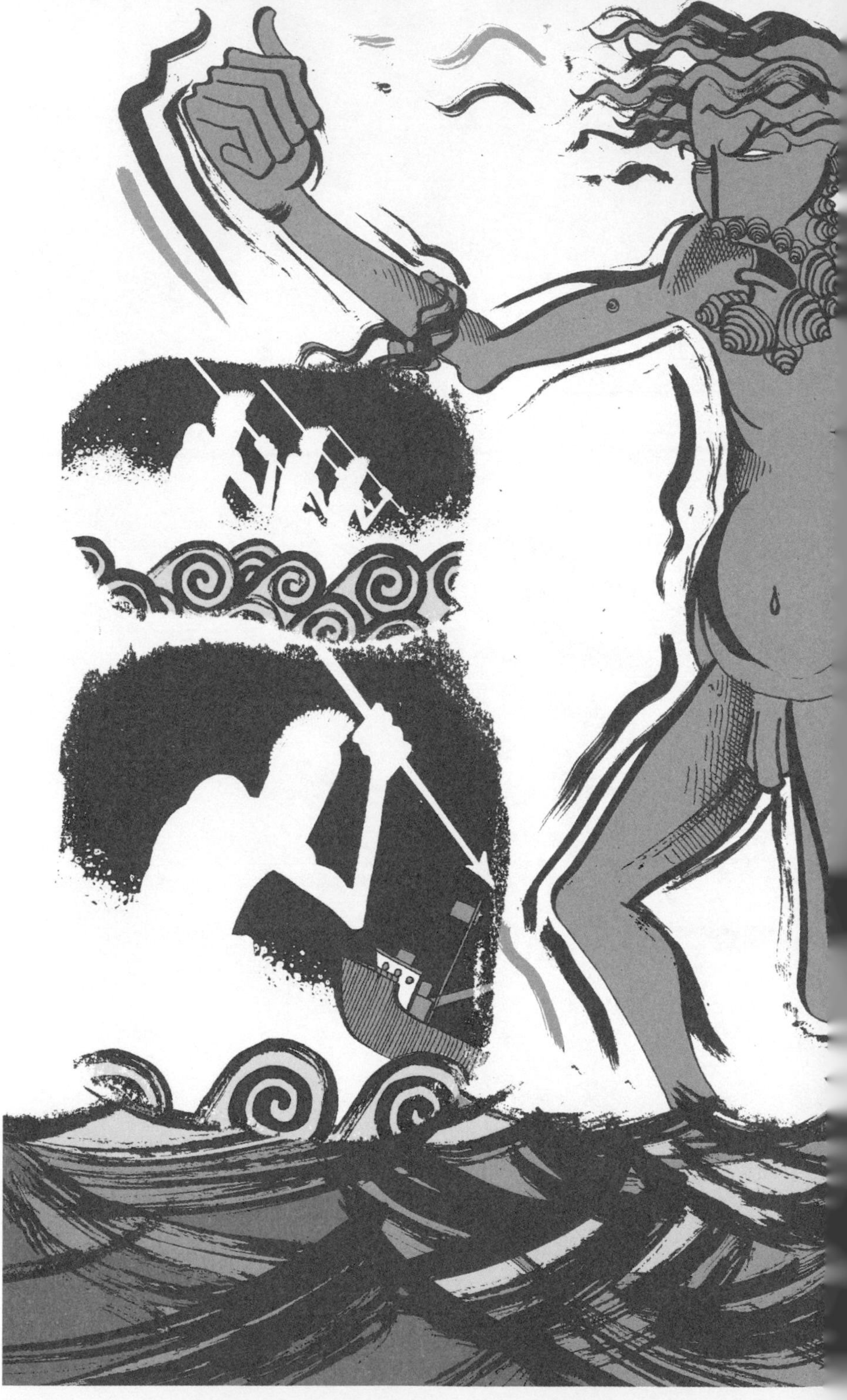

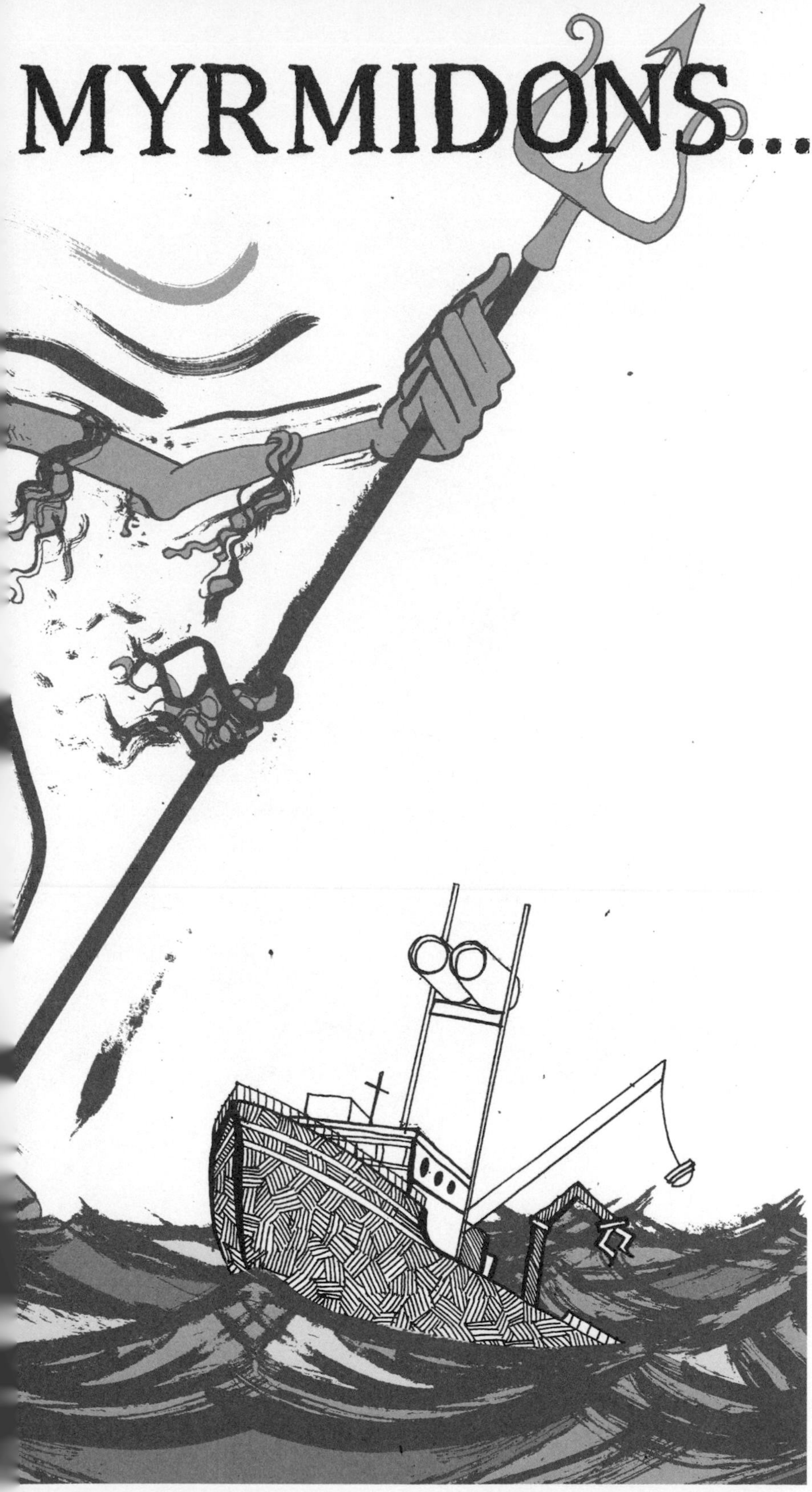
MYRMIDONS...

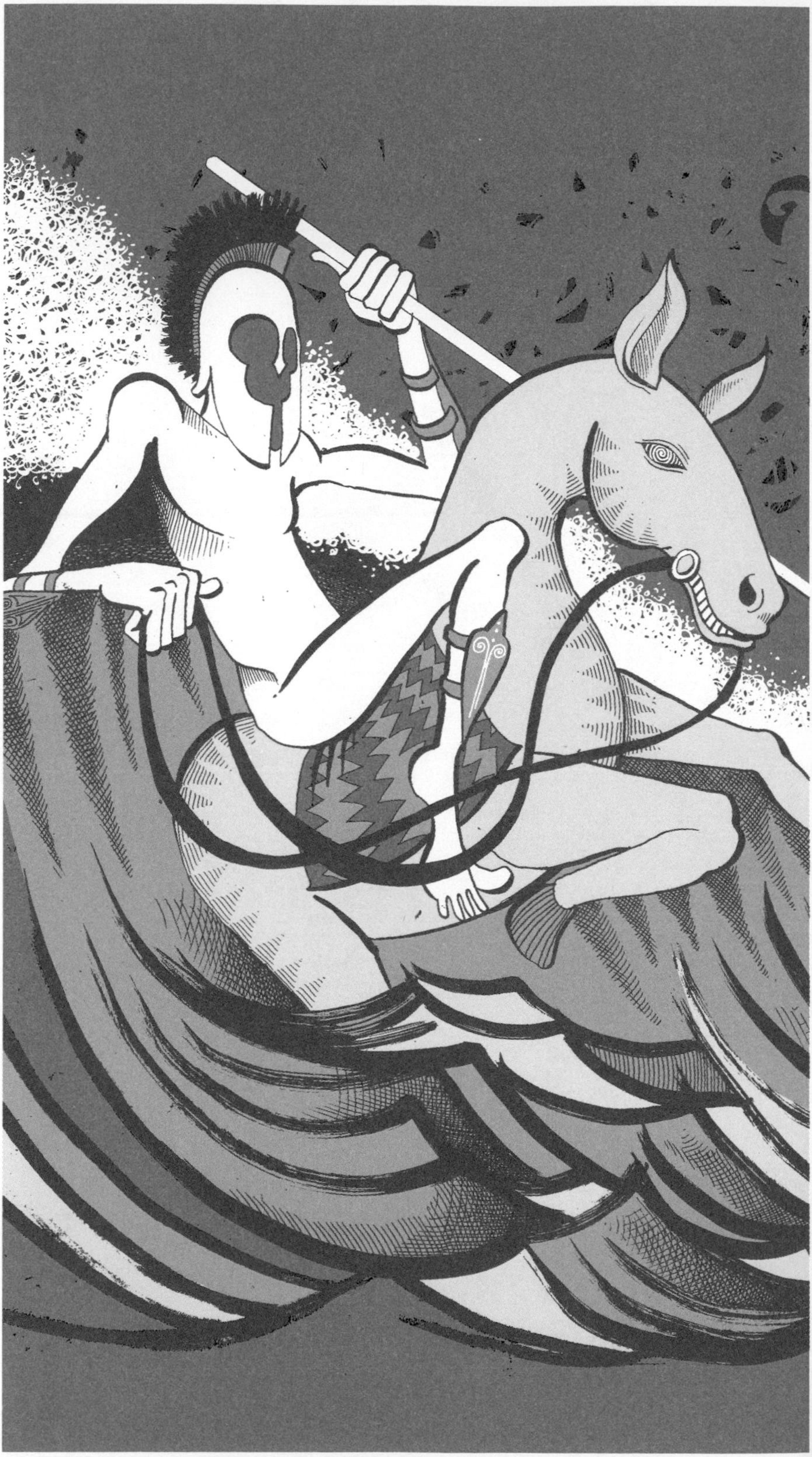

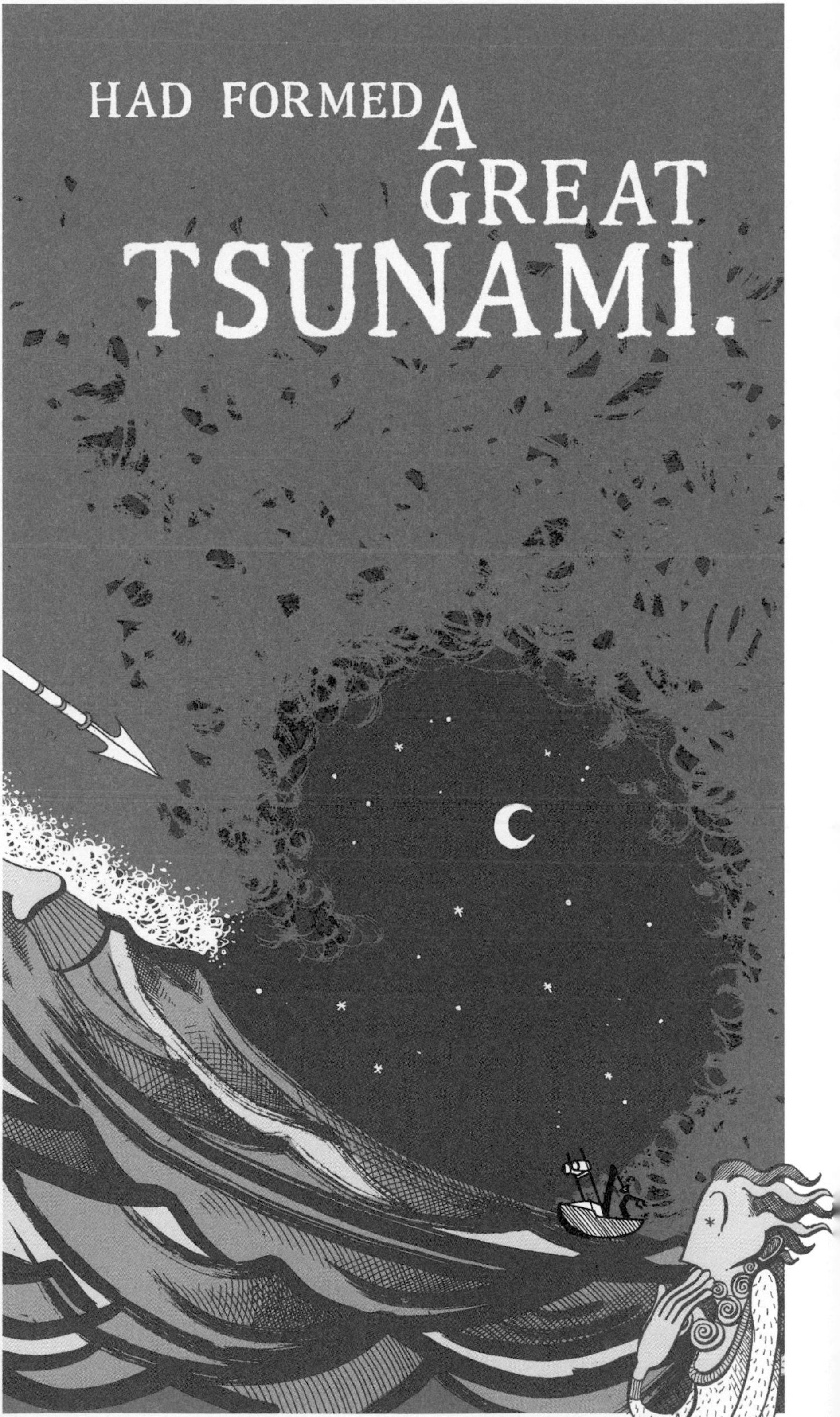
HAD FORMED A GREAT TSUNAMI.

TIME STOOD STILL...

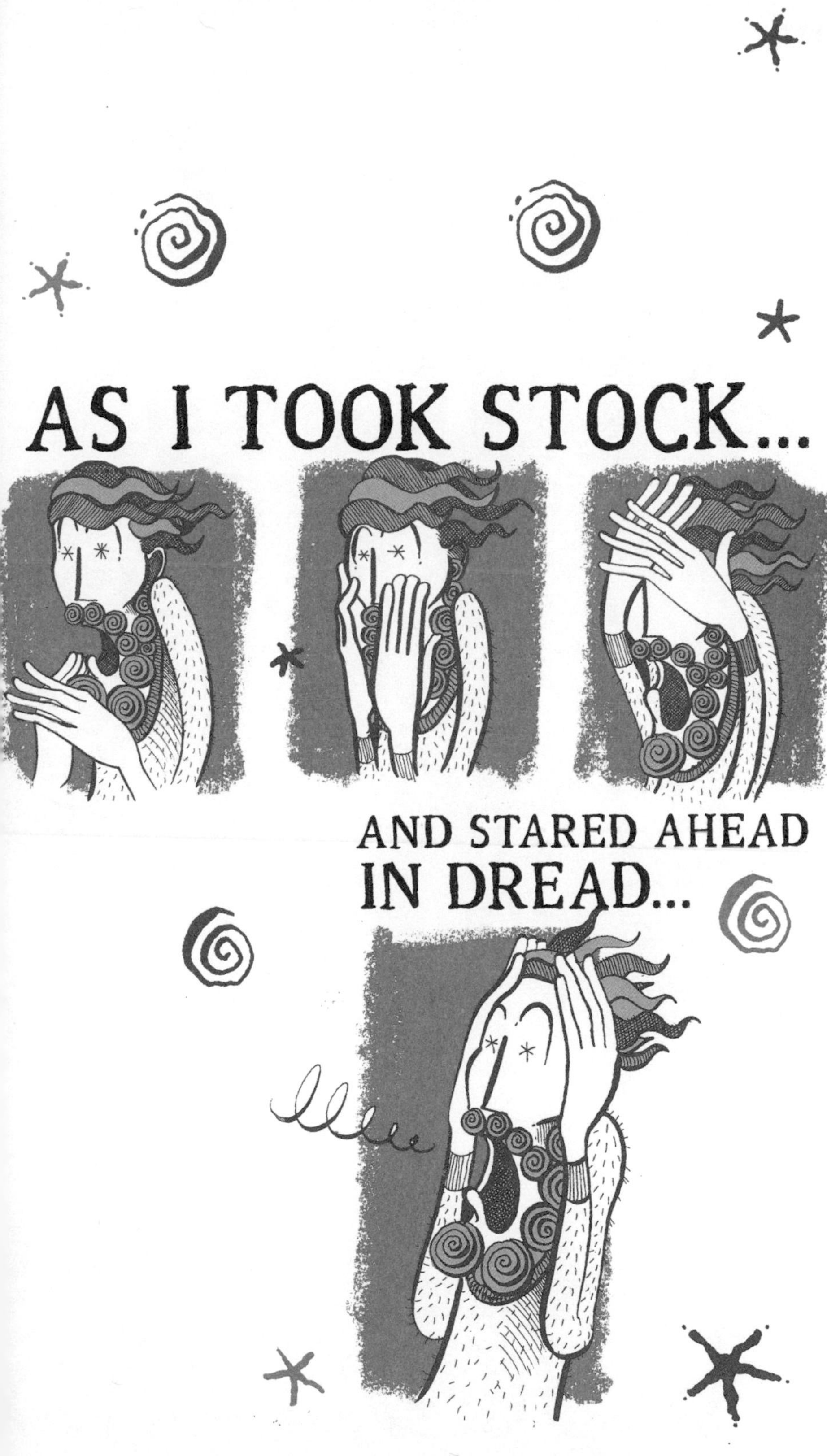
AS I TOOK STOCK...
AND STARED AHEAD
IN DREAD...

AT A WATERY FOREST OF REDWOOD PINES

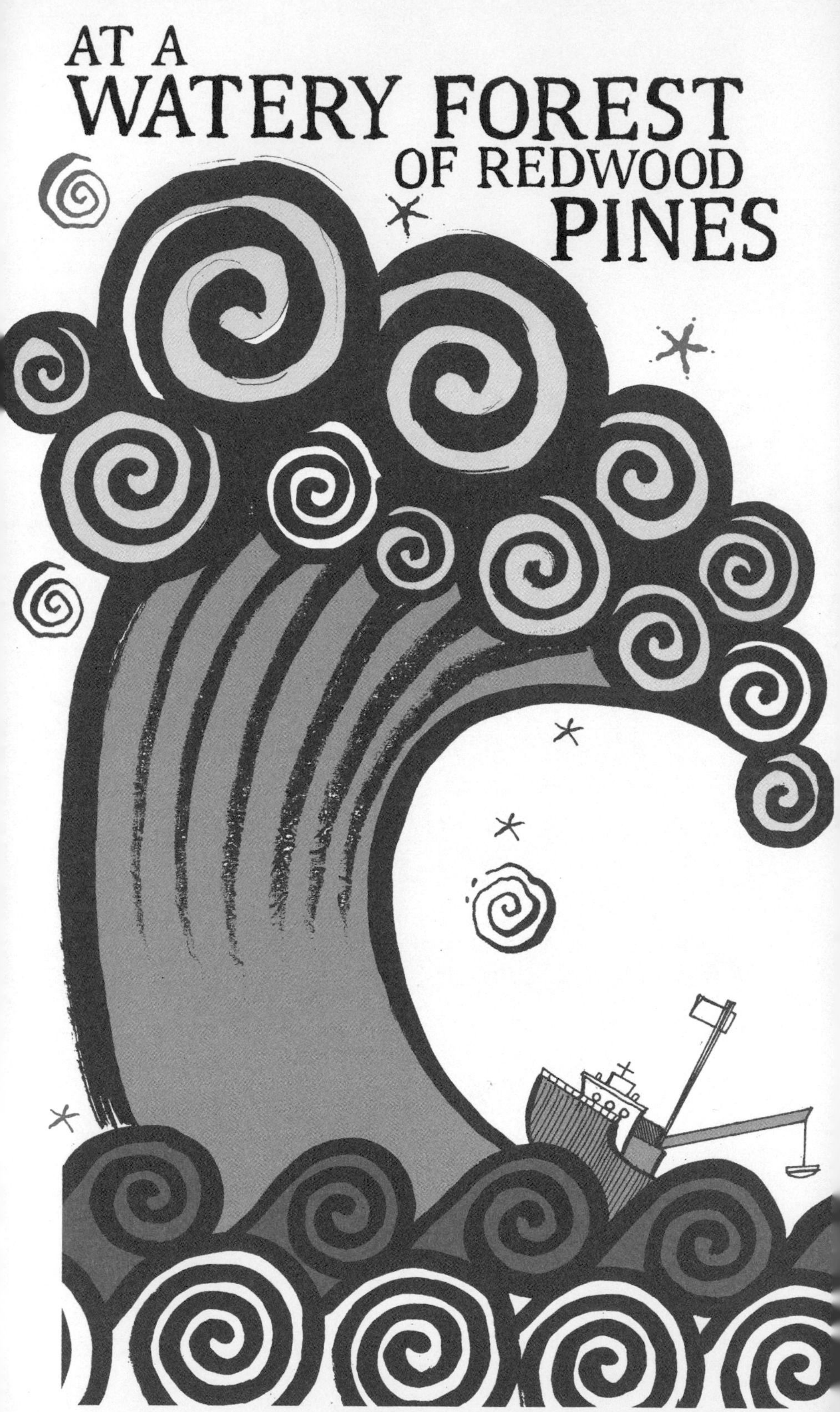

THAT
LOOMED
ABOVE
MY
HEAD.

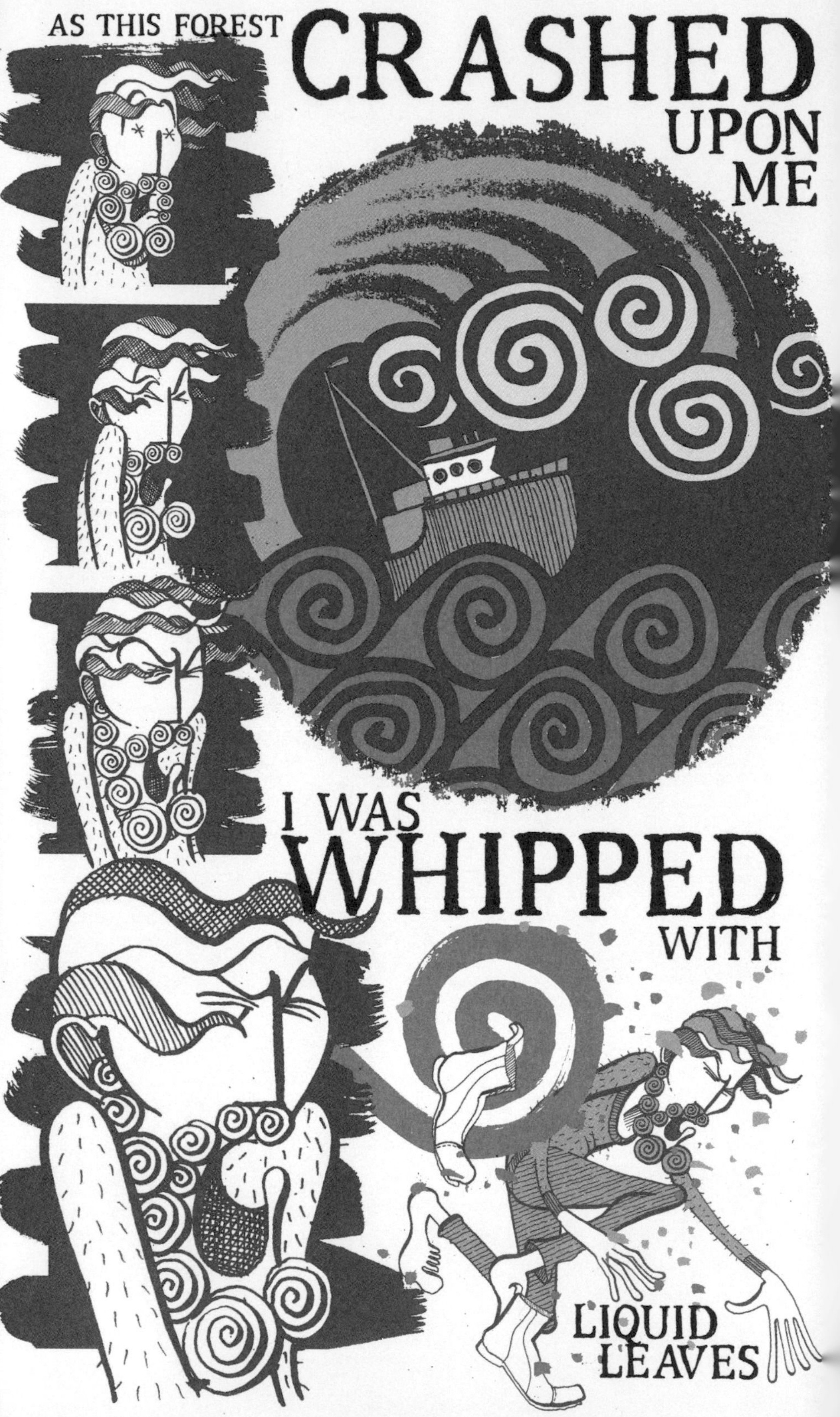
AS THIS FOREST CRASHED UPON ME
I WAS WHIPPED WITH
LIQUID LEAVES

THAT WRENCHED ME UP OFF MY FEET

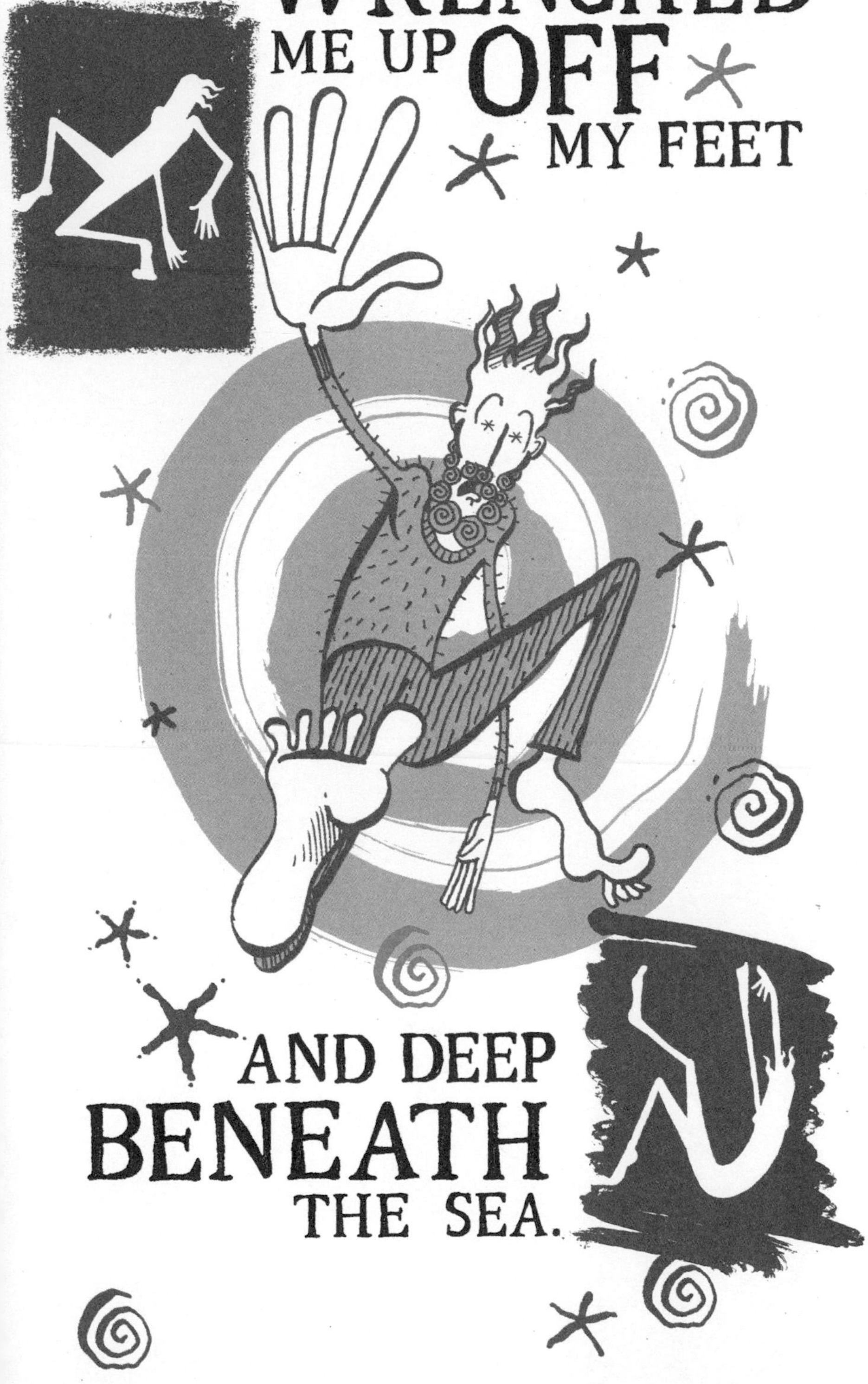

AND DEEP BENEATH THE SEA.

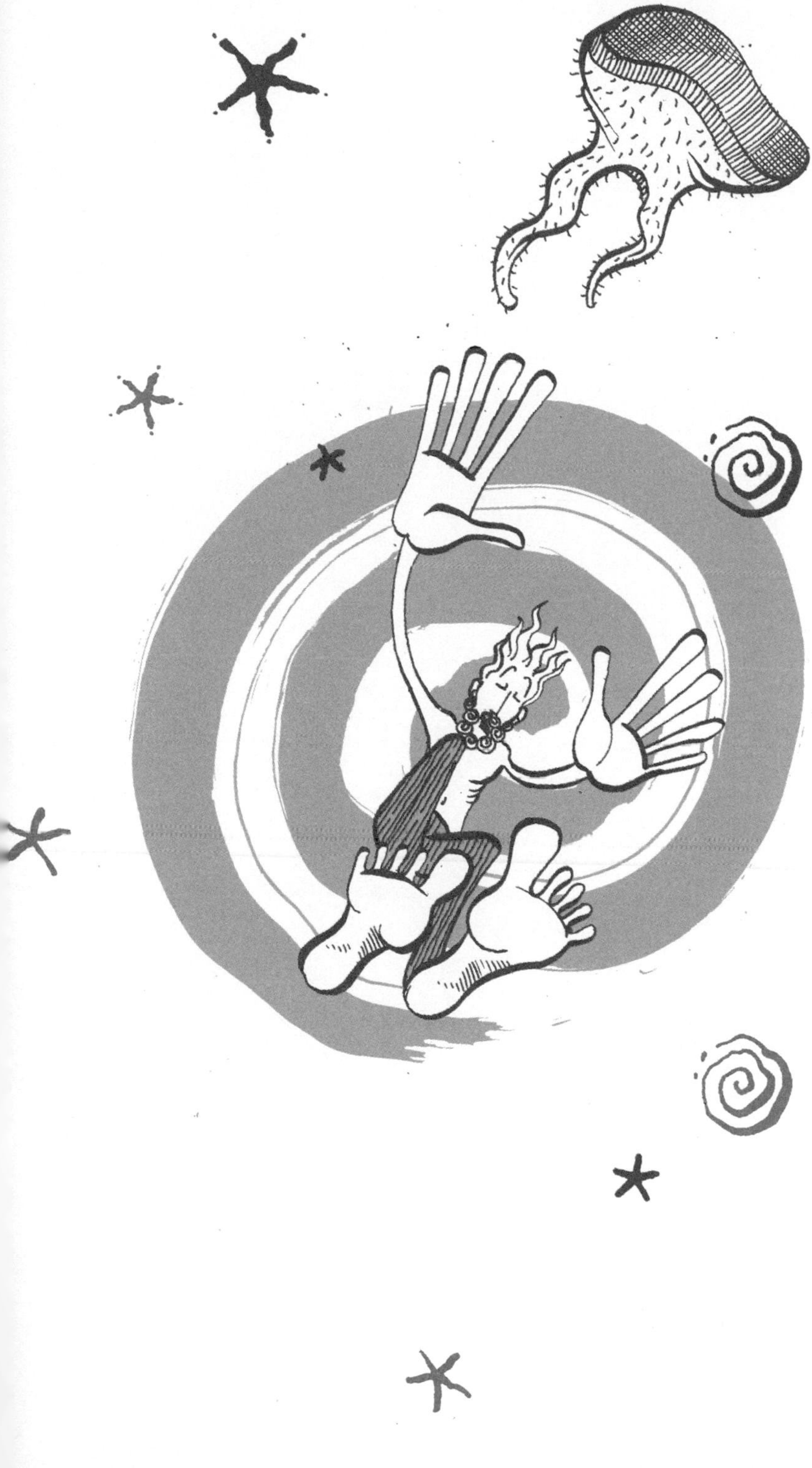

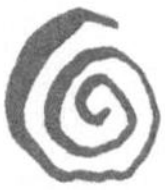

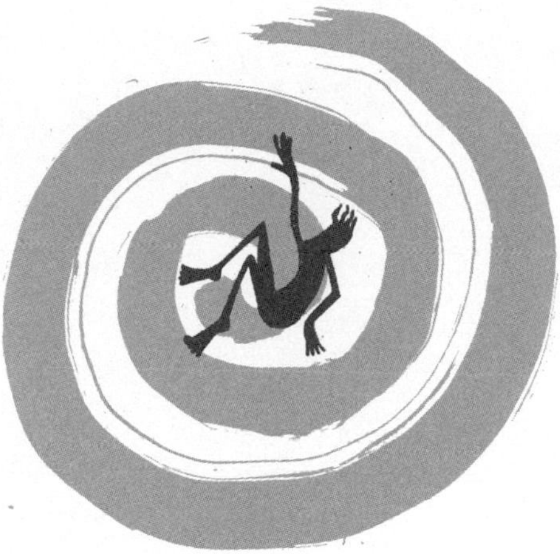

PART SIX

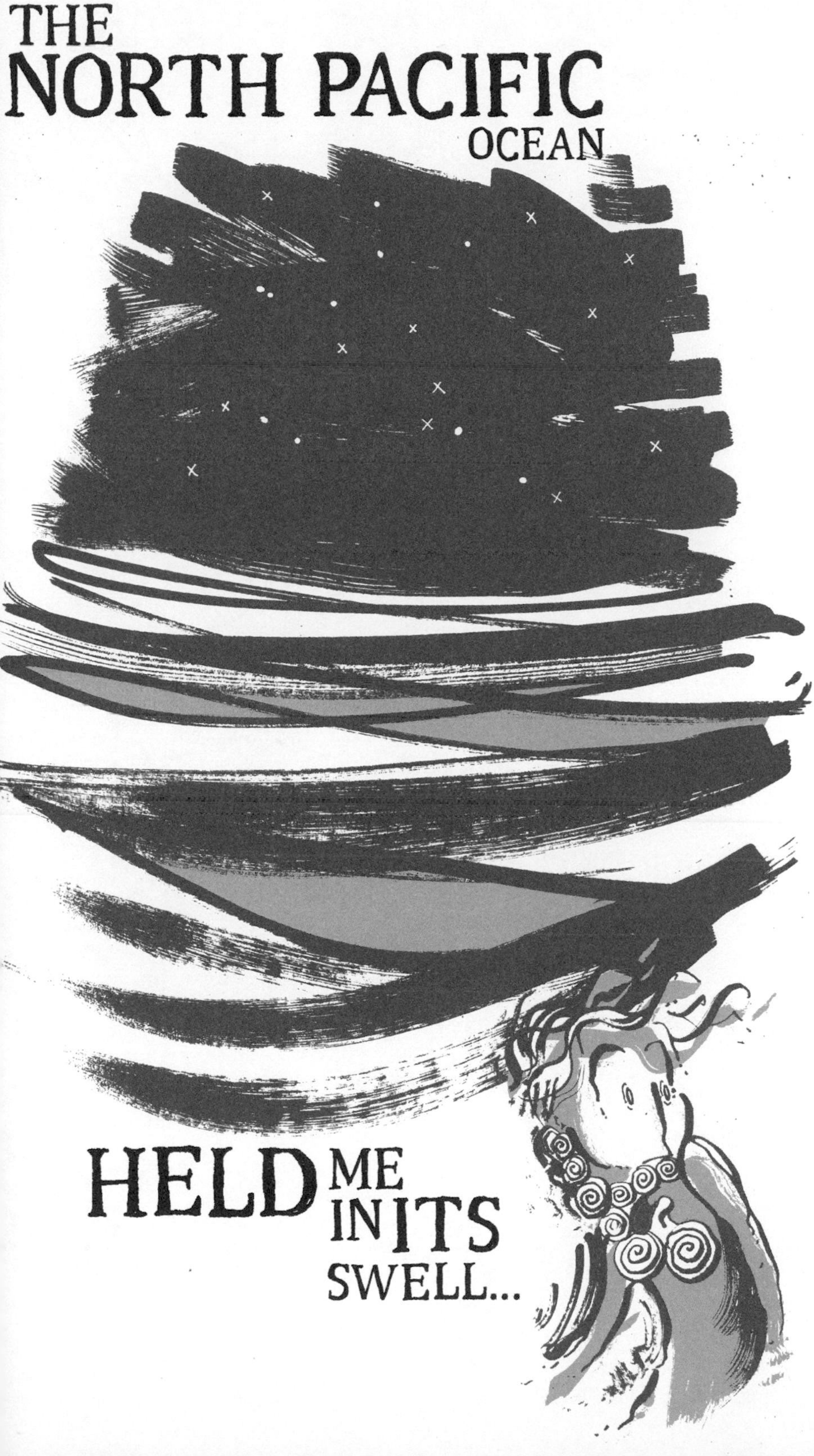
THE NORTH PACIFIC OCEAN
HELD ME IN ITS SWELL...

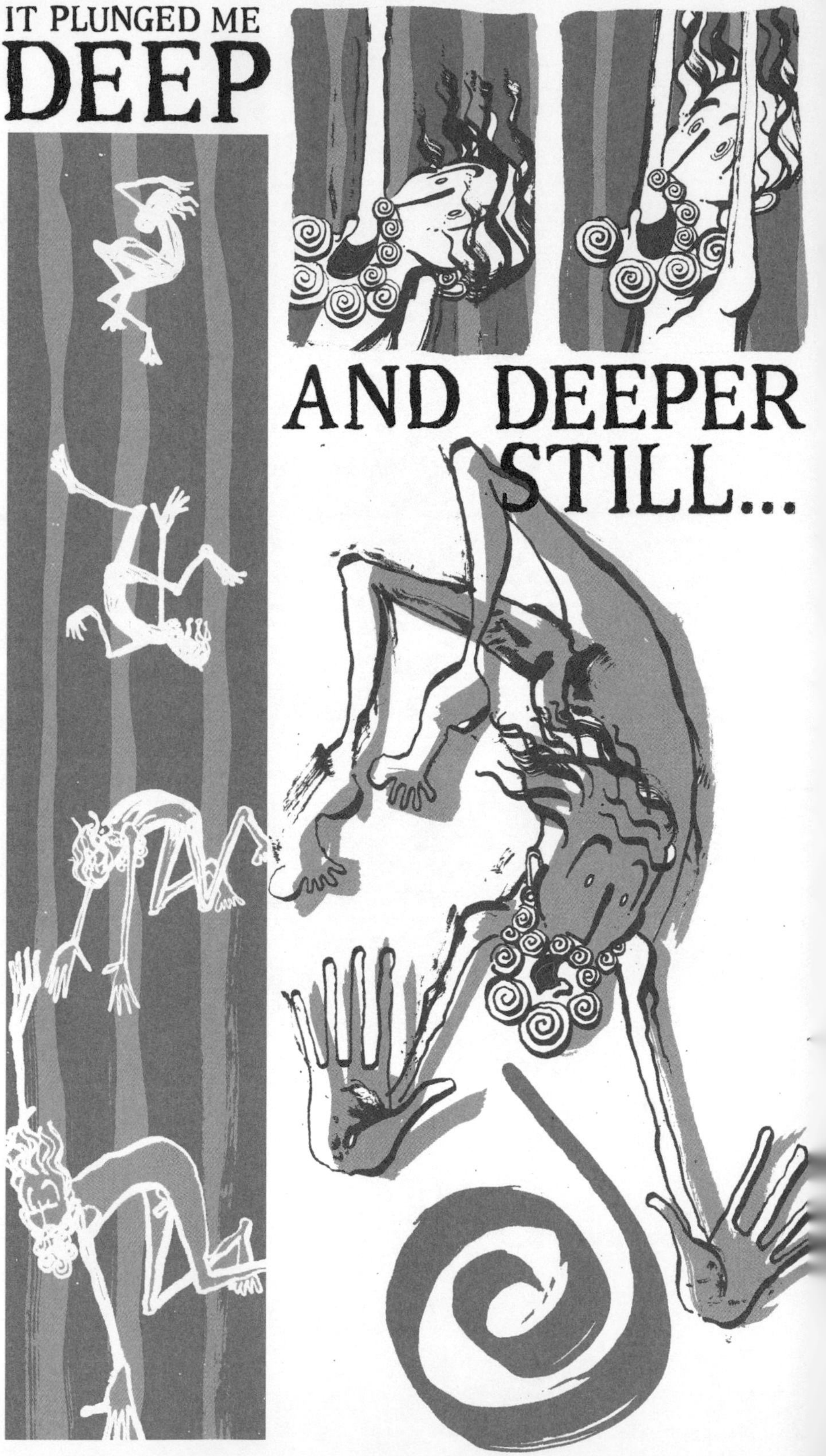
IT PLUNGED ME
DEEP
AND DEEPER
STILL...

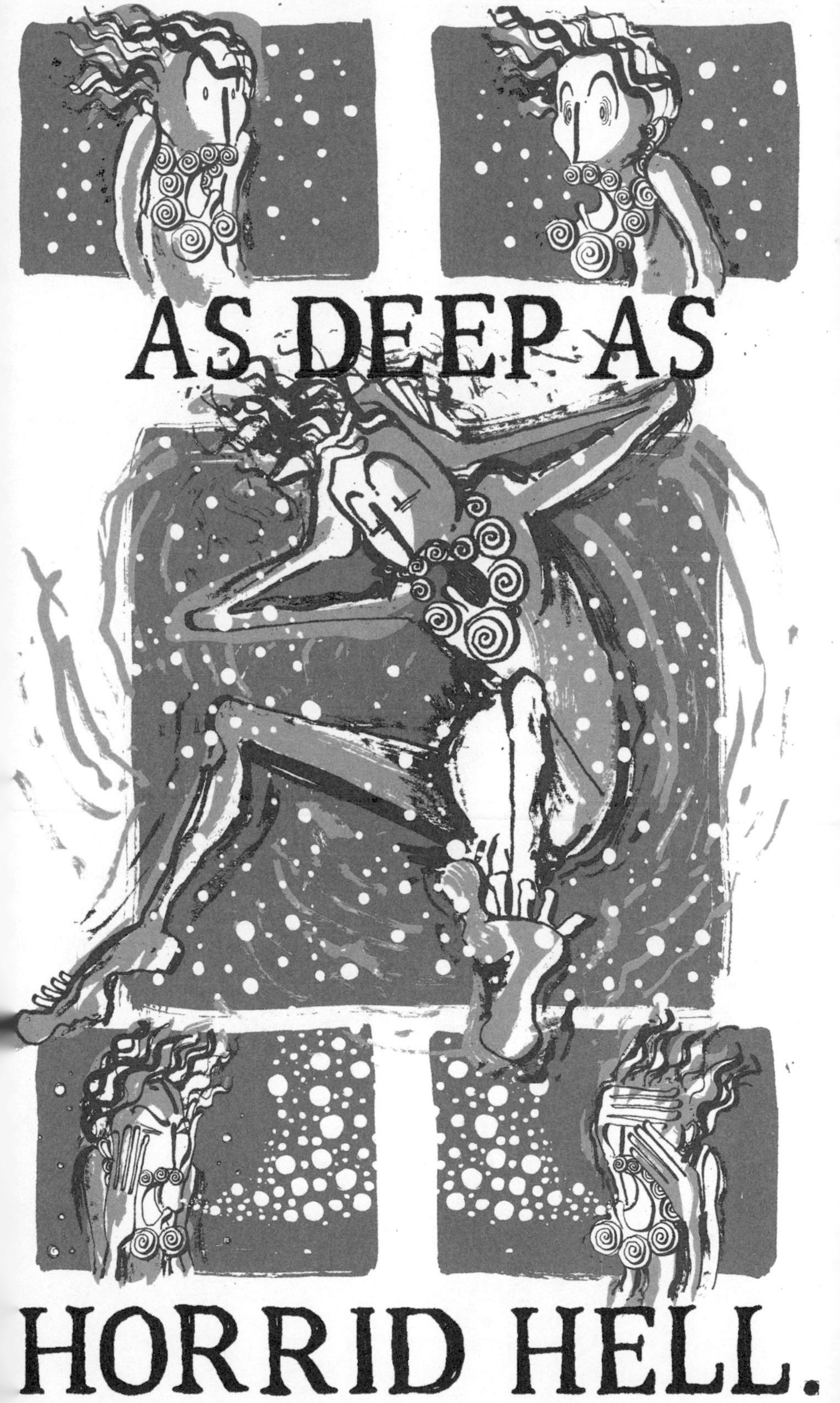

AS DEEP AS

HORRID HELL.

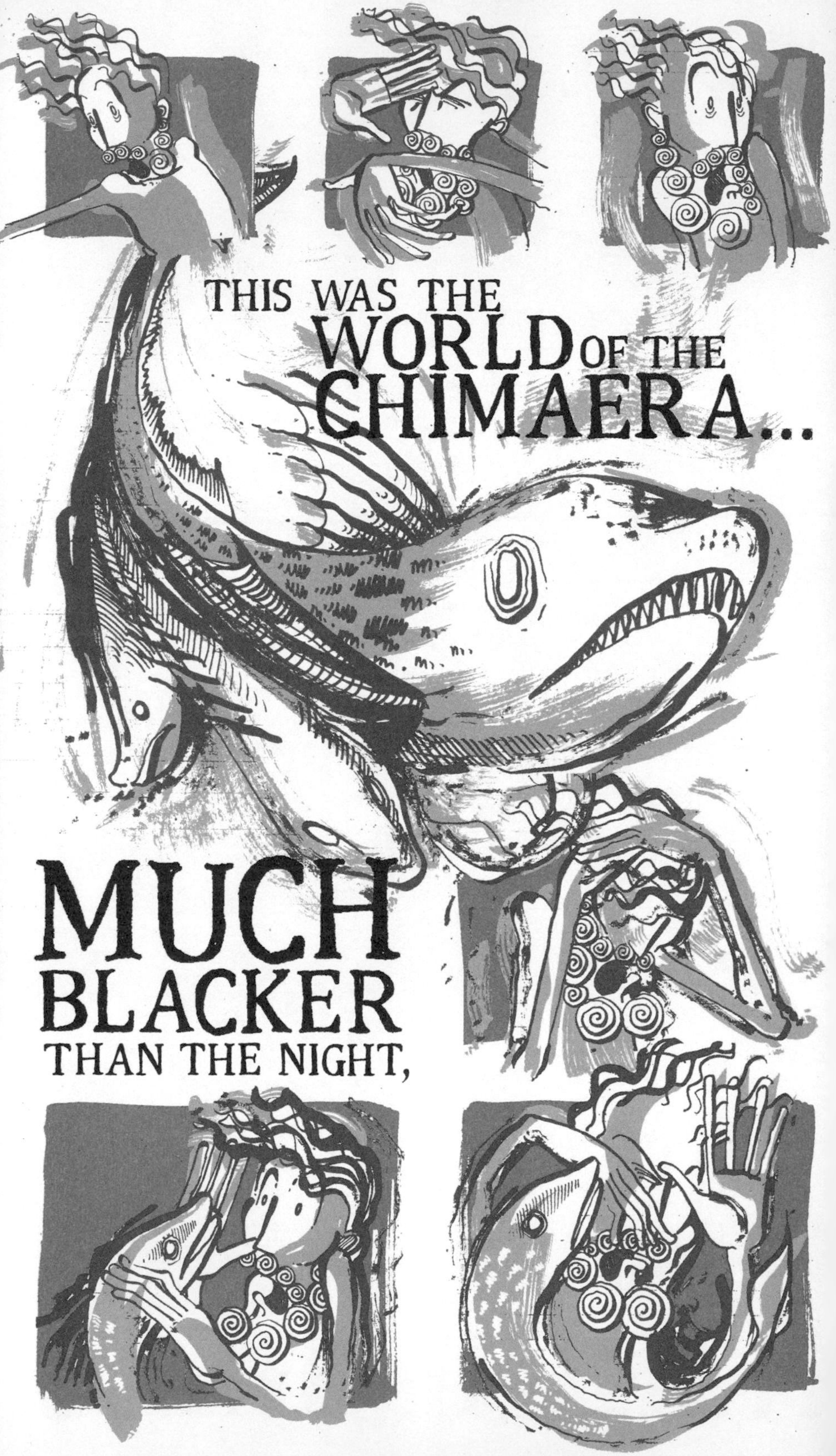
THIS WAS THE WORLD OF THE CHIMAERA...
MUCH BLACKER THAN THE NIGHT,

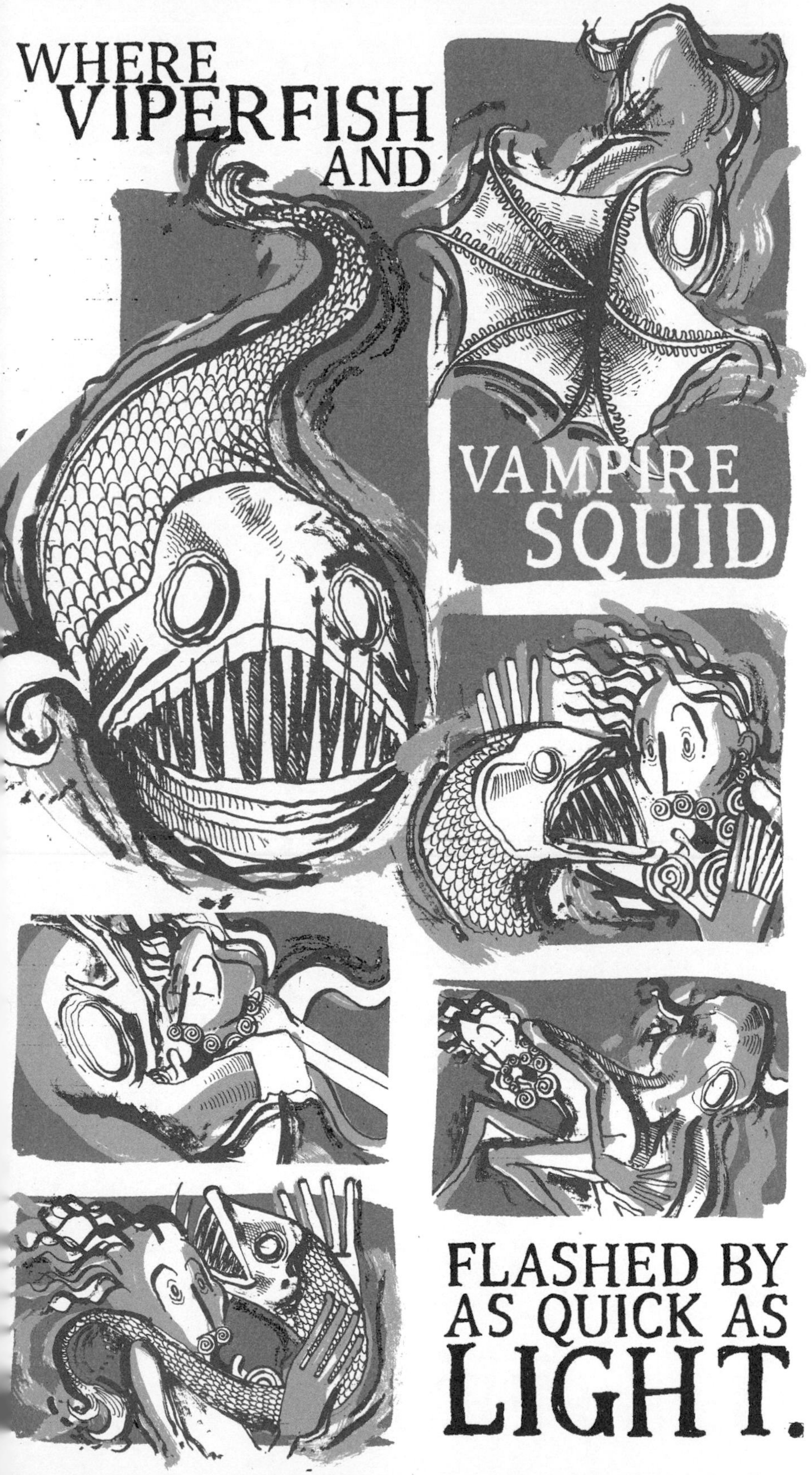
WHERE VIPERFISH AND
VAMPIRE SQUID
FLASHED BY AS QUICK AS LIGHT.

THEMISTO GAUDICHAUDII

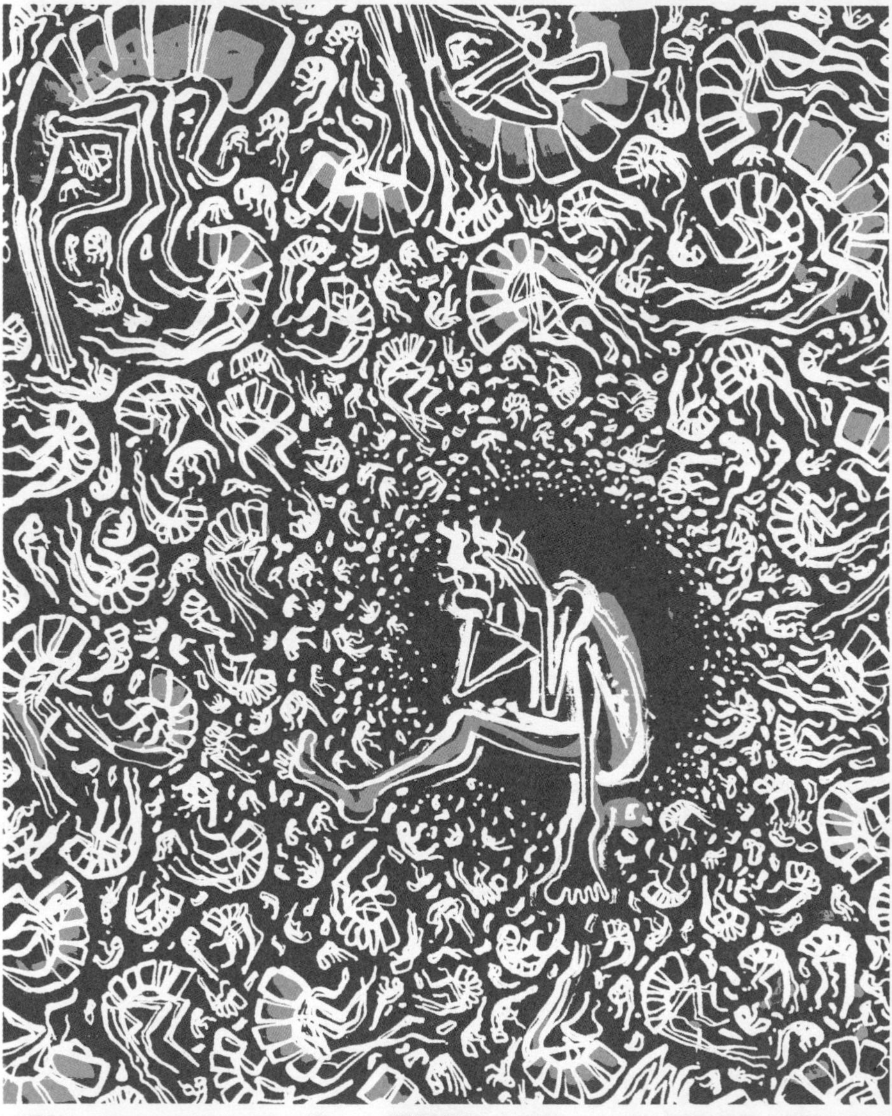

SWARMED
LIKE FEEDING FLIES

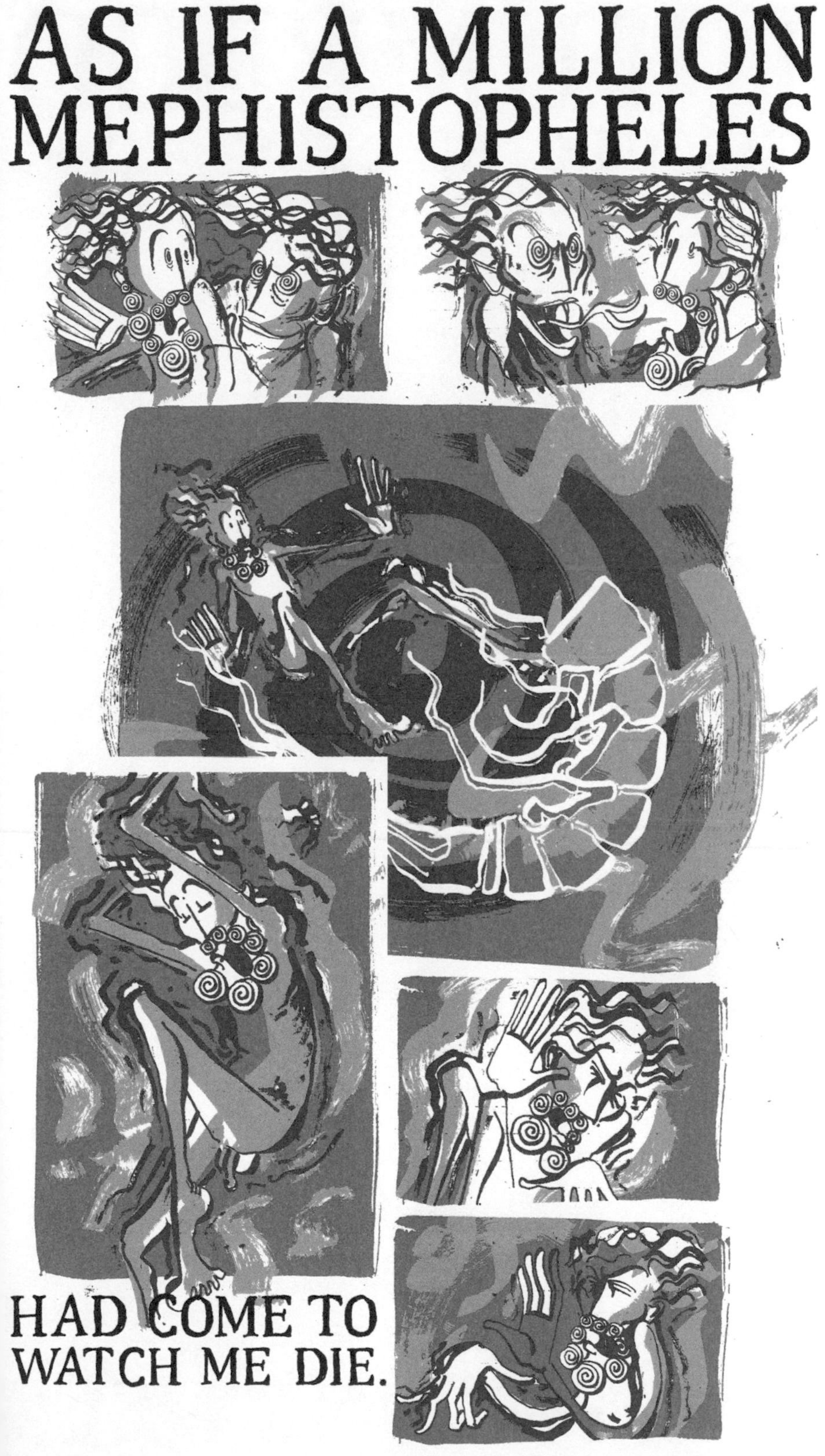
AS IF A MILLION MEPHISTOPHELES
HAD COME TO WATCH ME DIE.

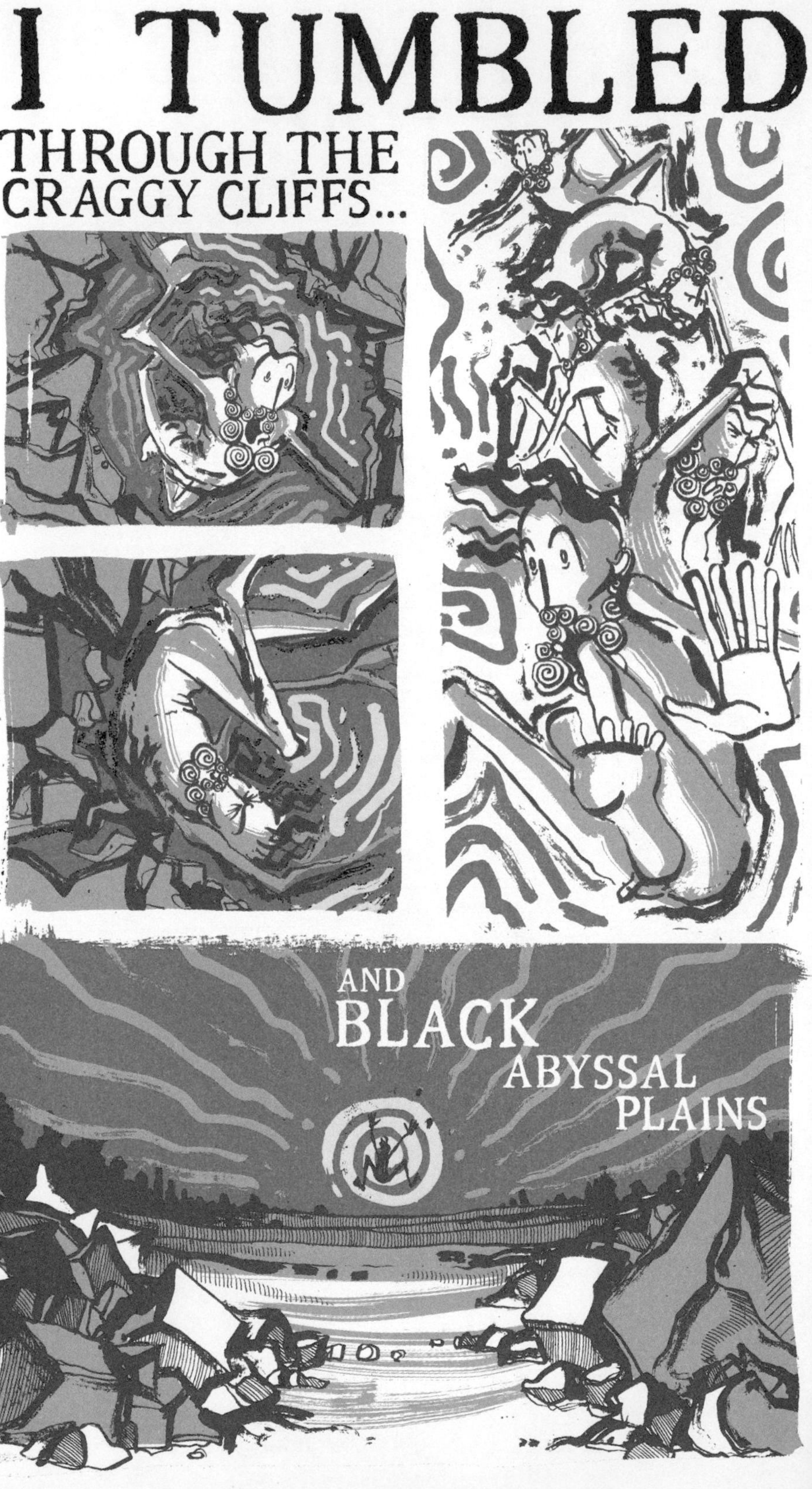
I TUMBLED
THROUGH THE
CRAGGY CLIFFS...
AND
BLACK
ABYSSAL
PLAINS

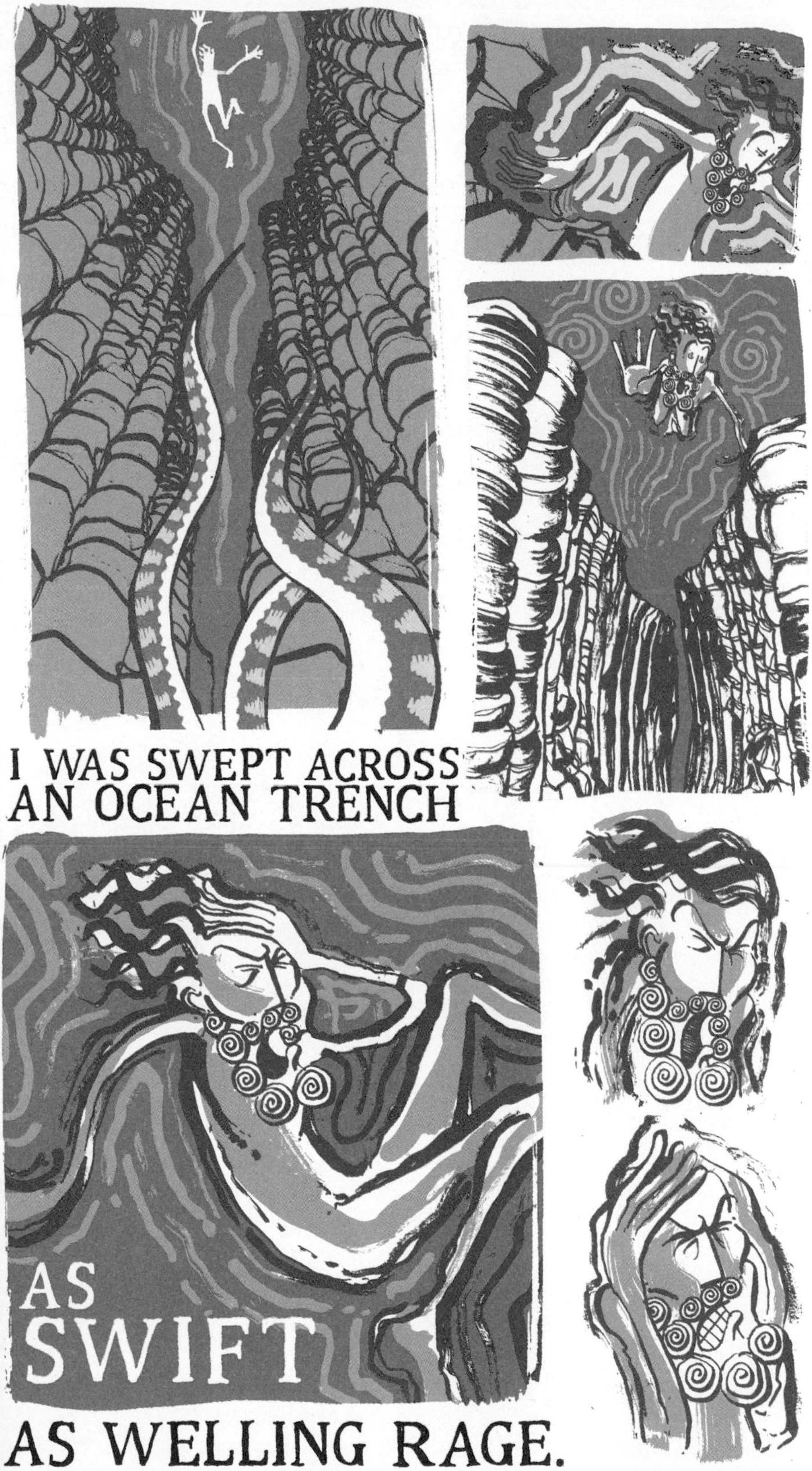
I WAS SWEPT ACROSS
AN OCEAN TRENCH
AS
SWIFT
AS WELLING RAGE.

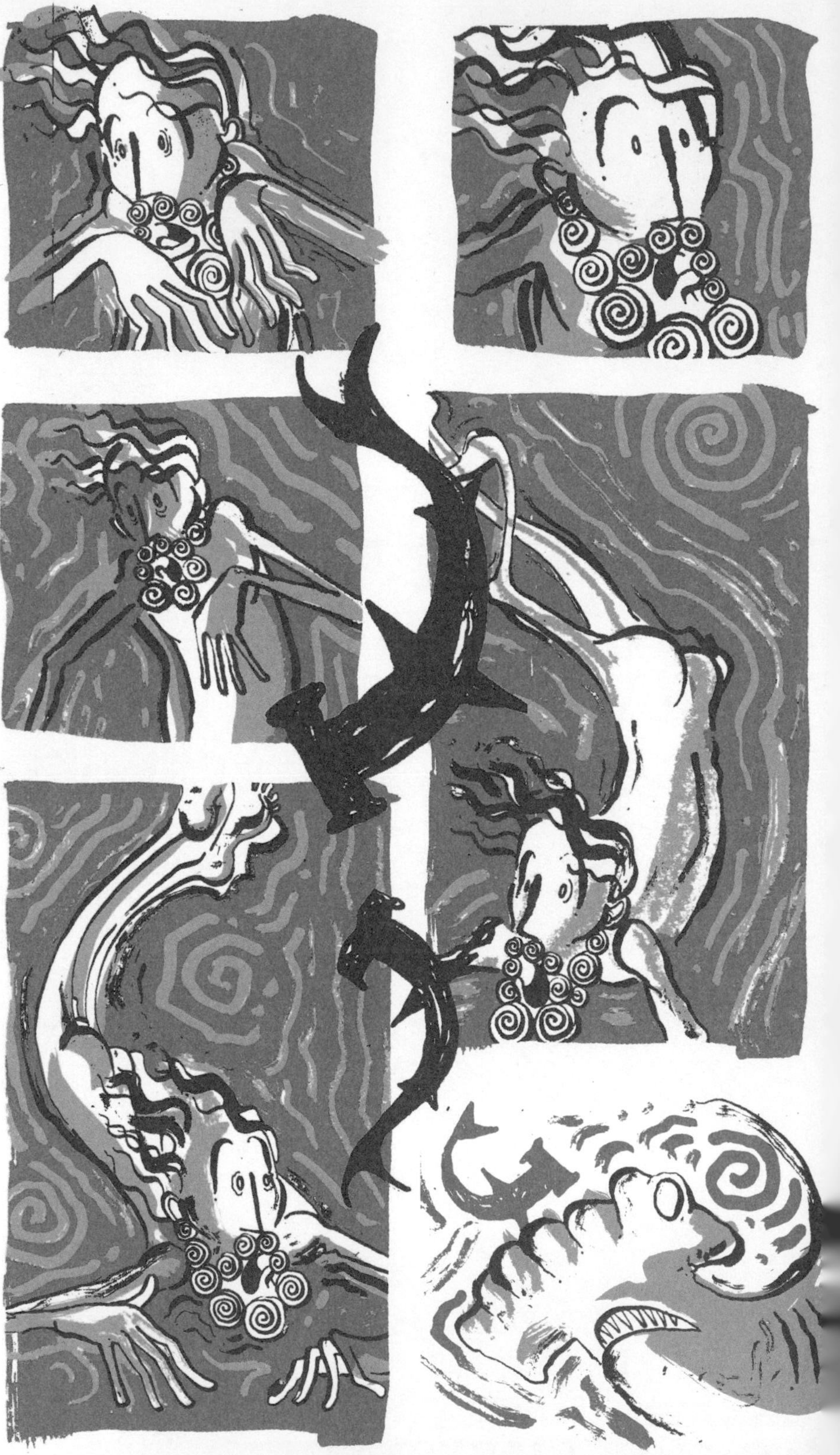

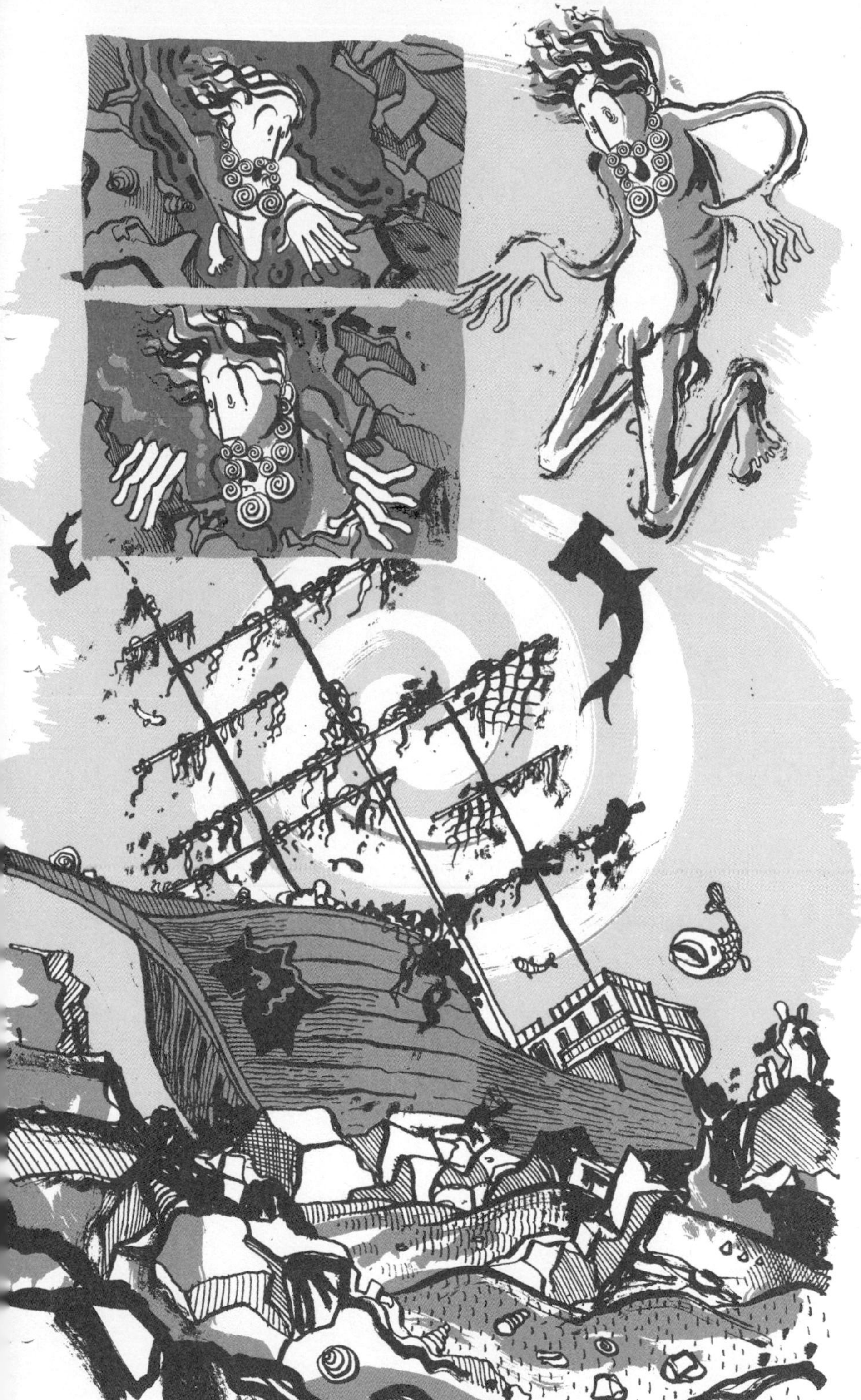

I SAW RELICS OF ENDEAVOURS...

TITANIC FEATS OF PRIDE...

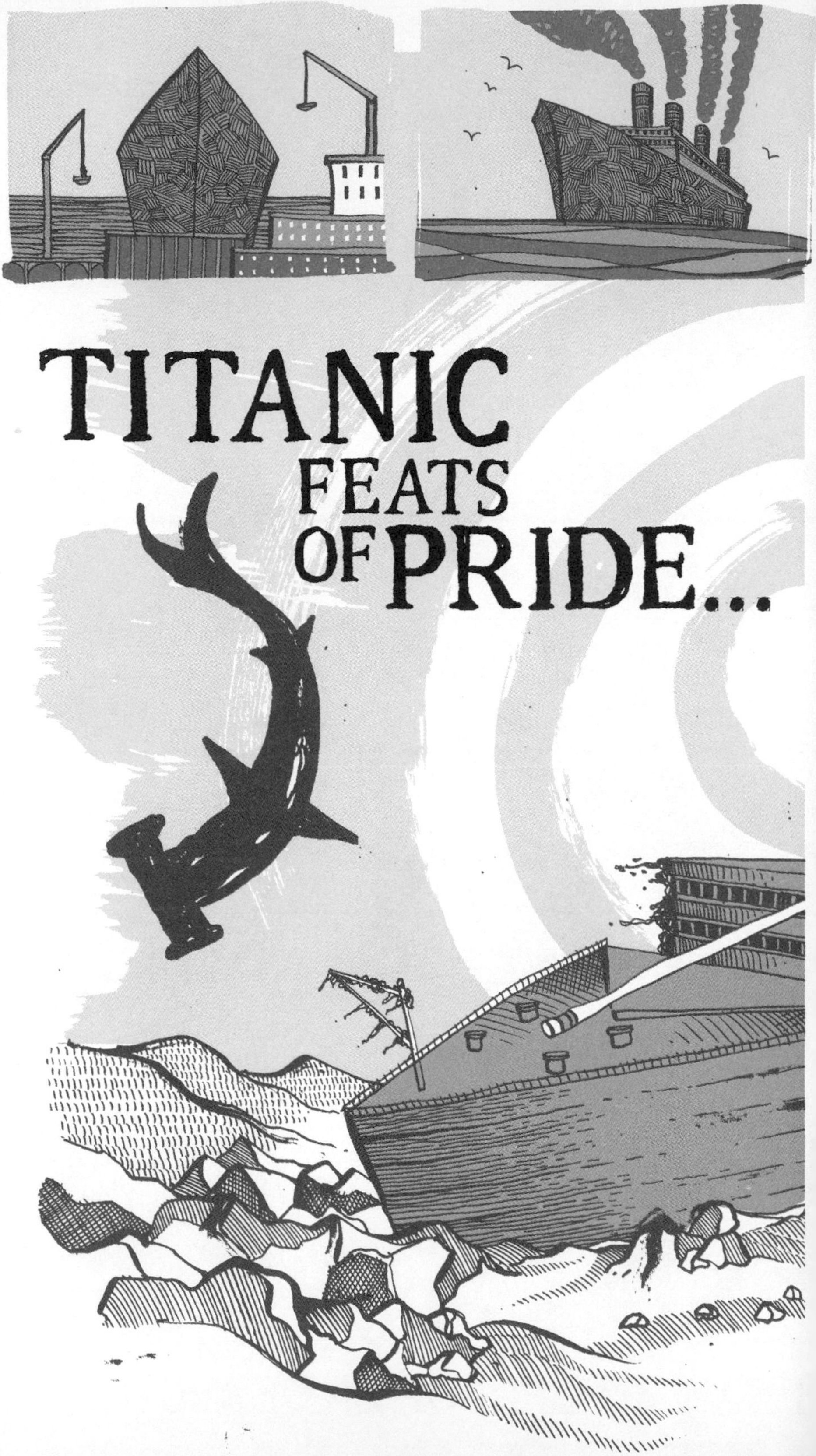

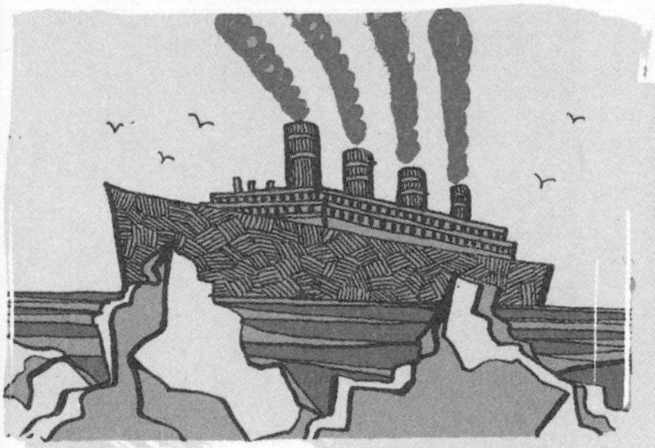

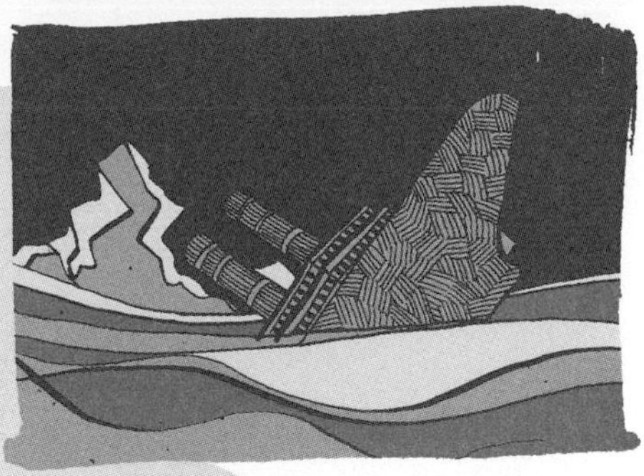

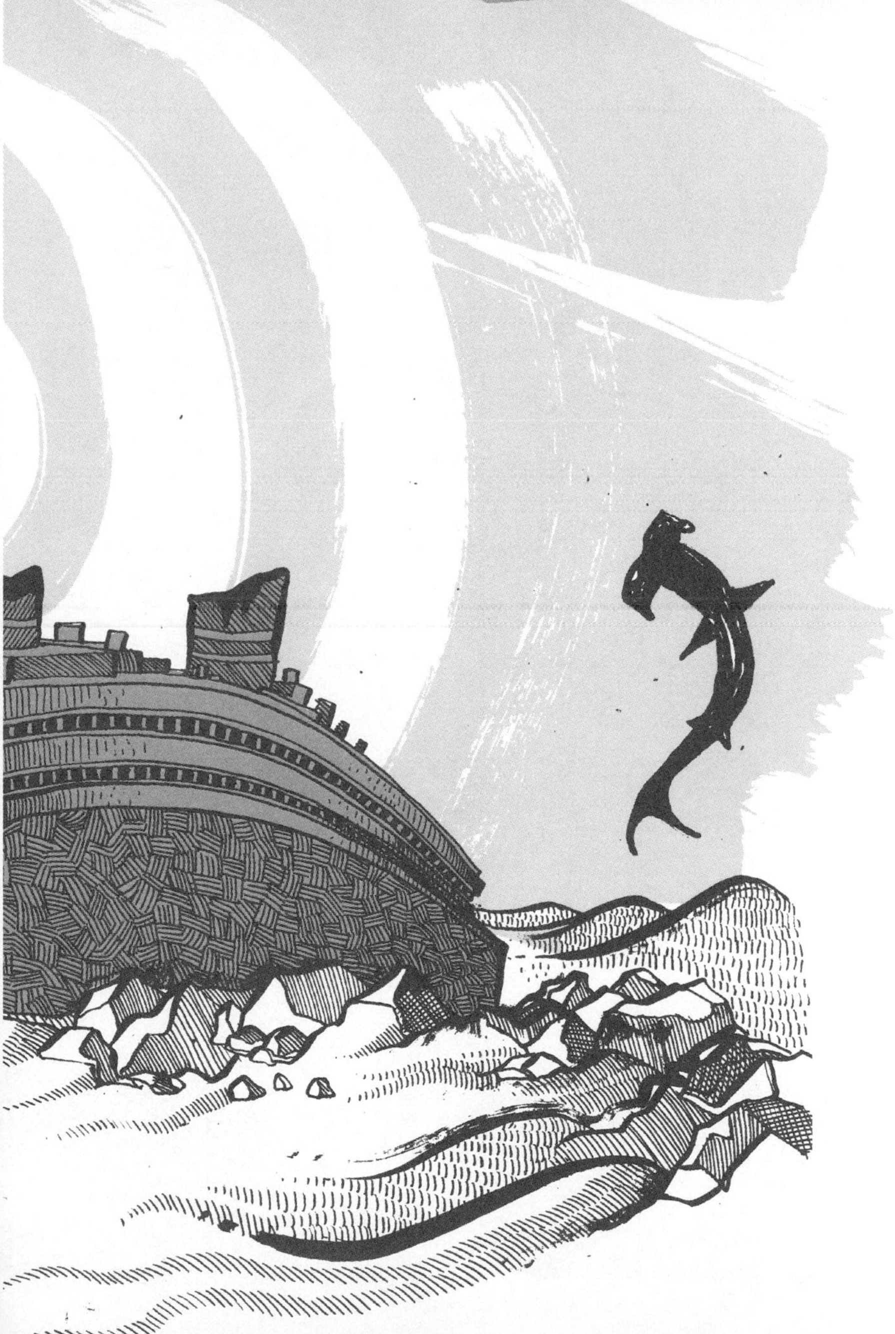

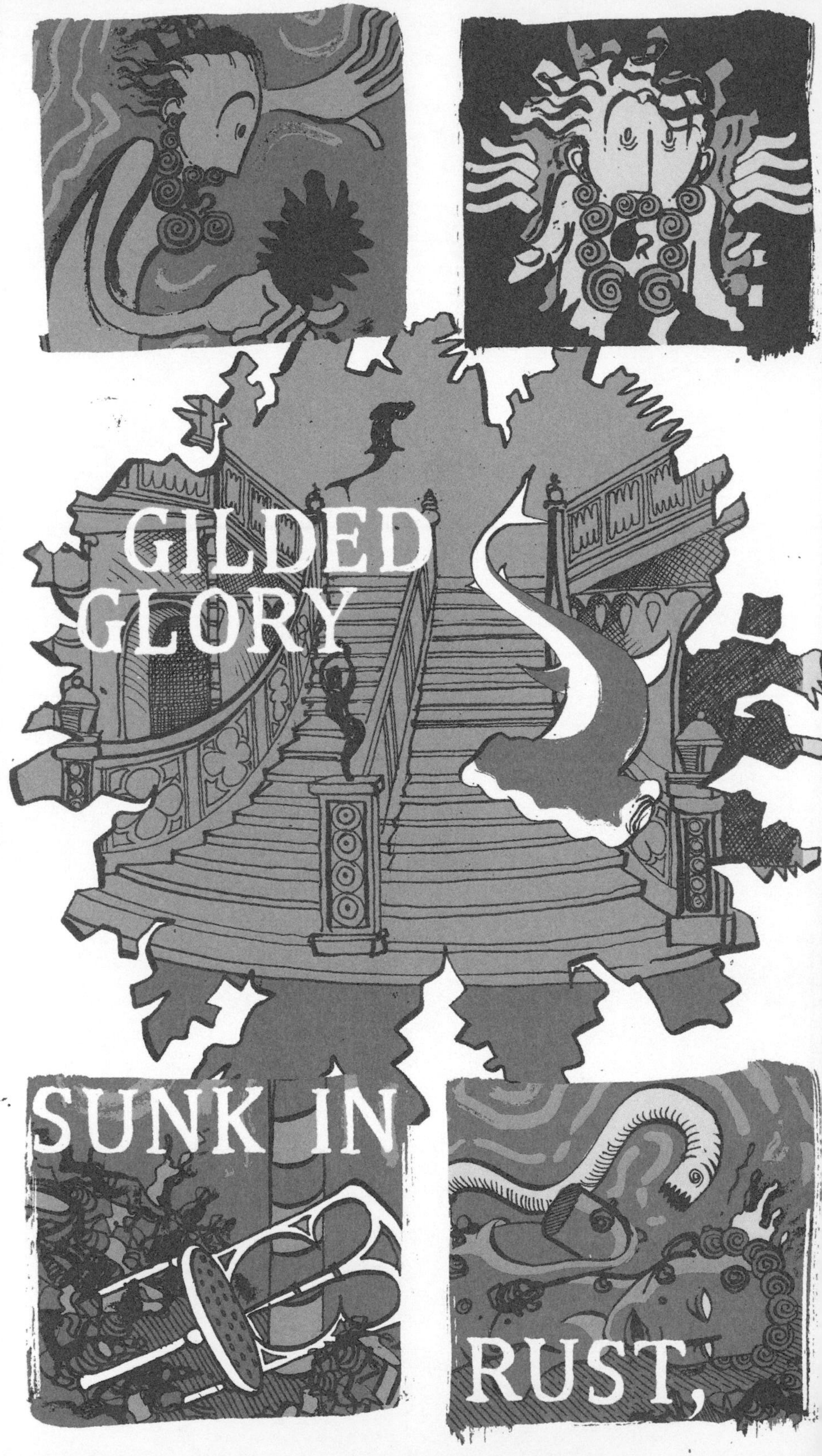
GILDED
GLORY
SUNK IN
RUST,

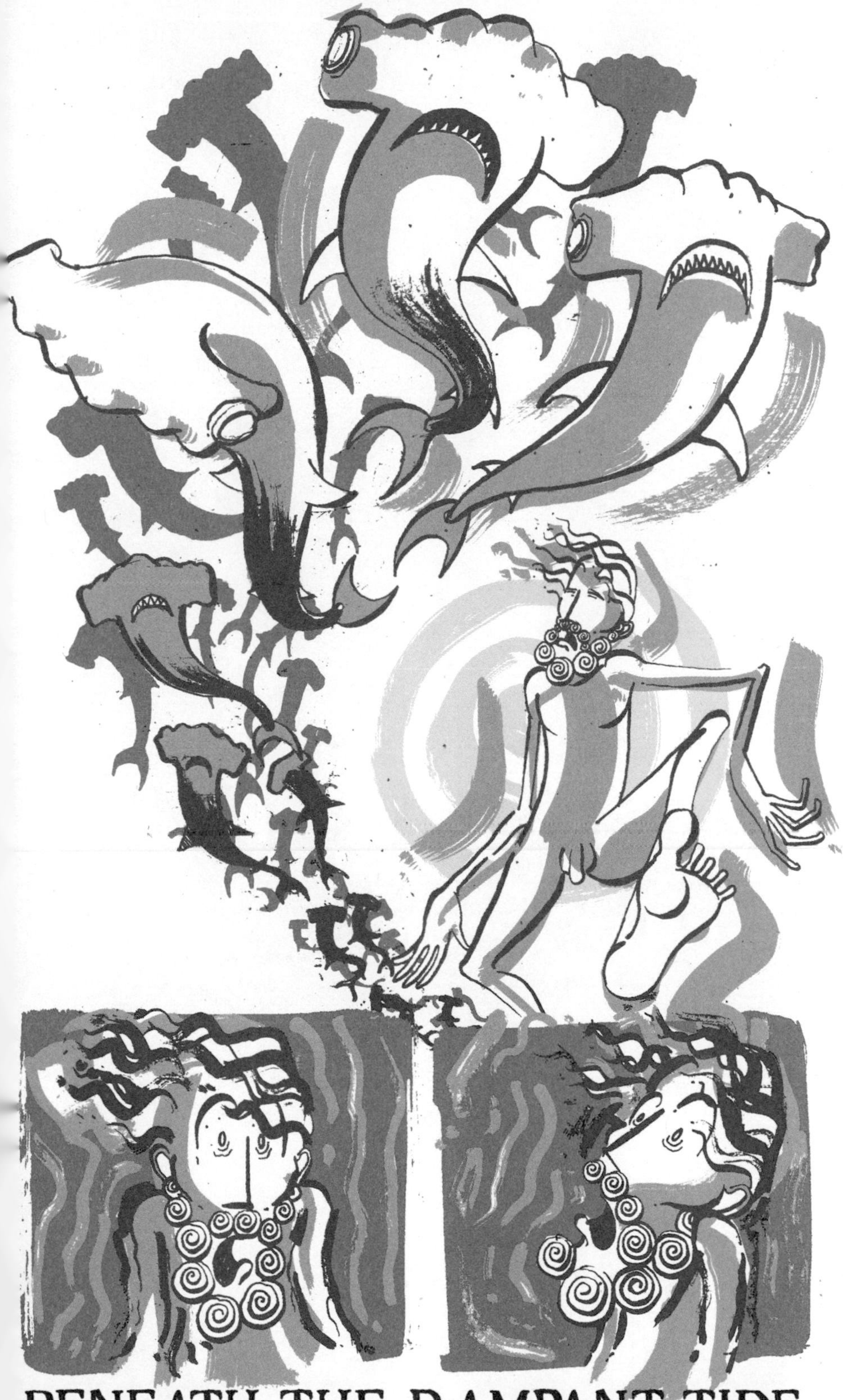

BENEATH THE RAMPANT TIDE.

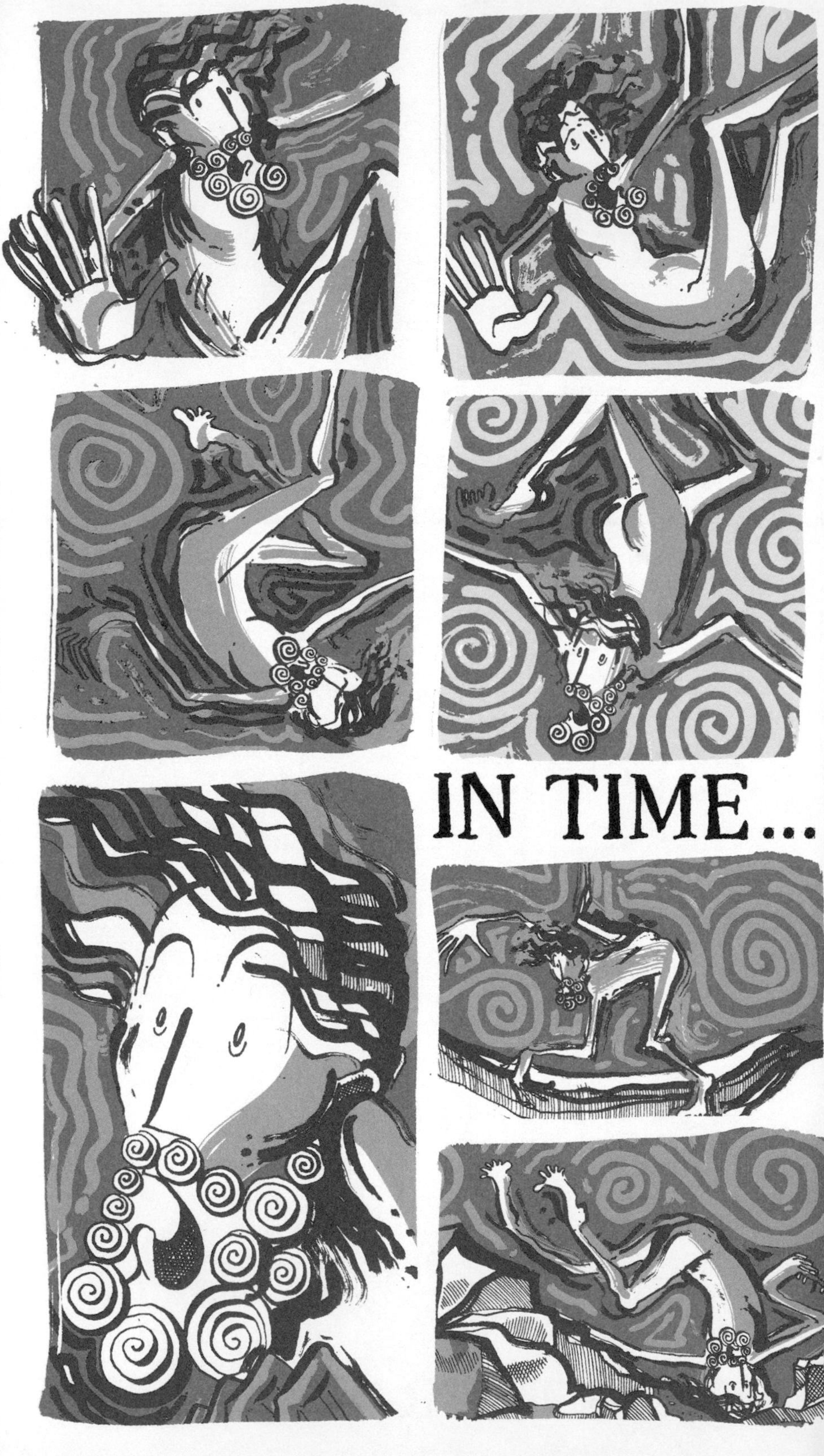
IN TIME...

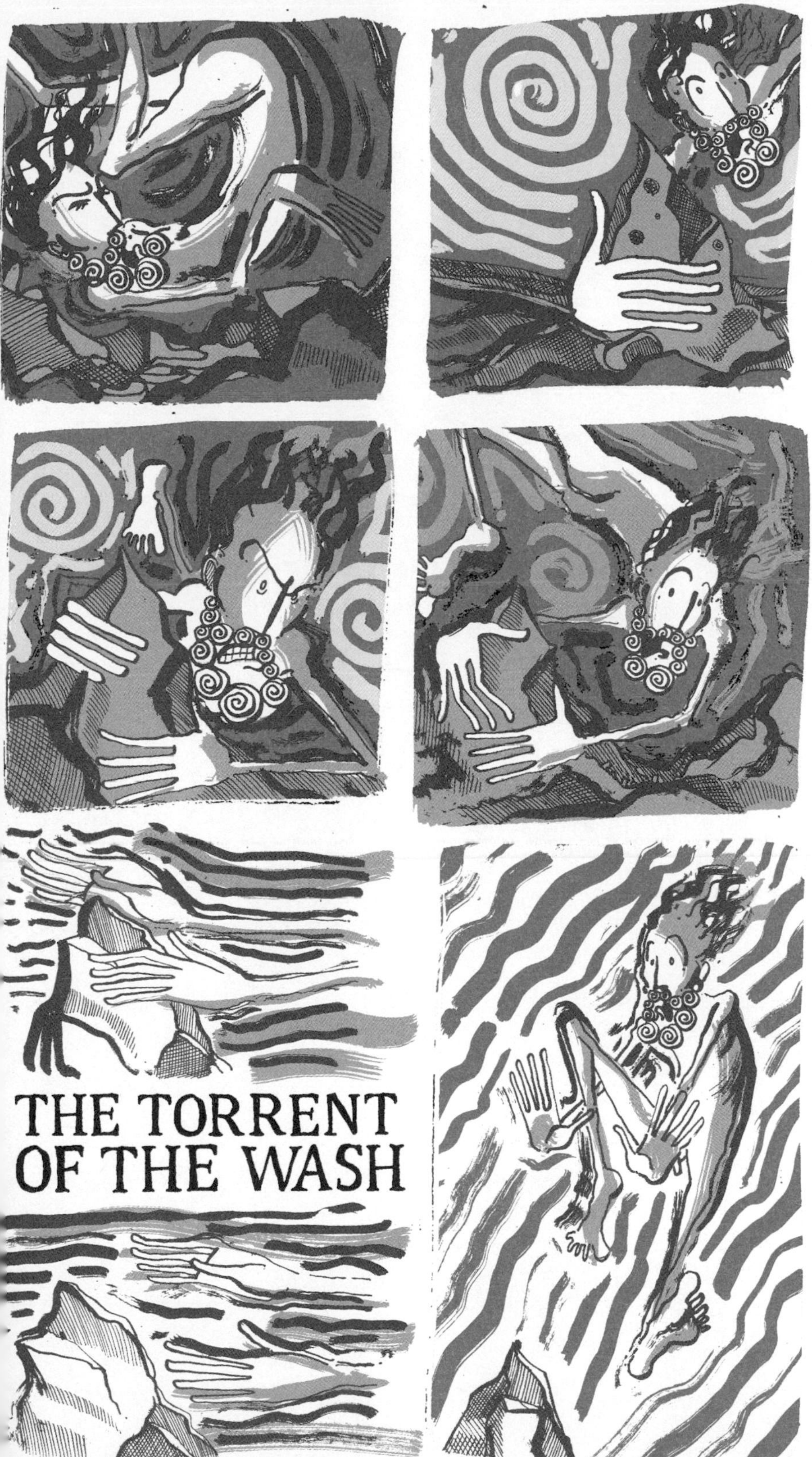
THE TORRENT
OF THE WASH

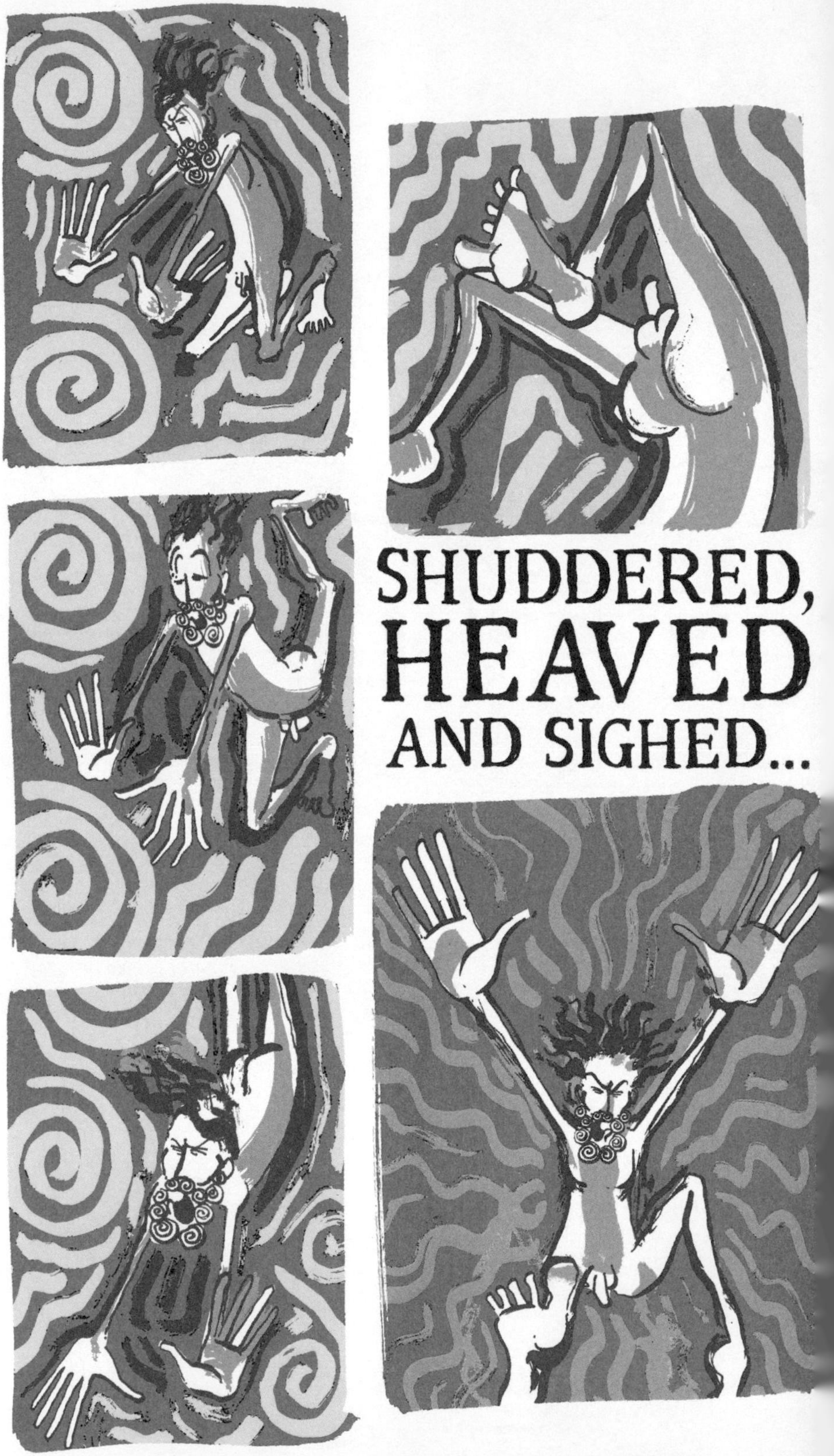
SHUDDERED,
HEAVED
AND SIGHED...

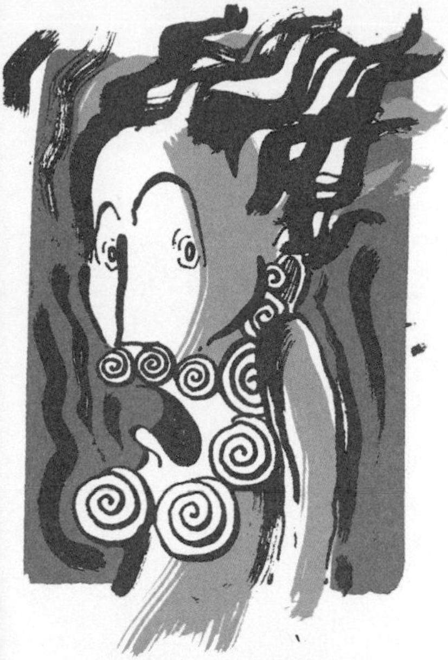

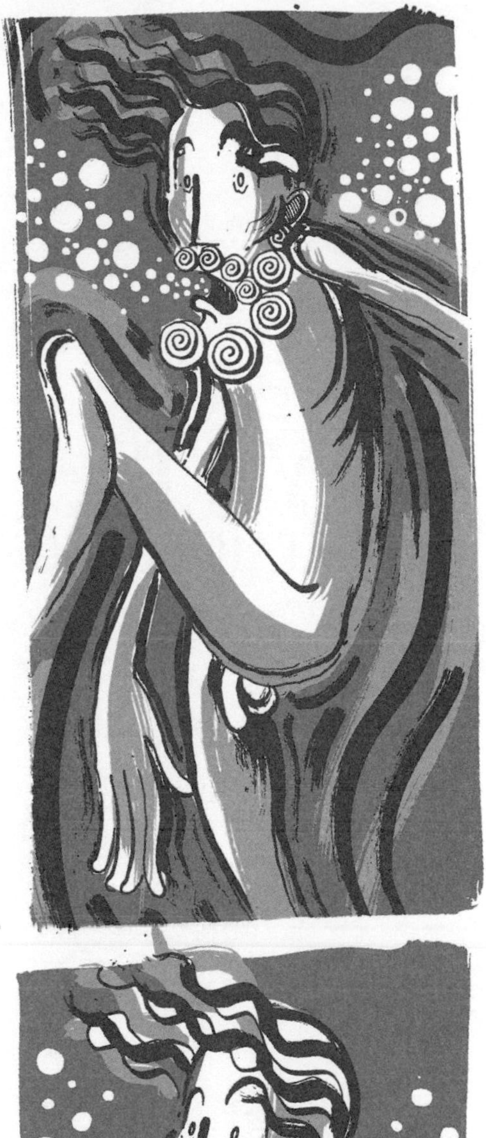

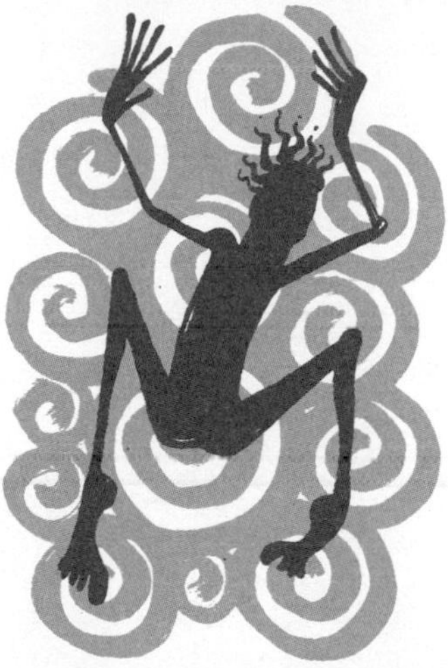

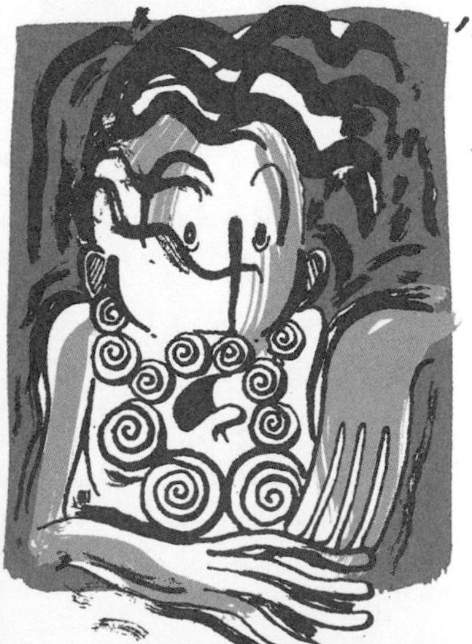

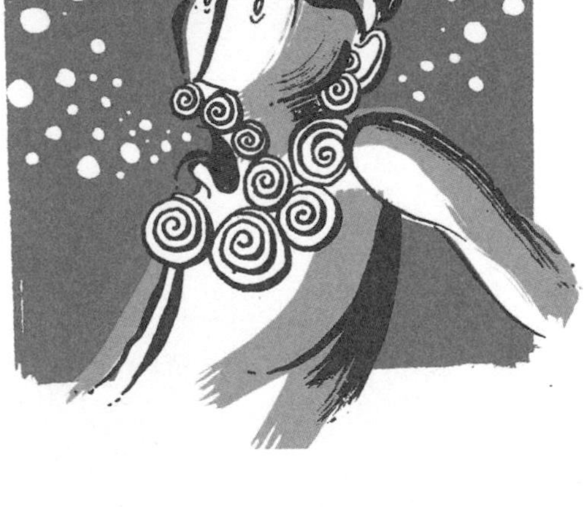

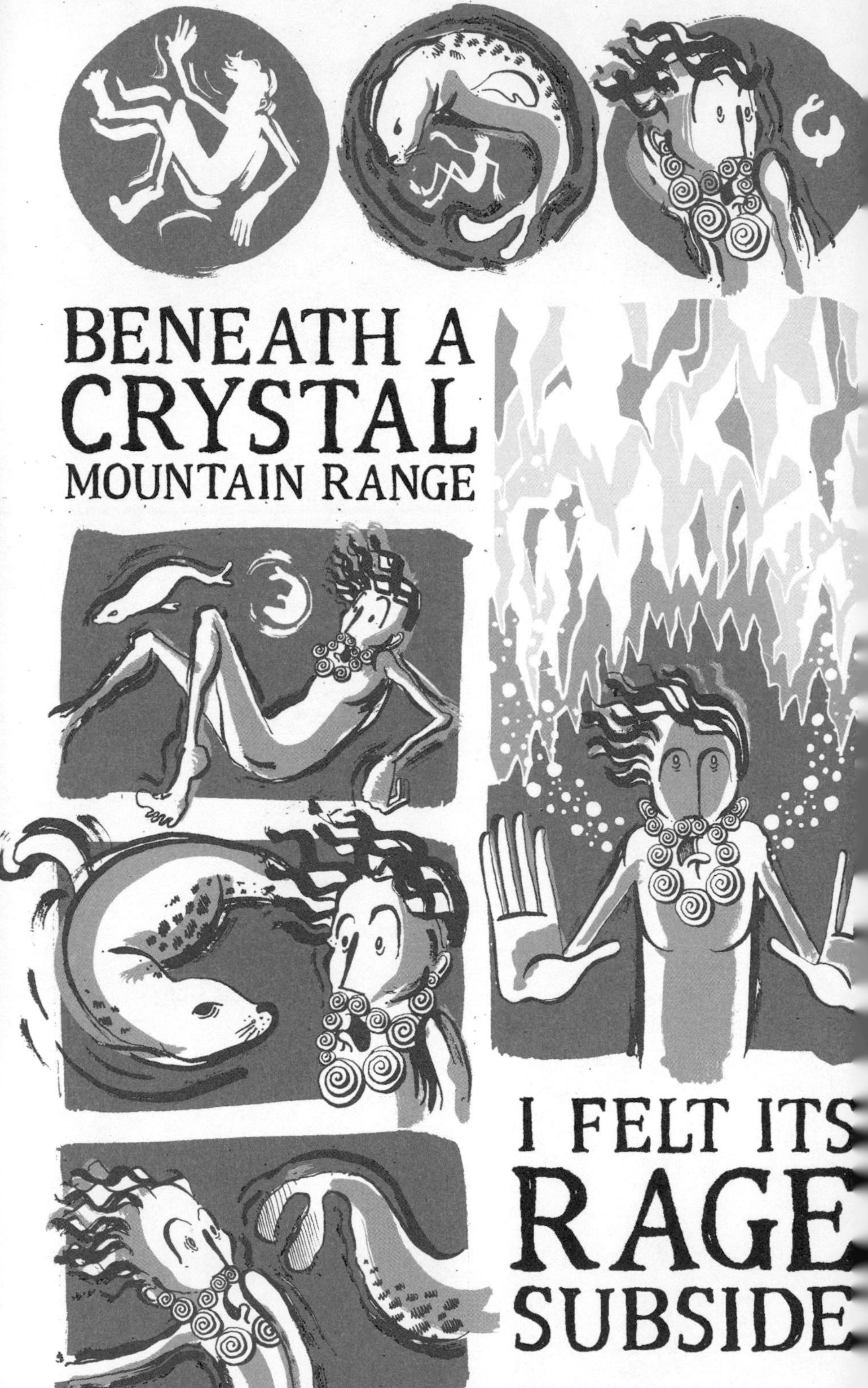
BENEATH A CRYSTAL MOUNTAIN RANGE
I FELT ITS RAGE SUBSIDE

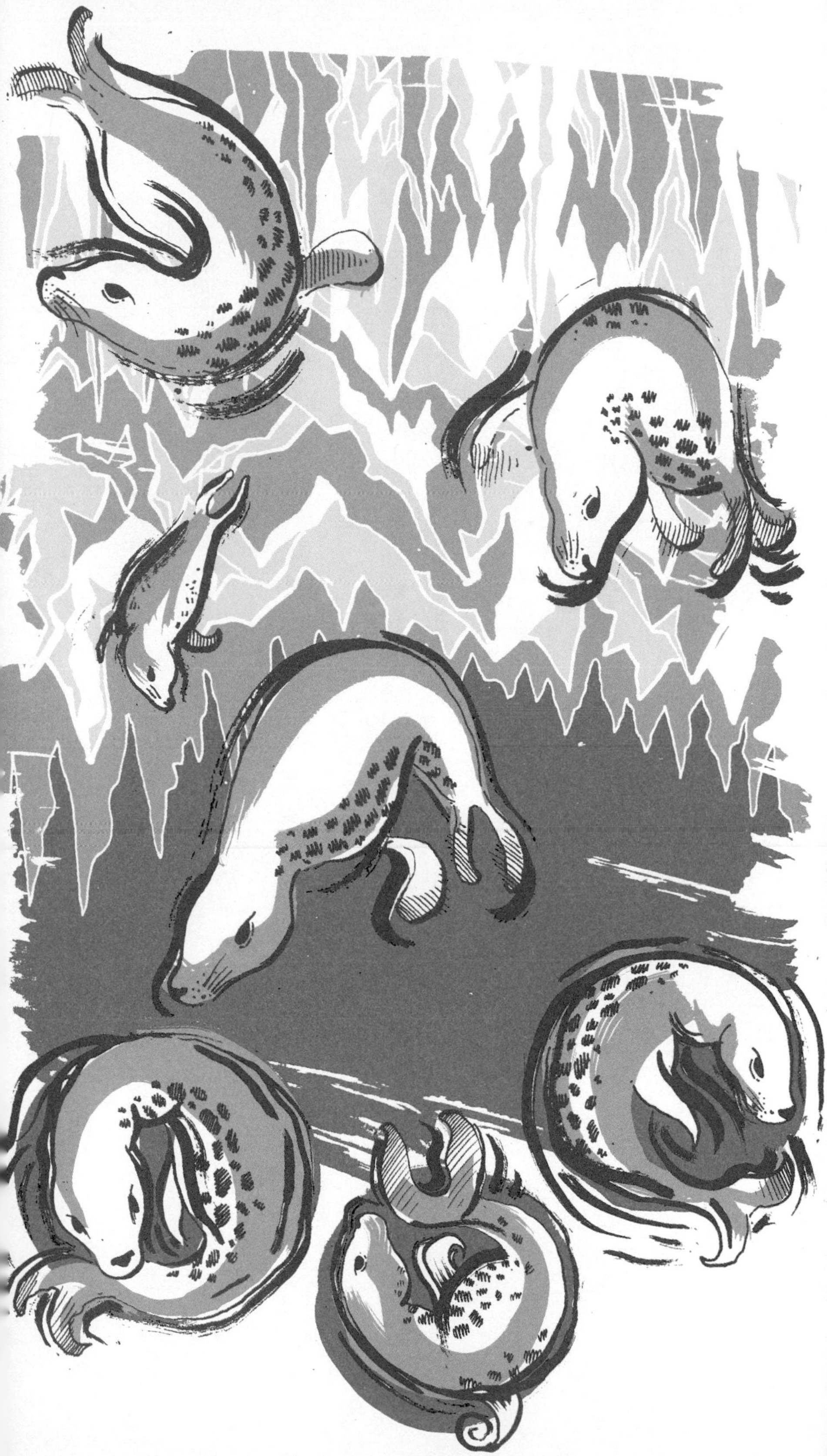

SHAFTS OF LIGHT
WERE VISIBLE

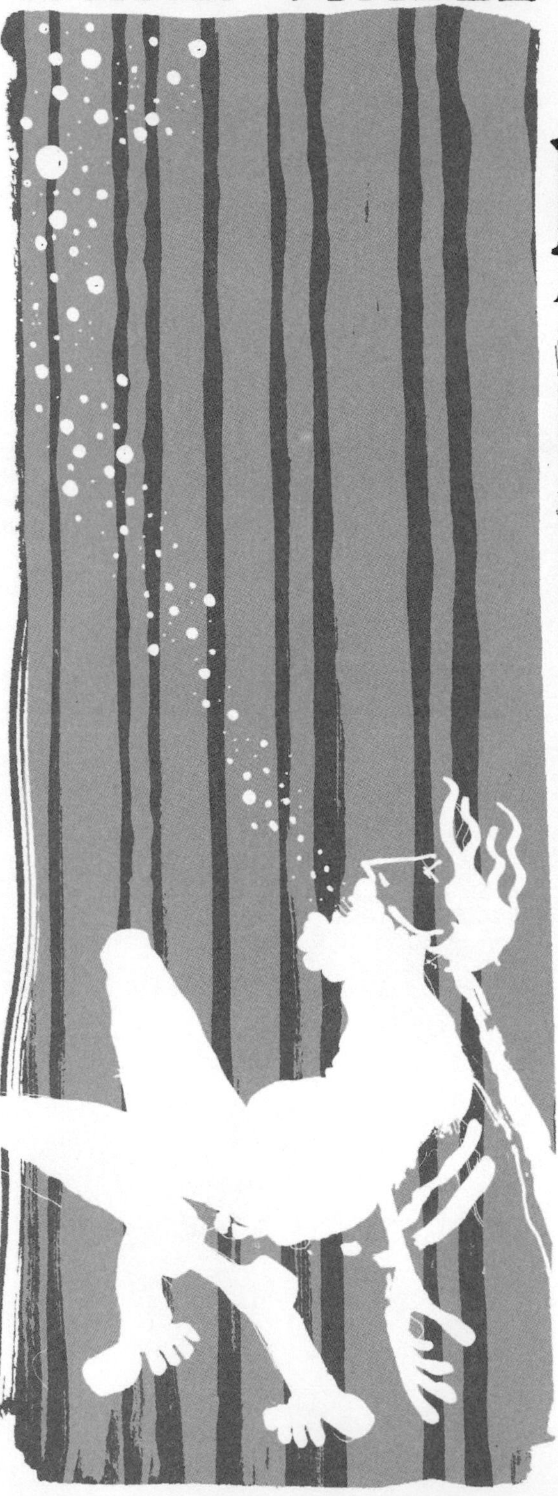

HIGH
ABOVE MY HEAD,

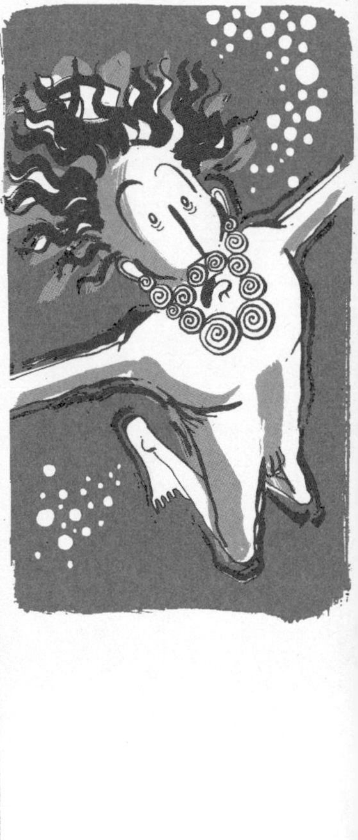

THAT LIT THE GENTLE CARBON SNOW

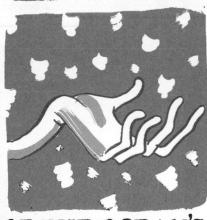

OF THE OCEAN'S NEWEST DEAD.

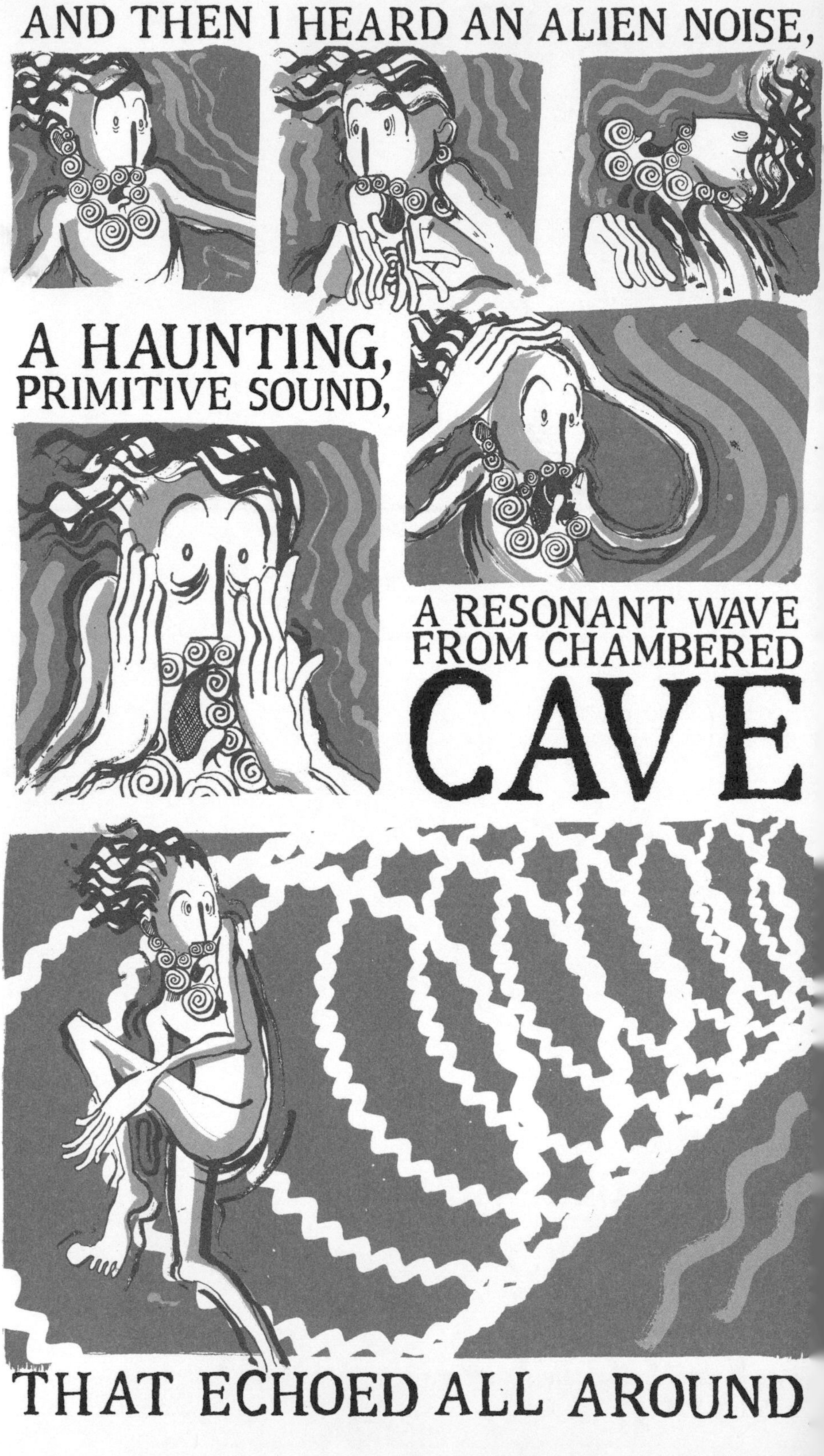
AND THEN I HEARD AN ALIEN NOISE,
A HAUNTING, PRIMITIVE SOUND,
A RESONANT WAVE FROM CHAMBERED CAVE
THAT ECHOED ALL AROUND

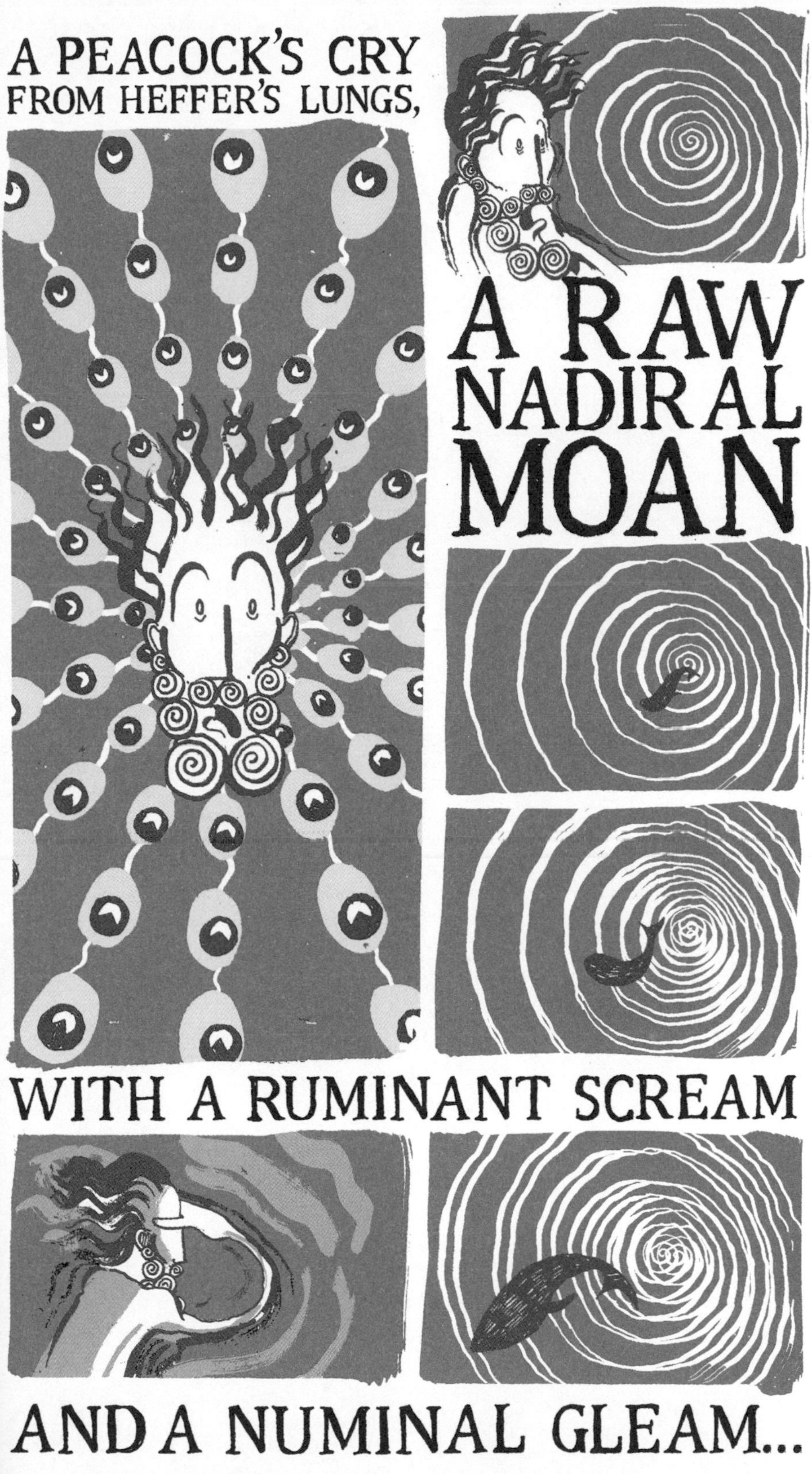
A PEACOCK'S CRY
FROM HEFFER'S LUNGS,
A RAW
NADIRAL
MOAN
WITH A RUMINANT SCREAM
AND A NUMINAL GLEAM...

A WHALE

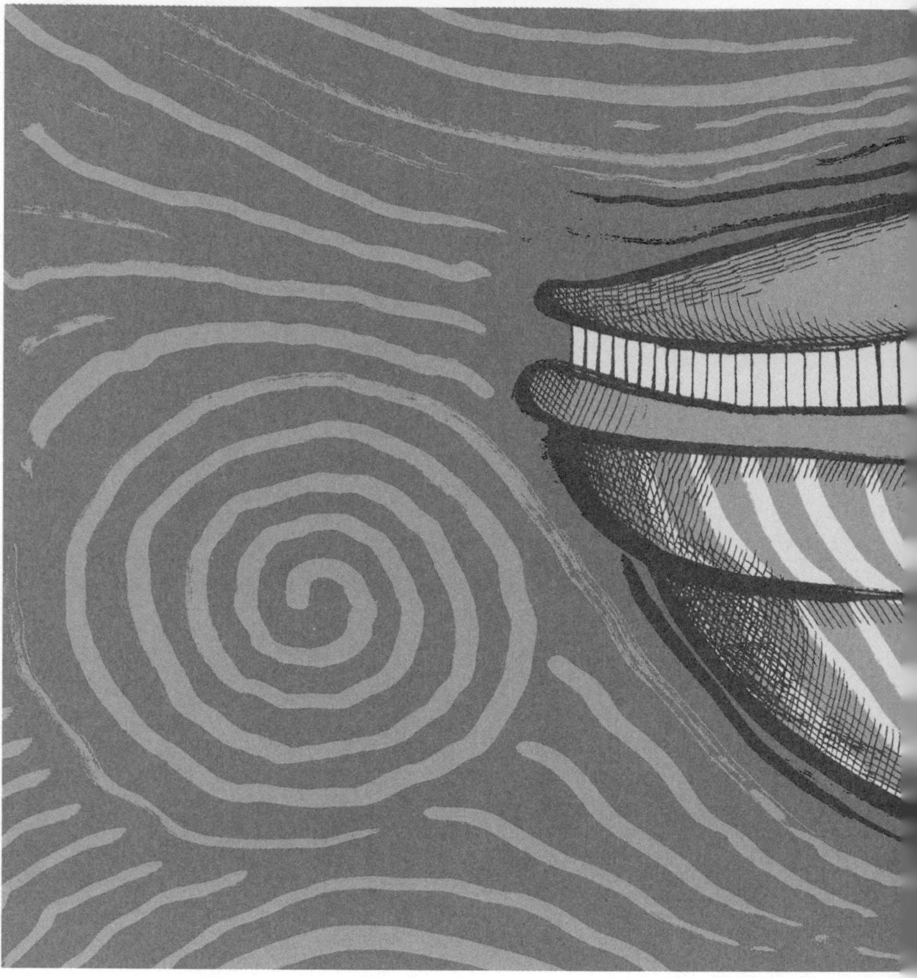

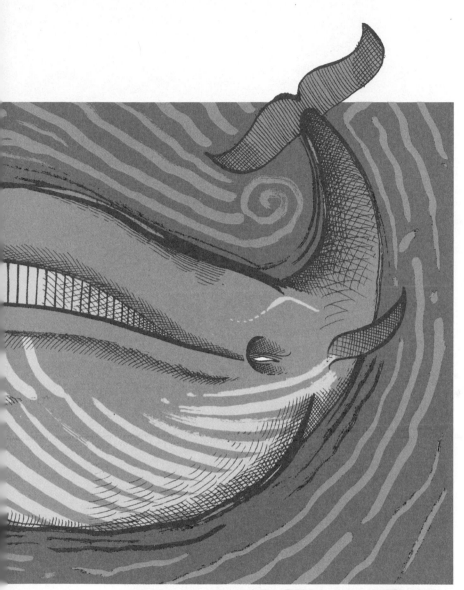

EMERGED
FROM THE GLOAM.

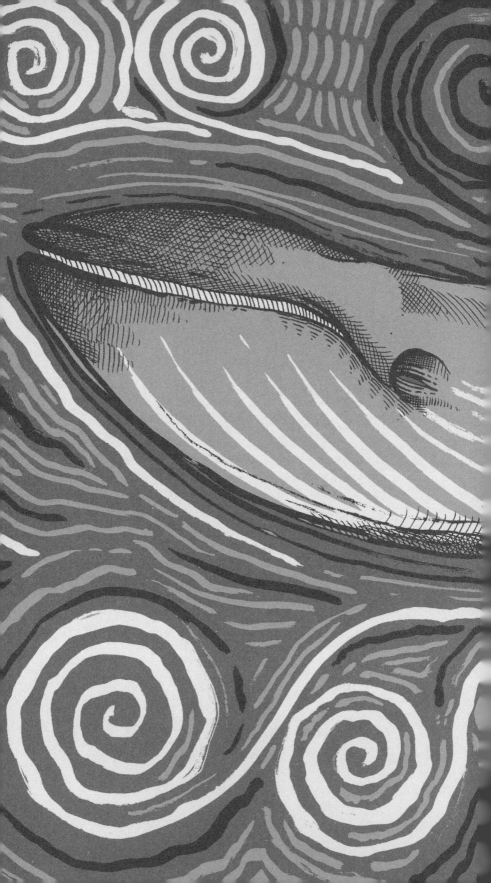

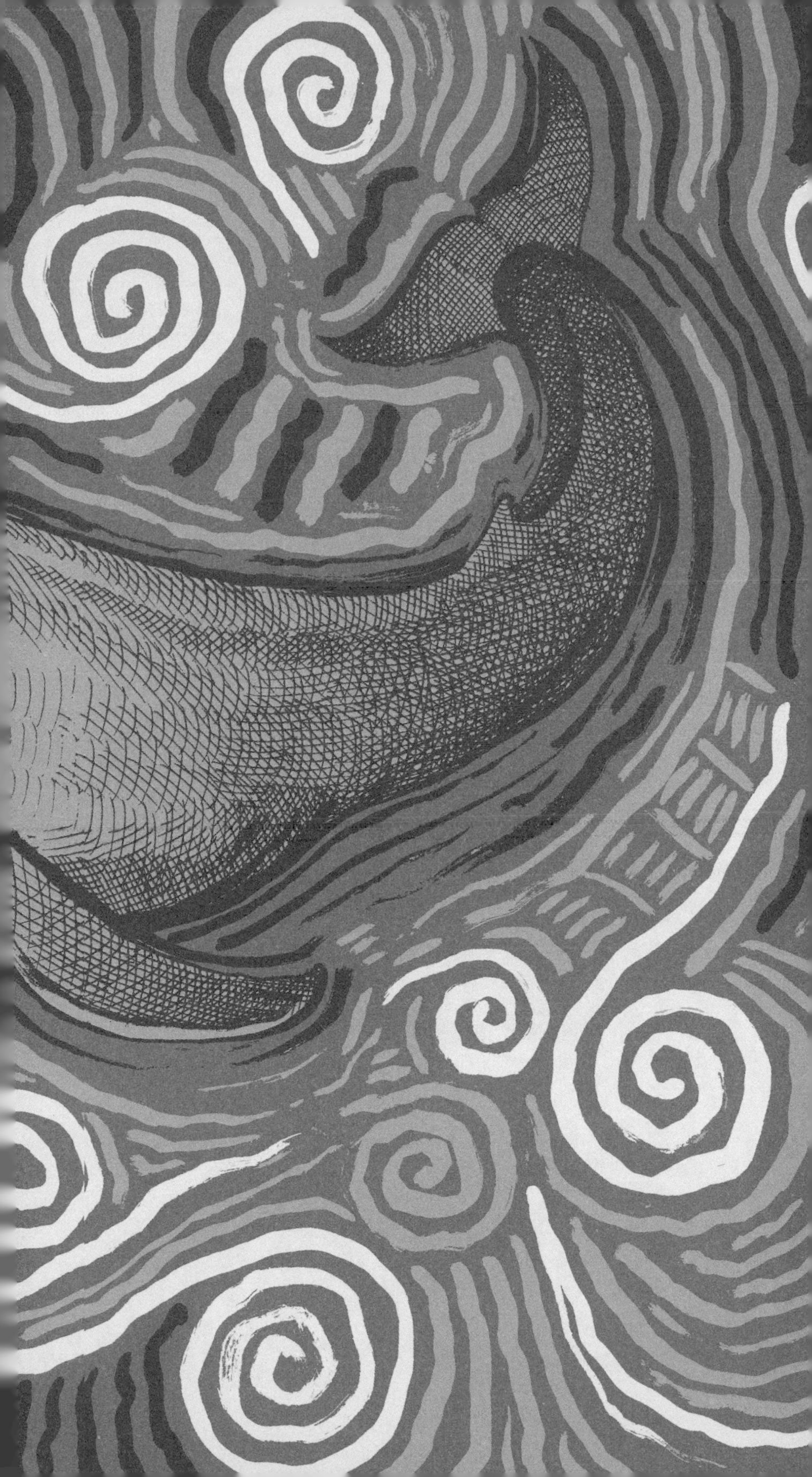

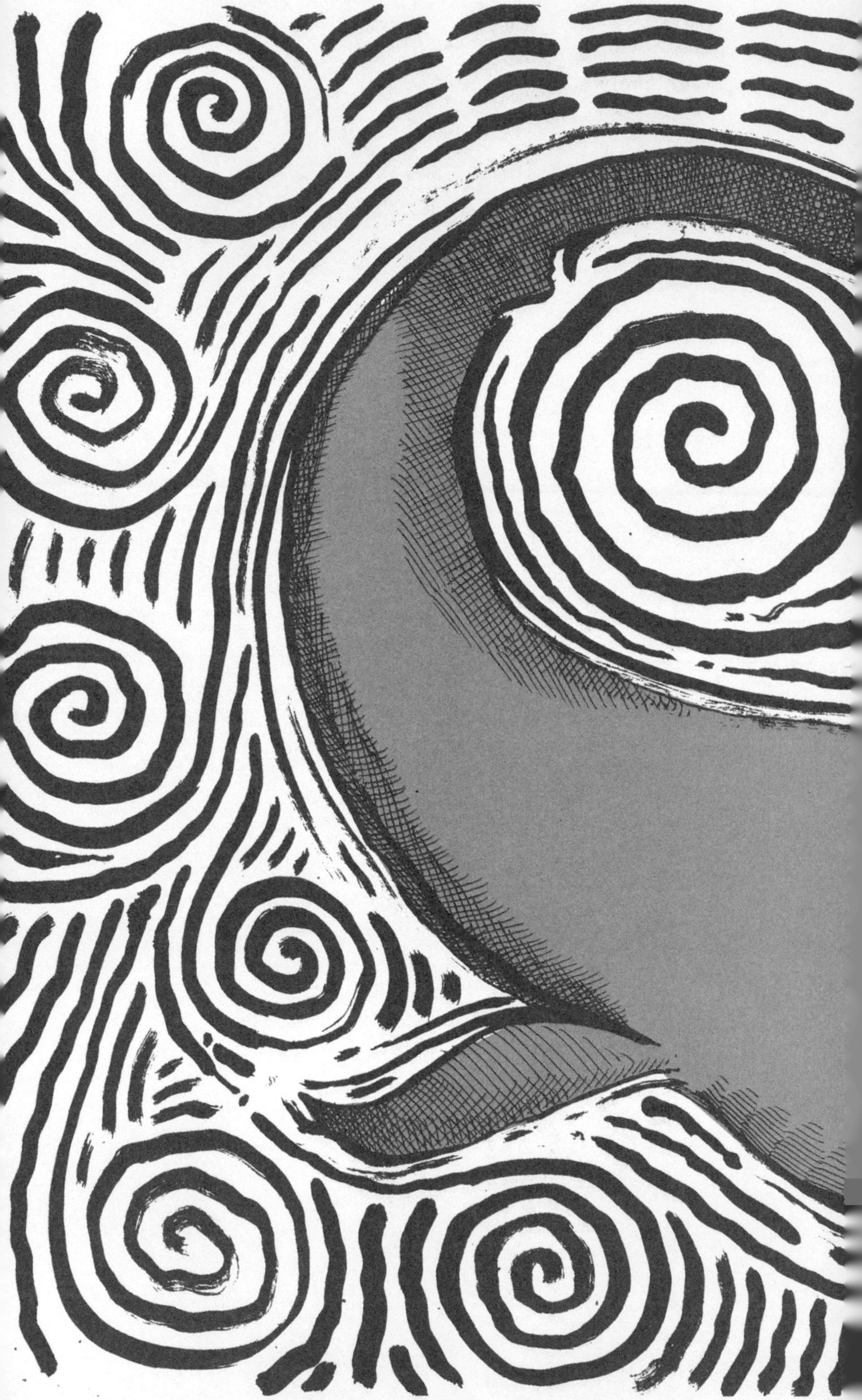

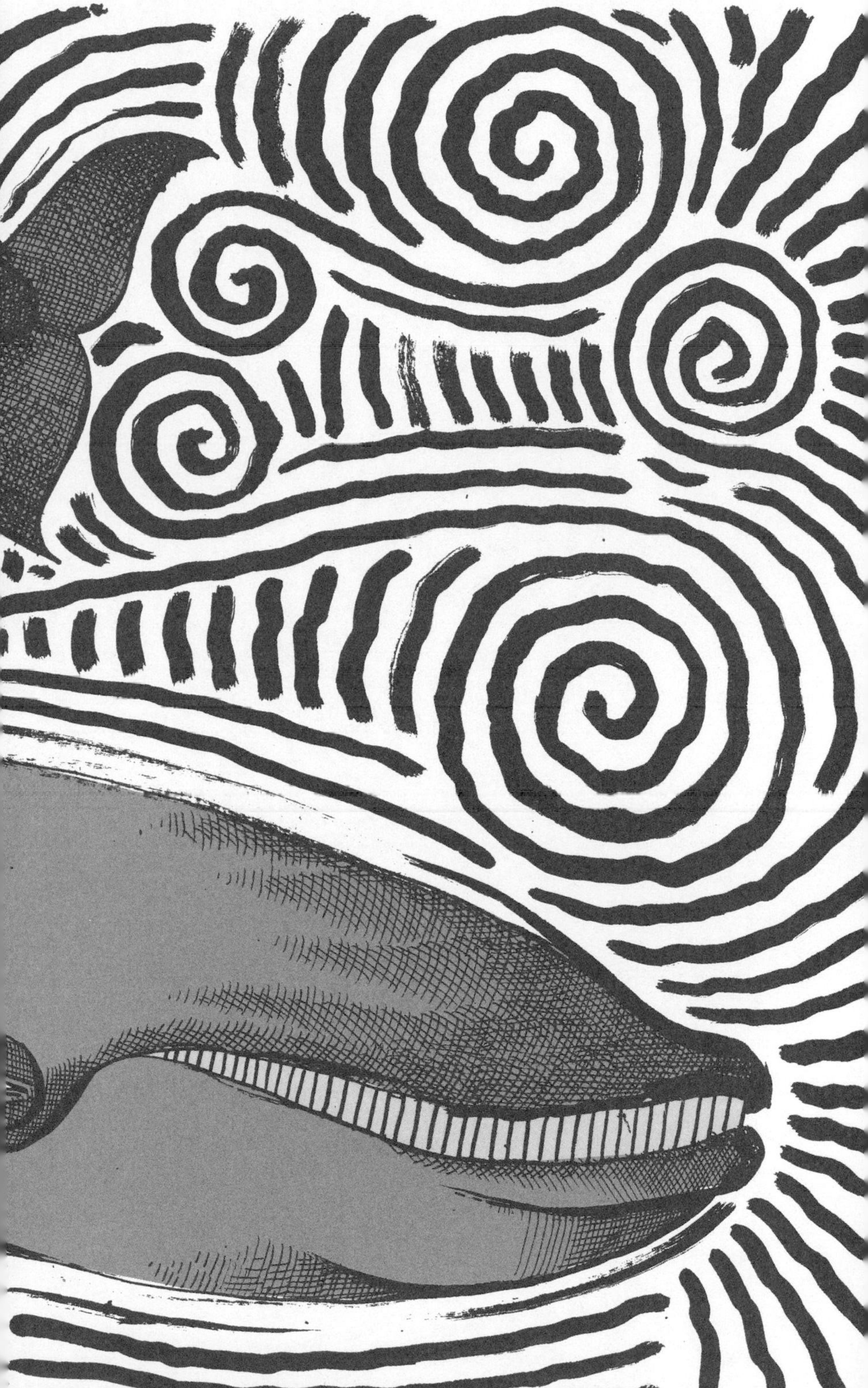

AS IT SLOWLY PASSED BEFORE ME,

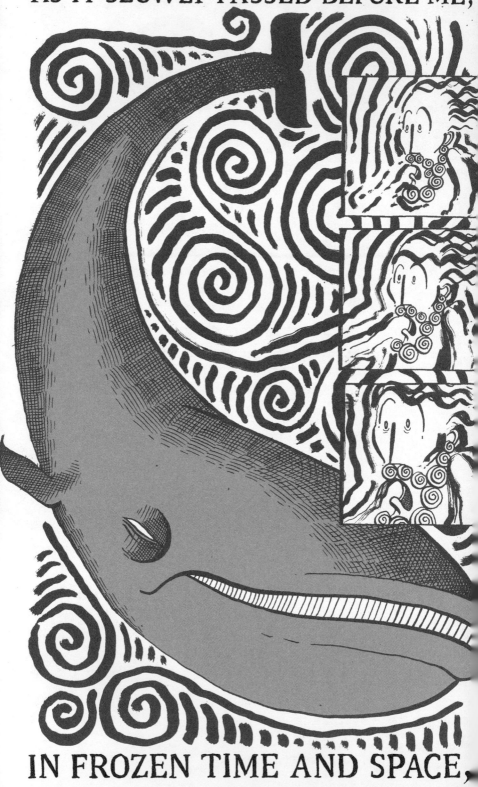

IN FROZEN TIME AND SPACE,

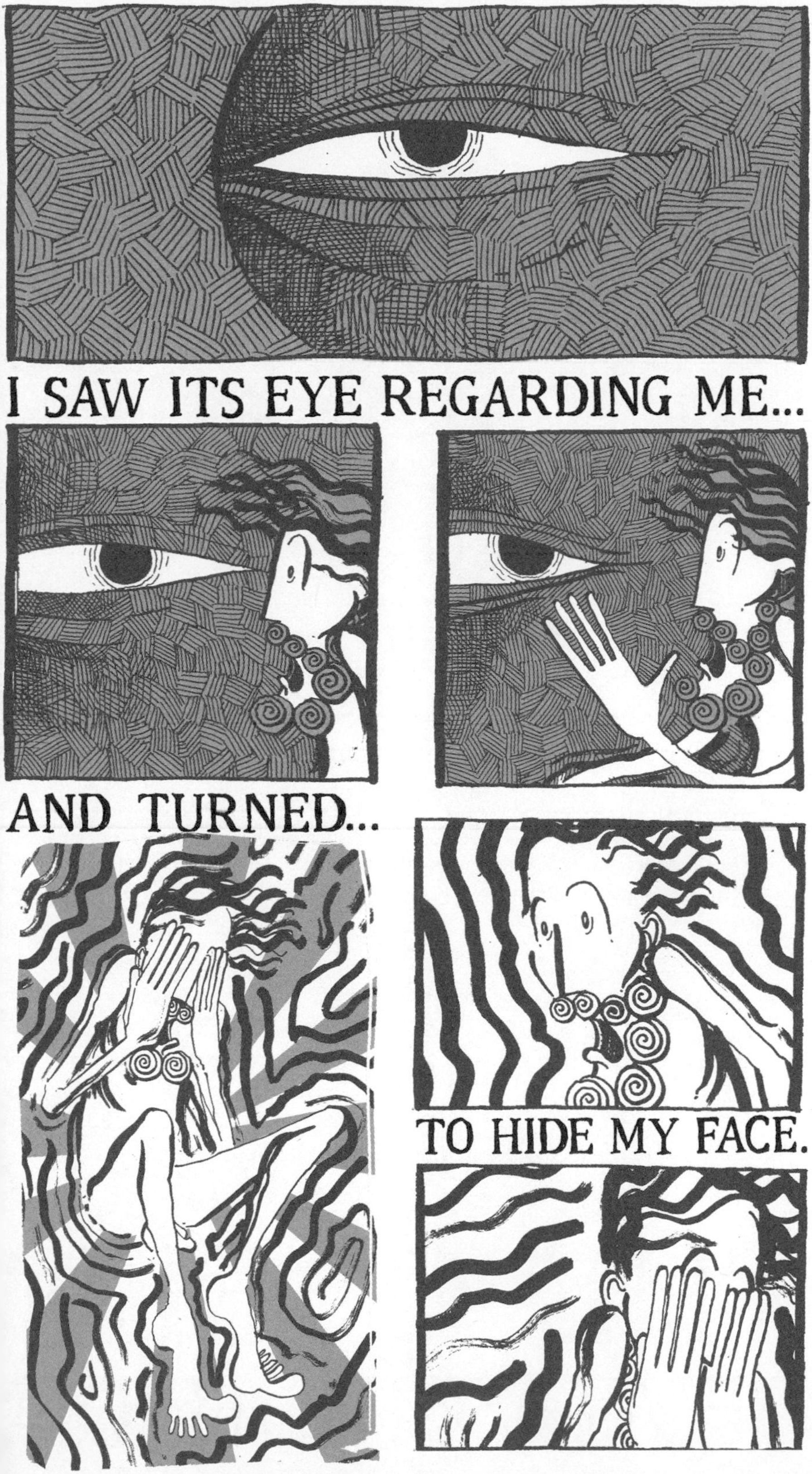
I SAW ITS EYE REGARDING ME...
AND TURNED...
TO HIDE MY FACE.

TWO HUNDRED TONNES
OF LIVING
FLESH,

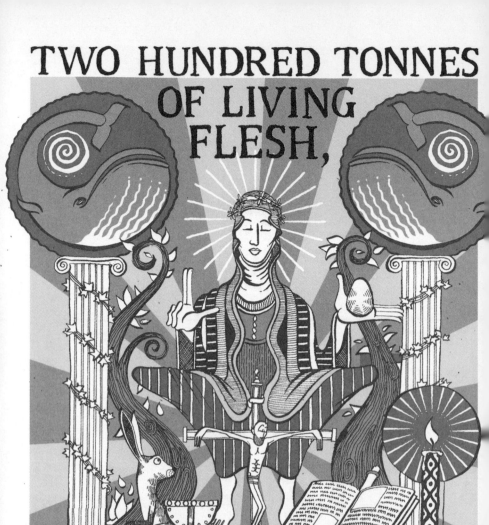

THE QUEEN
OF ALL CREATION

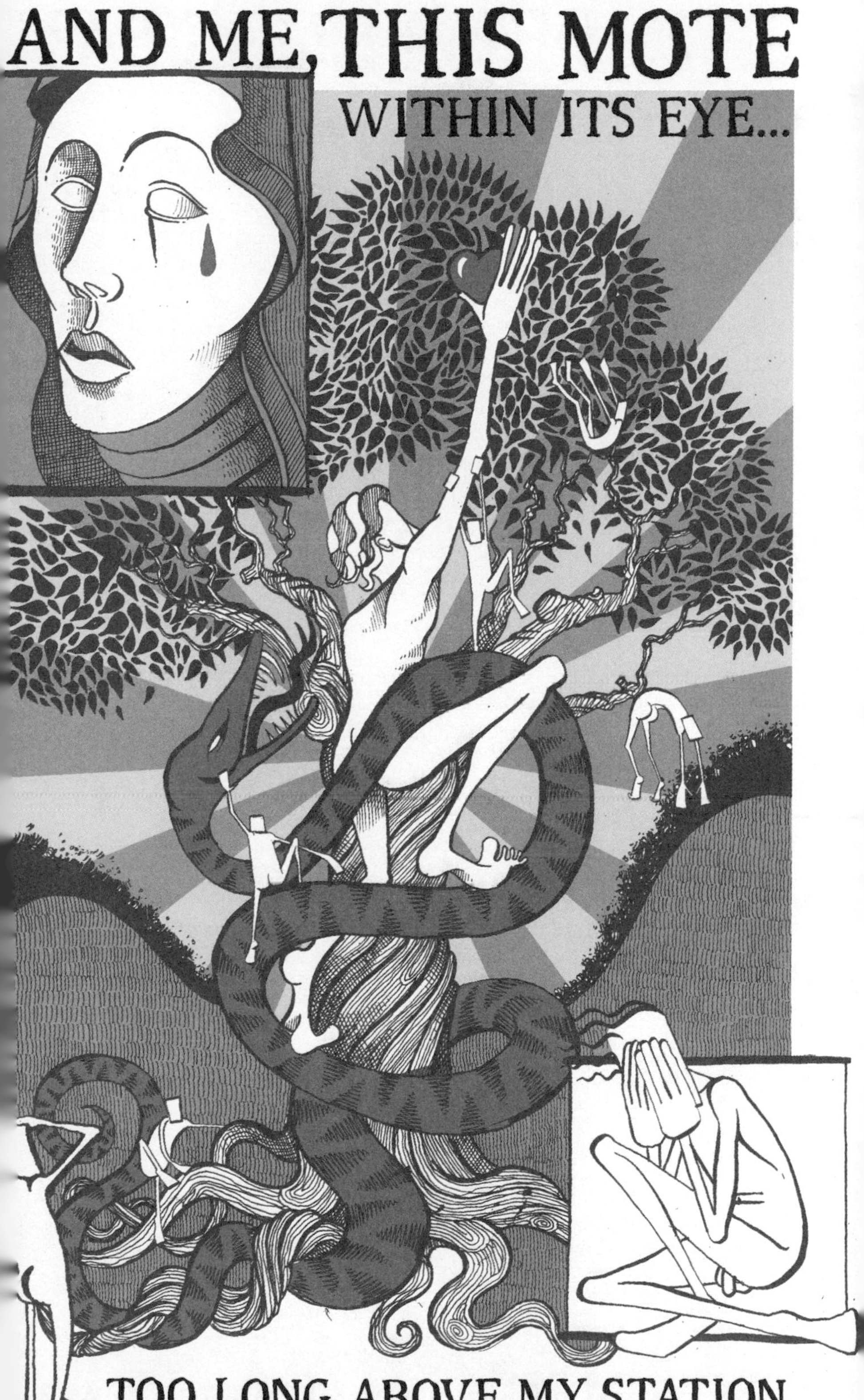
AND ME, THIS MOTE
WITHIN ITS EYE...
TOO LONG ABOVE MY STATION.

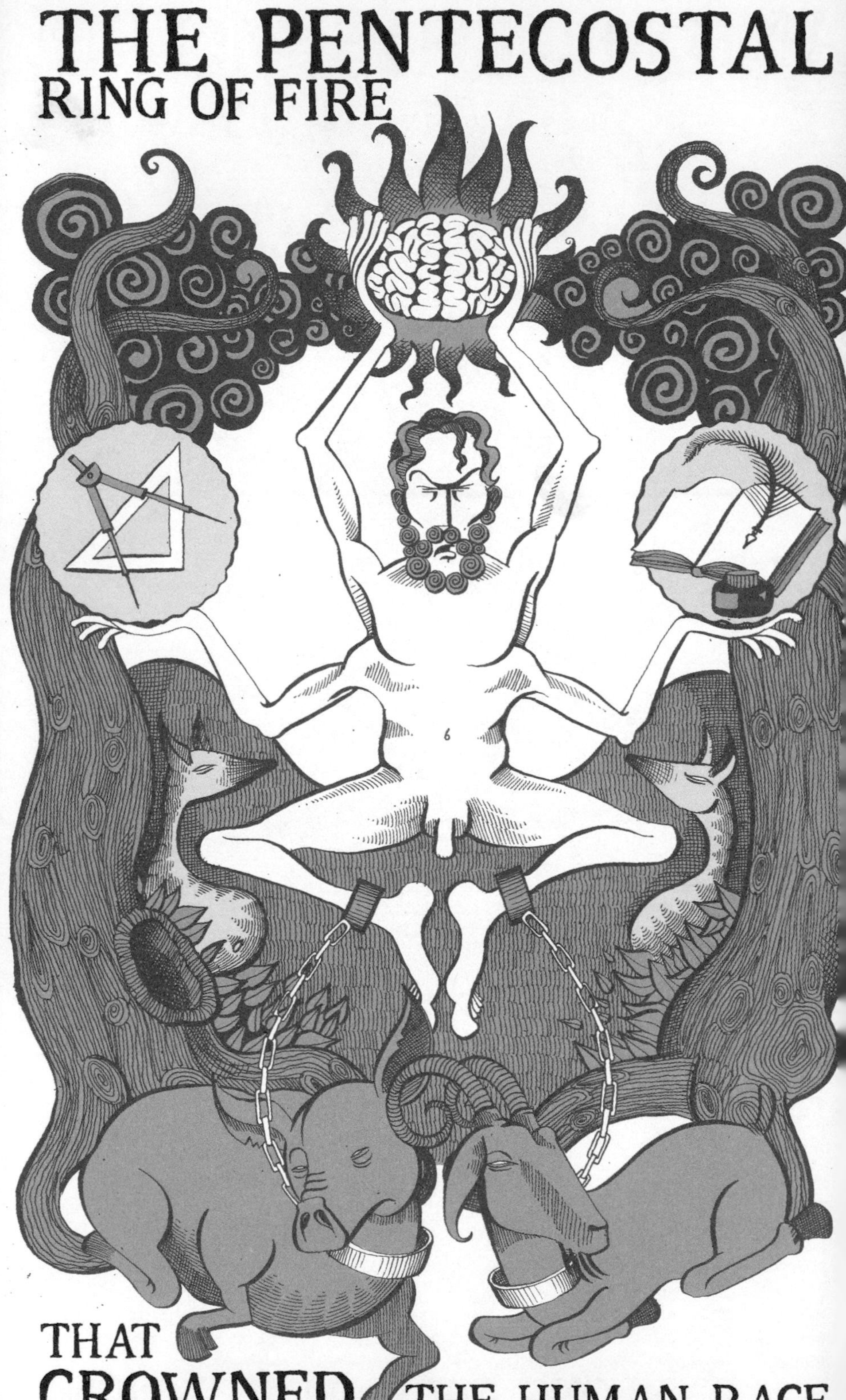
THE PENTECOSTAL
RING OF FIRE
THAT
CROWNED THE HUMAN RACE

WAS AL-JAZARI'S CANDLE CLOCK,

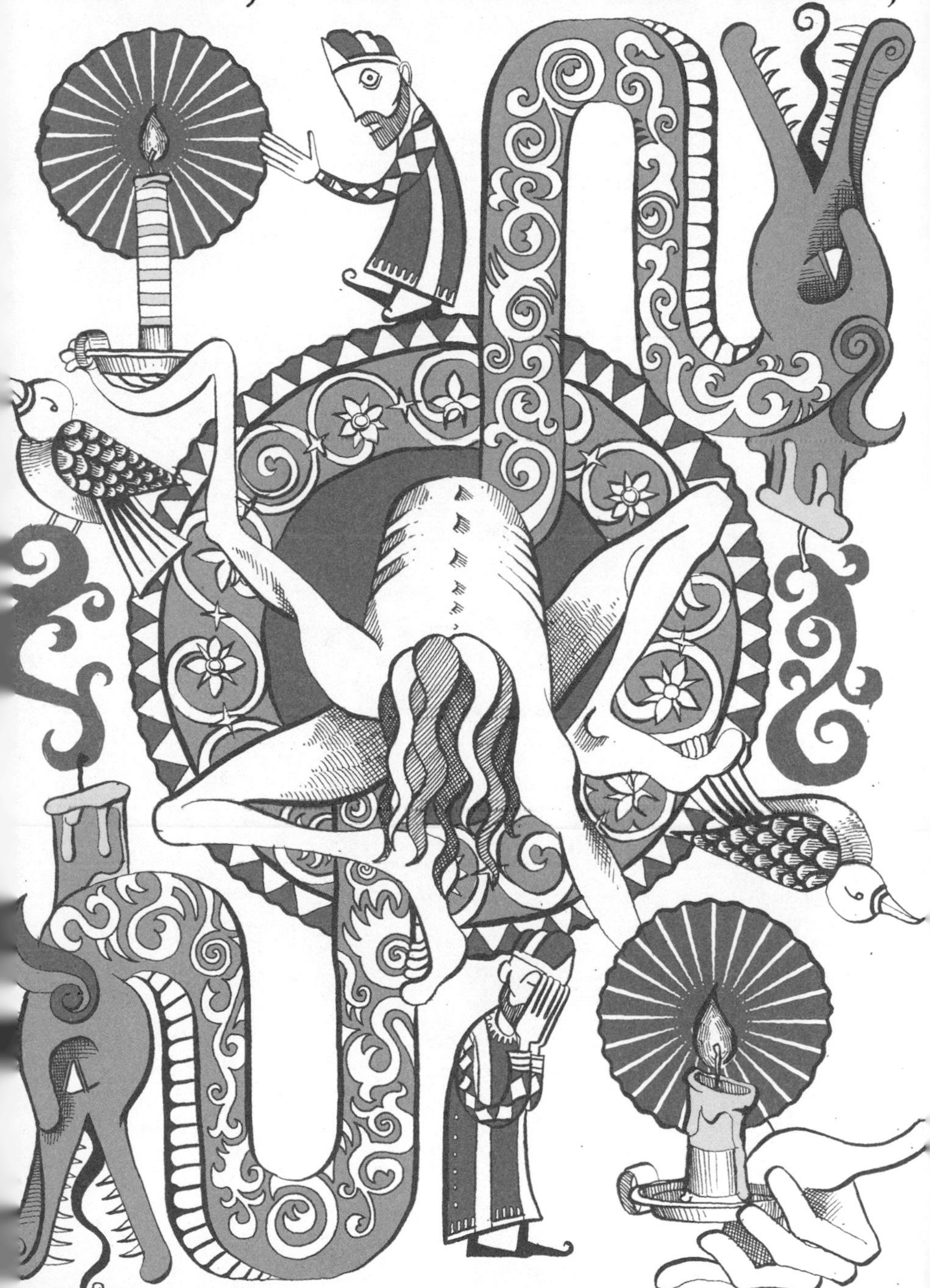

BURNING

AT ITS BASE.

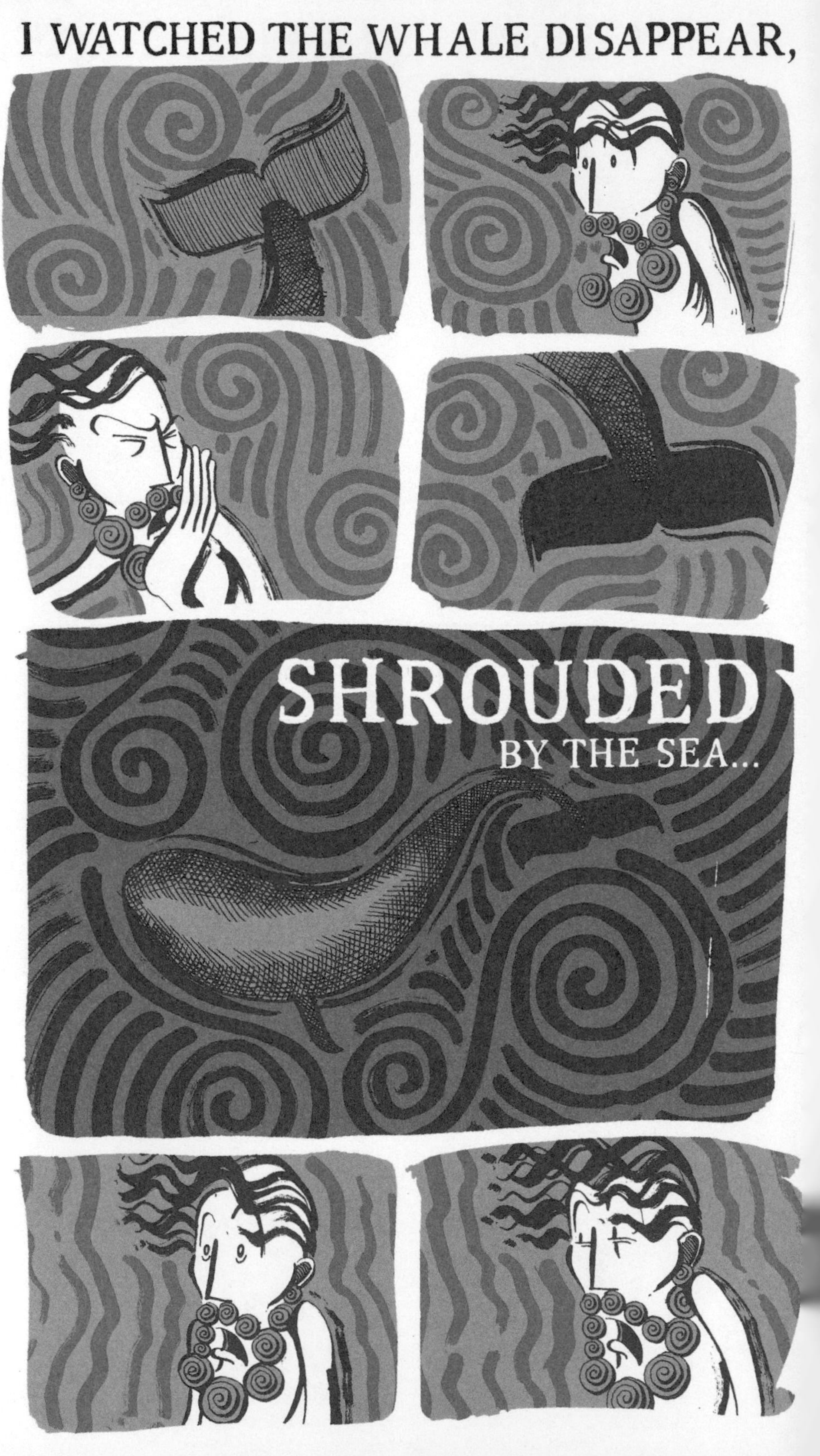
I WATCHED THE WHALE DISAPPEAR,
SHROUDED
BY THE SEA...

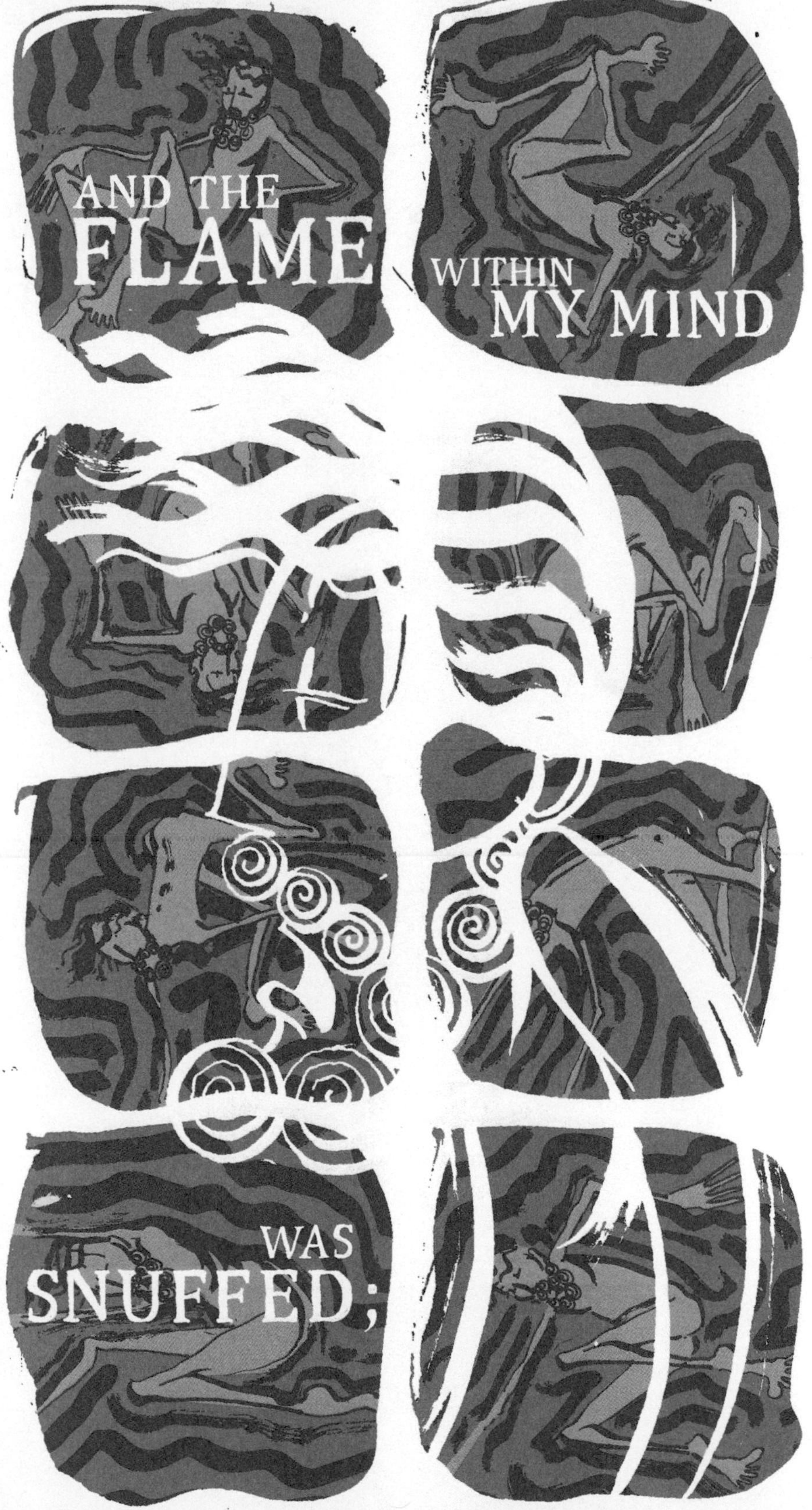
AND THE
FLAME
WITHIN
MY MIND
WAS
SNUFFED;

THIS SCENE
HAD CEASED

TO BE.

PART SEVEN

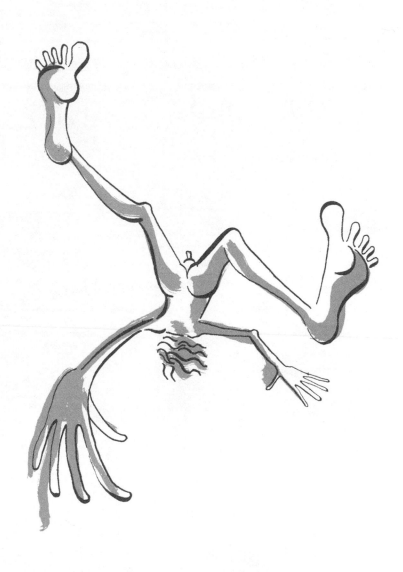

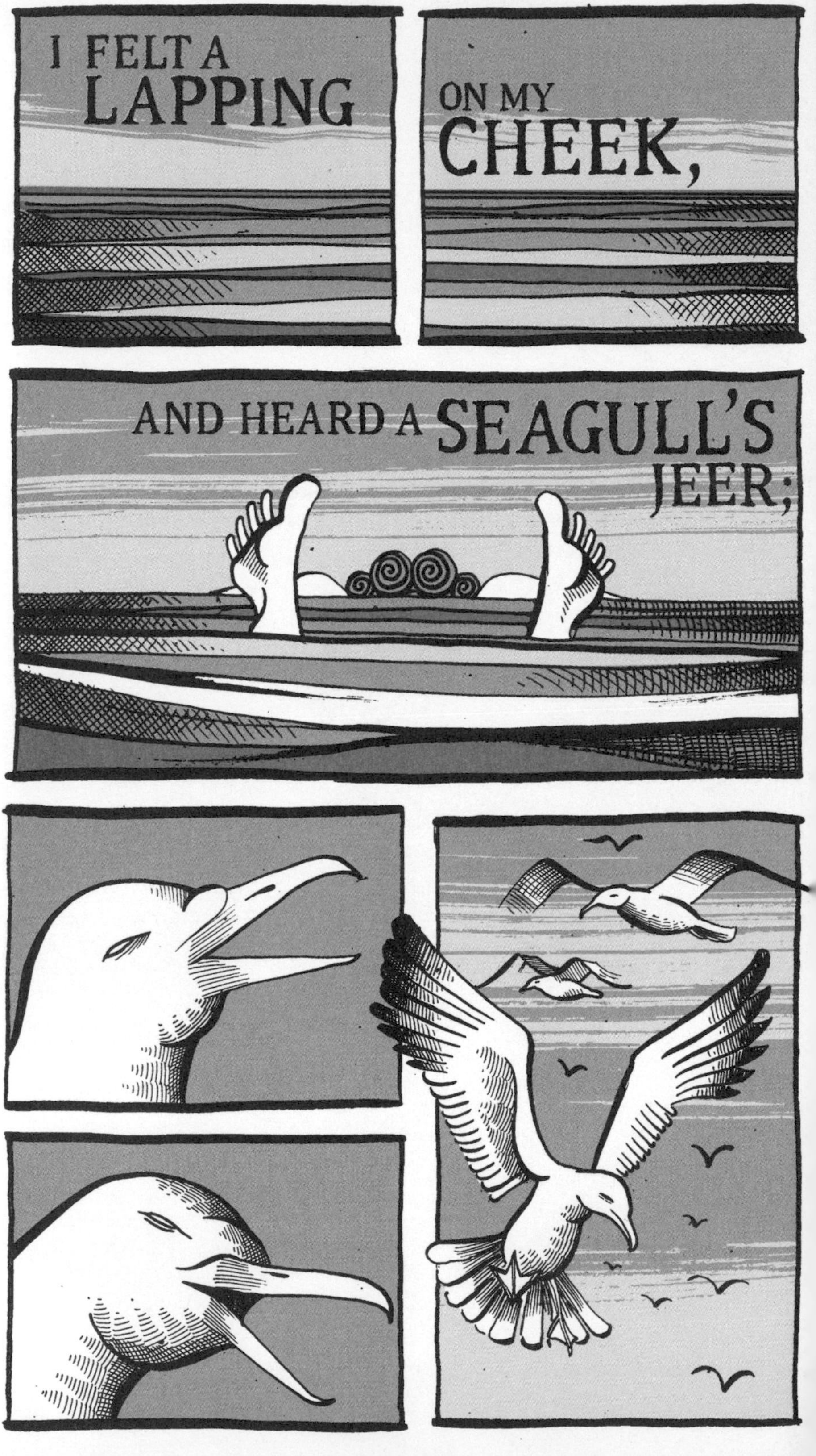
I FELT A LAPPING
ON MY CHEEK,
AND HEARD A SEAGULL'S JEER;

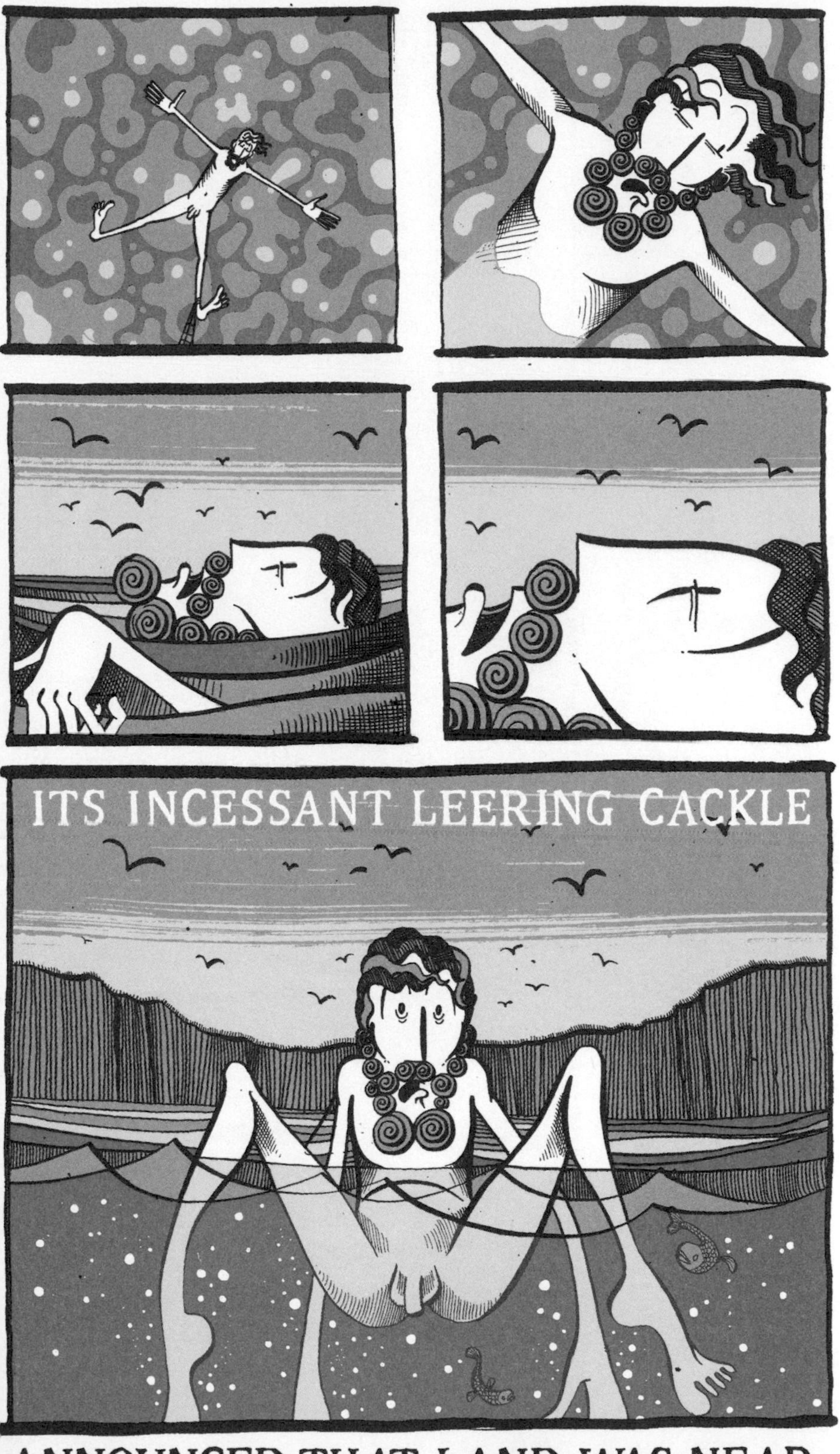
ITS INCESSANT LEERING CACKLE

ANNOUNCED THAT LAND WAS NEAR.

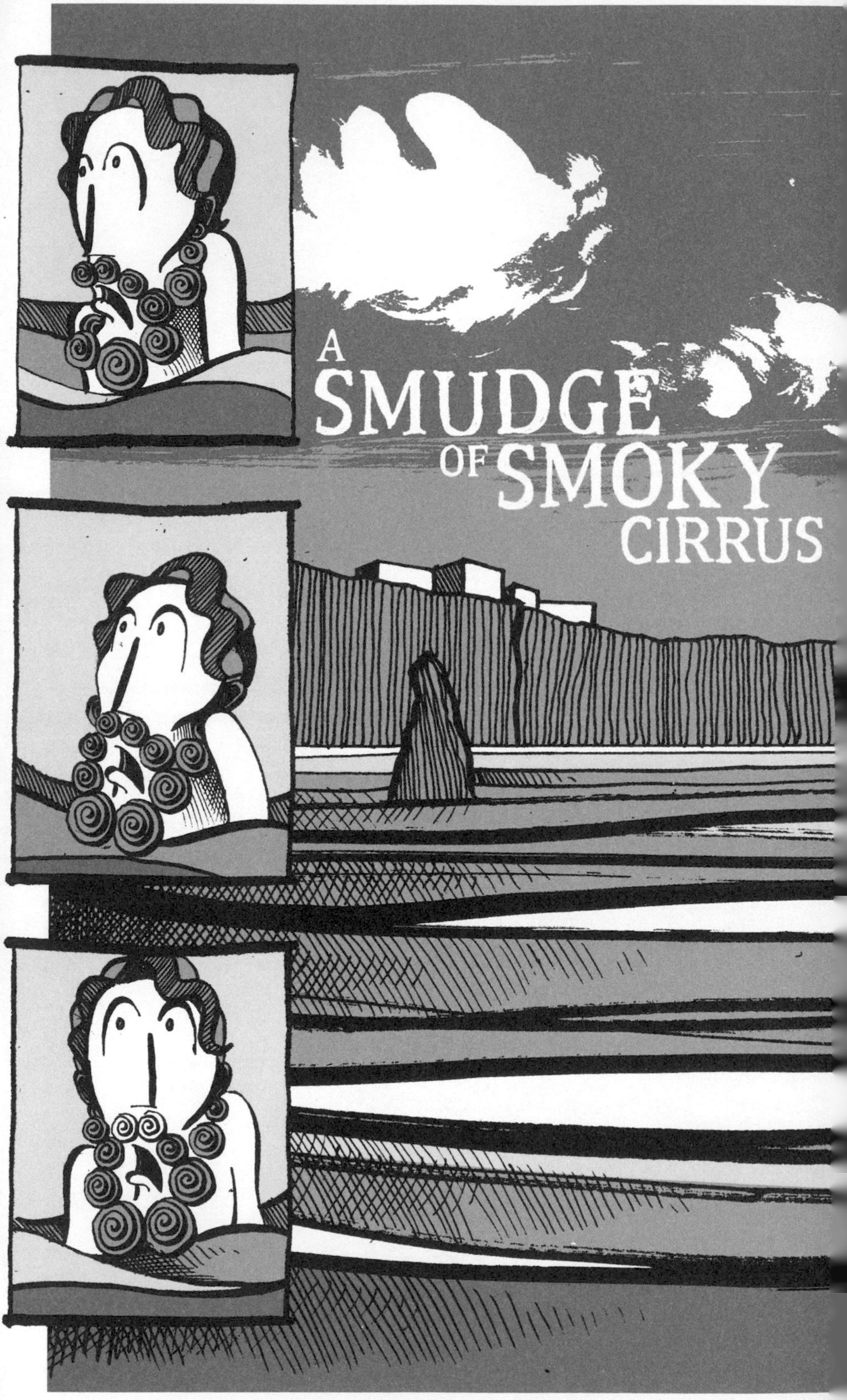
A
SMUDGE
OF SMOKY
CIRRUS

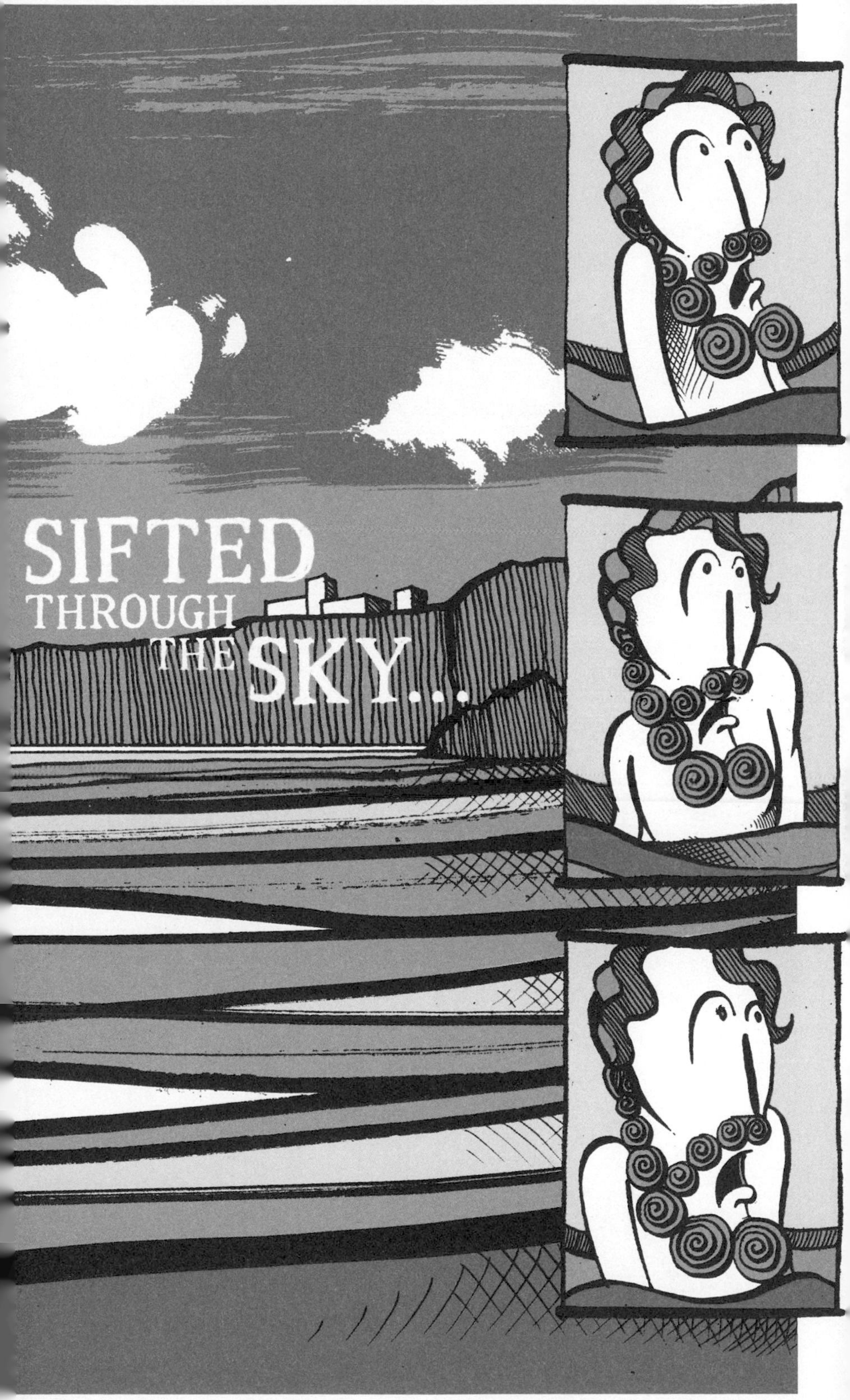
SIFTED THROUGH THE SKY...

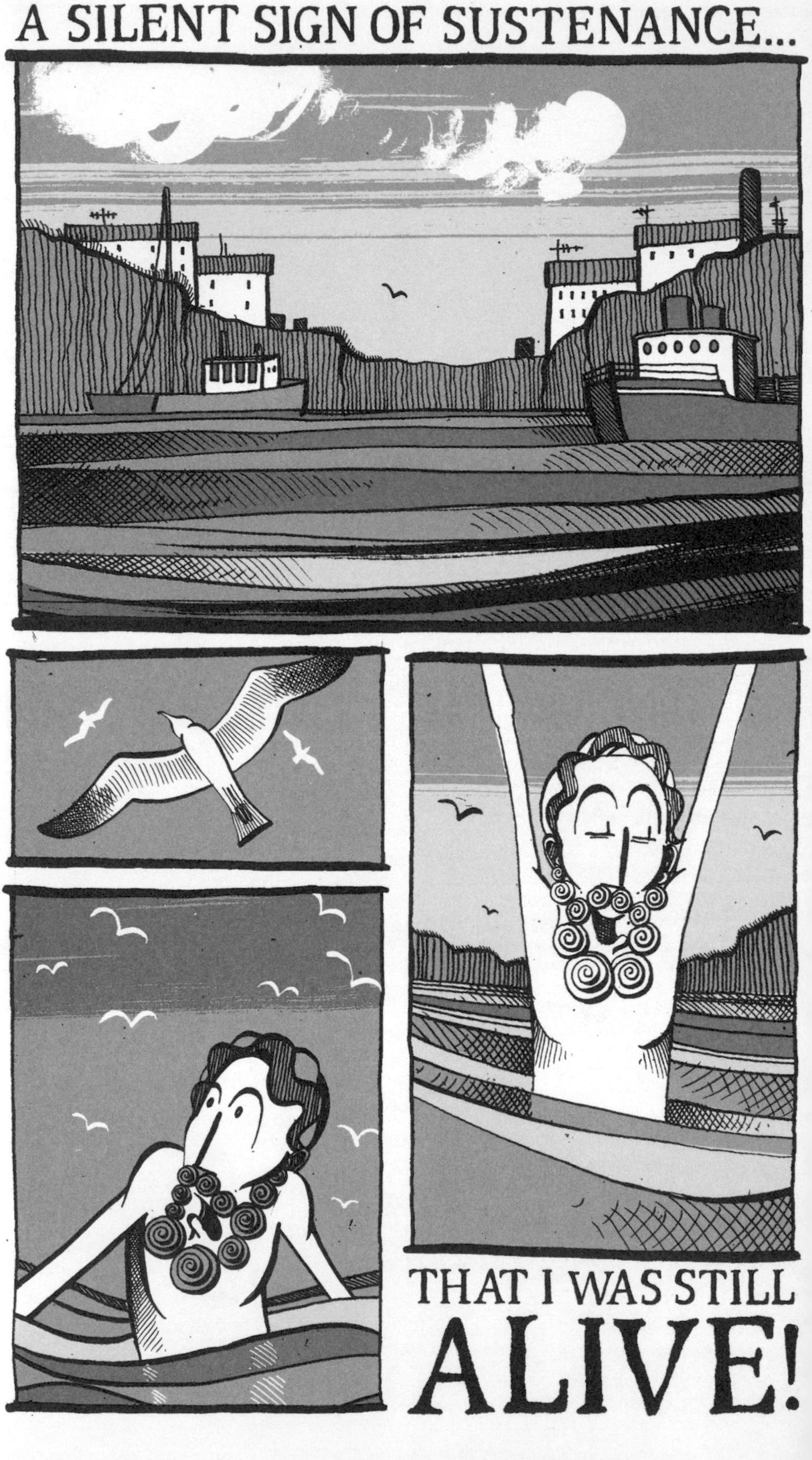
A SILENT SIGN OF SUSTENANCE...
THAT I WAS STILL
ALIVE!

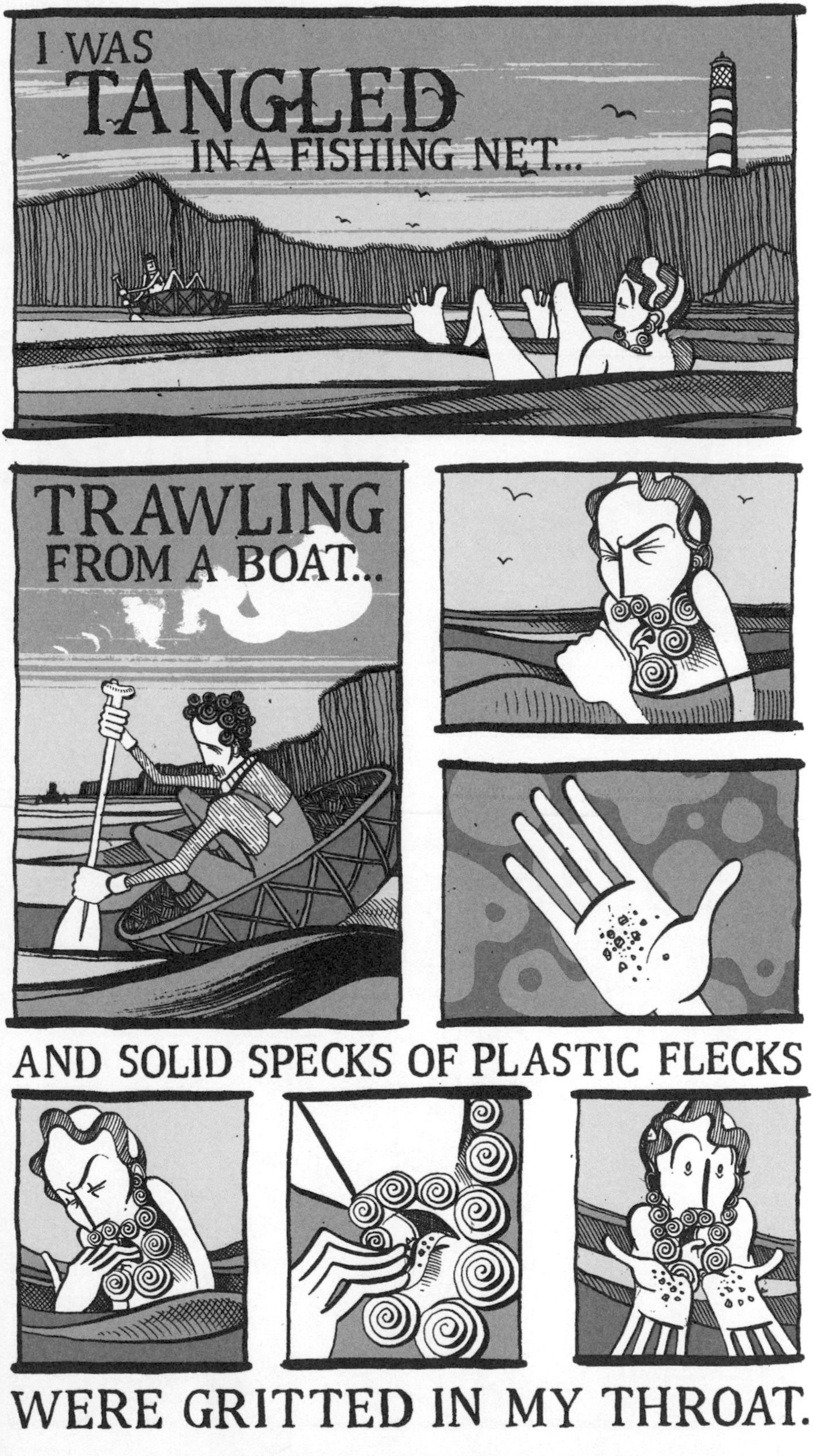
I WAS TANGLED IN A FISHING NET...
TRAWLING FROM A BOAT...
AND SOLID SPECKS OF PLASTIC FLECKS
WERE GRITTED IN MY THROAT.

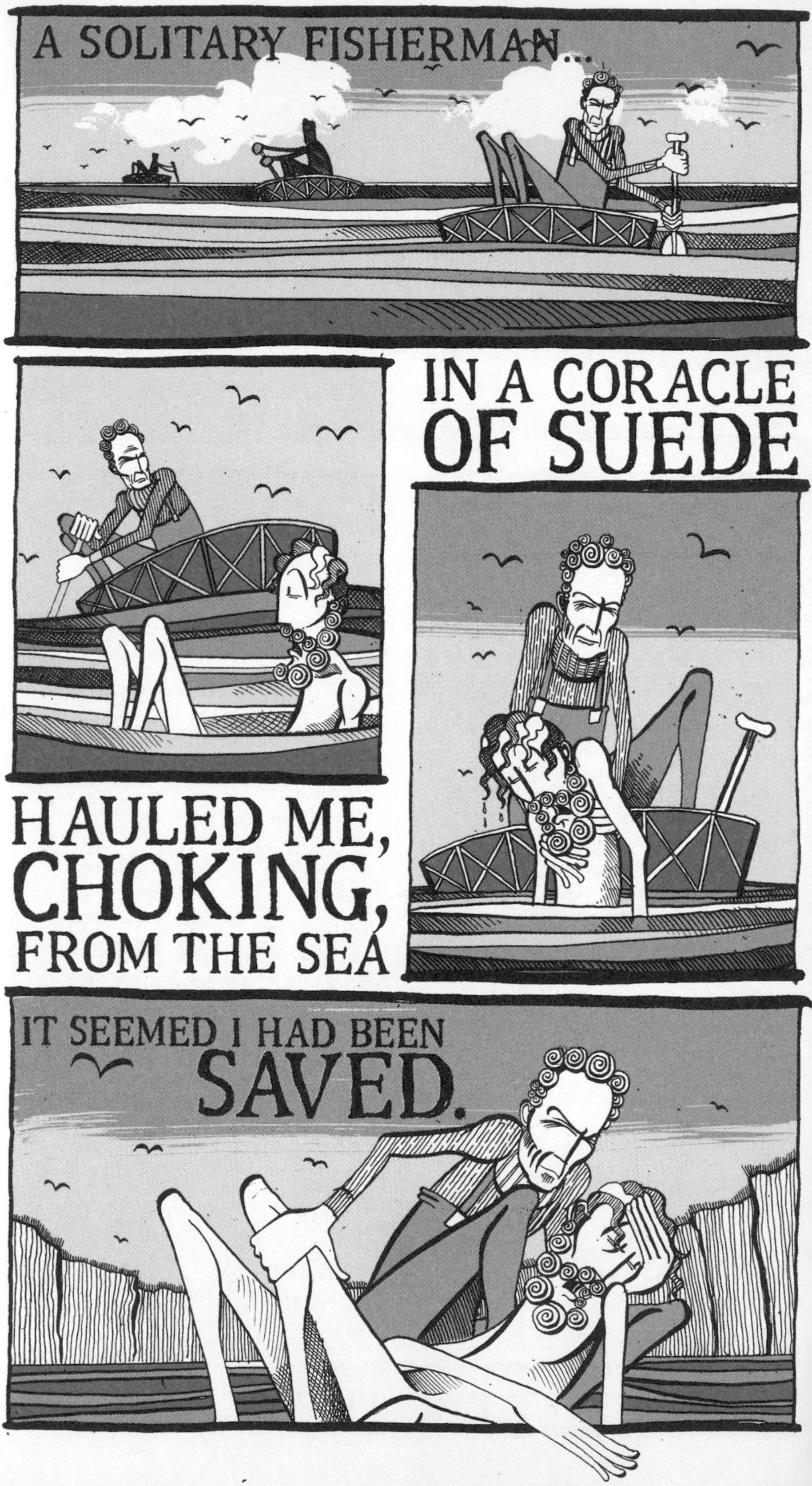
A SOLITARY FISHERMAN...
IN A CORACLE OF SUEDE
HAULED ME, CHOKING, FROM THE SEA
IT SEEMED I HAD BEEN SAVED.

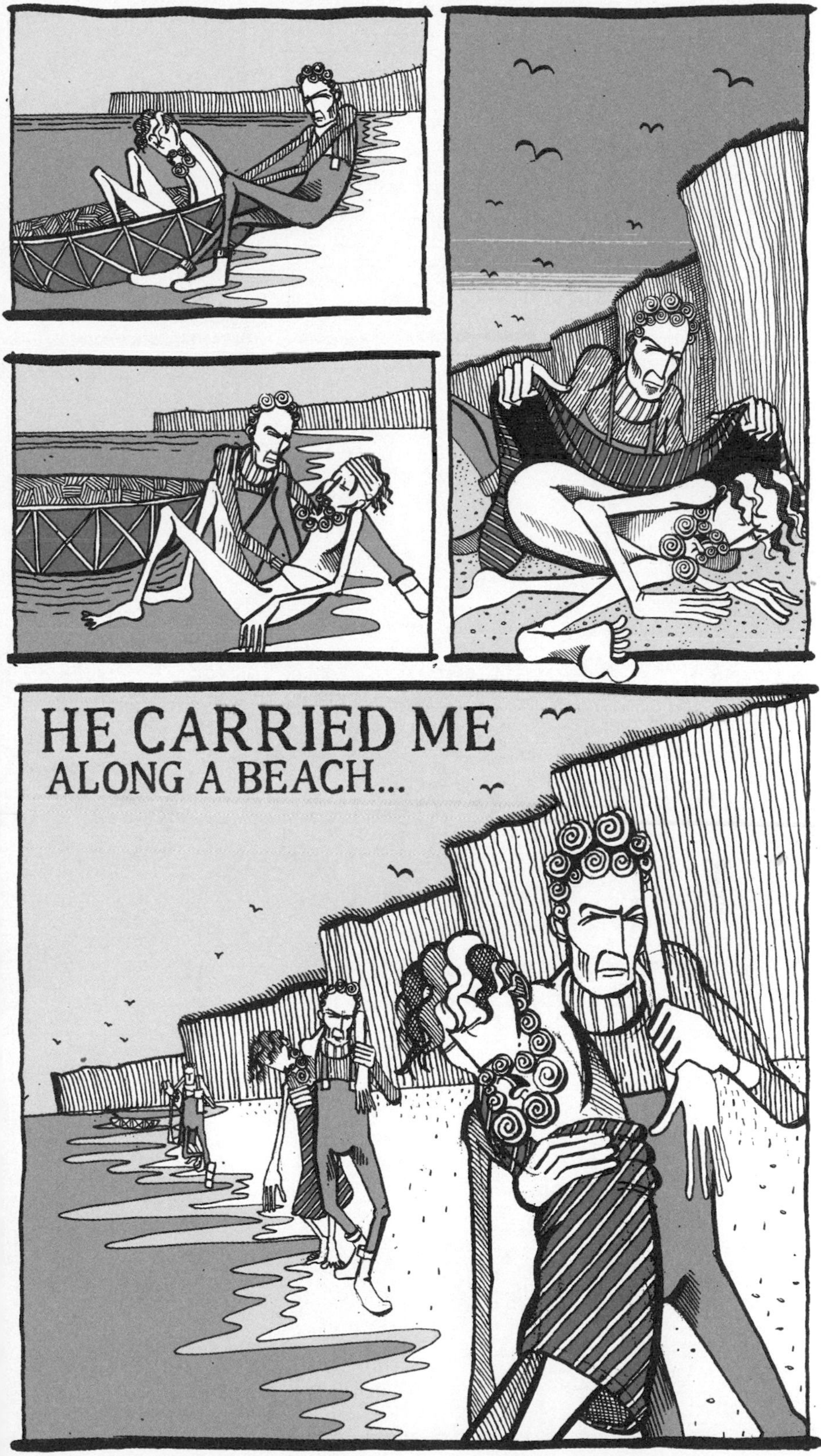
HE CARRIED ME
ALONG A BEACH...

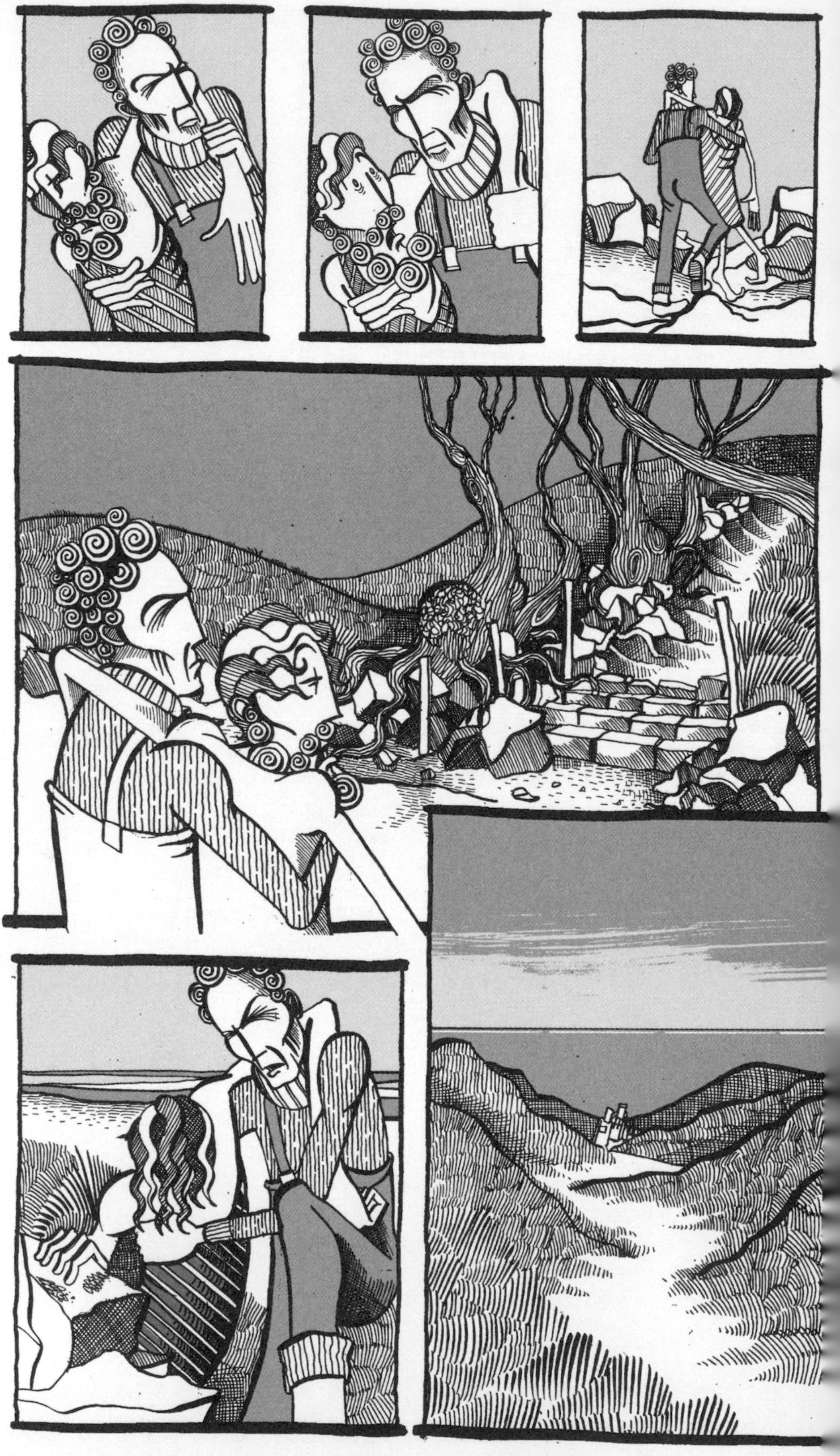

ON A PATH TOWARDS HIS HOME...

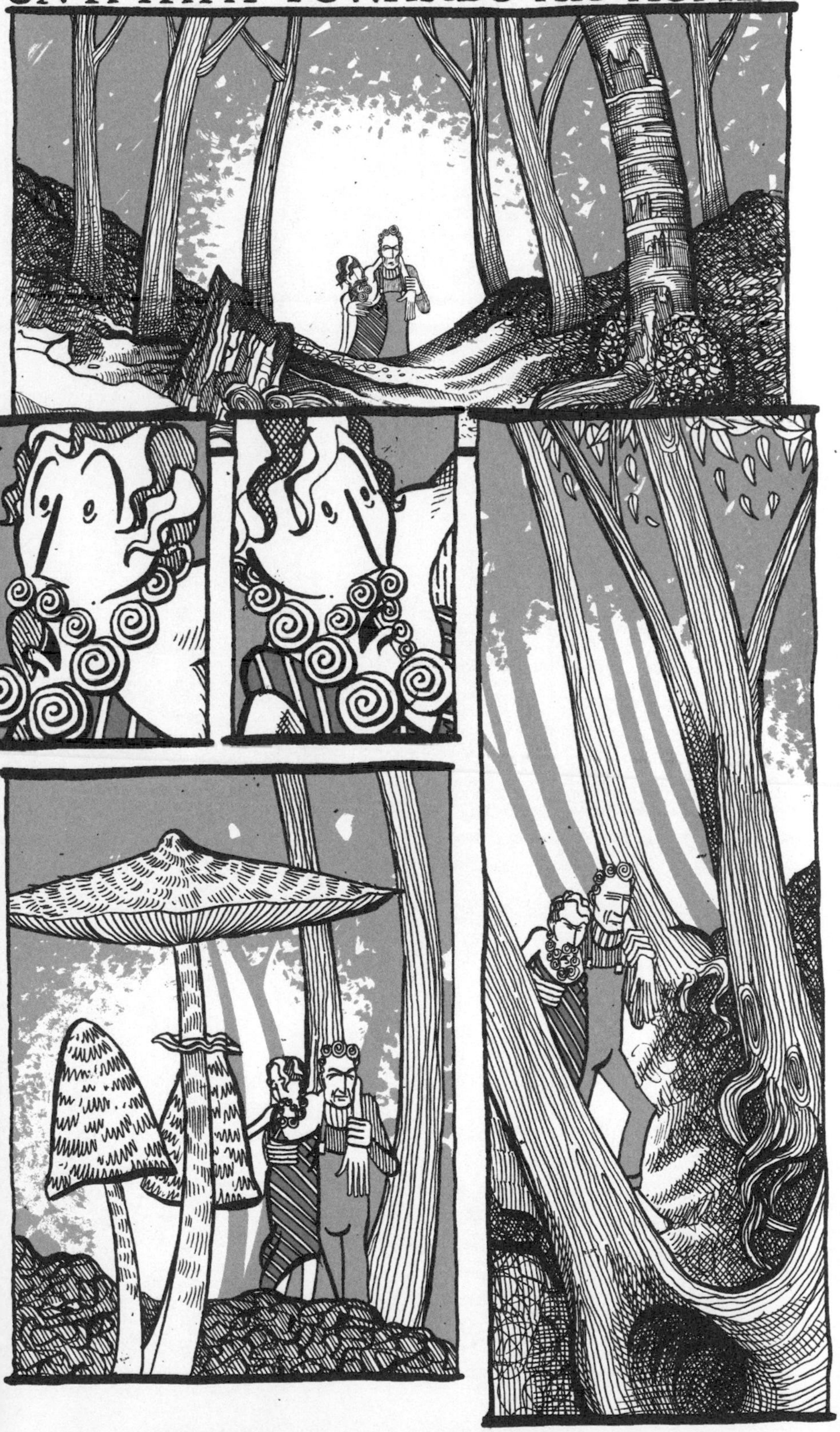

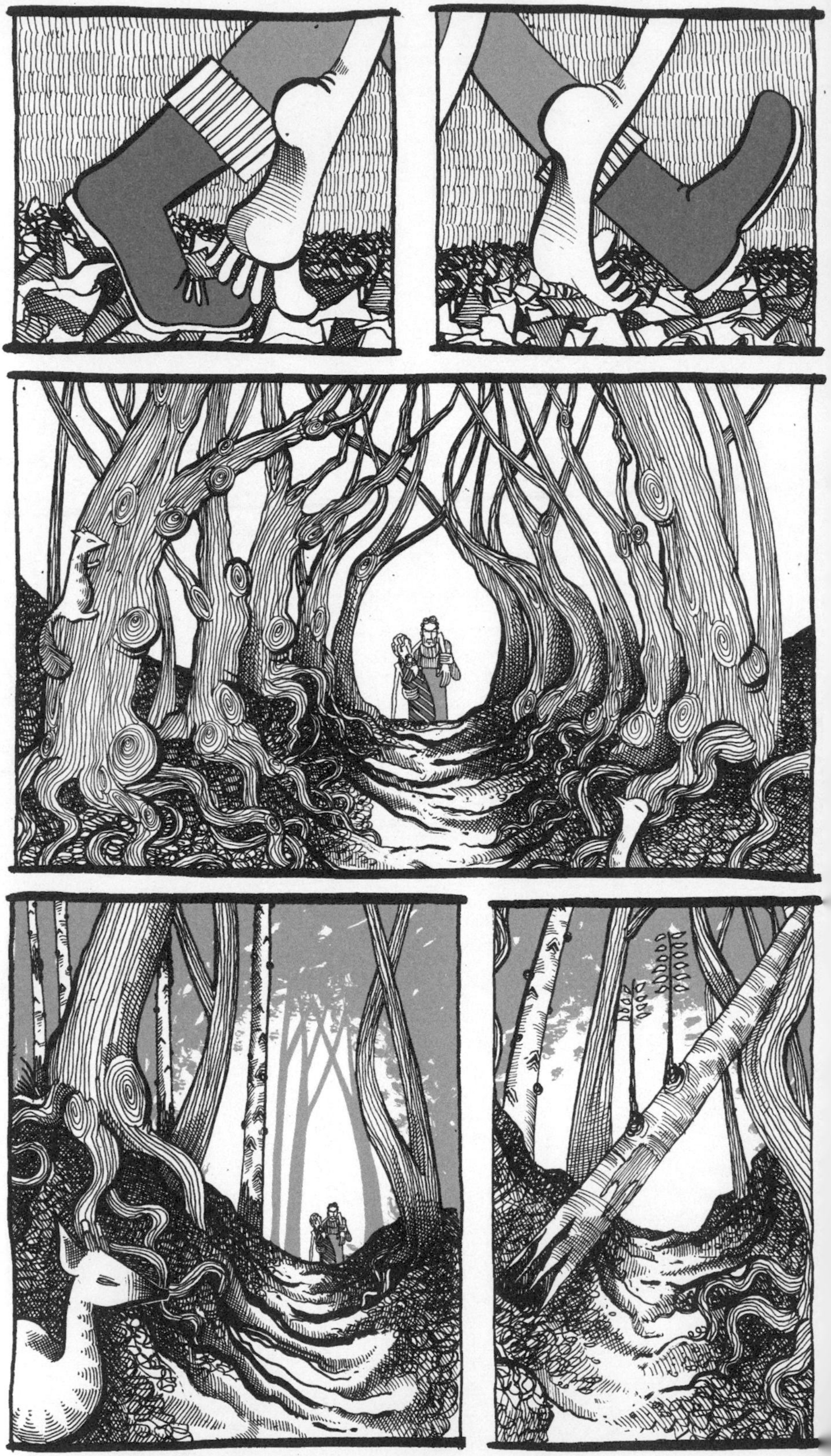

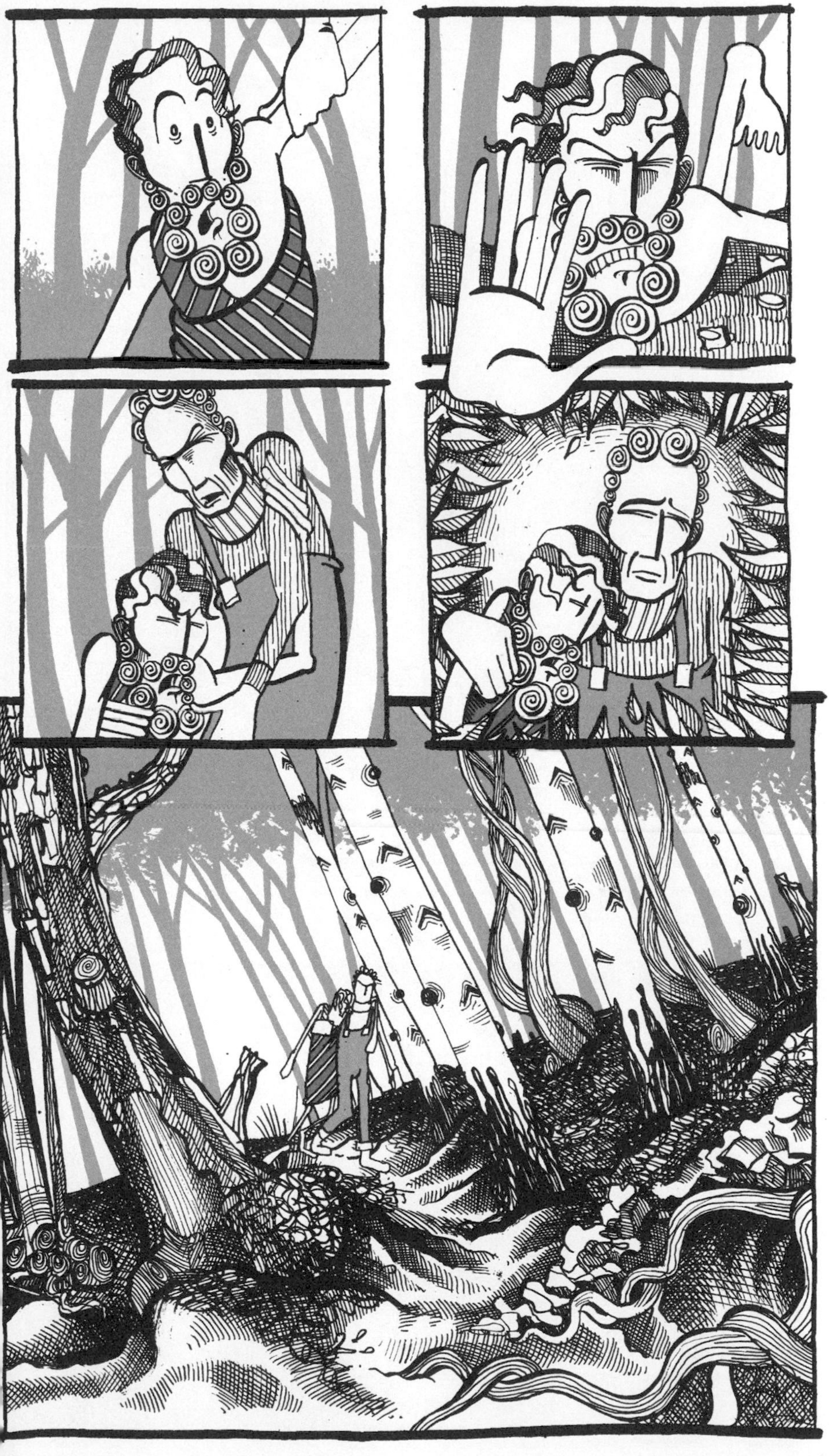

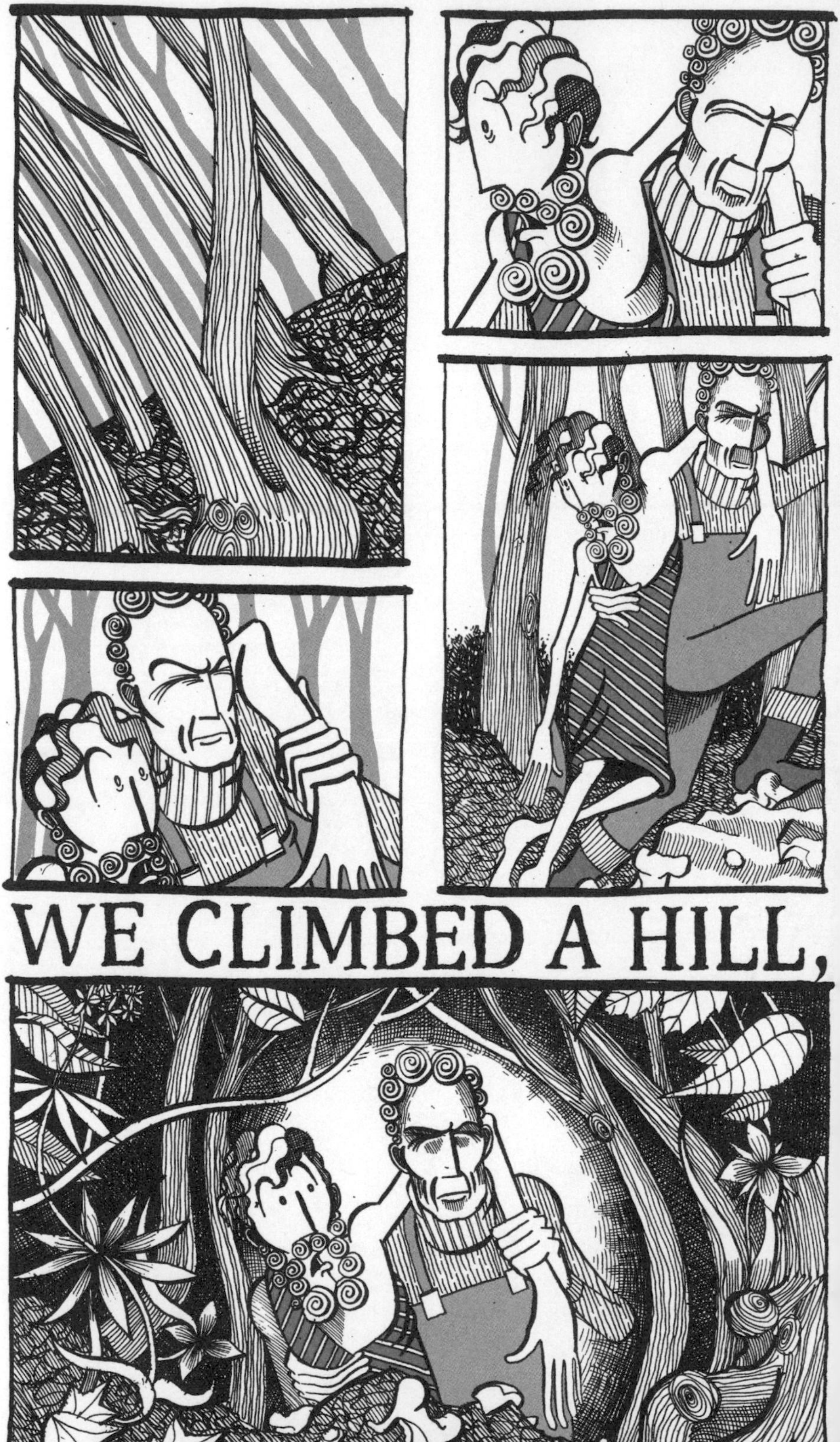
WE CLIMBED A HILL,

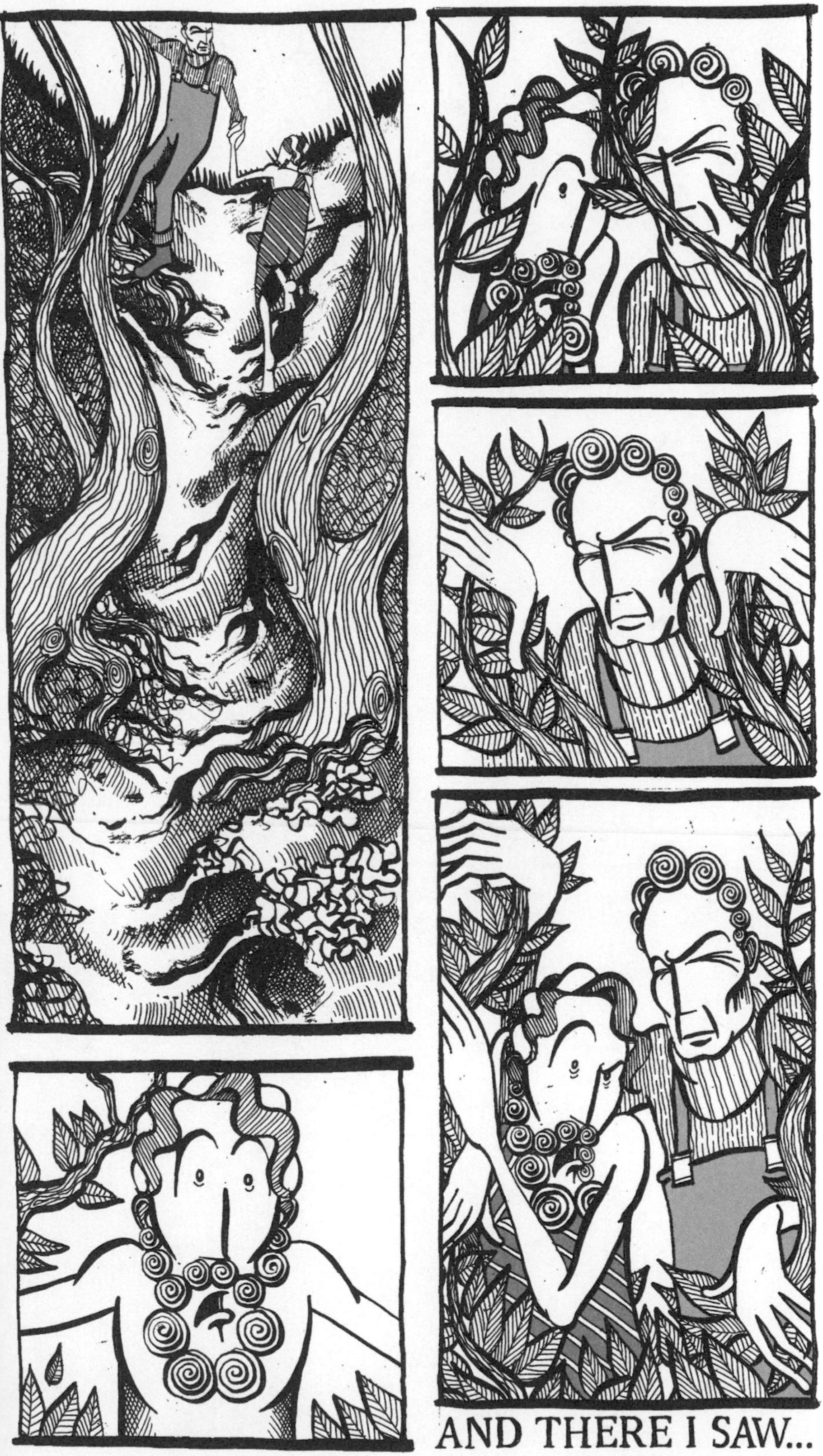
AND THERE I SAW...

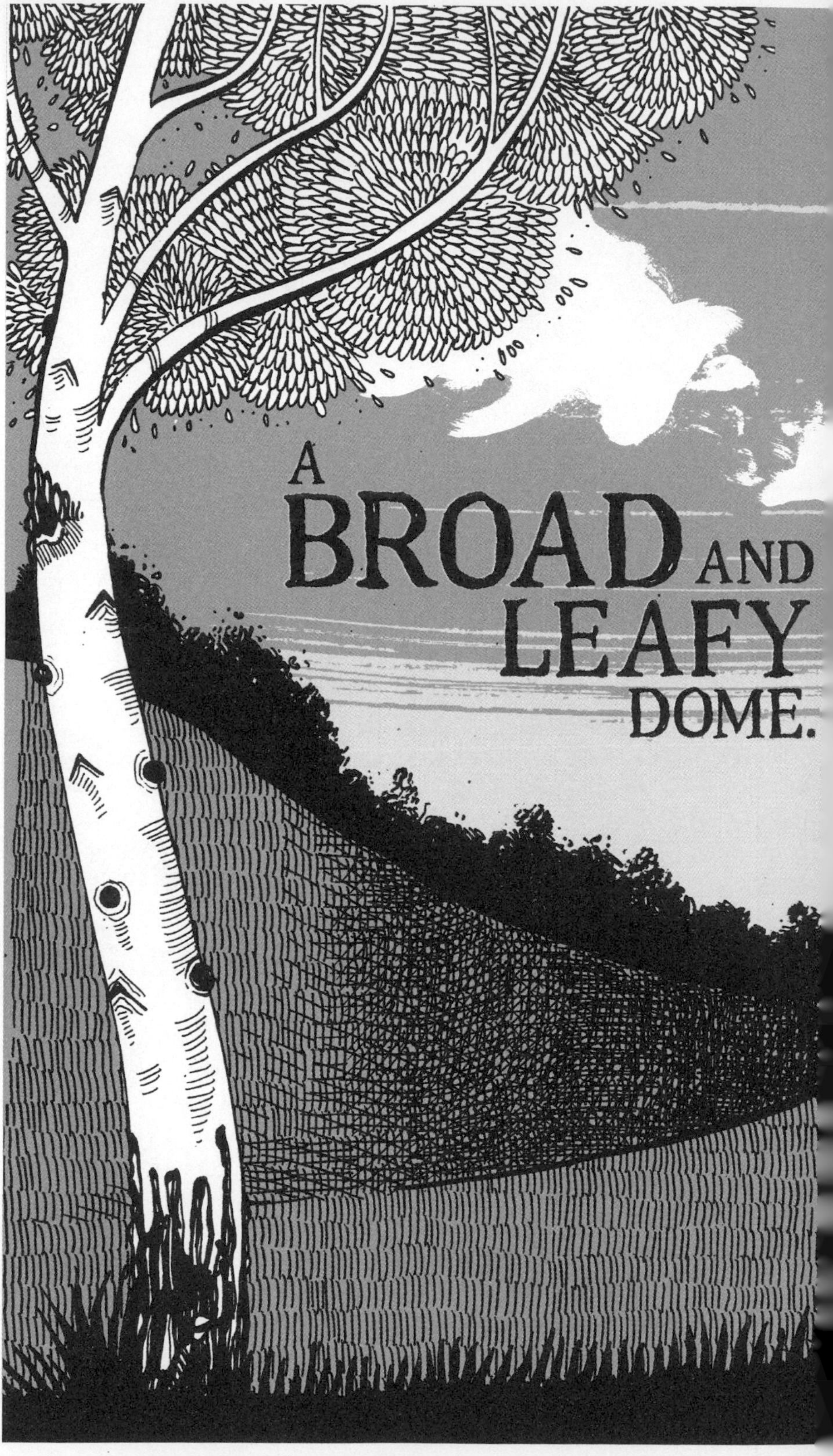
A BROAD AND LEAFY DOME.

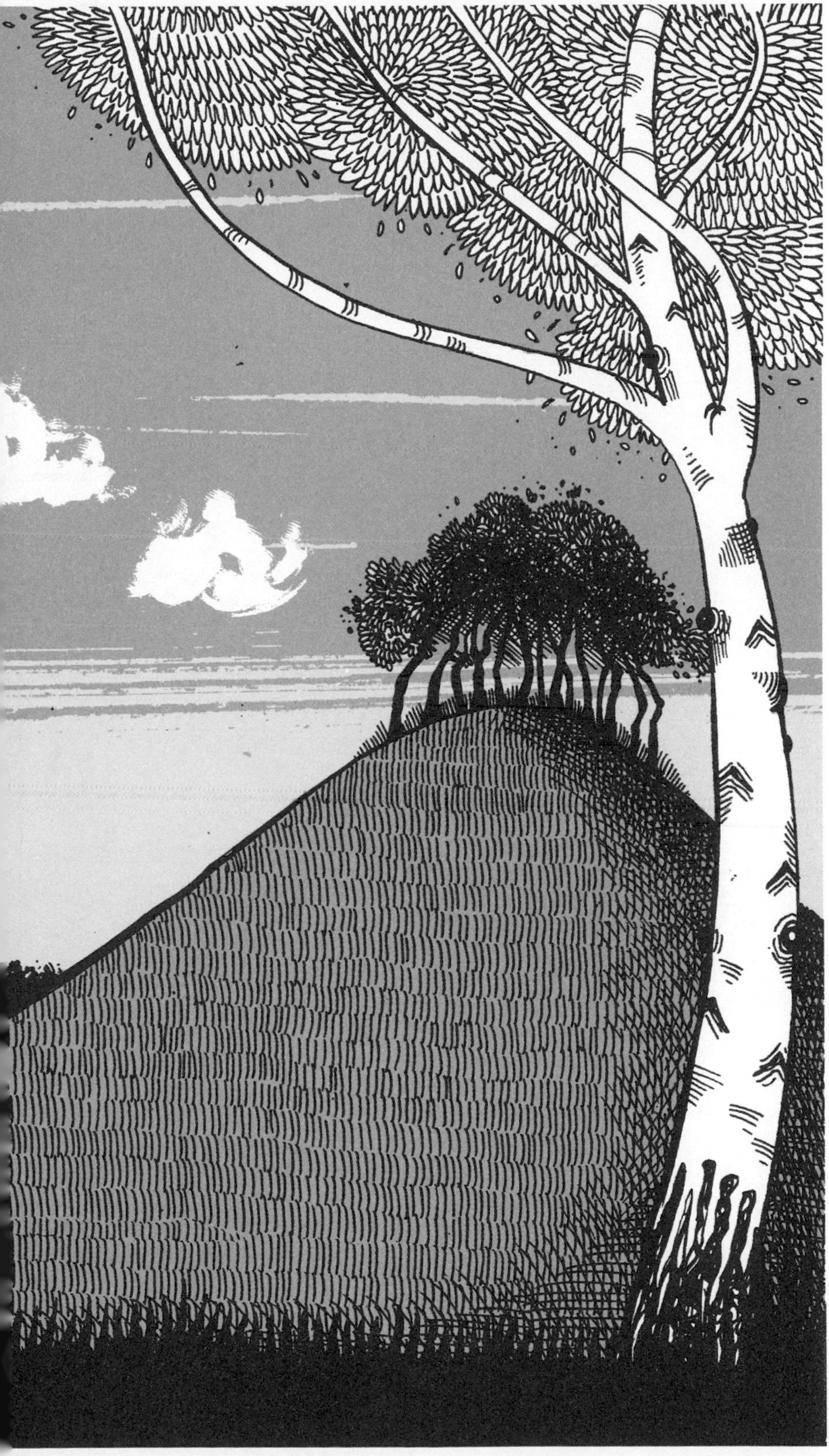

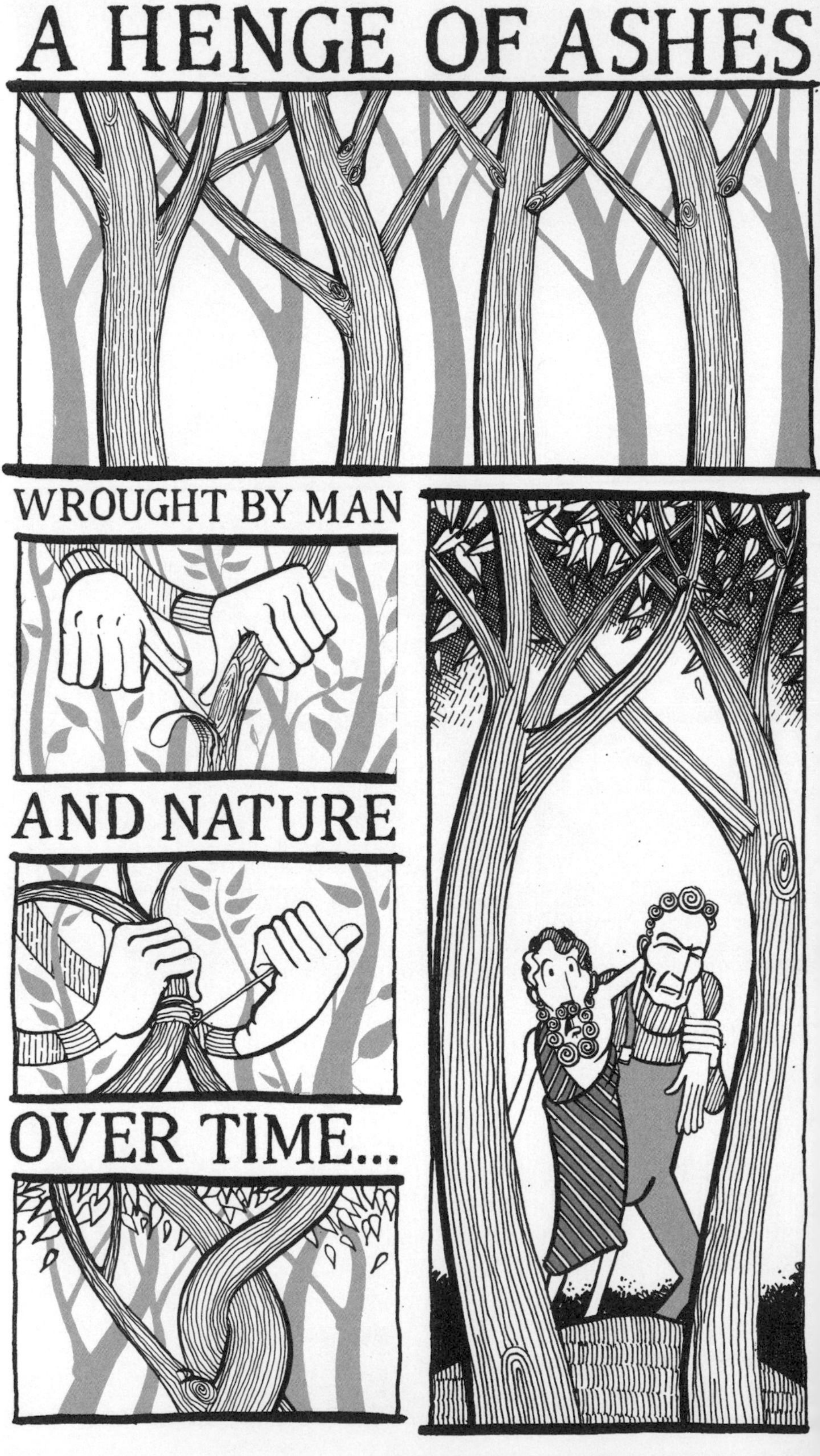
A HENGE OF ASHES
WROUGHT BY MAN
AND NATURE
OVER TIME...

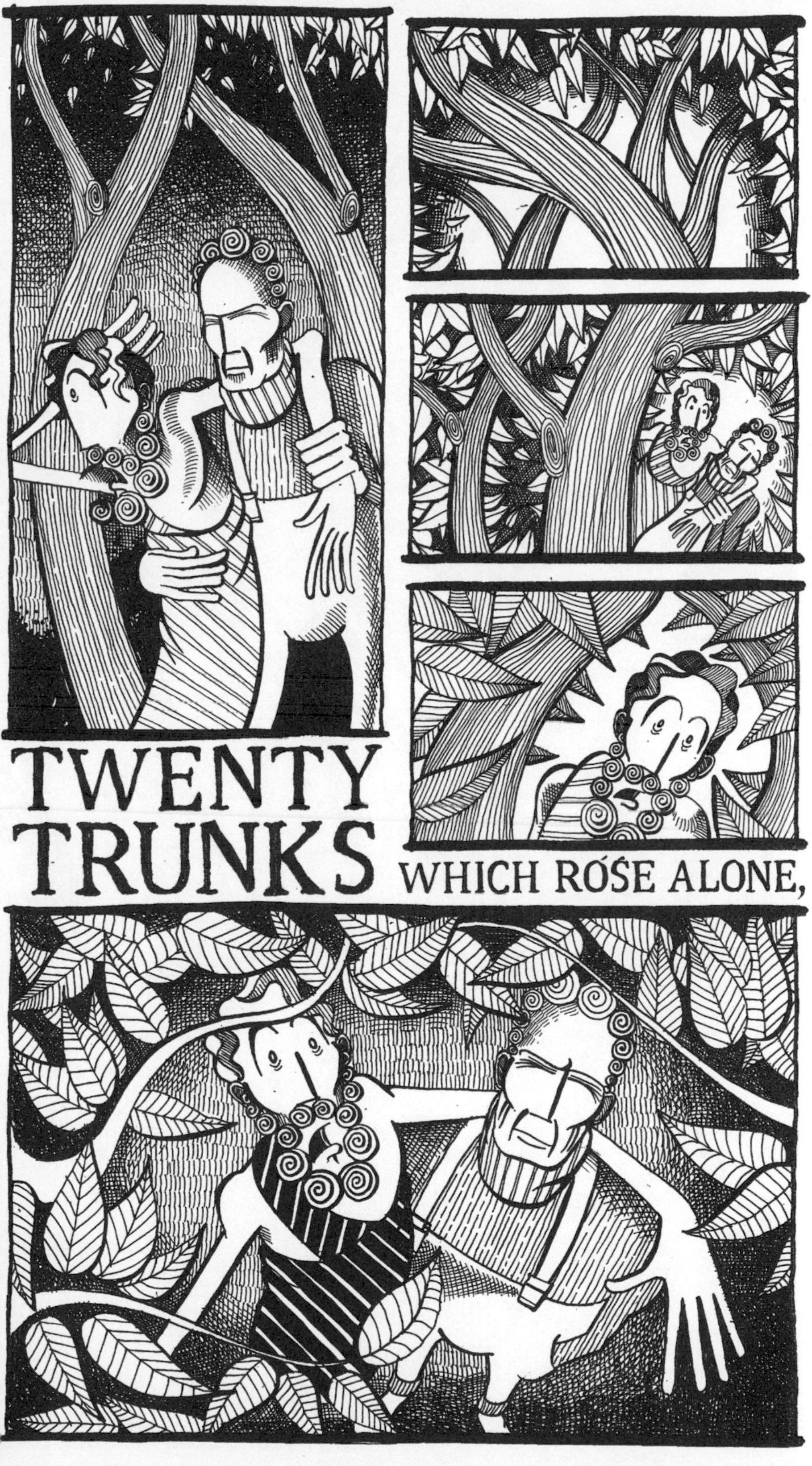
TWENTY
TRUNKS
WHICH ROSE ALONE,

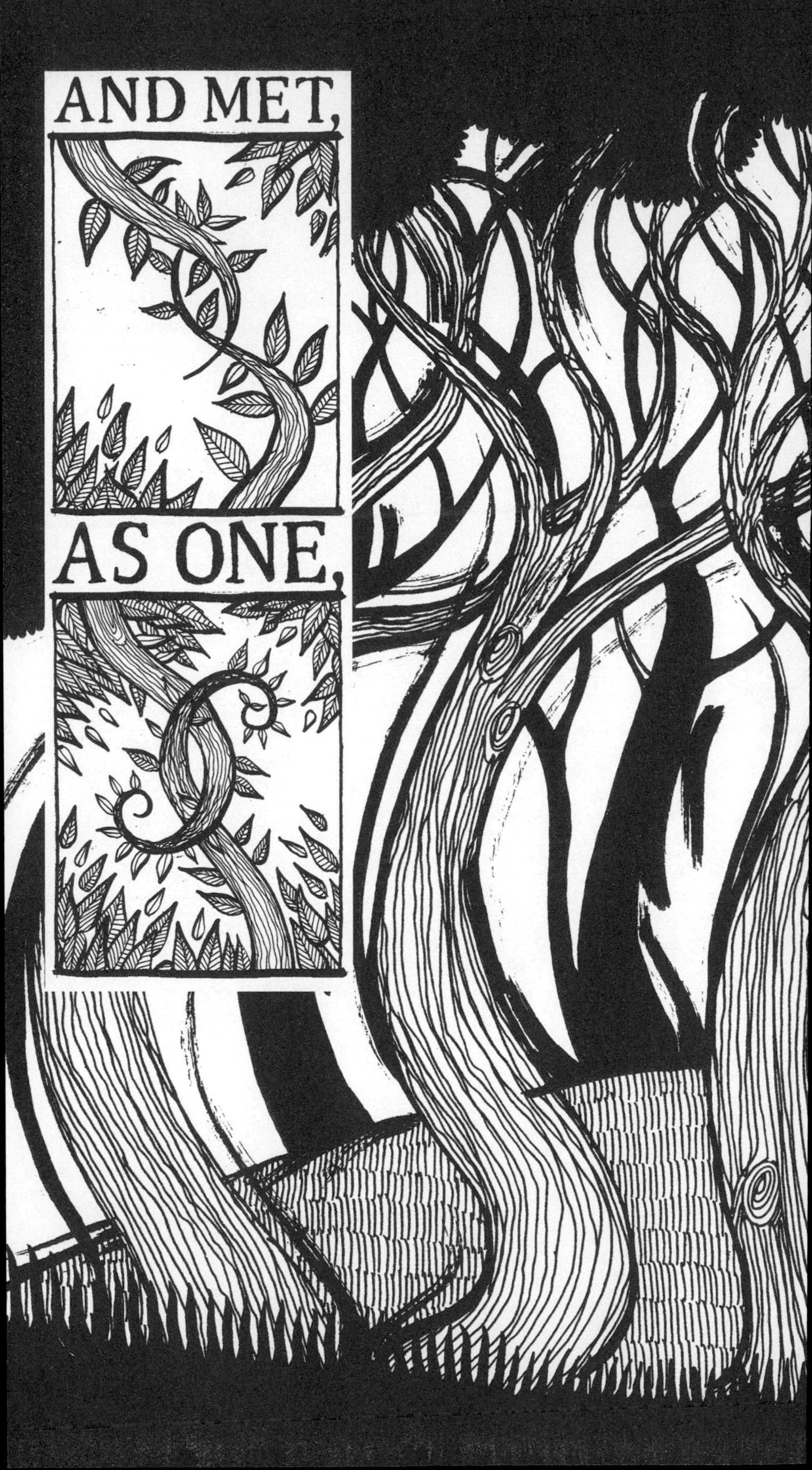
AND MET,
AS ONE,

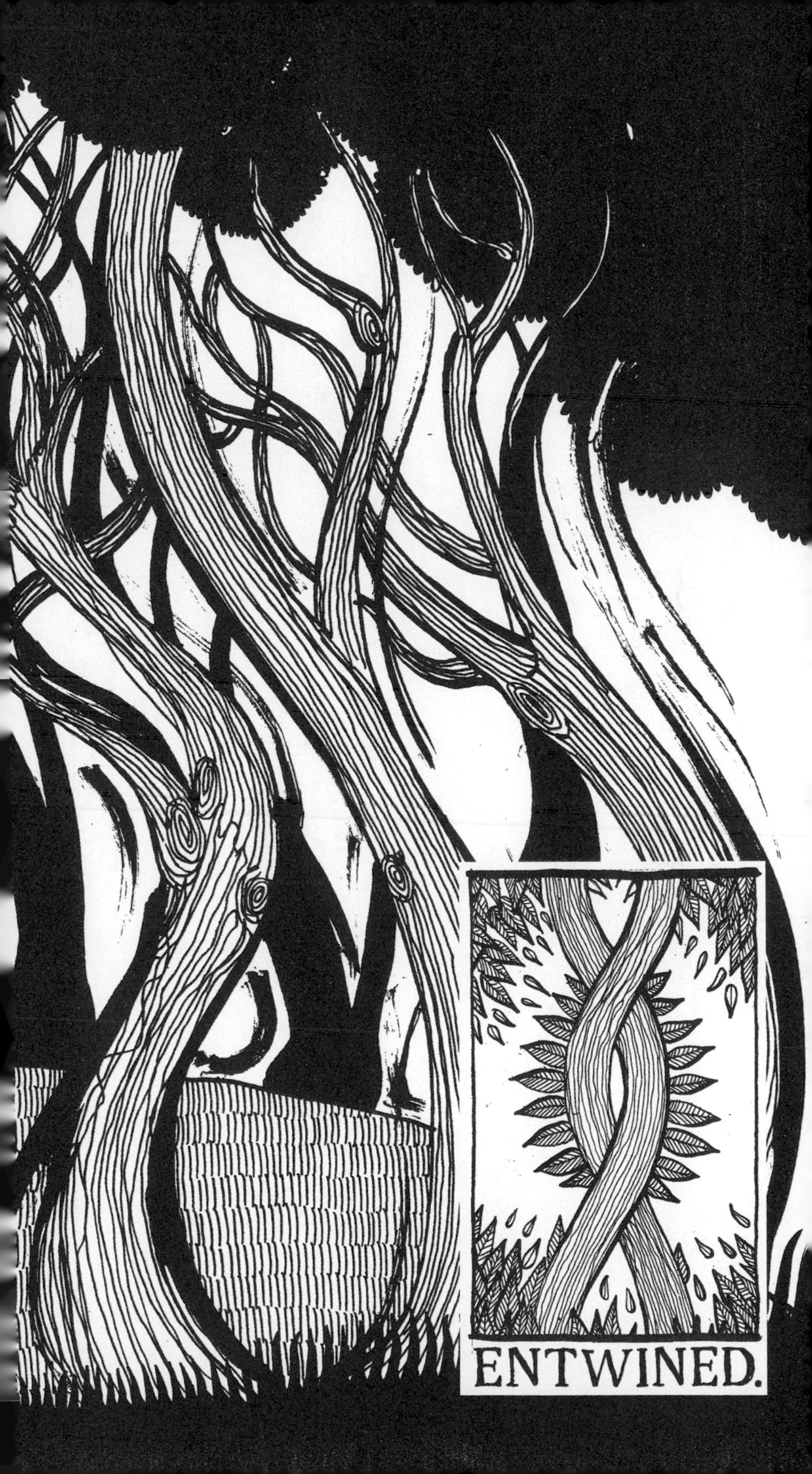
ENTWINED.

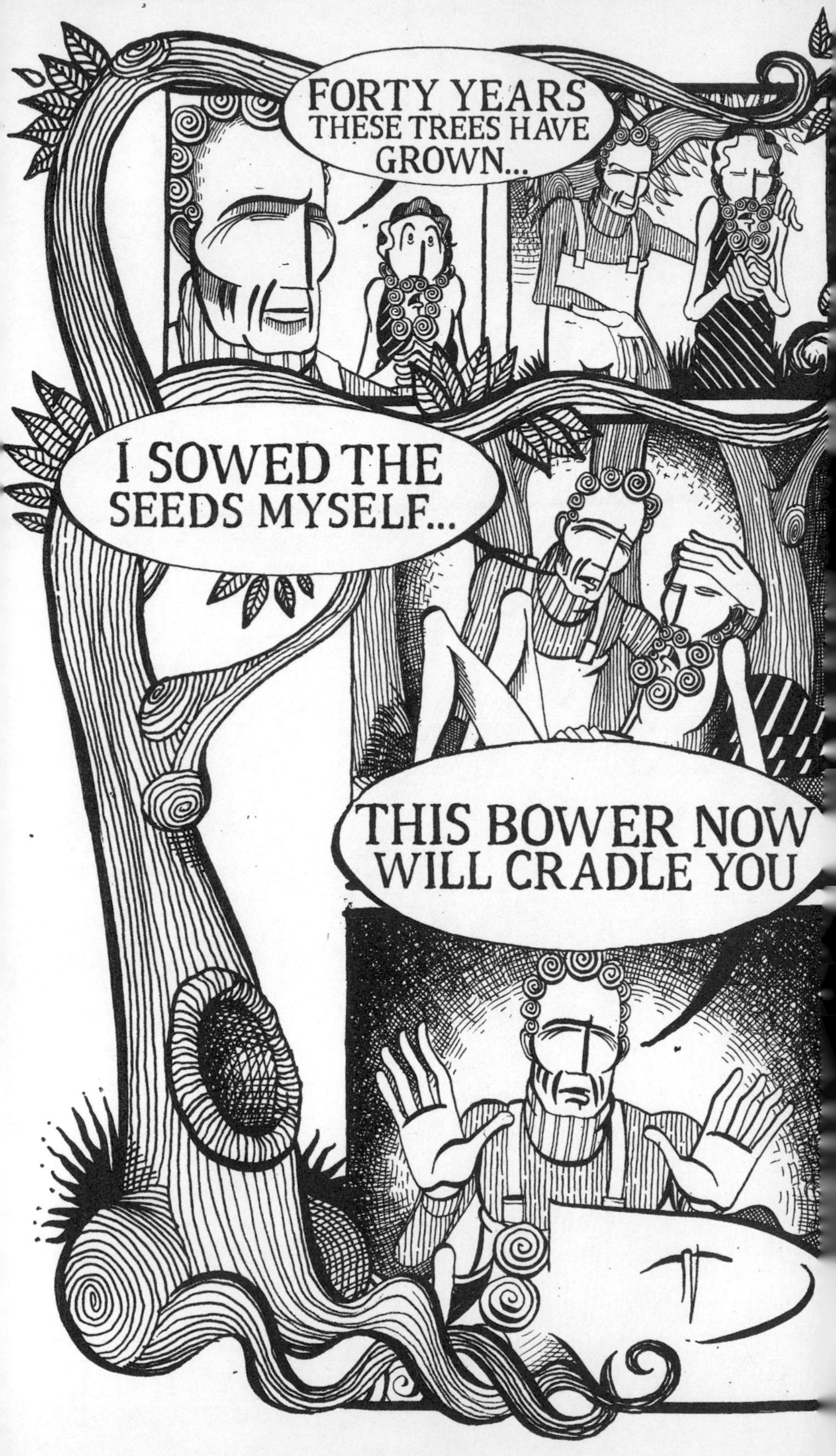
FORTY YEARS THESE TREES HAVE GROWN...
I SOWED THE SEEDS MYSELF...
THIS BOWER NOW WILL CRADLE YOU

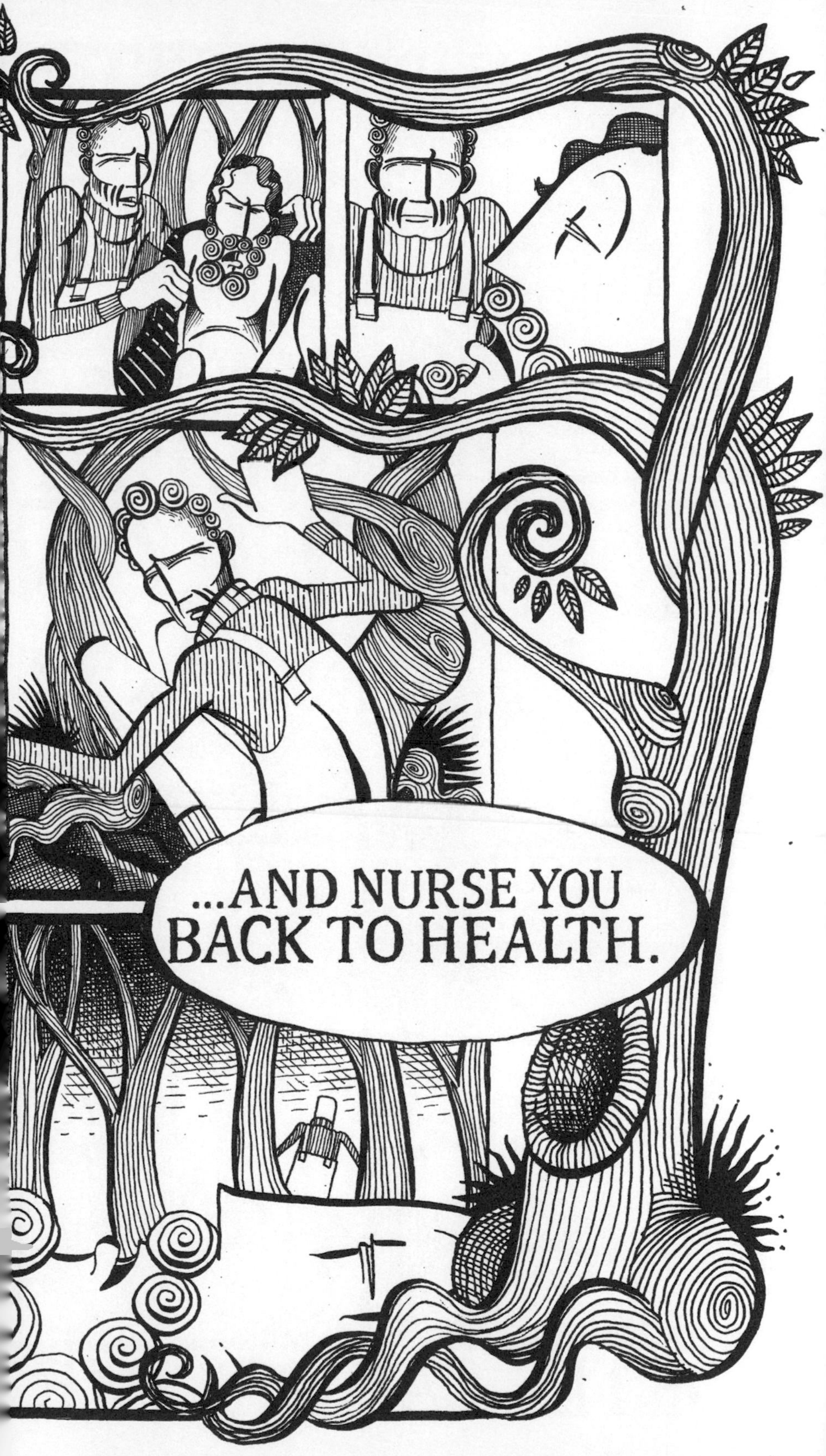
...AND NURSE YOU BACK TO HEALTH.

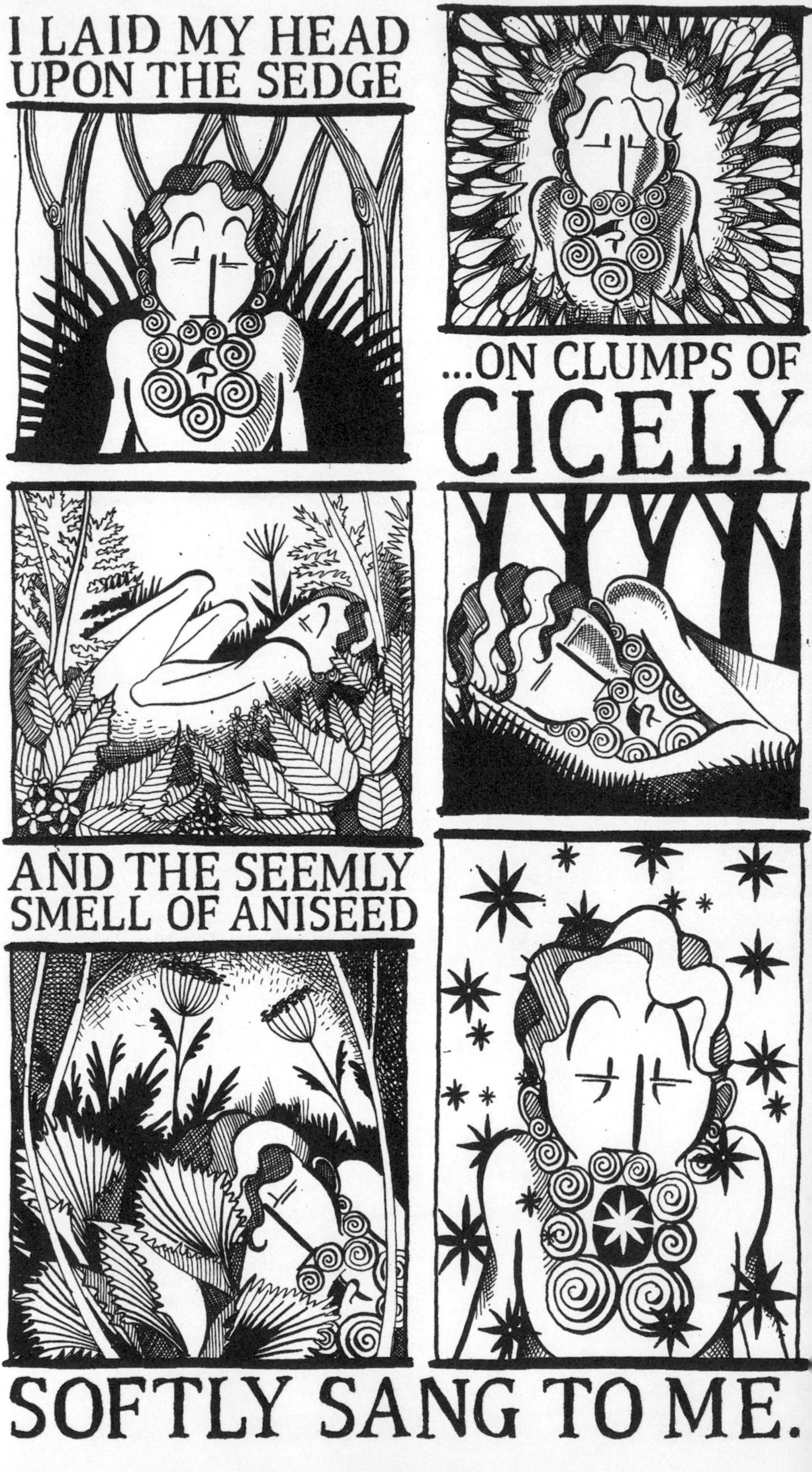
I LAID MY HEAD UPON THE SEDGE
...ON CLUMPS OF CICELY
AND THE SEEMLY SMELL OF ANISEED
SOFTLY SANG TO ME.

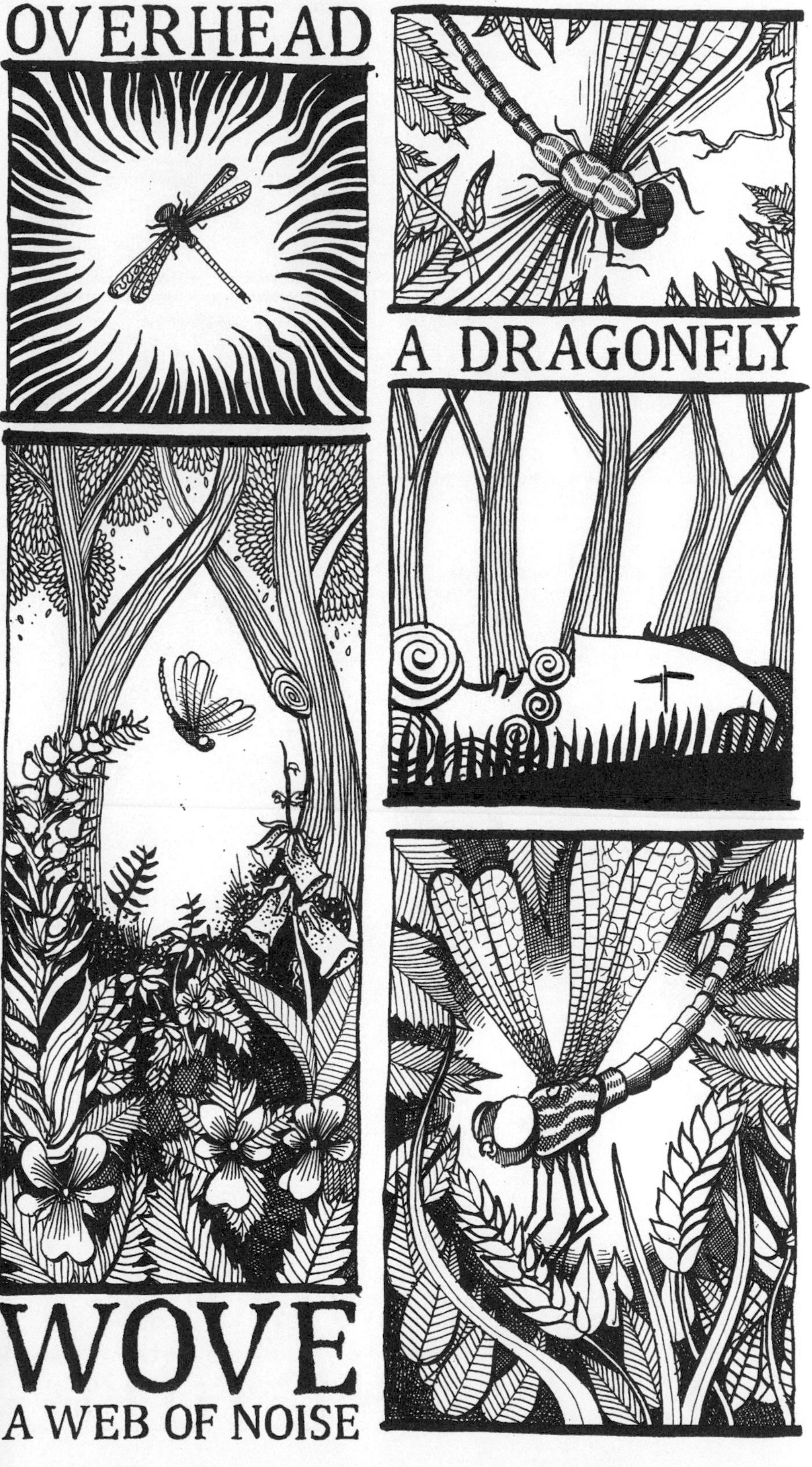
OVERHEAD
A DRAGONFLY
WOVE
A WEB OF NOISE

AND HIGHER STILL

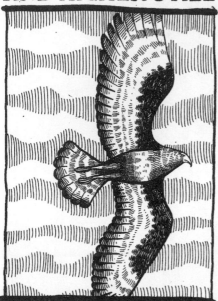

A BUZZARD HUNG

SILENTLY

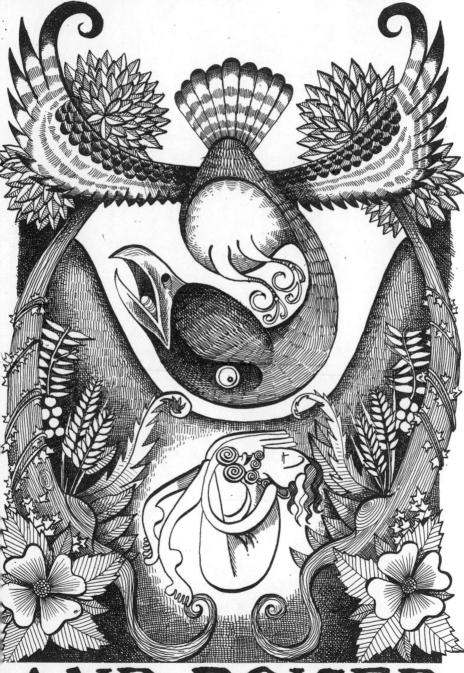

AND POISED.

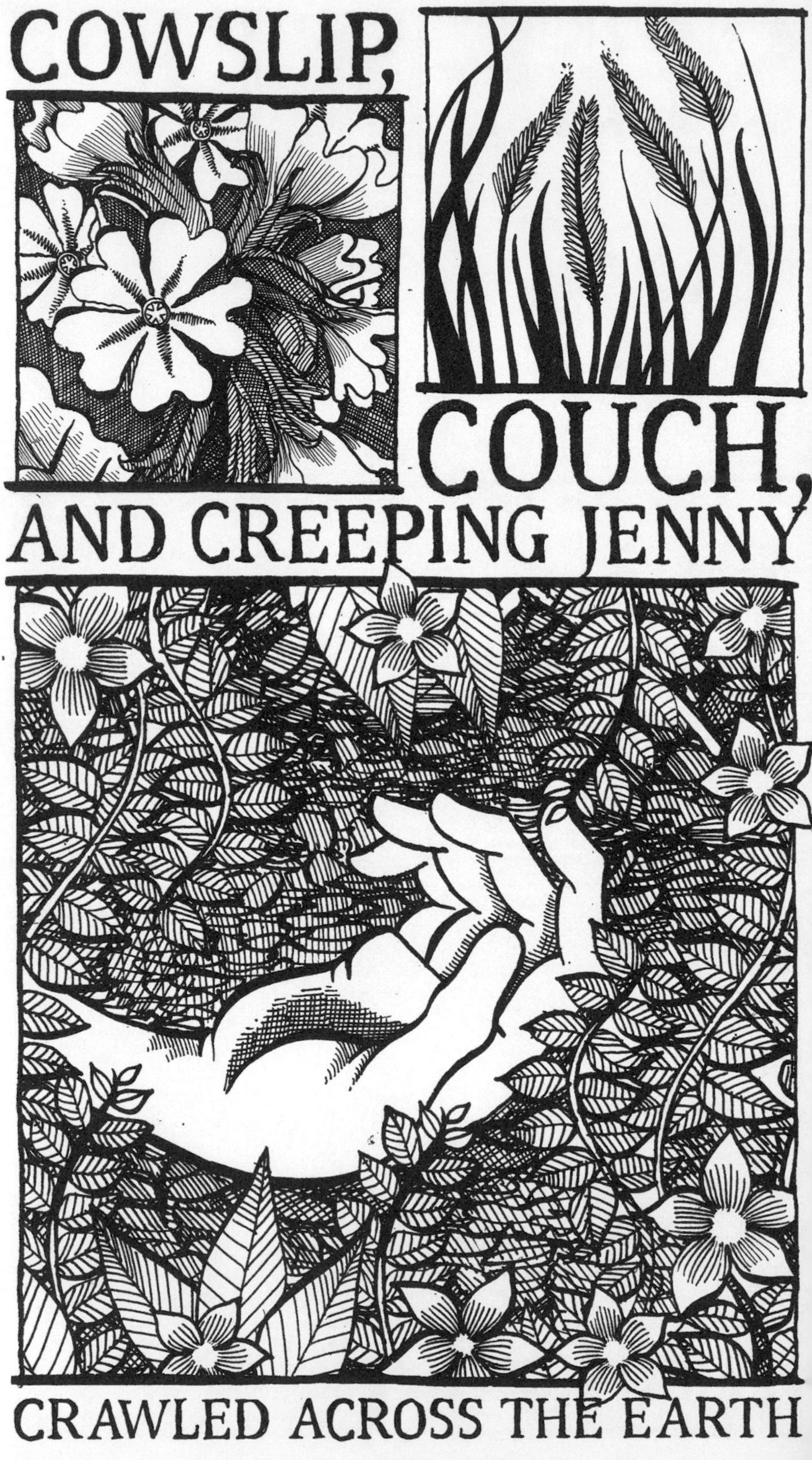
COWSLIP,
COUCH,
AND CREEPING JENNY
CRAWLED ACROSS THE EARTH

AND ANCIENT
IVY

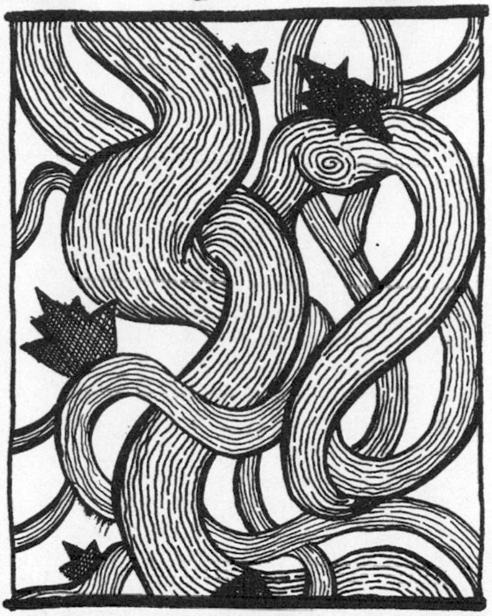

CLIMBED THE
TREES

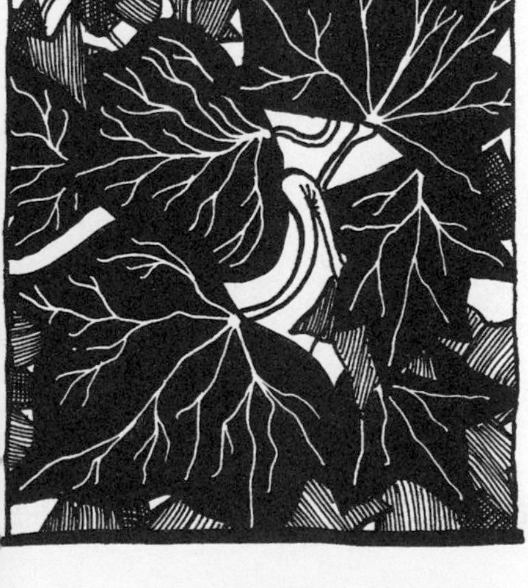

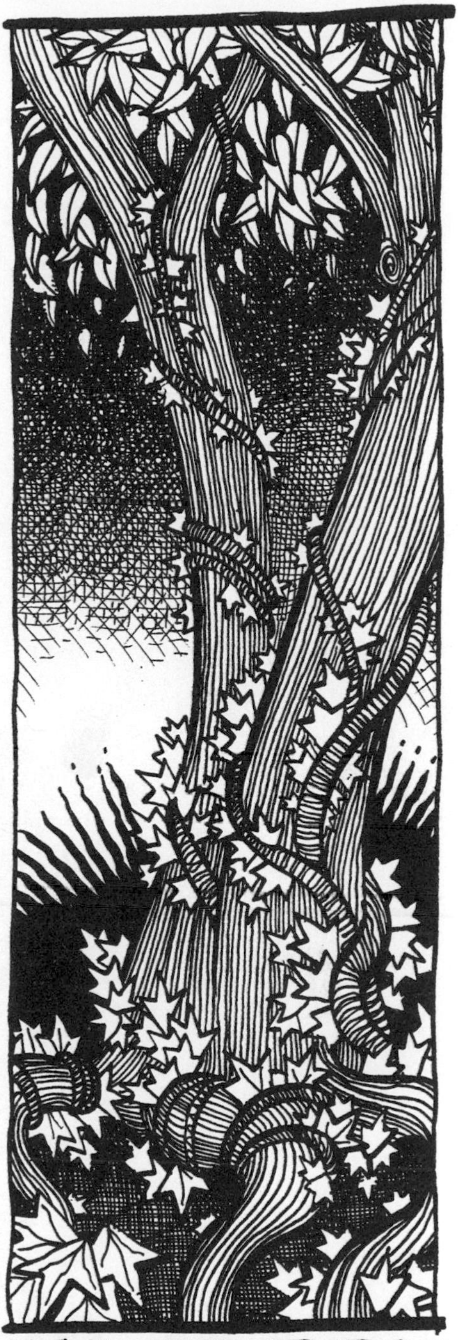

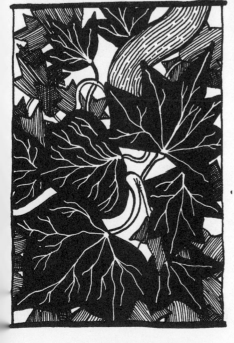

IN GREEN
RENEWING
BIRTH.

THE EARTH WAS BREATHING

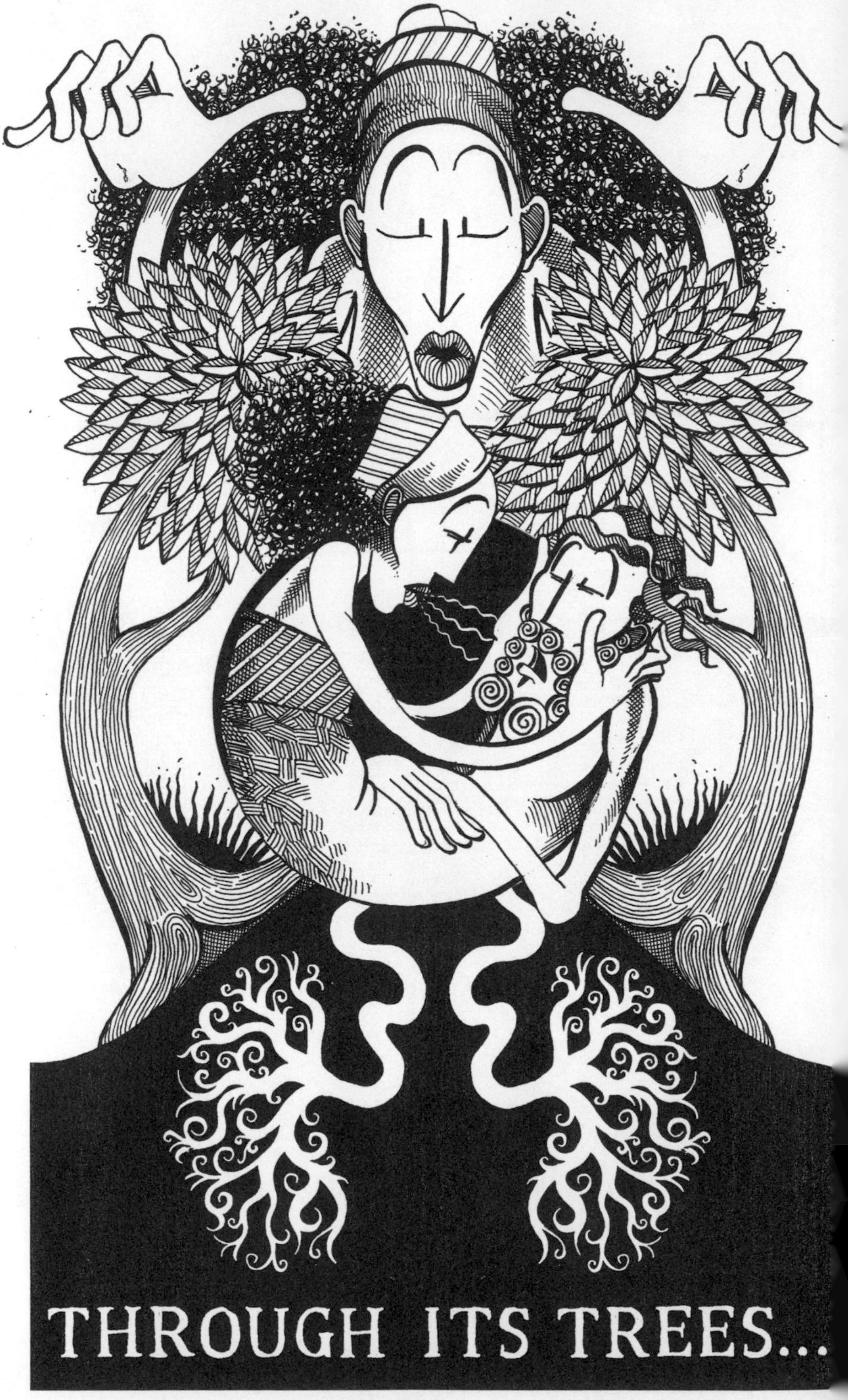
THROUGH ITS TREES...

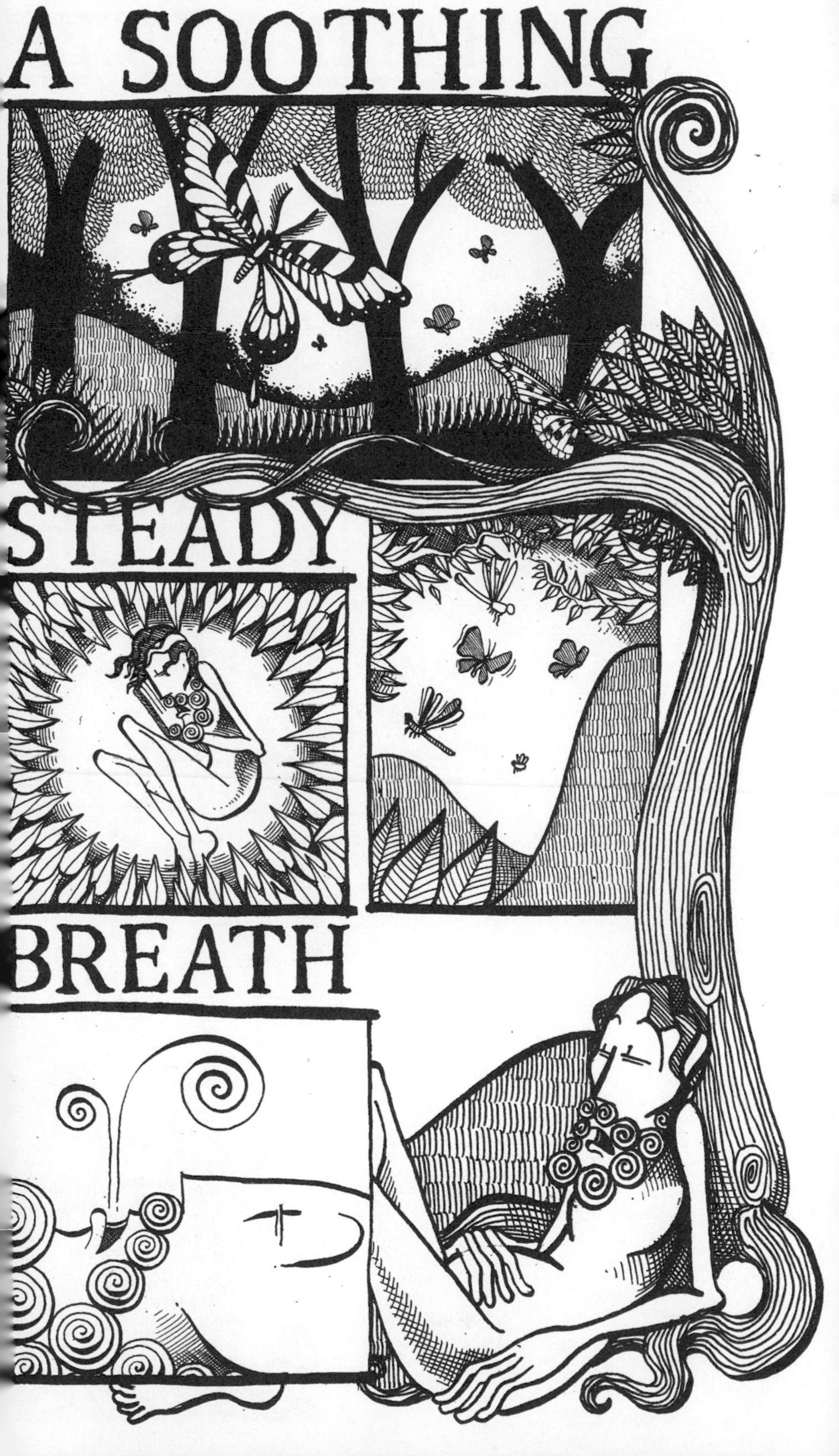
A SOOTHING
STEADY
BREATH

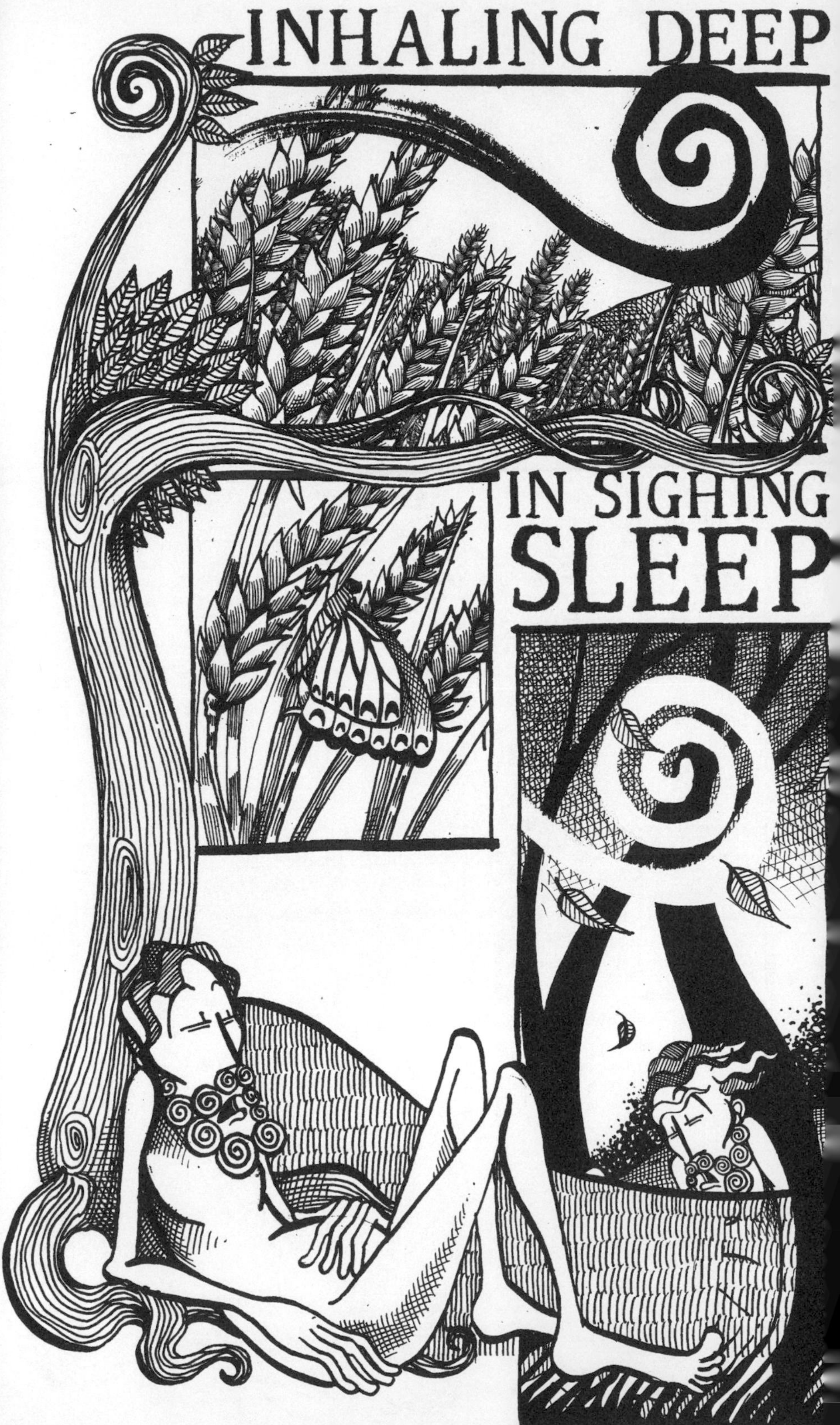
INHALING DEEP
IN SIGHING
SLEEP

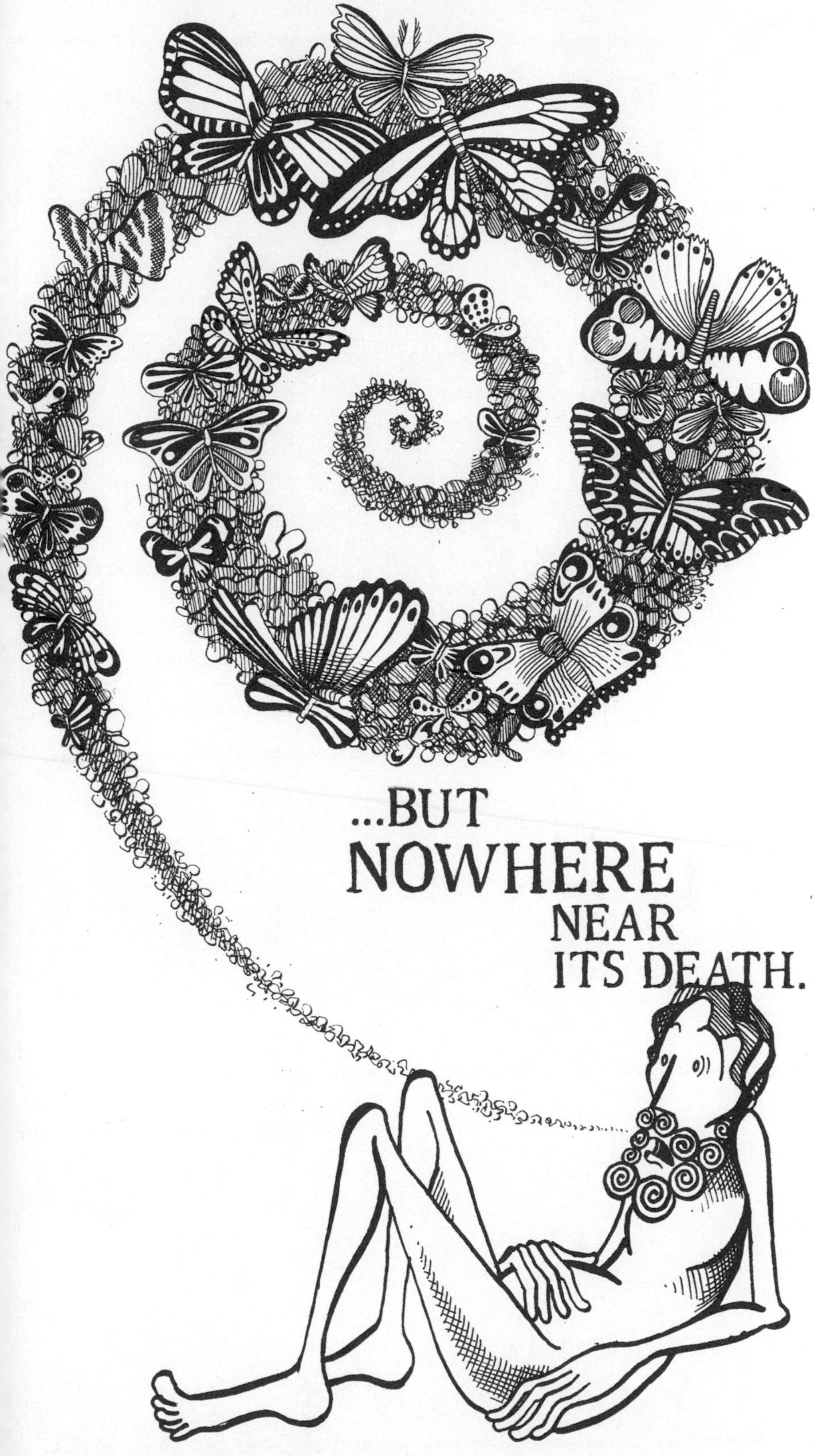
...BUT
NOWHERE
NEAR
ITS DEATH.

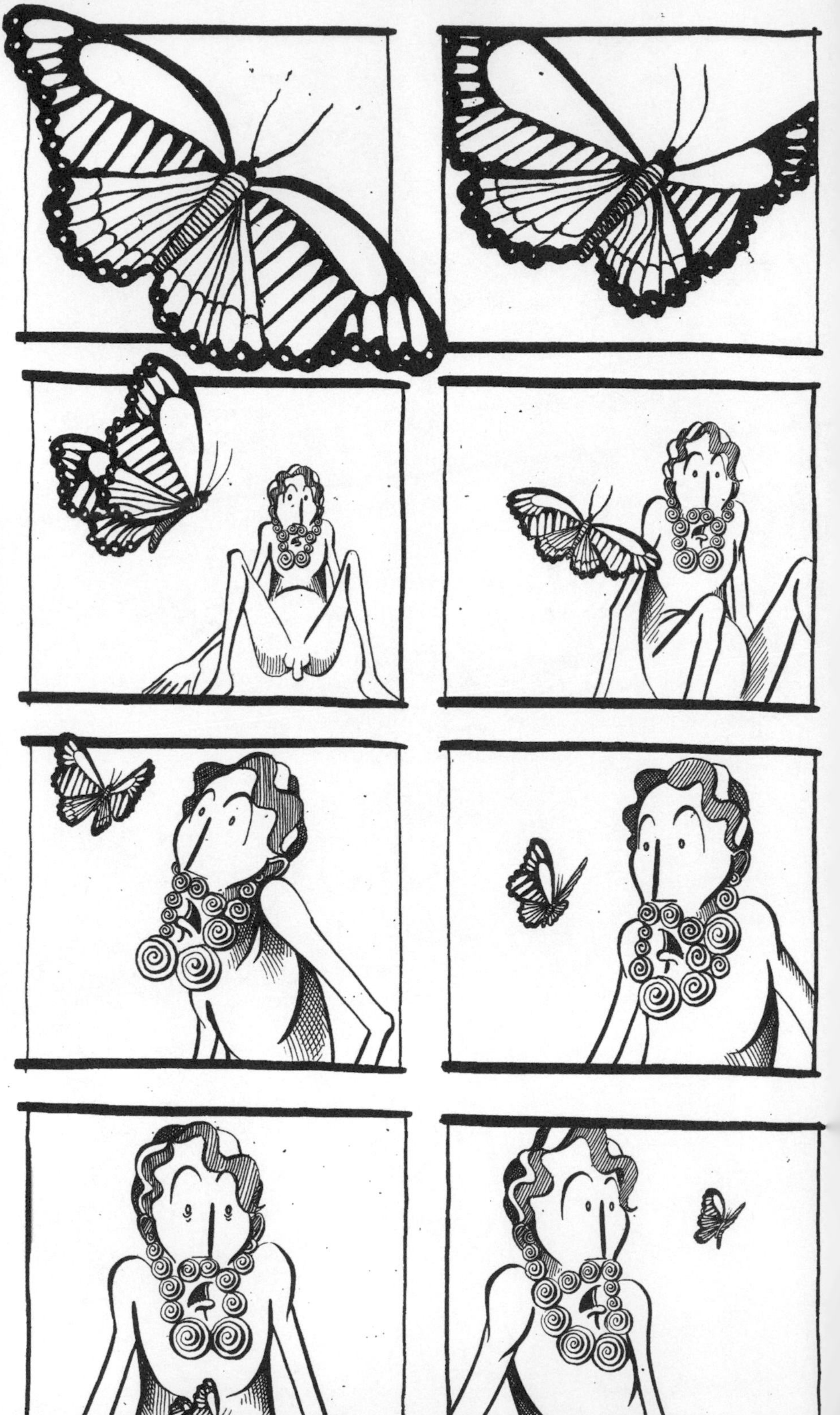

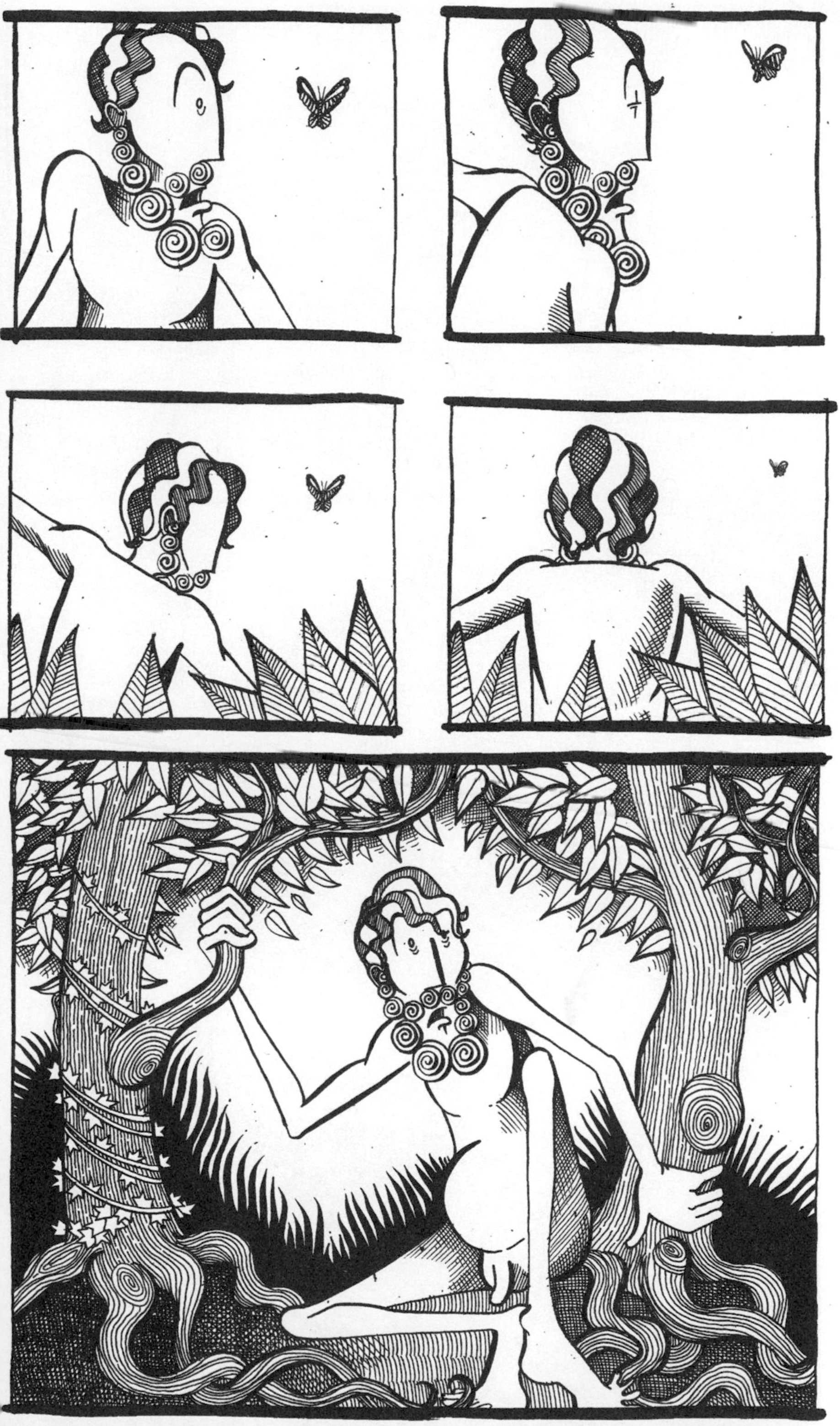

I RAISED MYSELF UPON A BED...

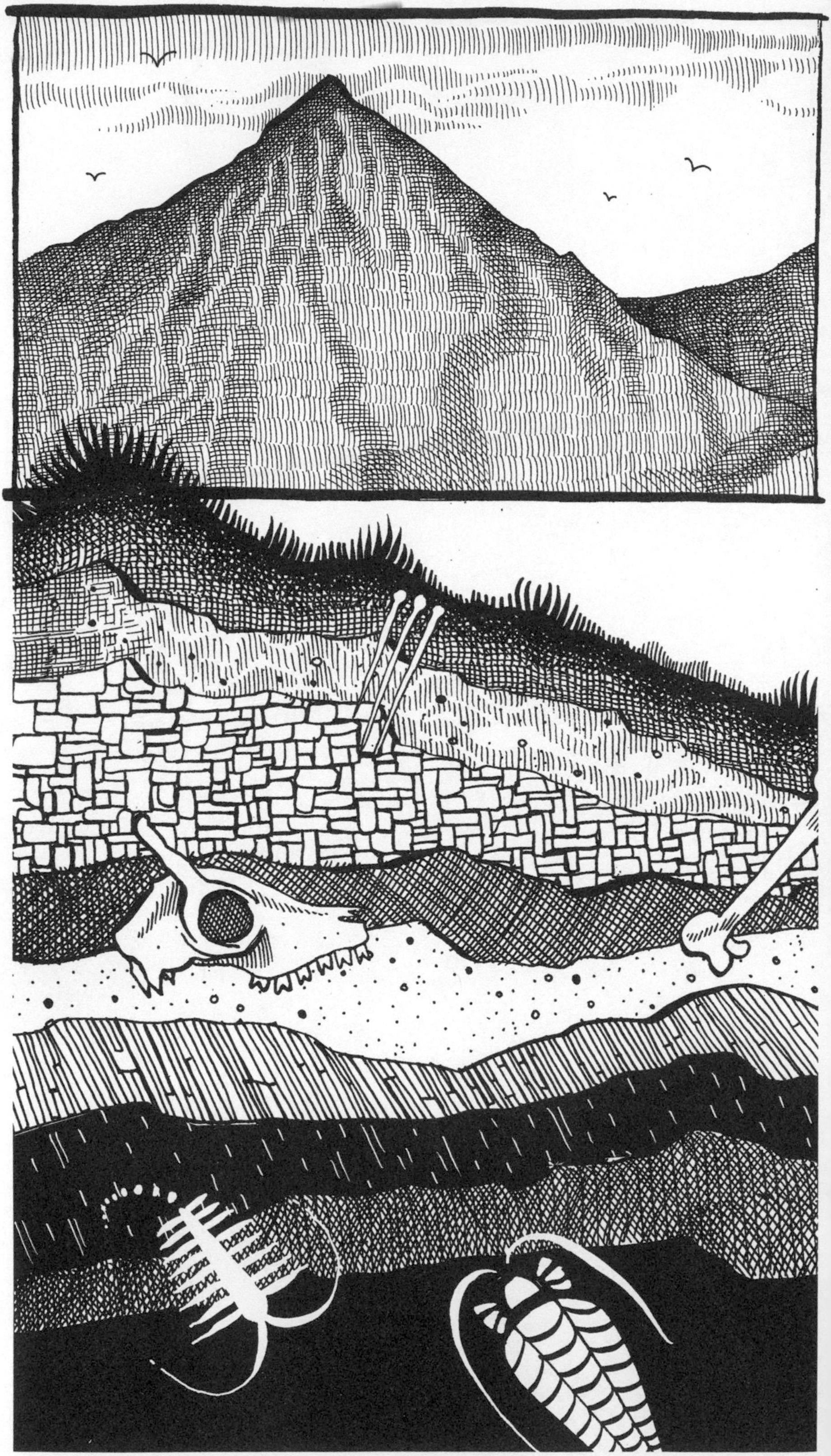

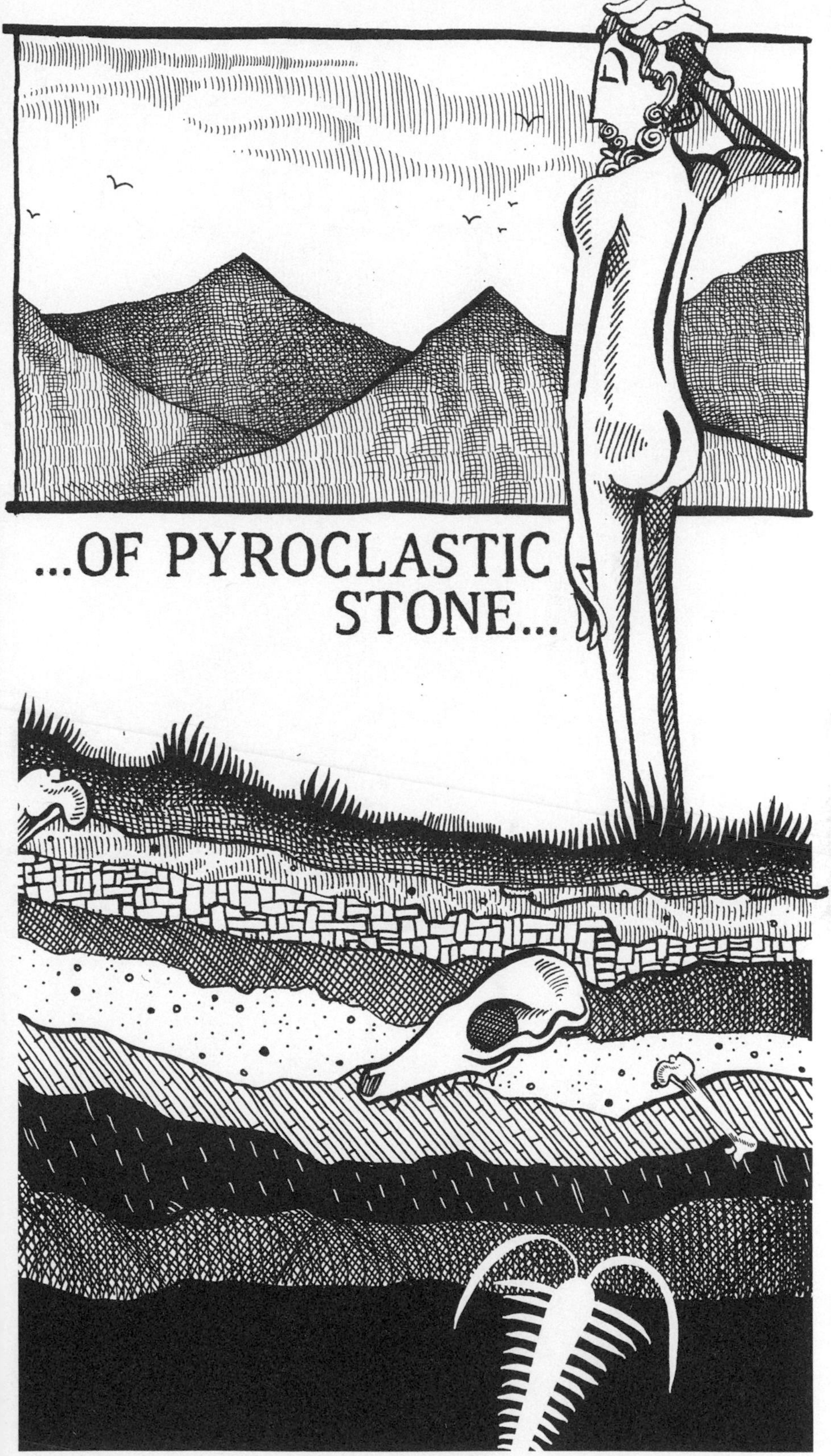
...OF PYROCLASTIC
STONE...

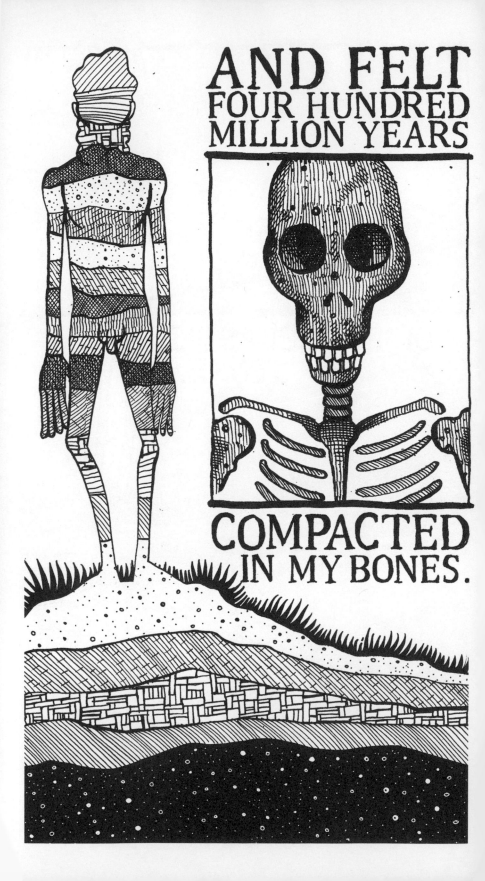

AND FELT
FOUR HUNDRED
MILLION YEARS

COMPACTED
IN MY BONES.

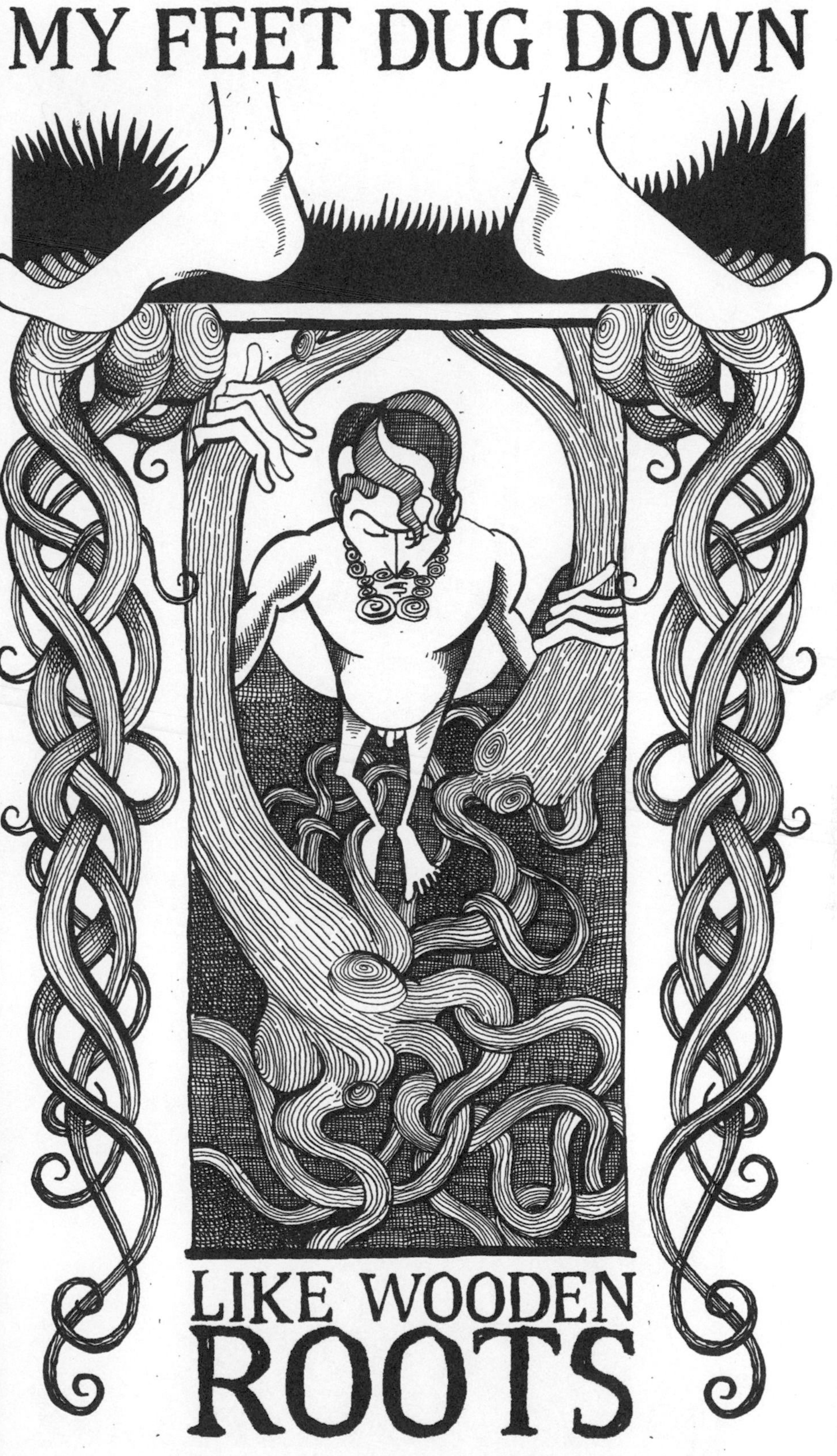
MY FEET DUG DOWN
LIKE WOODEN
ROOTS

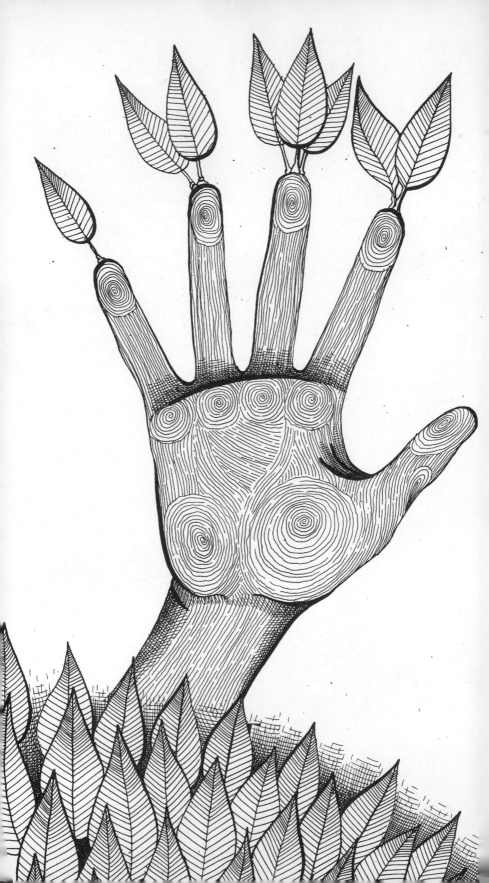

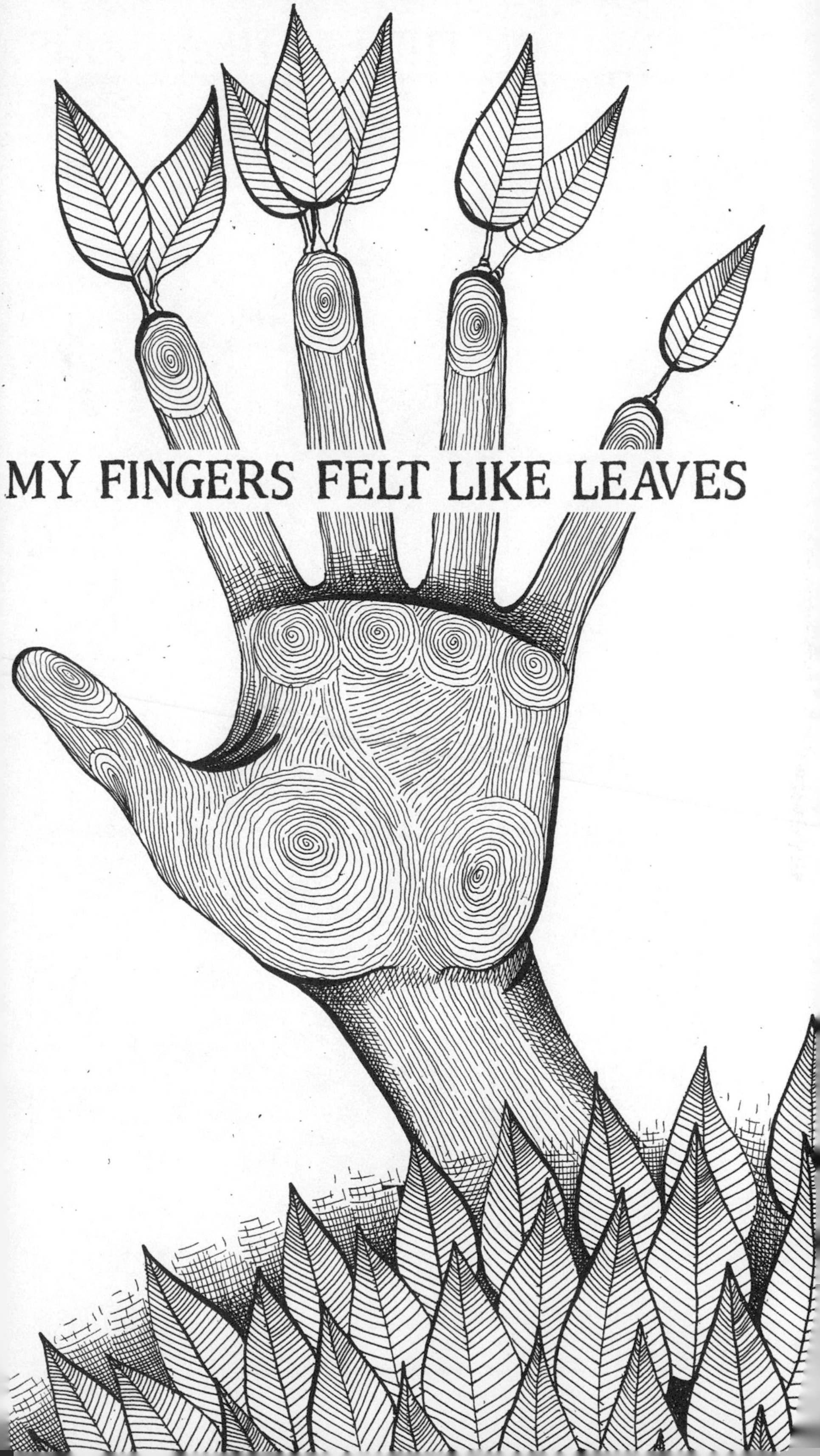
MY FINGERS FELT LIKE LEAVES

I DREW UPON THE EARTH AND AIR,

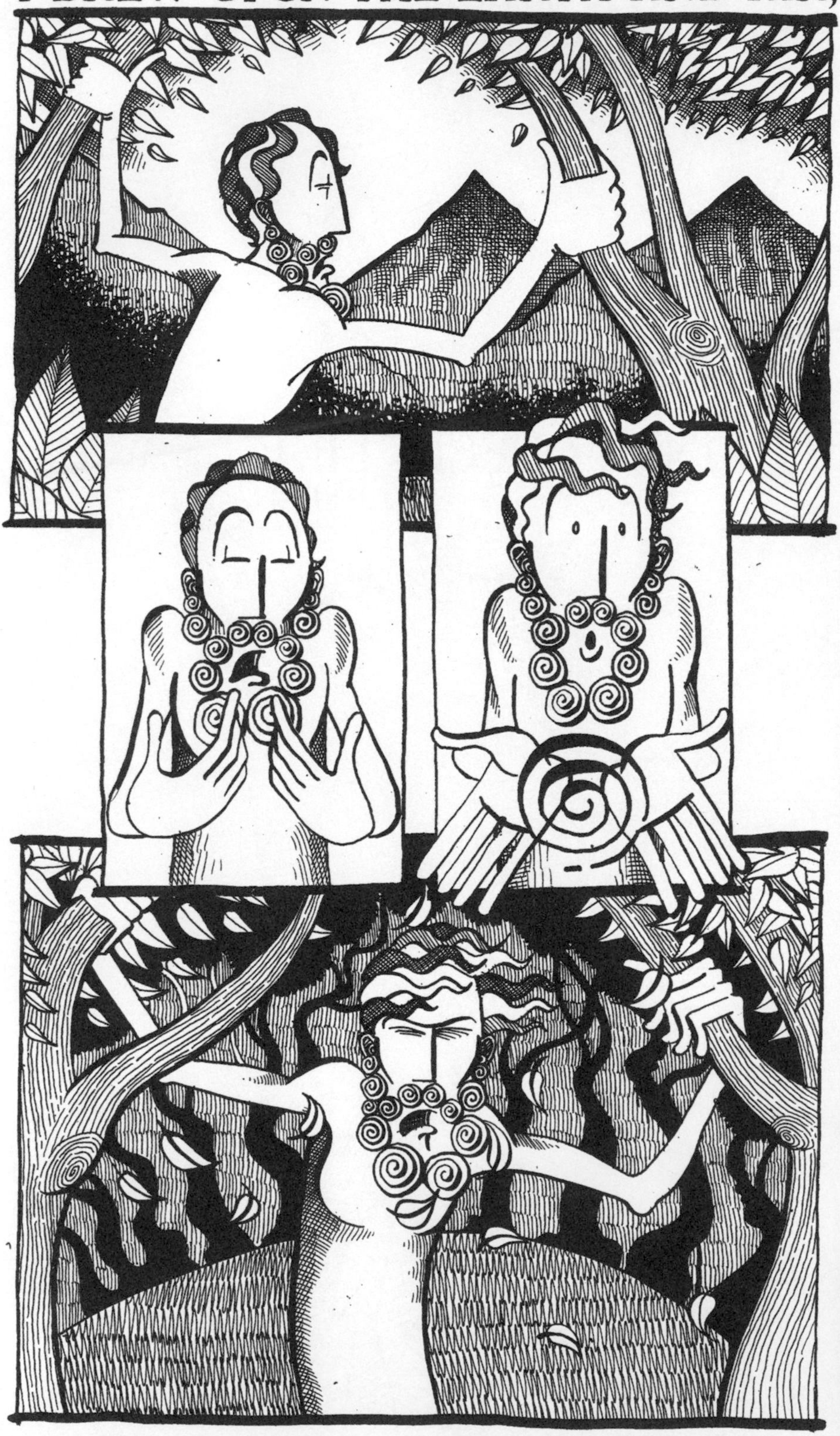

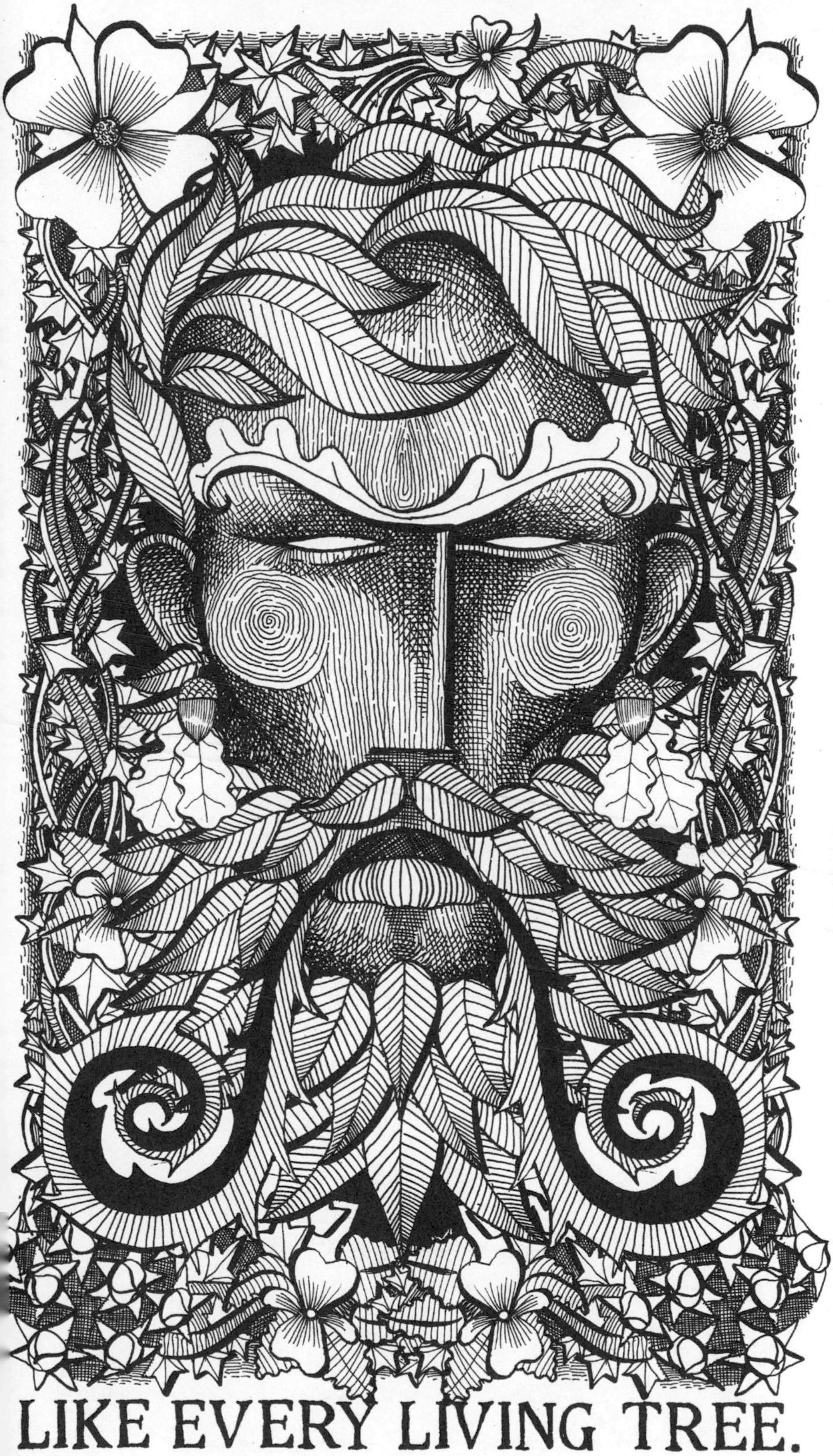

LIKE EVERY LIVING TREE.

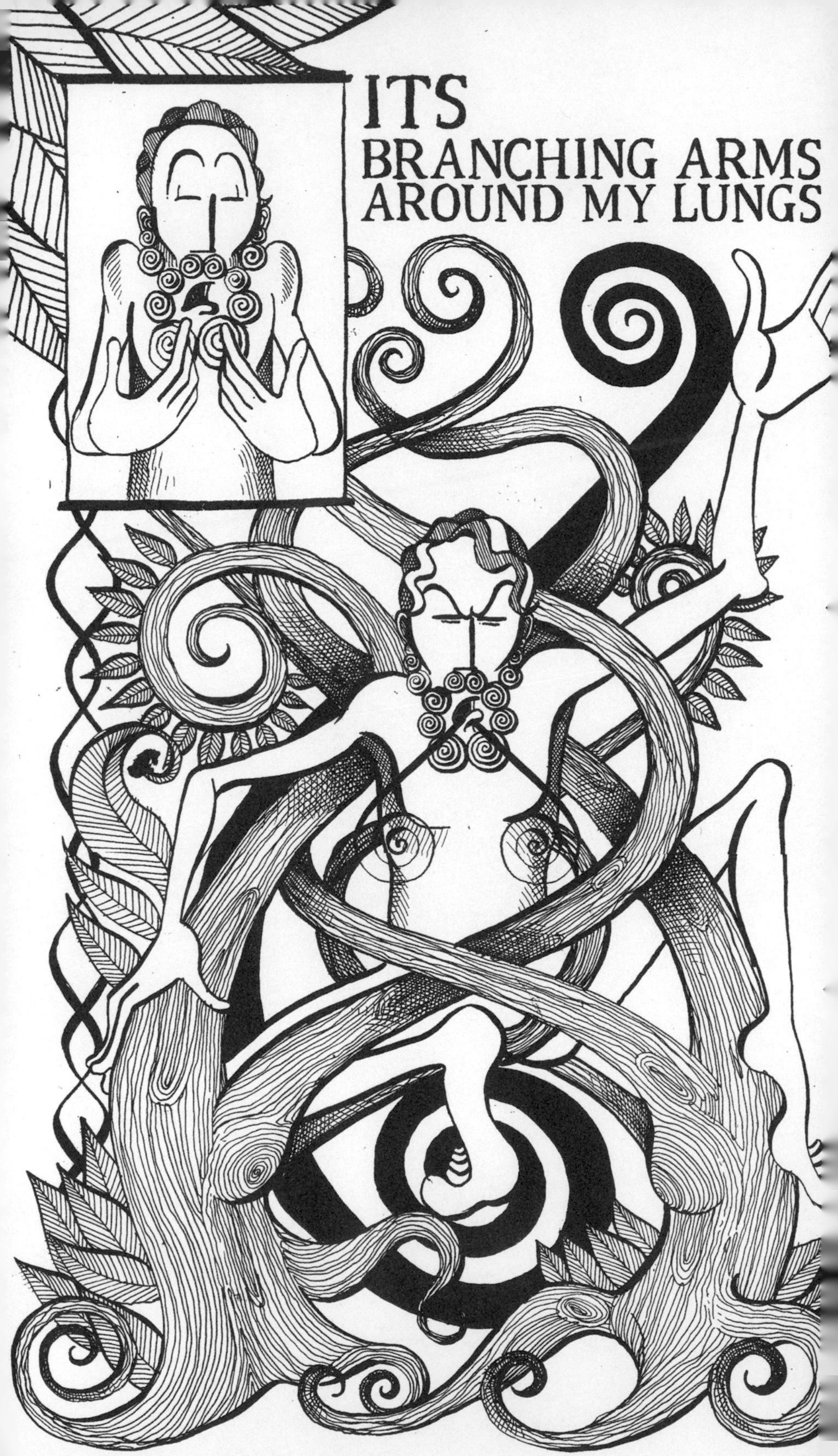
ITS
BRANCHING ARMS
AROUND MY LUNGS

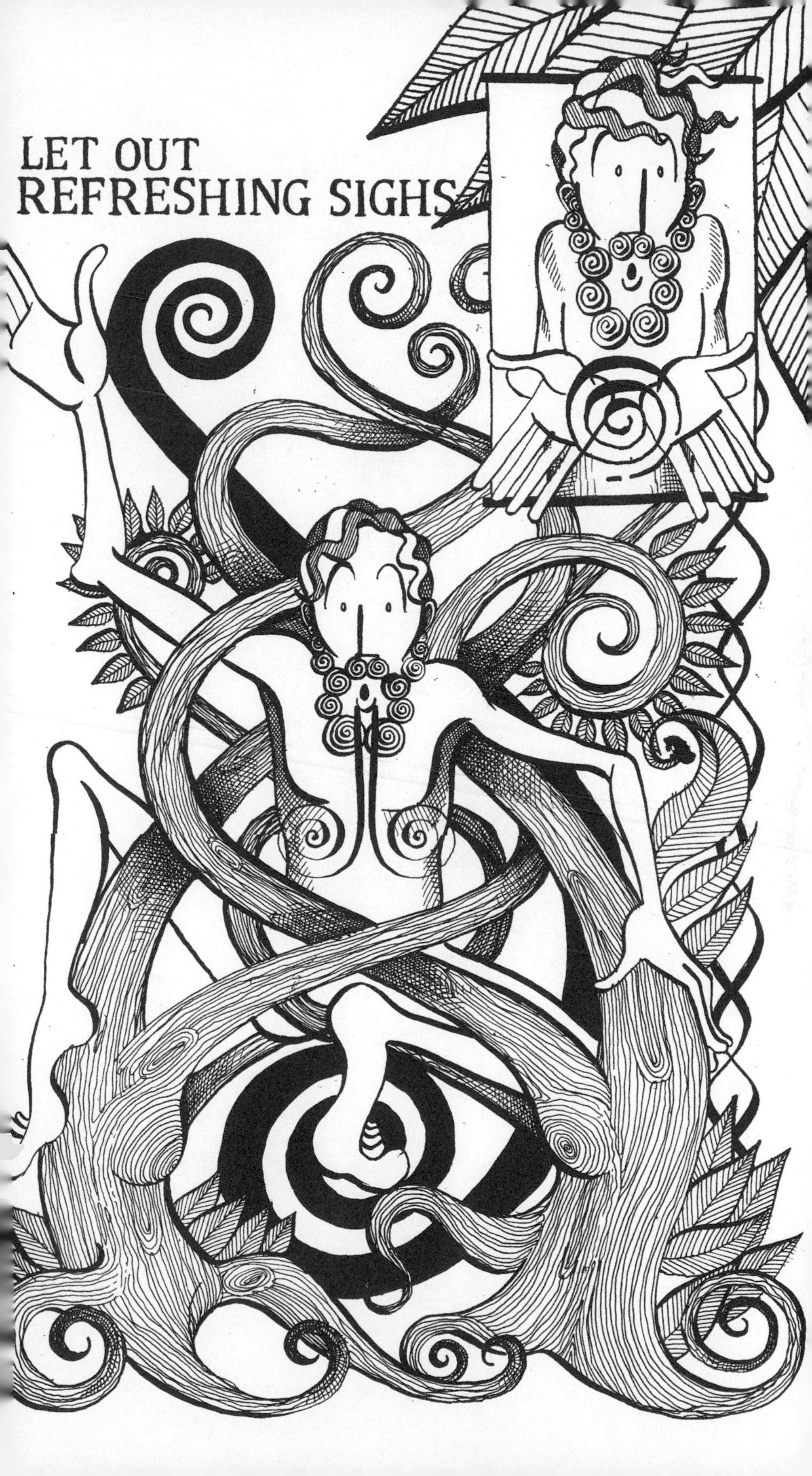
LET OUT
REFRESHING SIGHS

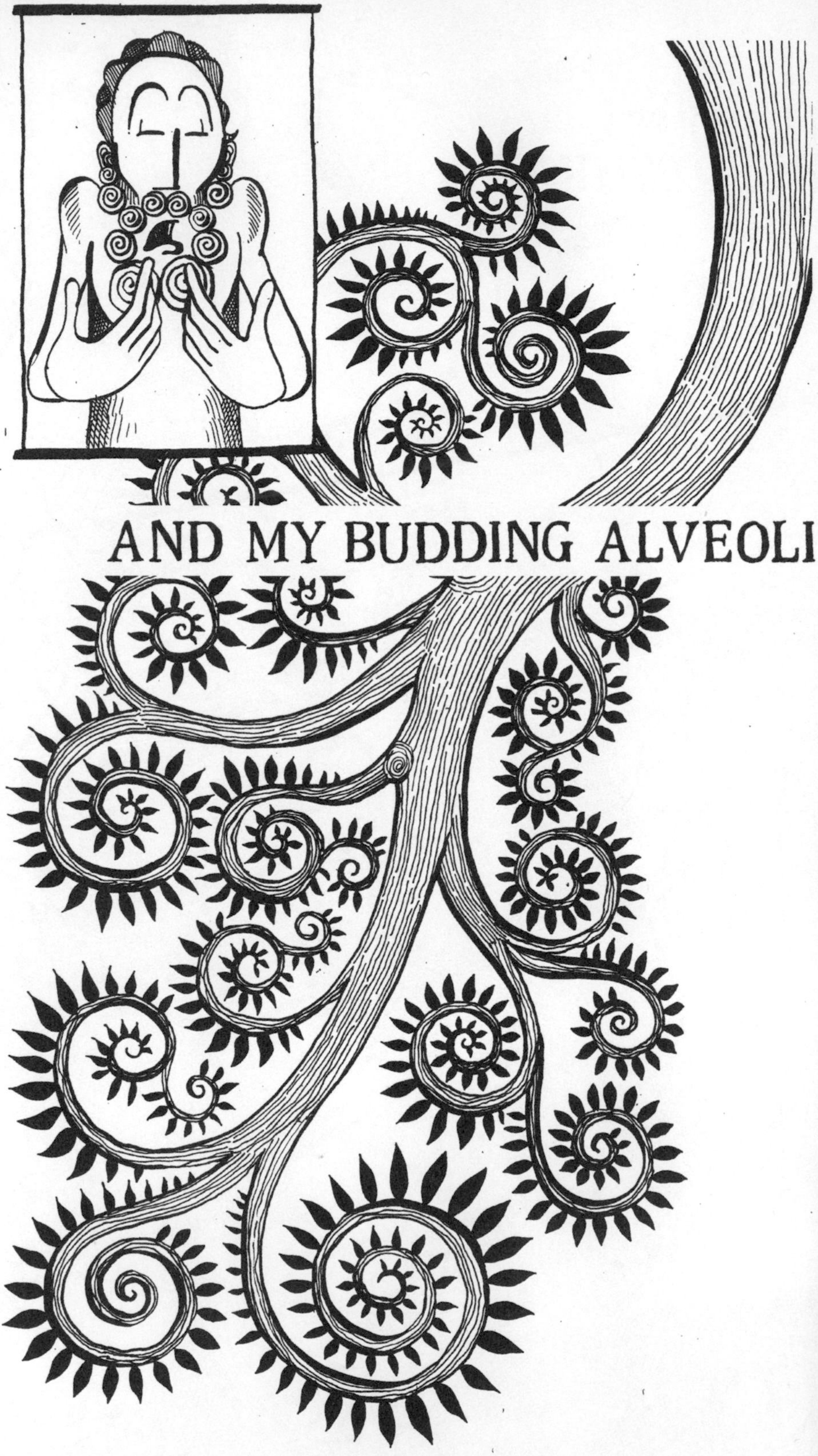
AND MY BUDDING ALVEOLI

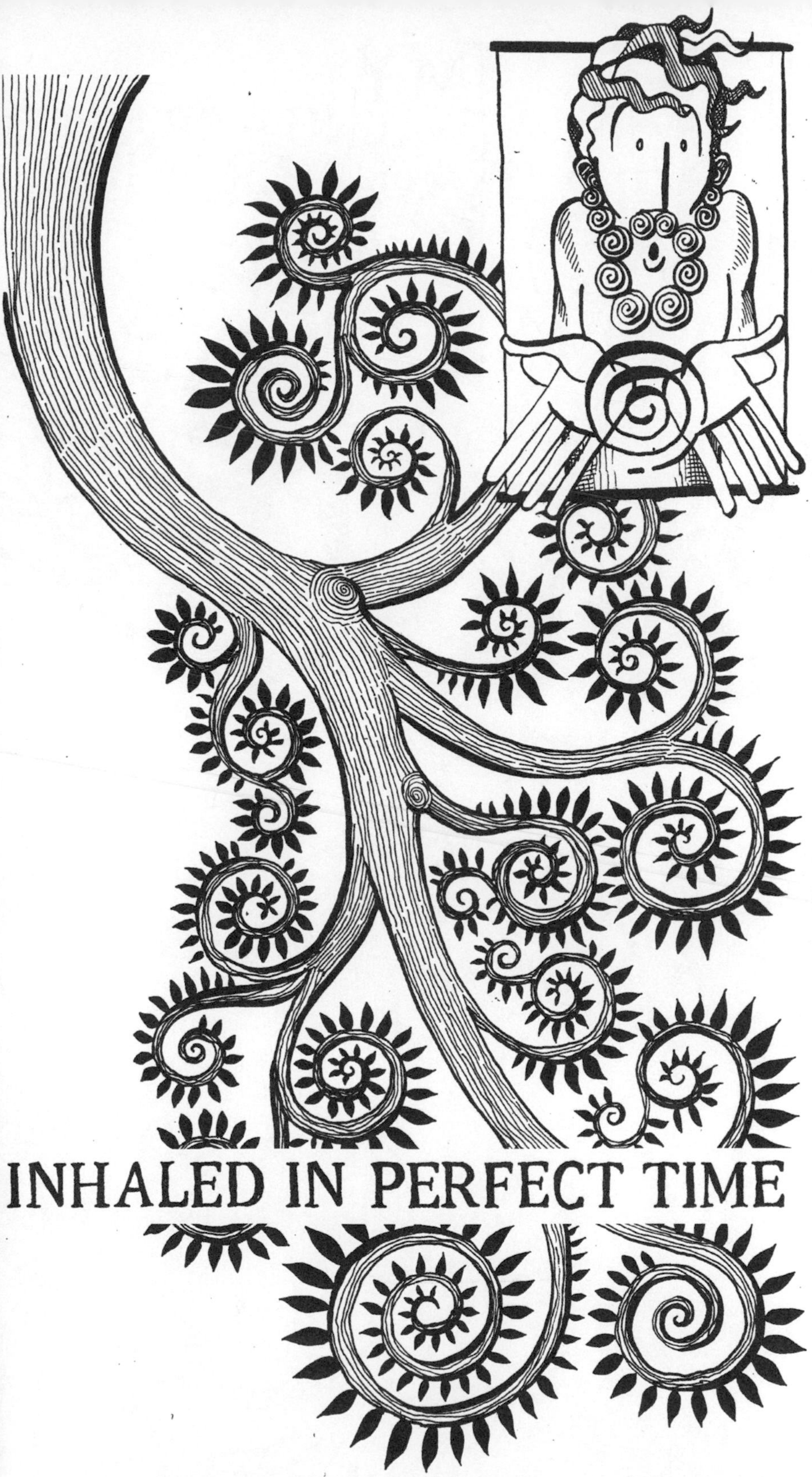

INHALED IN PERFECT TIME

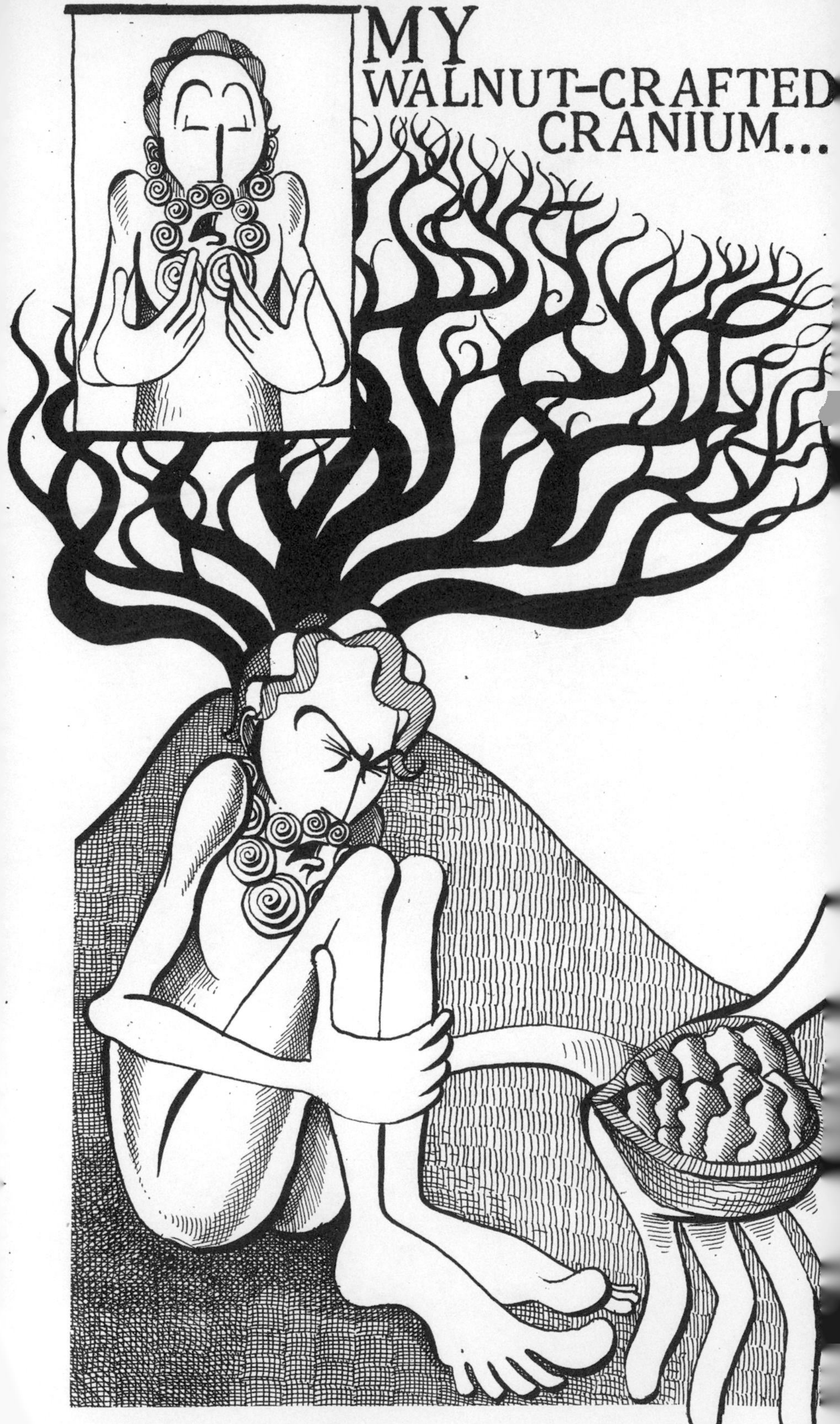
MY
WALNUT-CRAFTED
CRANIUM...

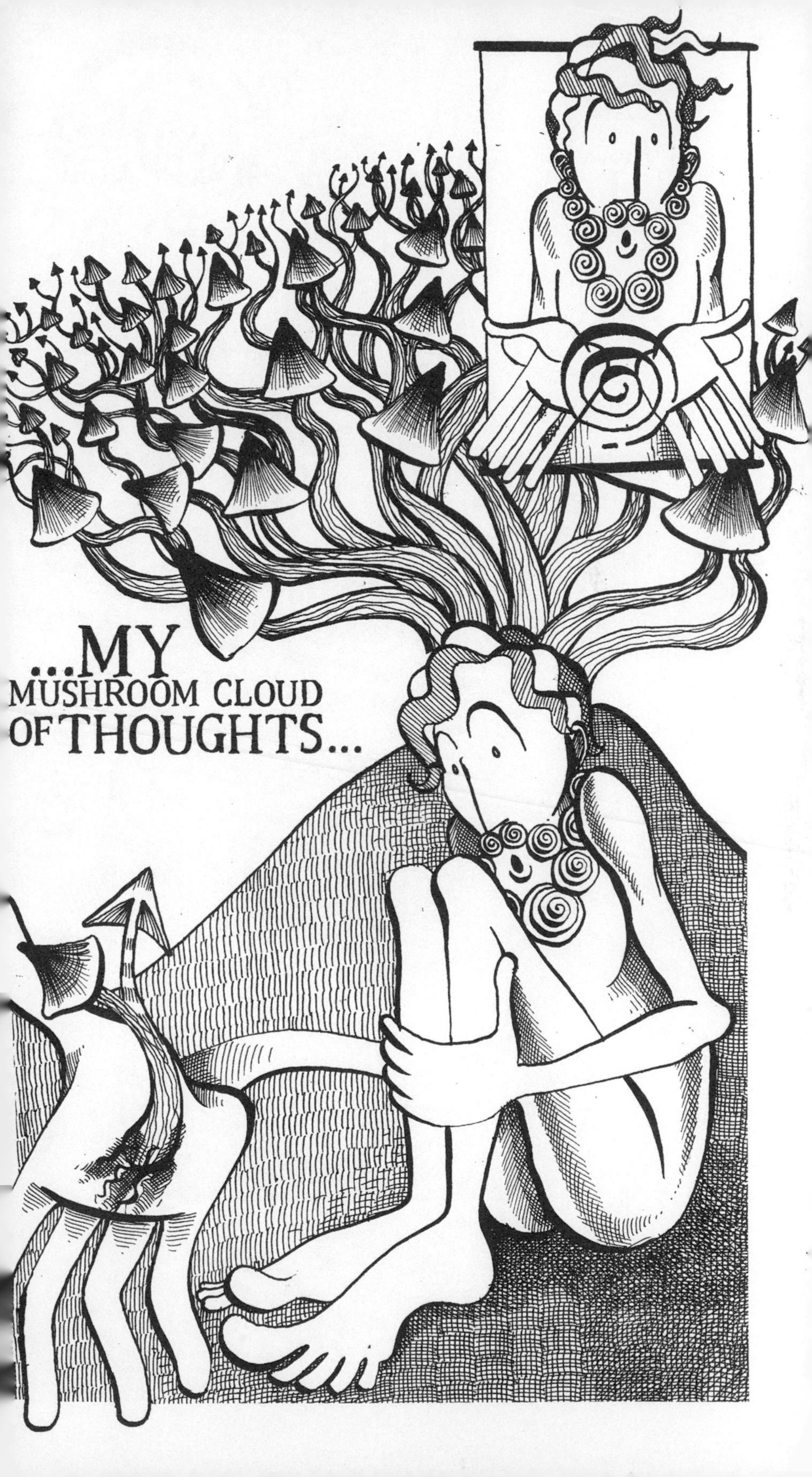
...MY
MUSHROOM CLOUD
OF THOUGHTS...

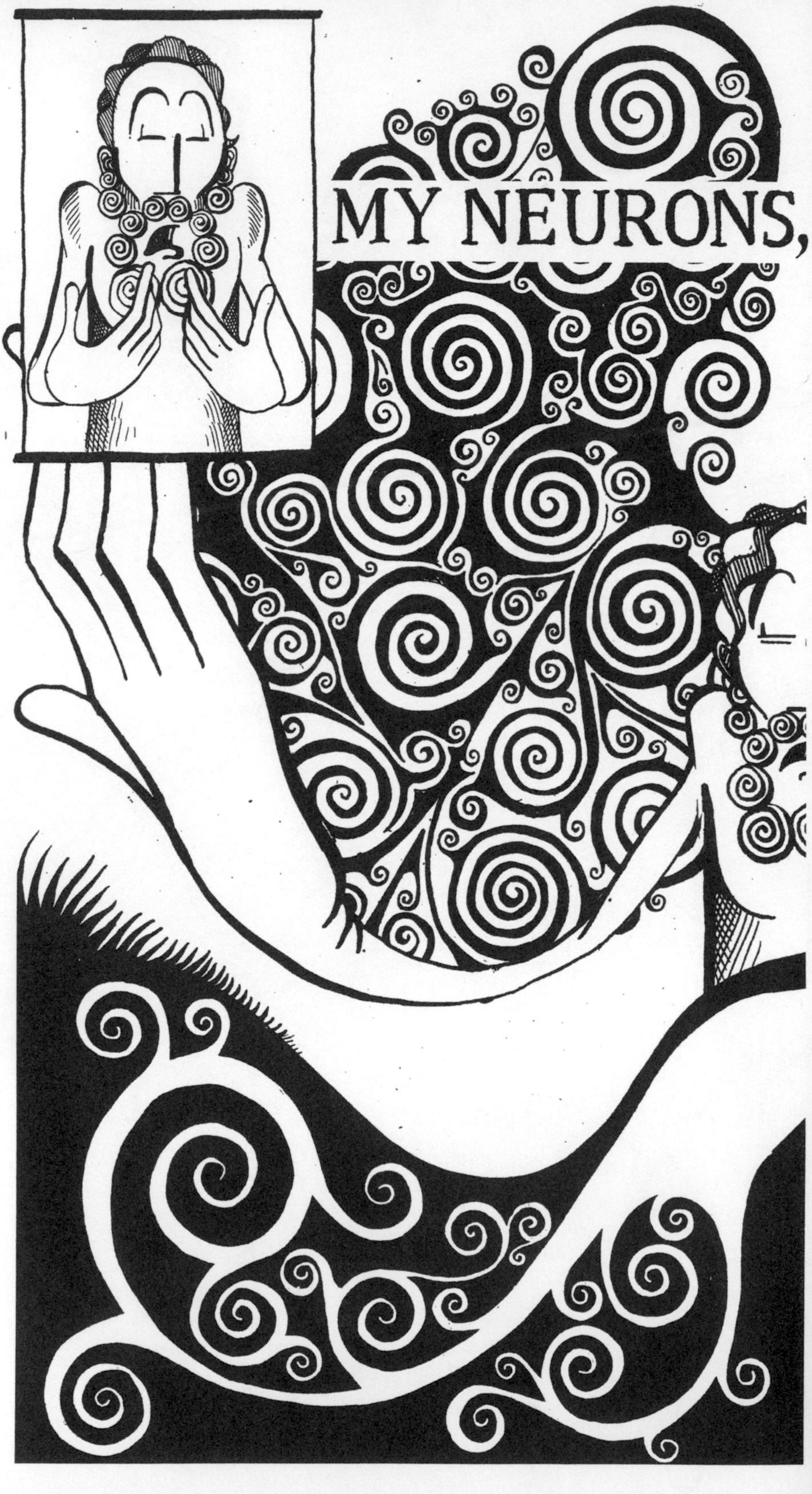
MY NEURONS,

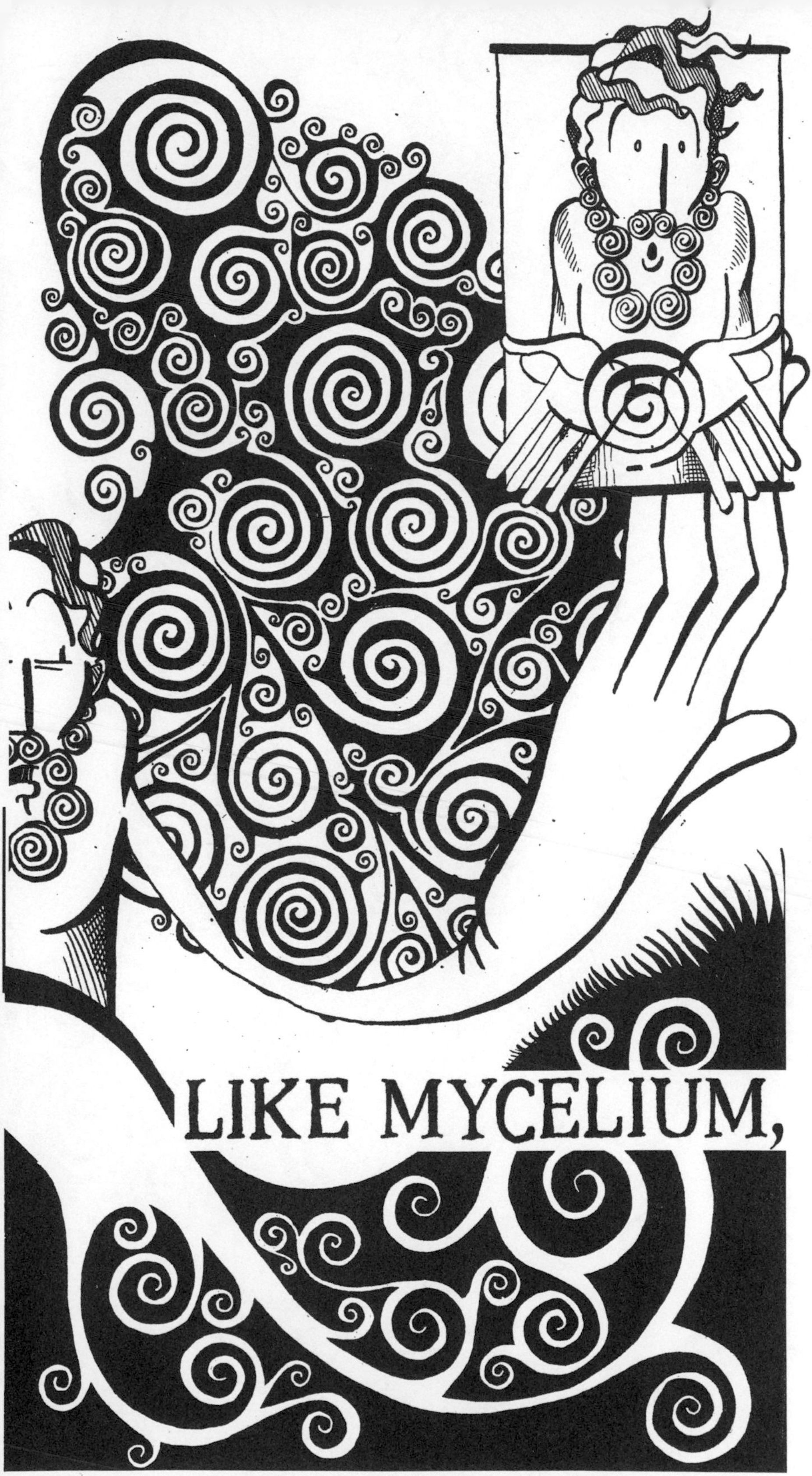
LIKE MYCELIUM,

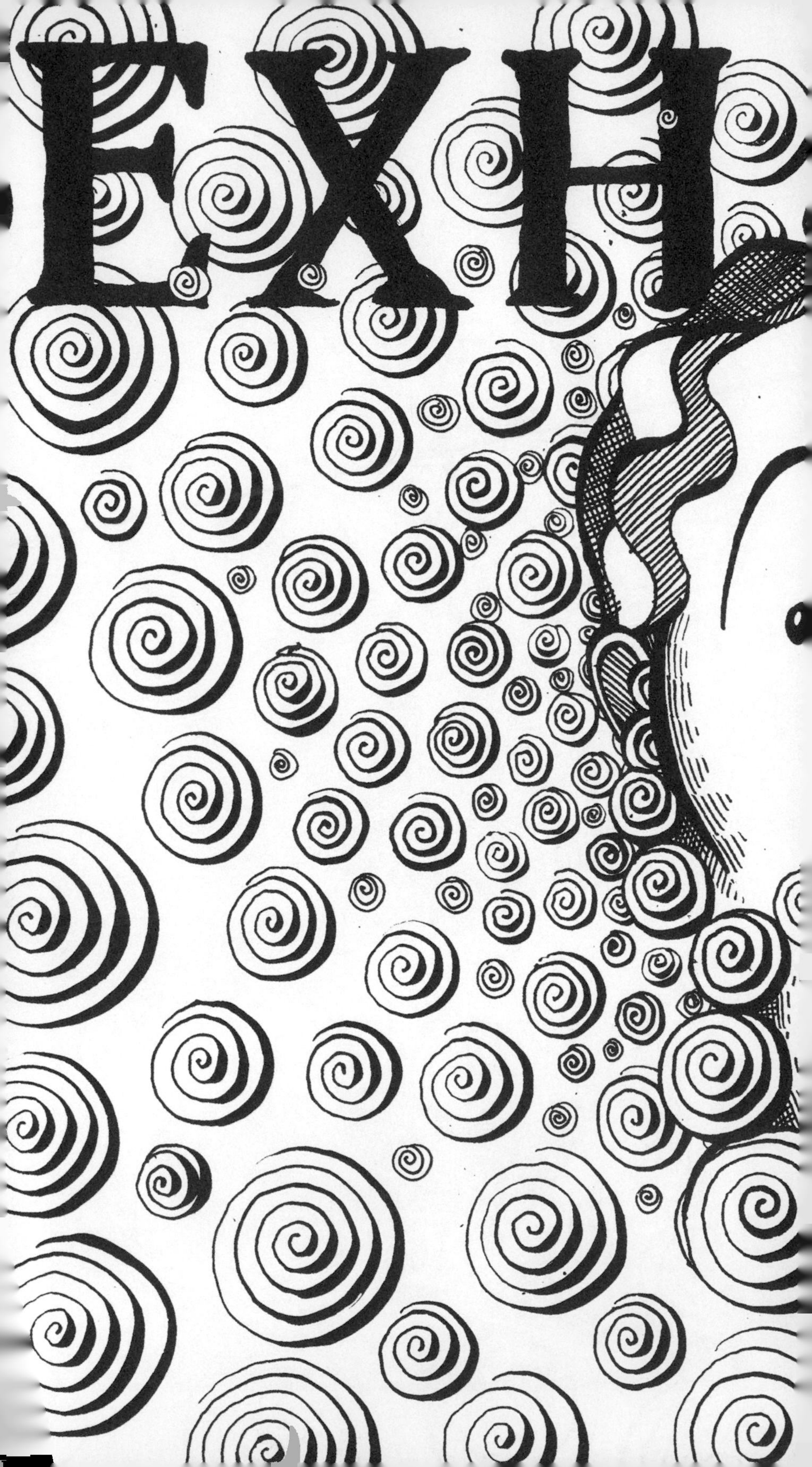
EXH

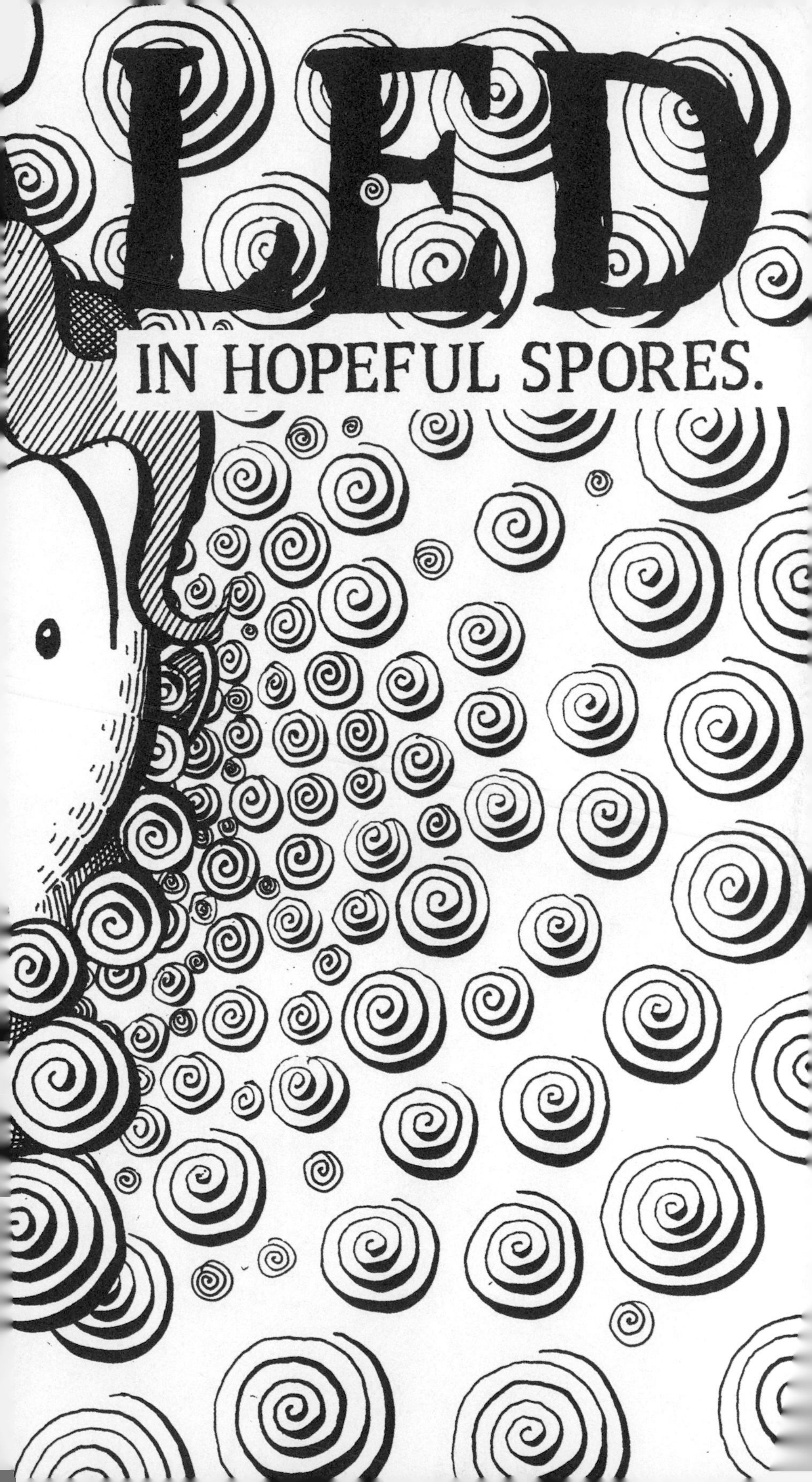
LED
IN HOPEFUL SPORES.

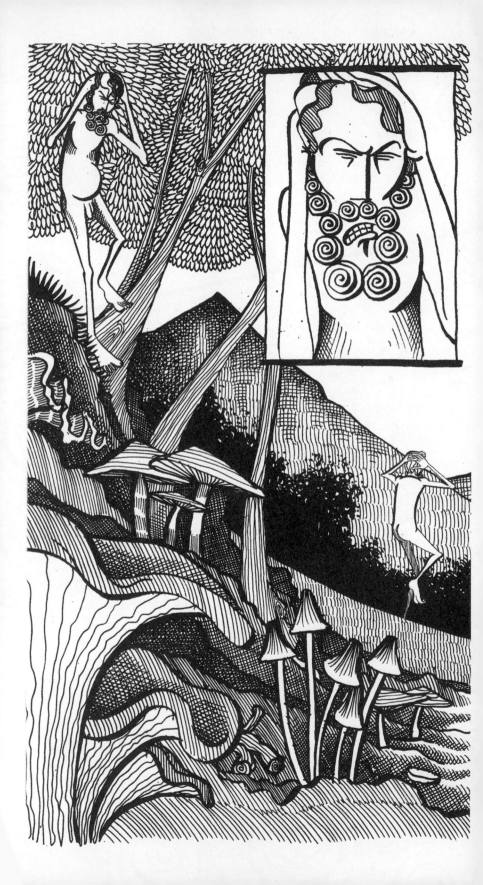

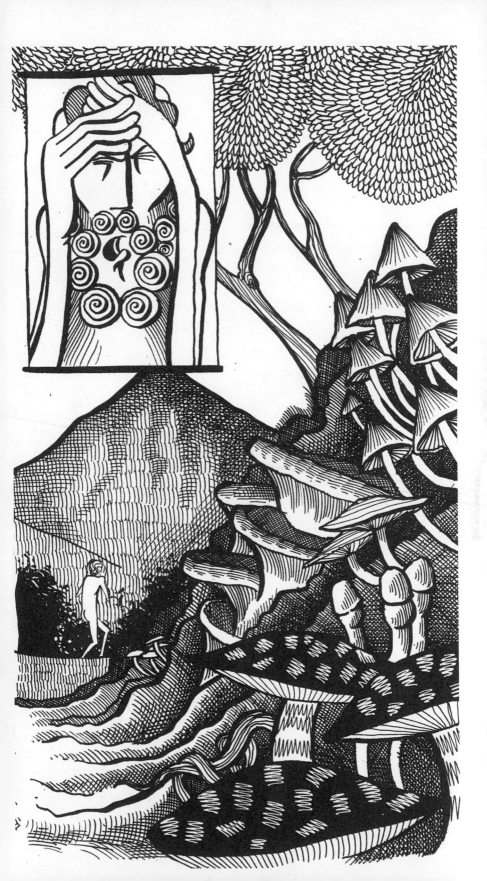

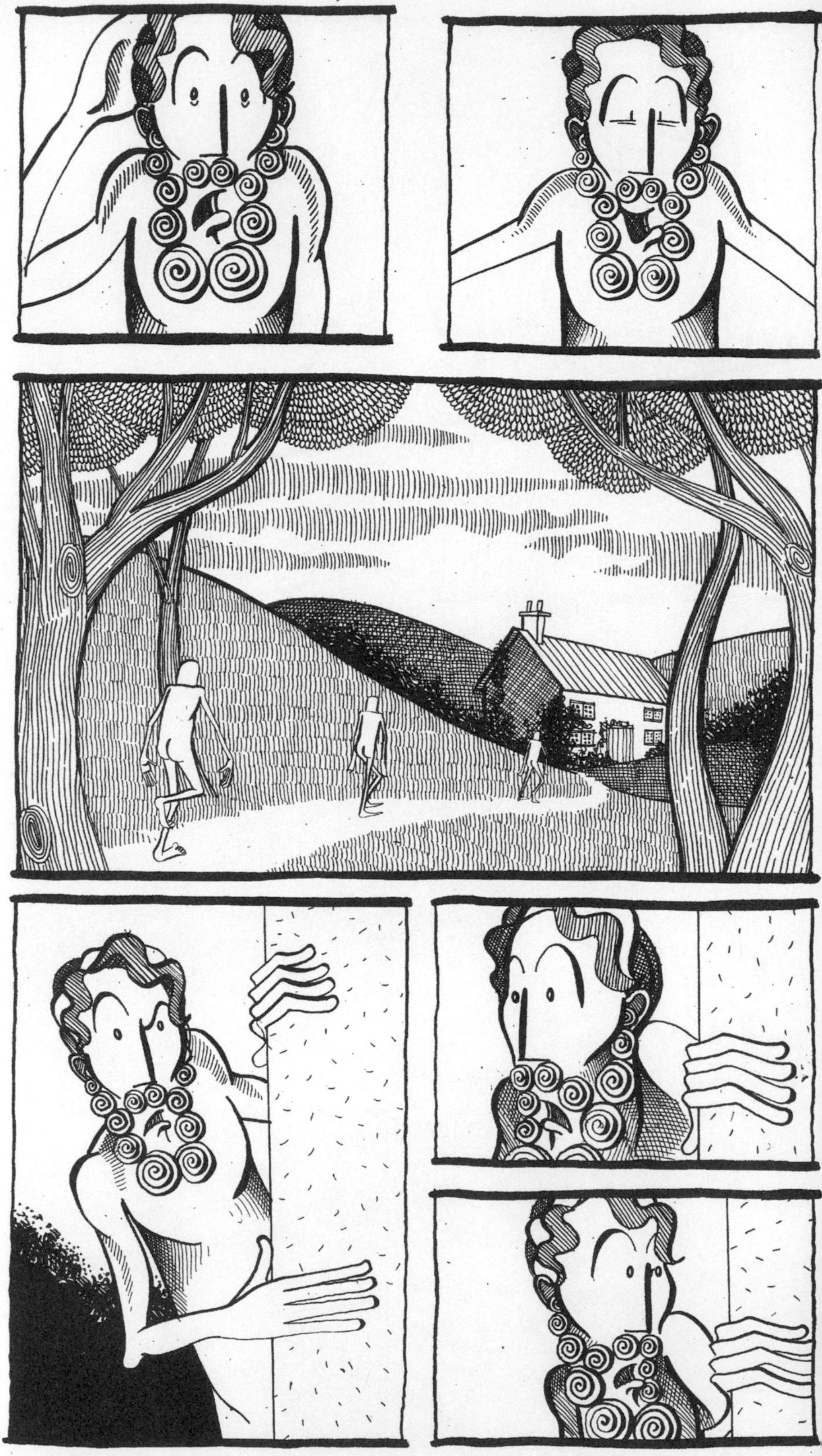

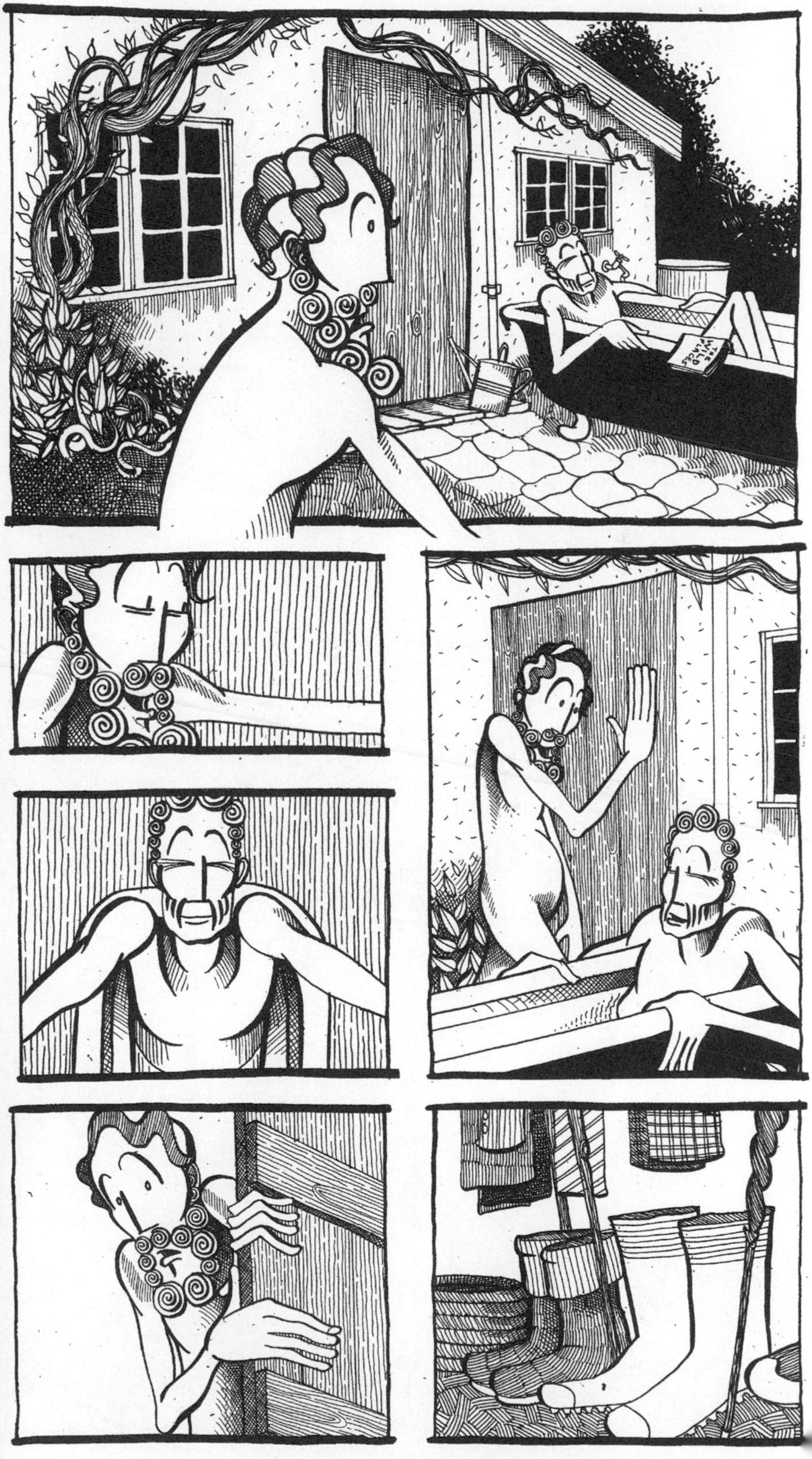
THE WILD PLACES

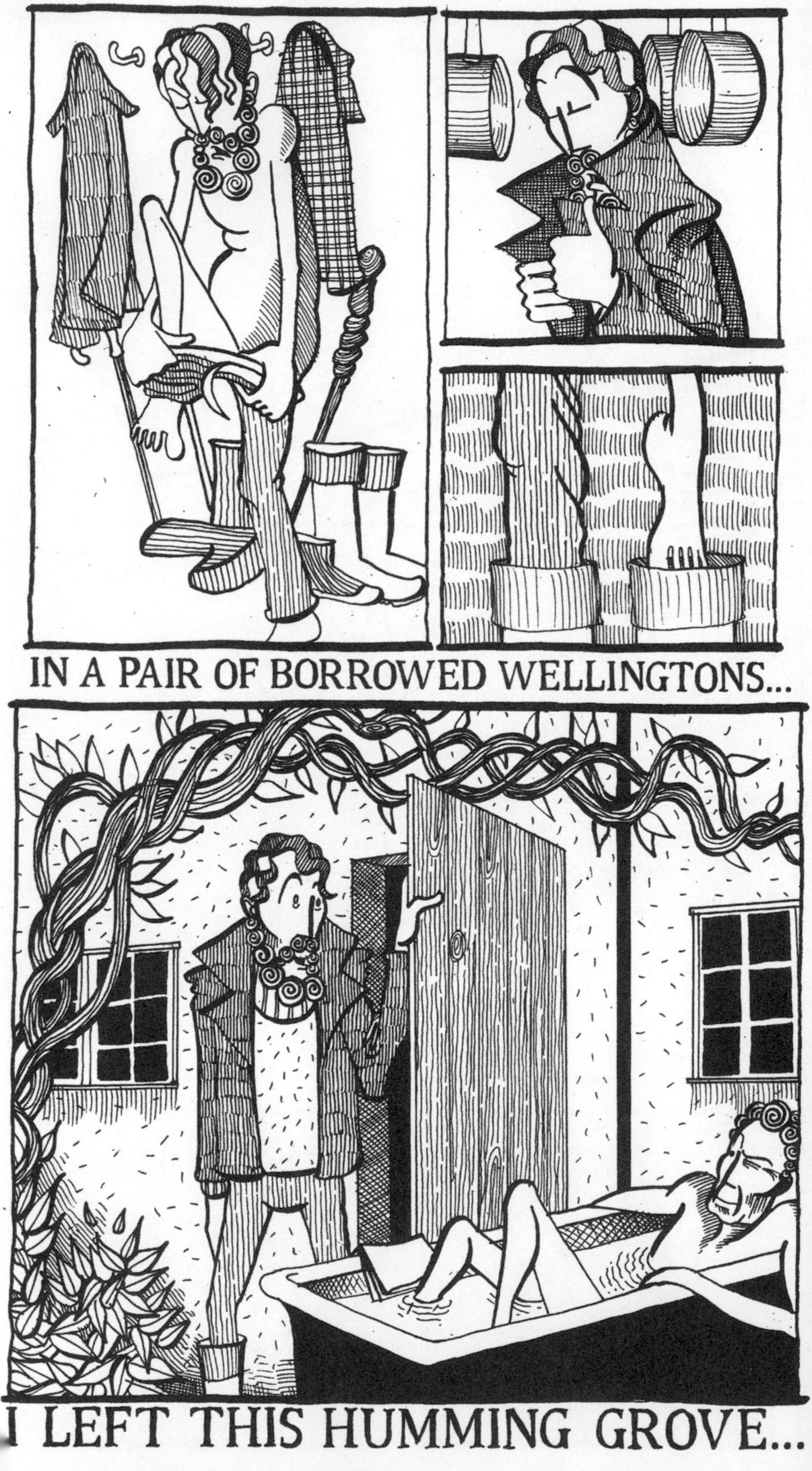
IN A PAIR OF BORROWED WELLINGTONS...
I LEFT THIS HUMMING GROVE...

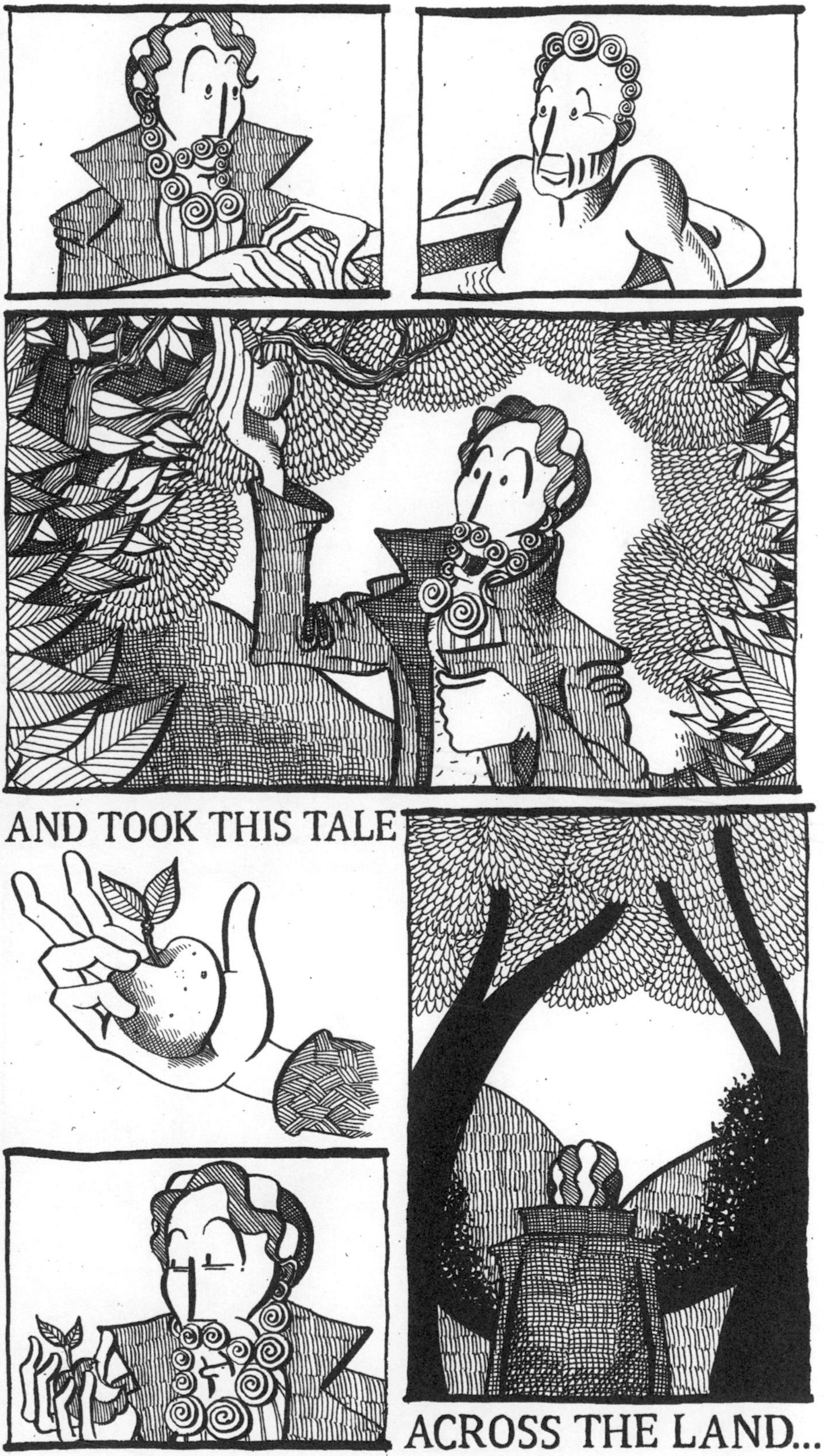
AND TOOK THIS TALE
ACROSS THE LAND...

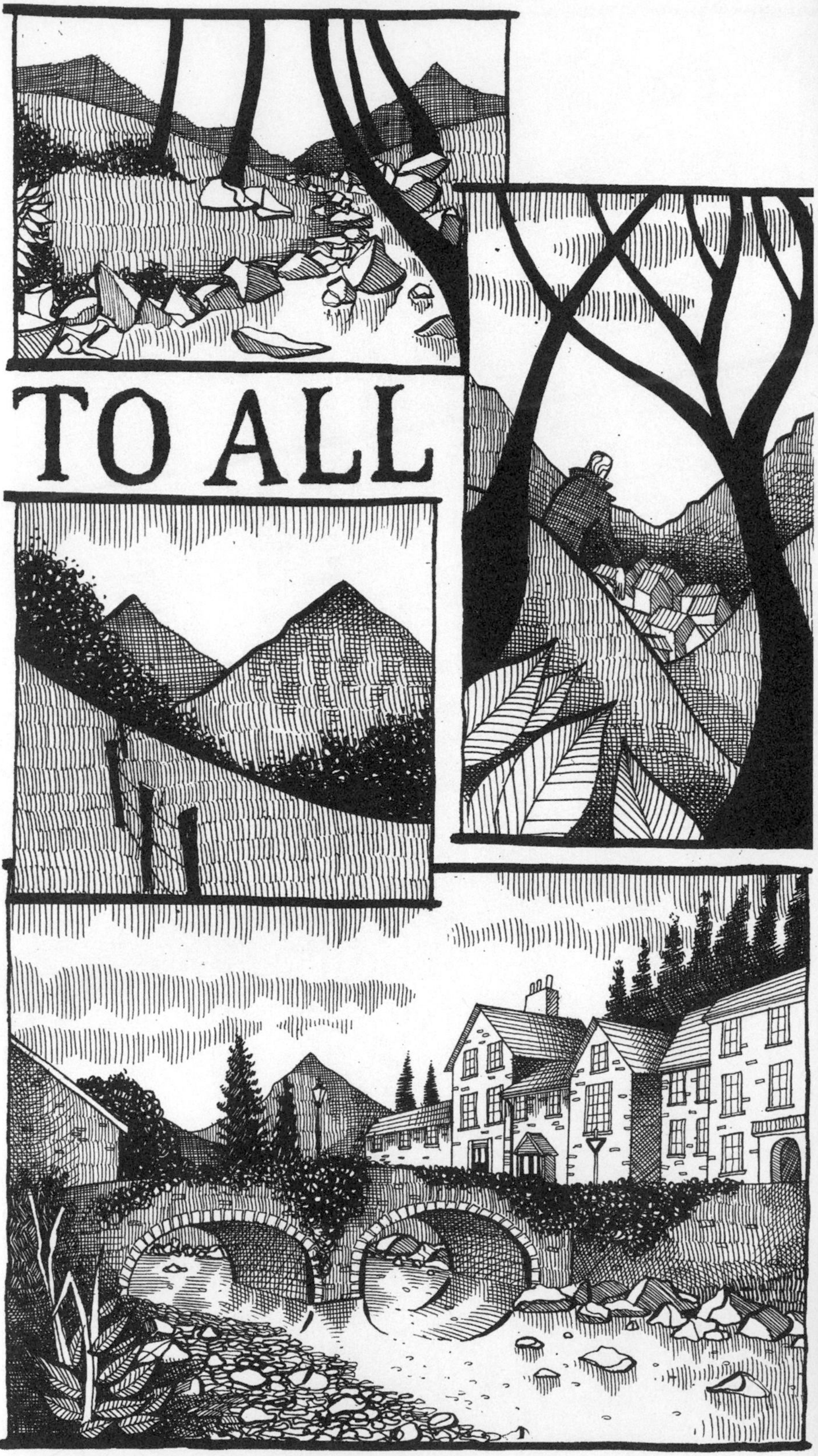
TO ALL

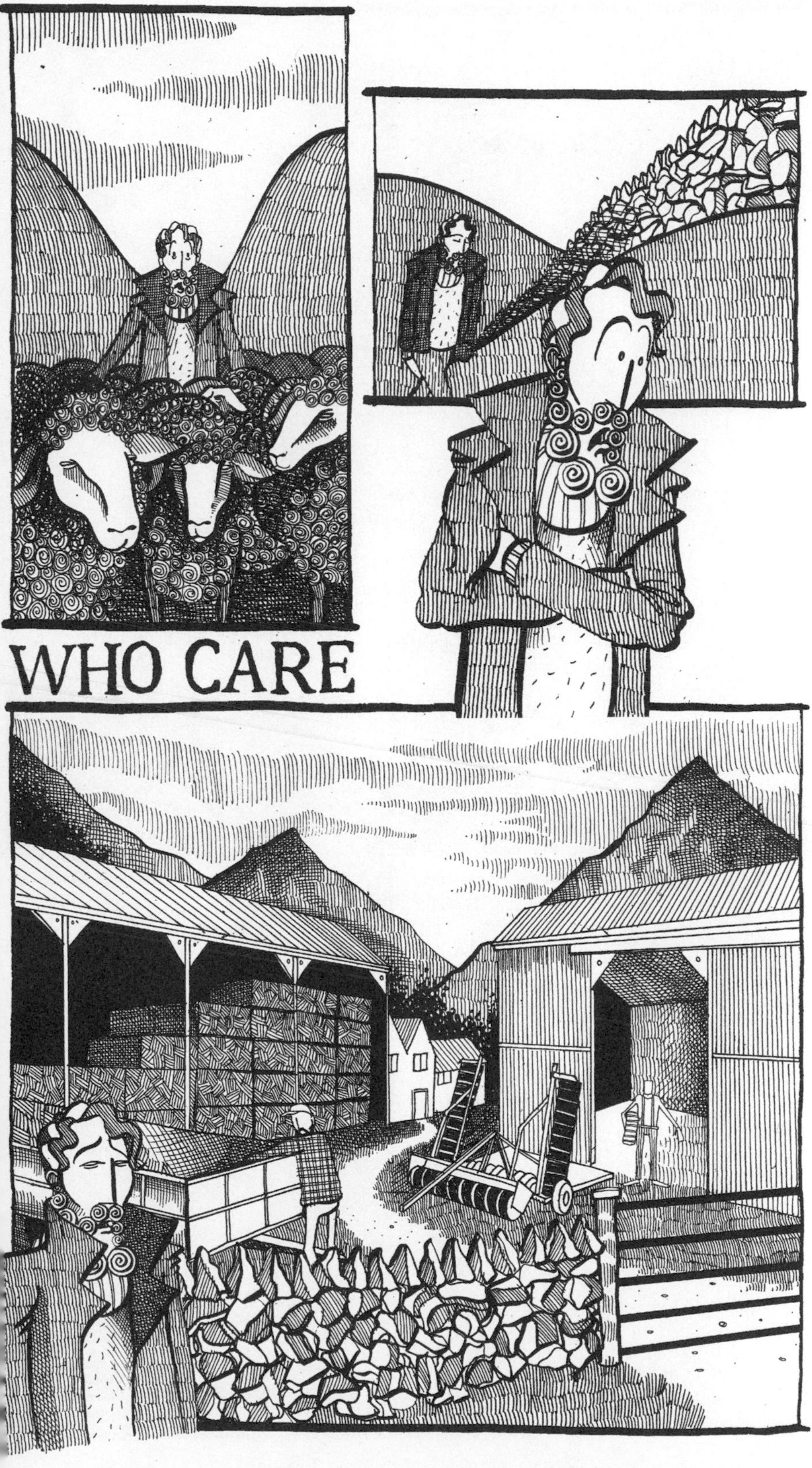
WHO CARE

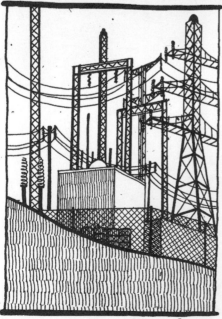

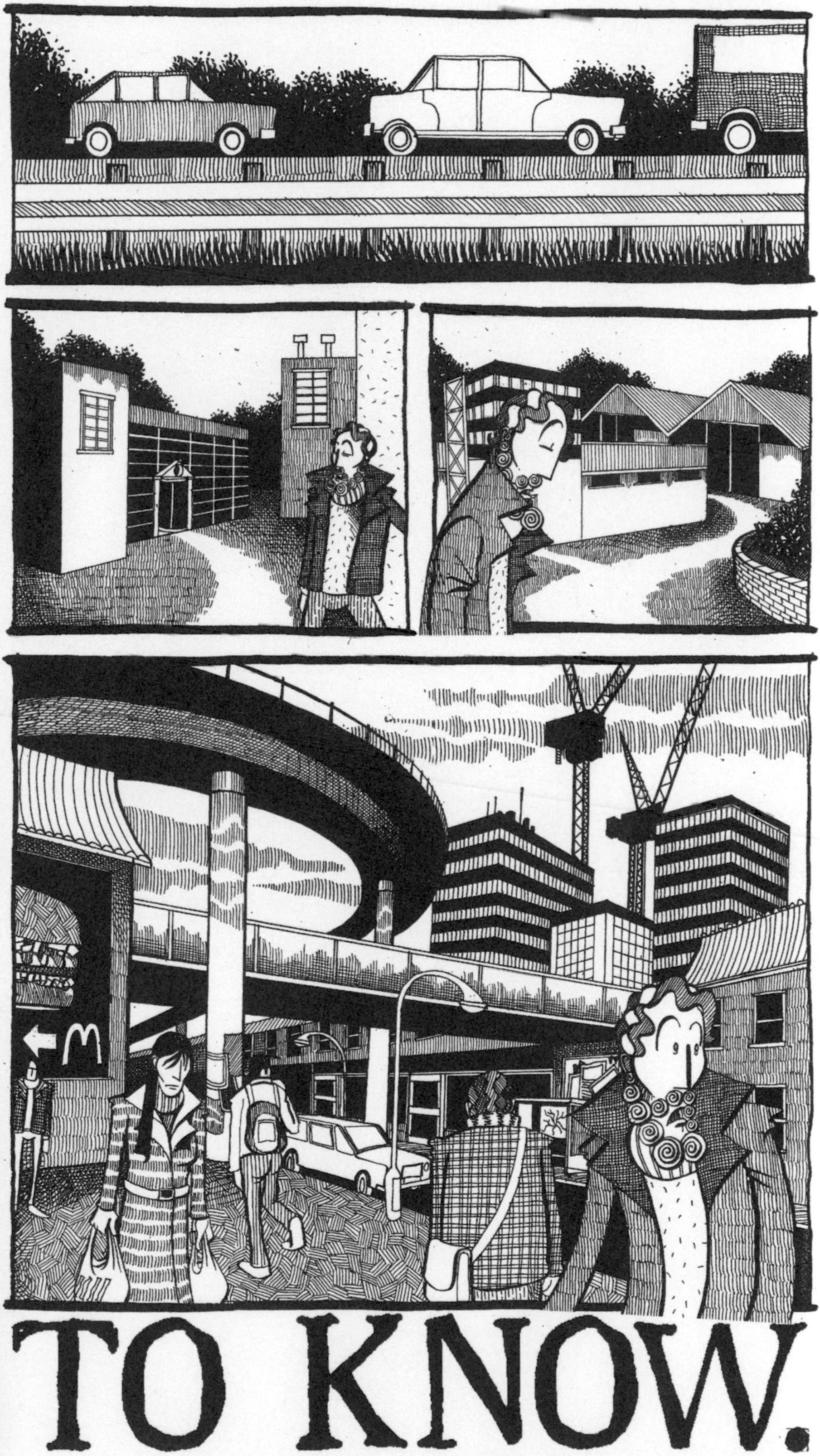

TO KNOW.

PART EIGHT

THE
MARINER

THEN TURNED
HIS HEAD...

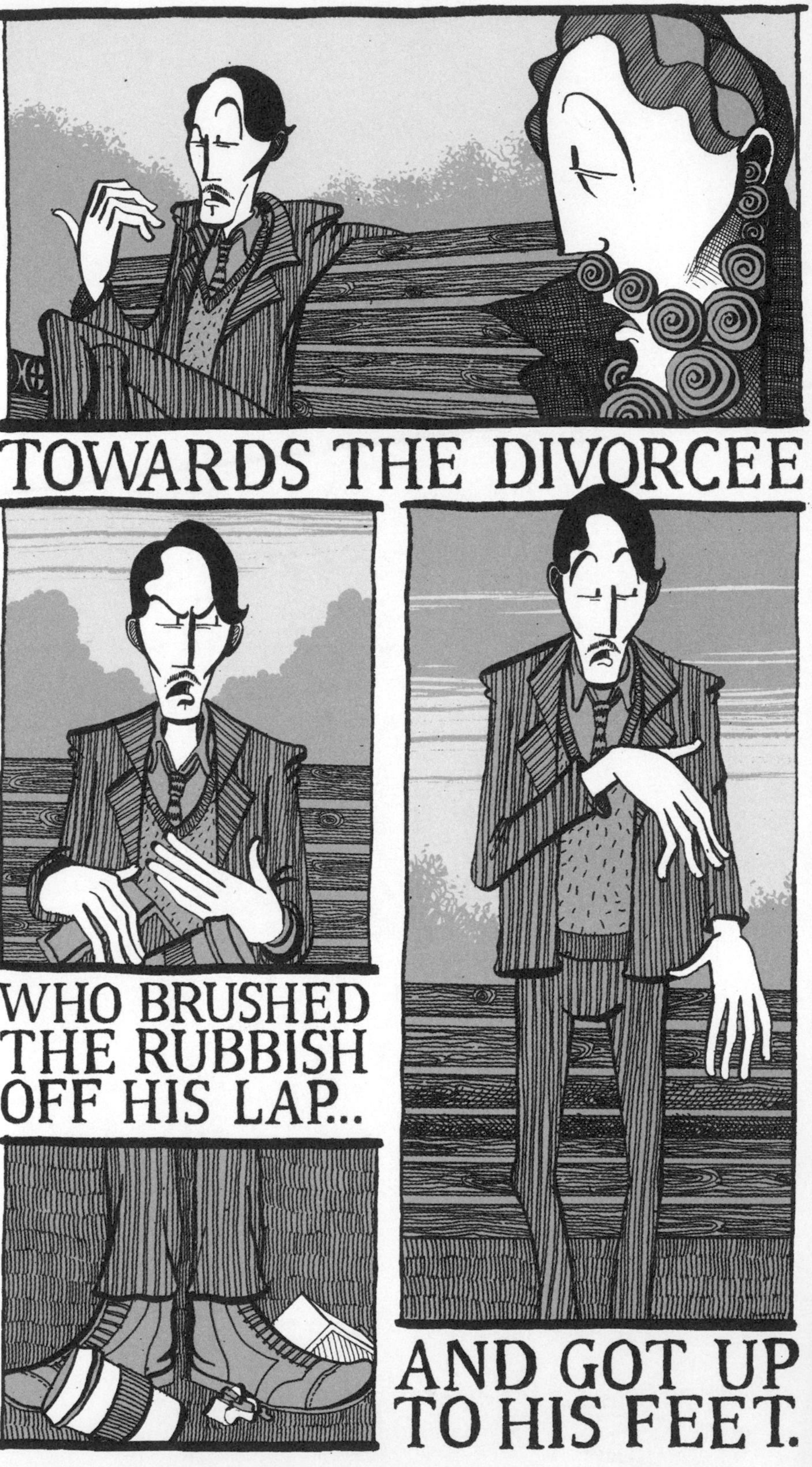
TOWARDS THE DIVORCEE
WHO BRUSHED THE RUBBISH OFF HIS LAP...
AND GOT UP TO HIS FEET.

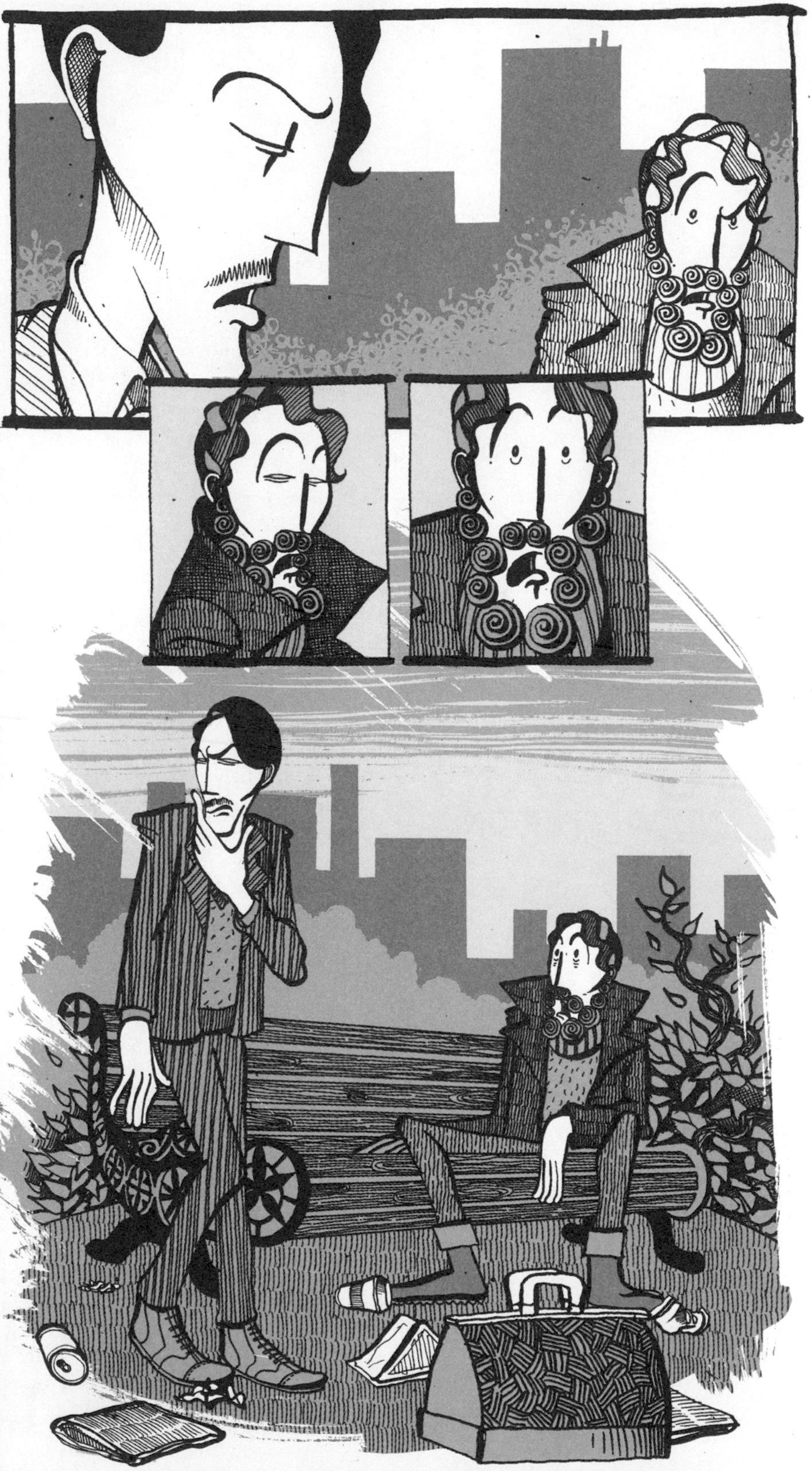

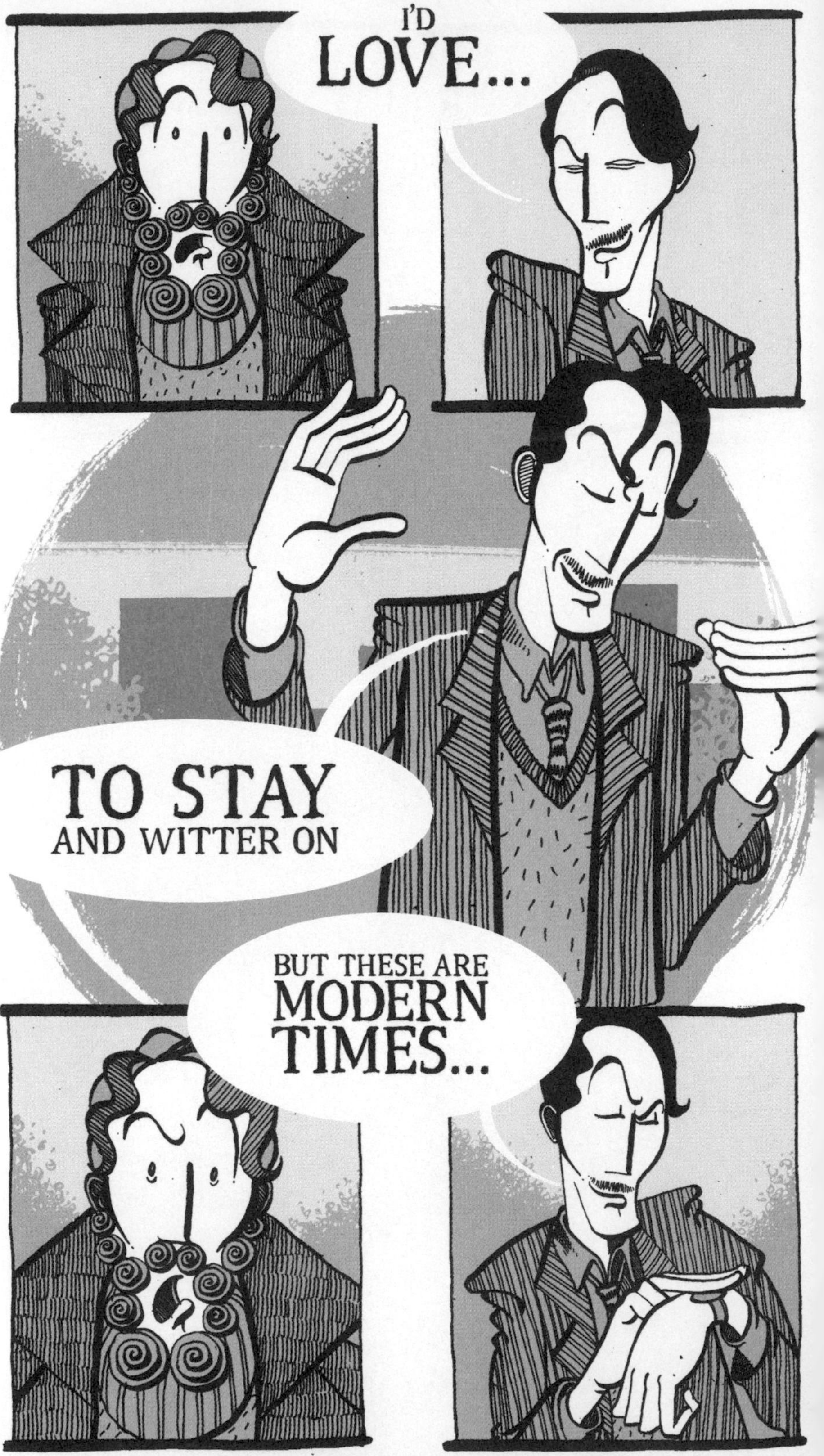
I'D LOVE...
TO STAY AND WITTER ON
BUT THESE ARE MODERN TIMES...

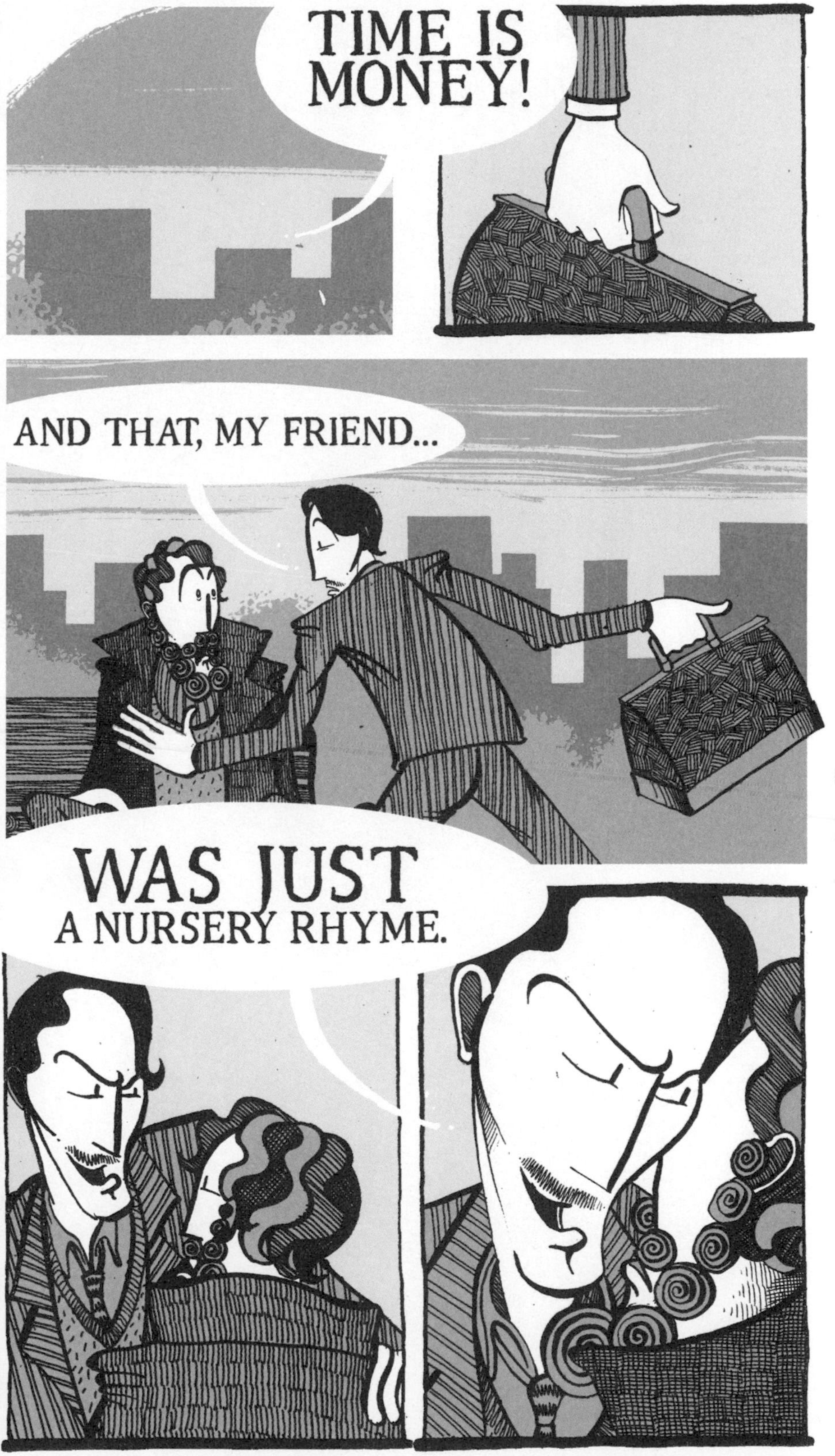
TIME IS MONEY!
AND THAT, MY FRIEND...
WAS JUST A NURSERY RHYME.

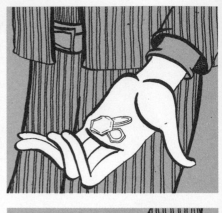

HE PAID THE SEAMAN
FOR HIS TIME

AND QUICKLY HURRIED ON

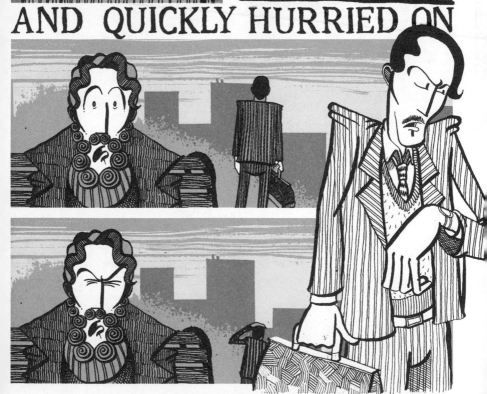

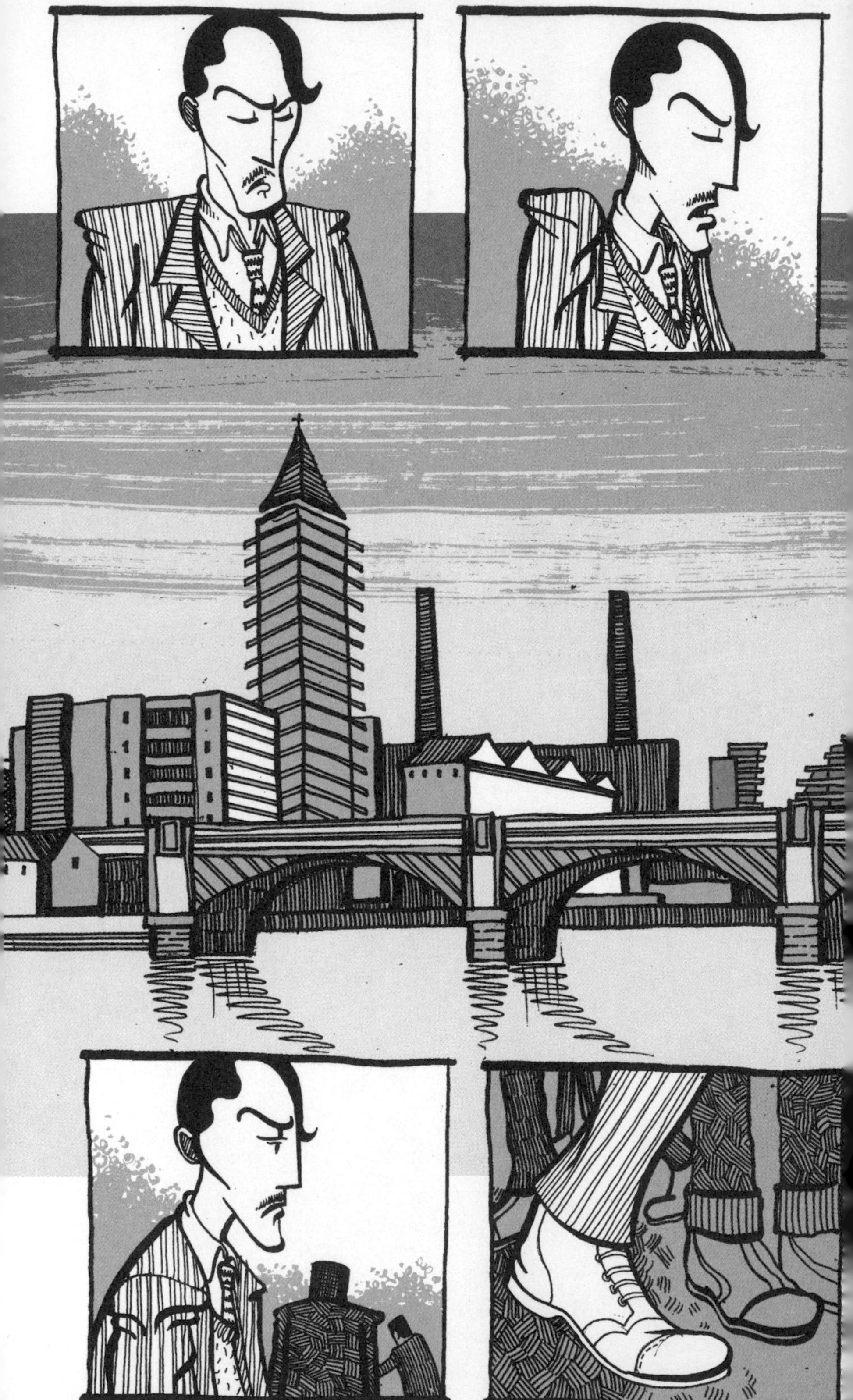

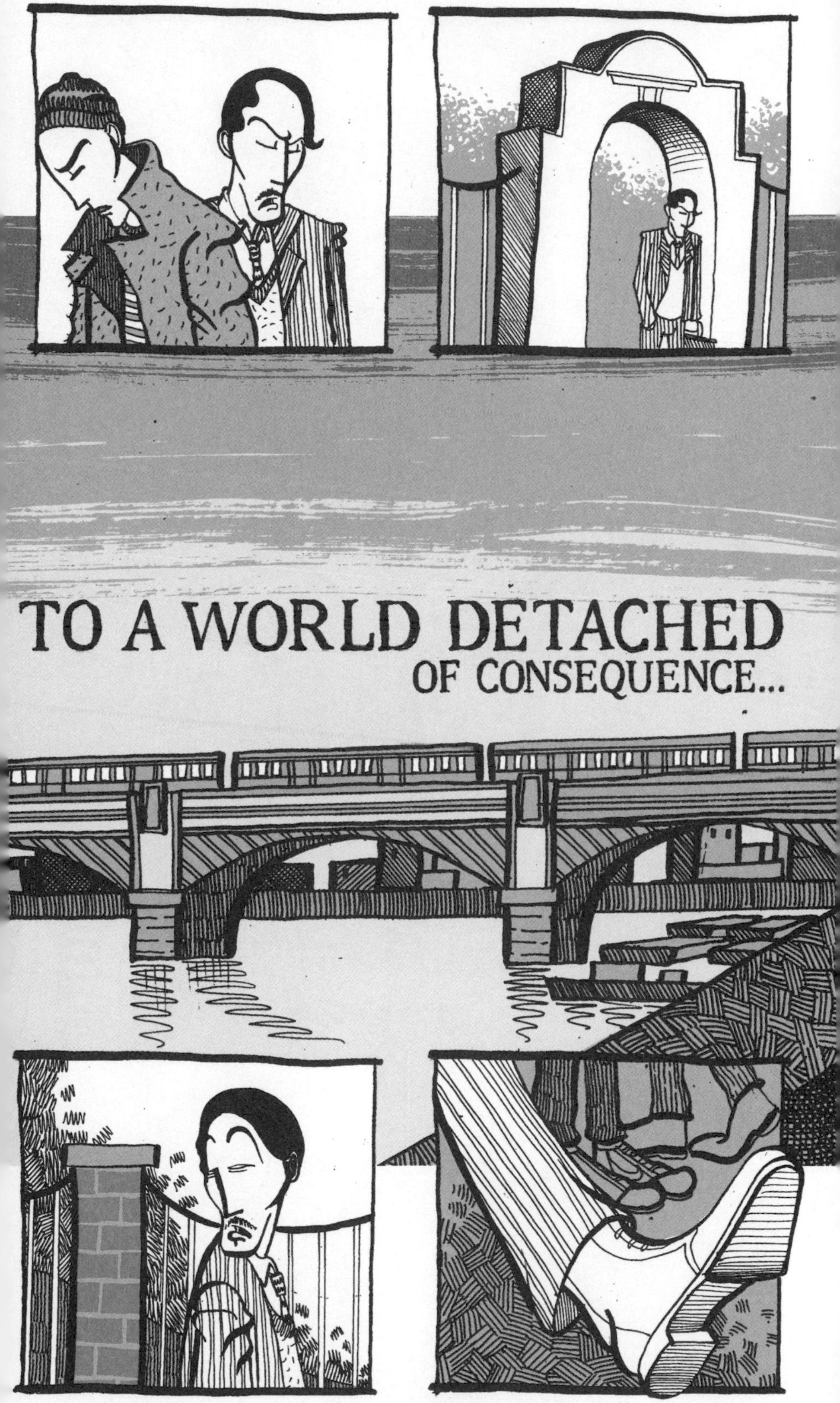
TO A WORLD DETACHED
OF CONSEQUENCE...

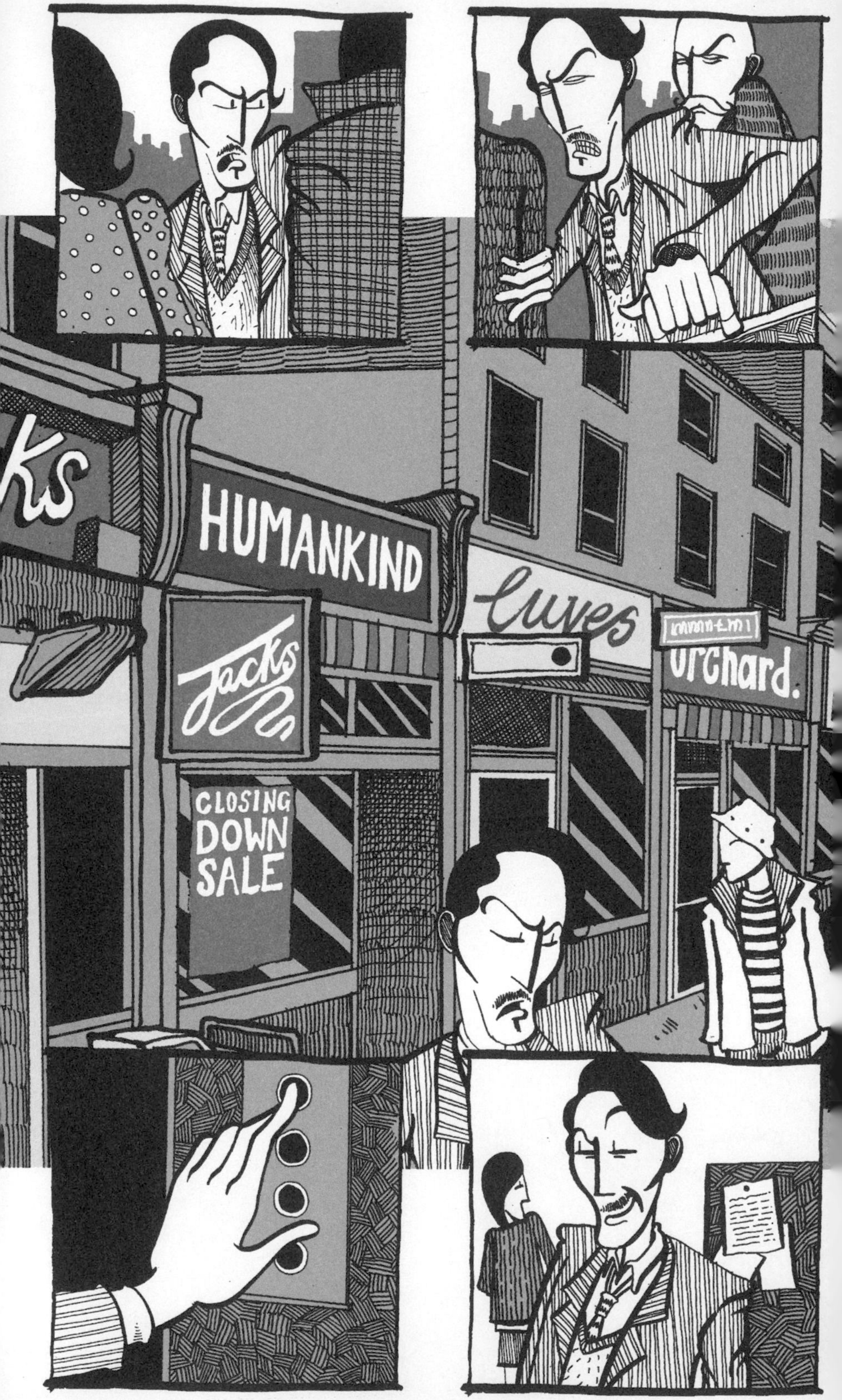
HUMANKIND
Jacks
Luves
Orchard.
CLOSING DOWN SALE

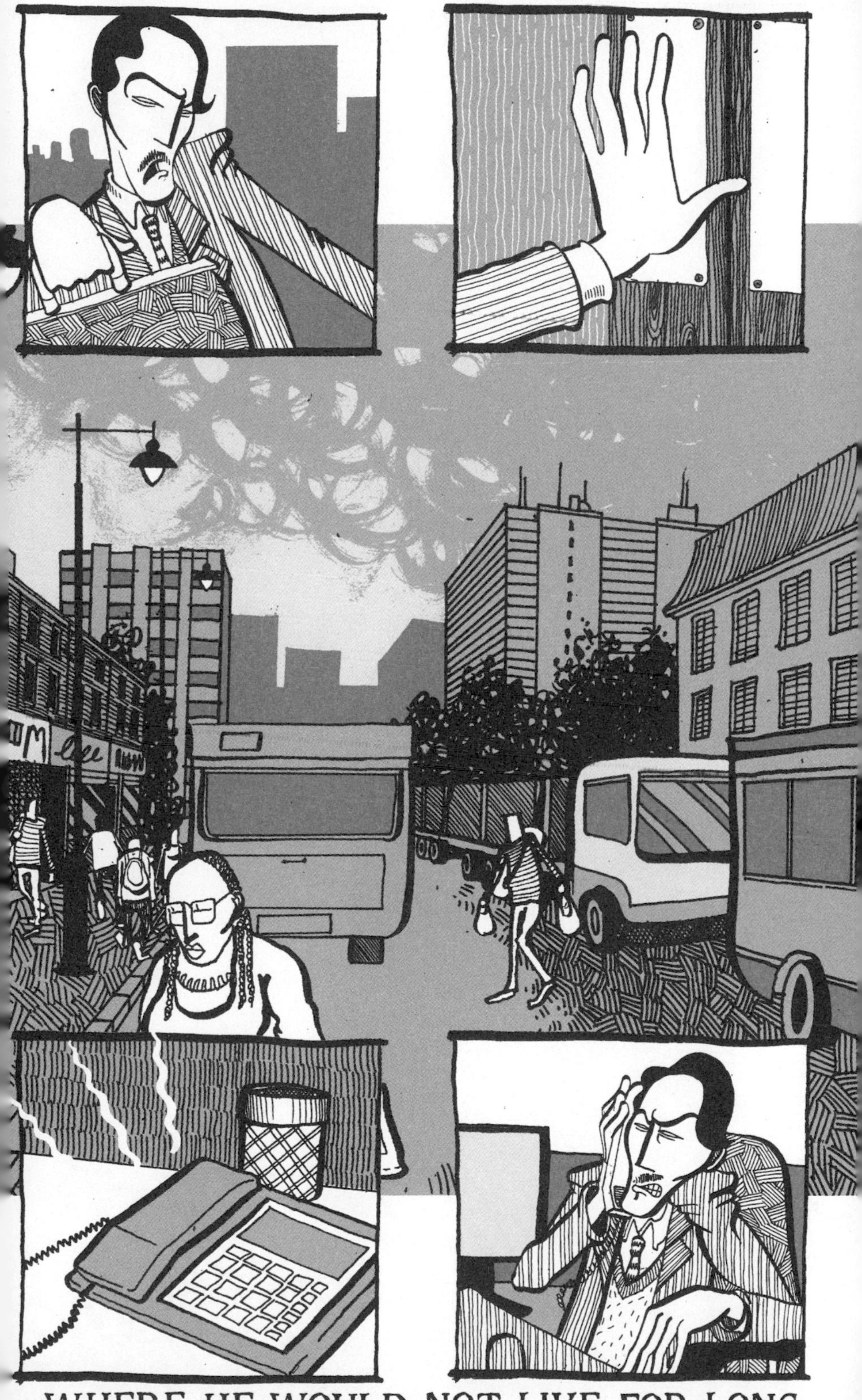

...WHERE HE WOULD NOT LIVE FOR LONG.

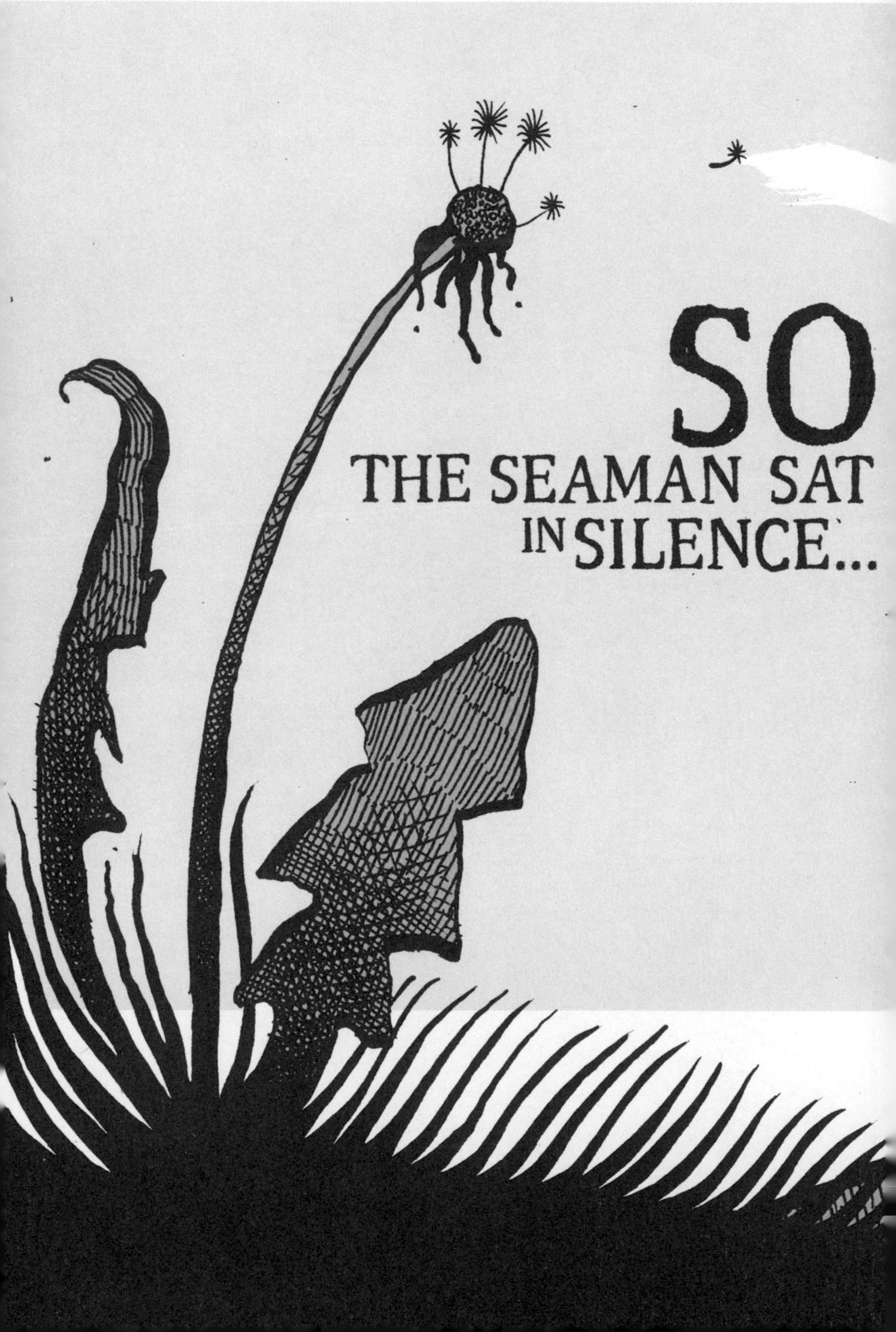
SO
THE SEAMAN SAT
IN SILENCE...

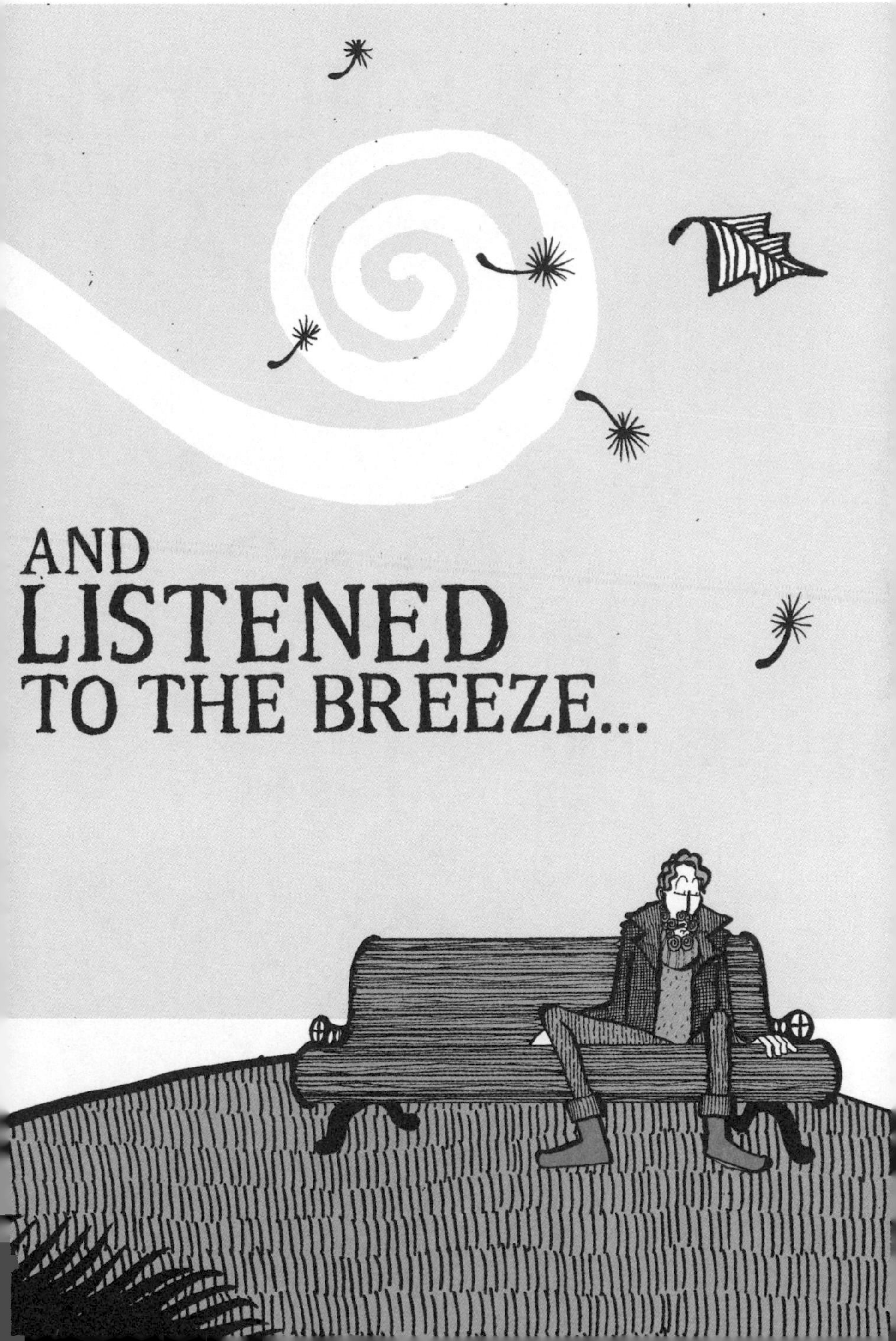
AND
LISTENED
TO THE BREEZE...

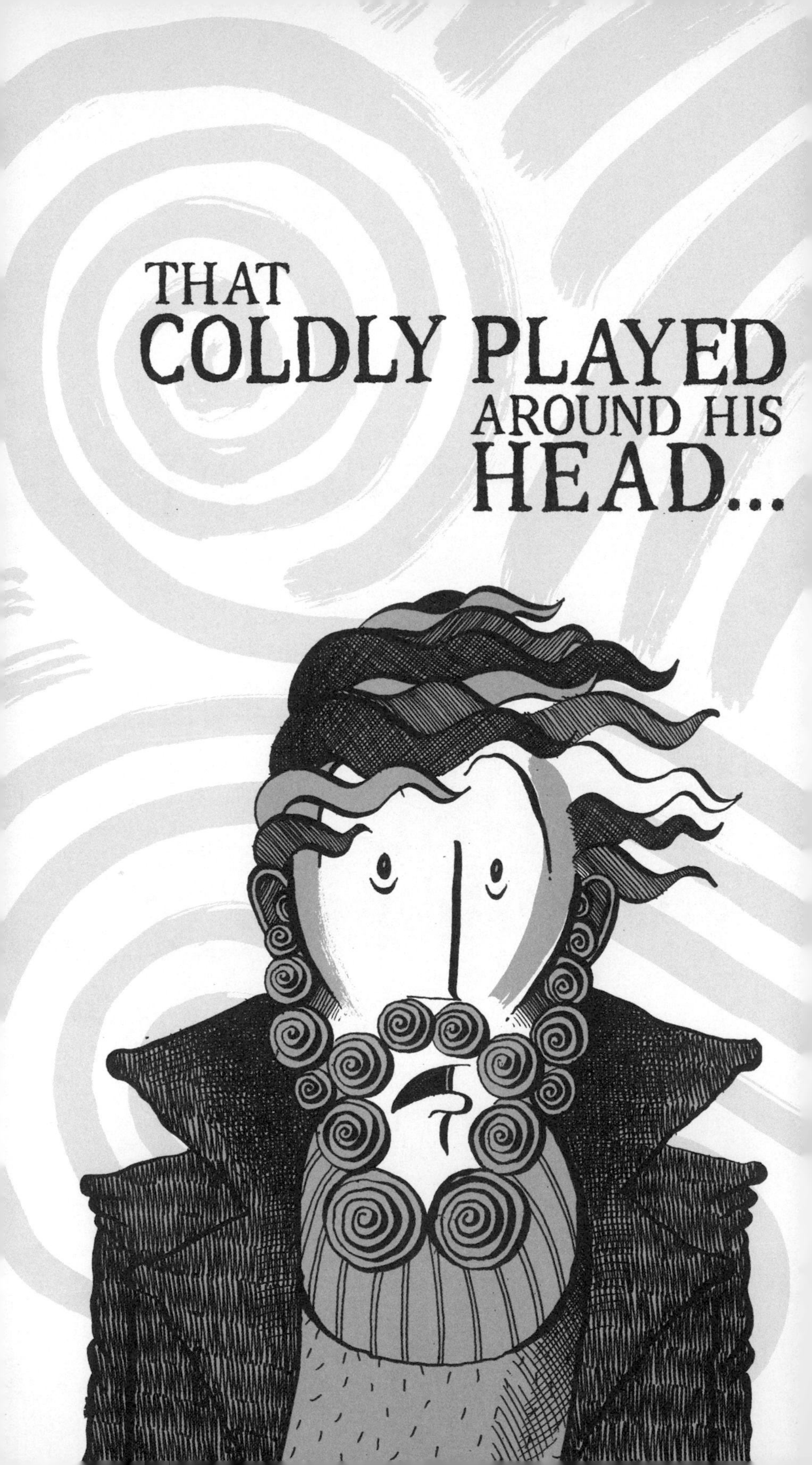
THAT
COLDLY PLAYED
AROUND HIS
HEAD...

IN BITTER MELODIES.

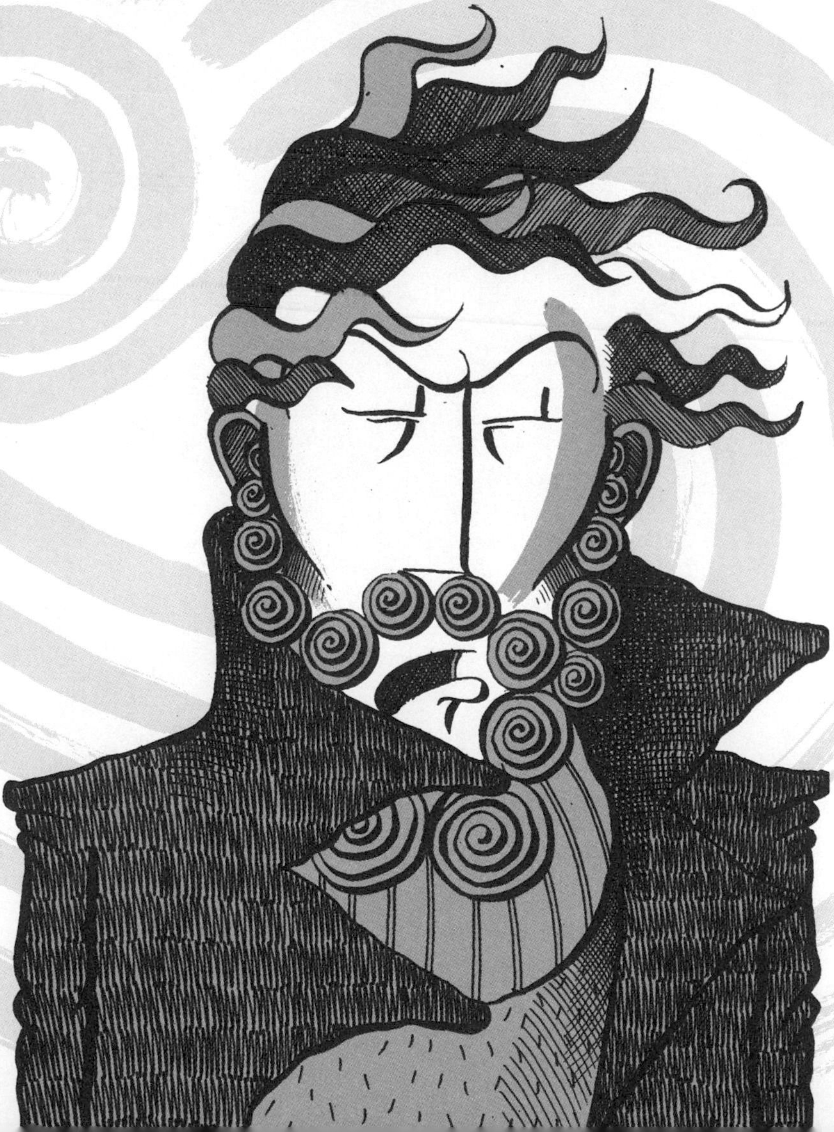

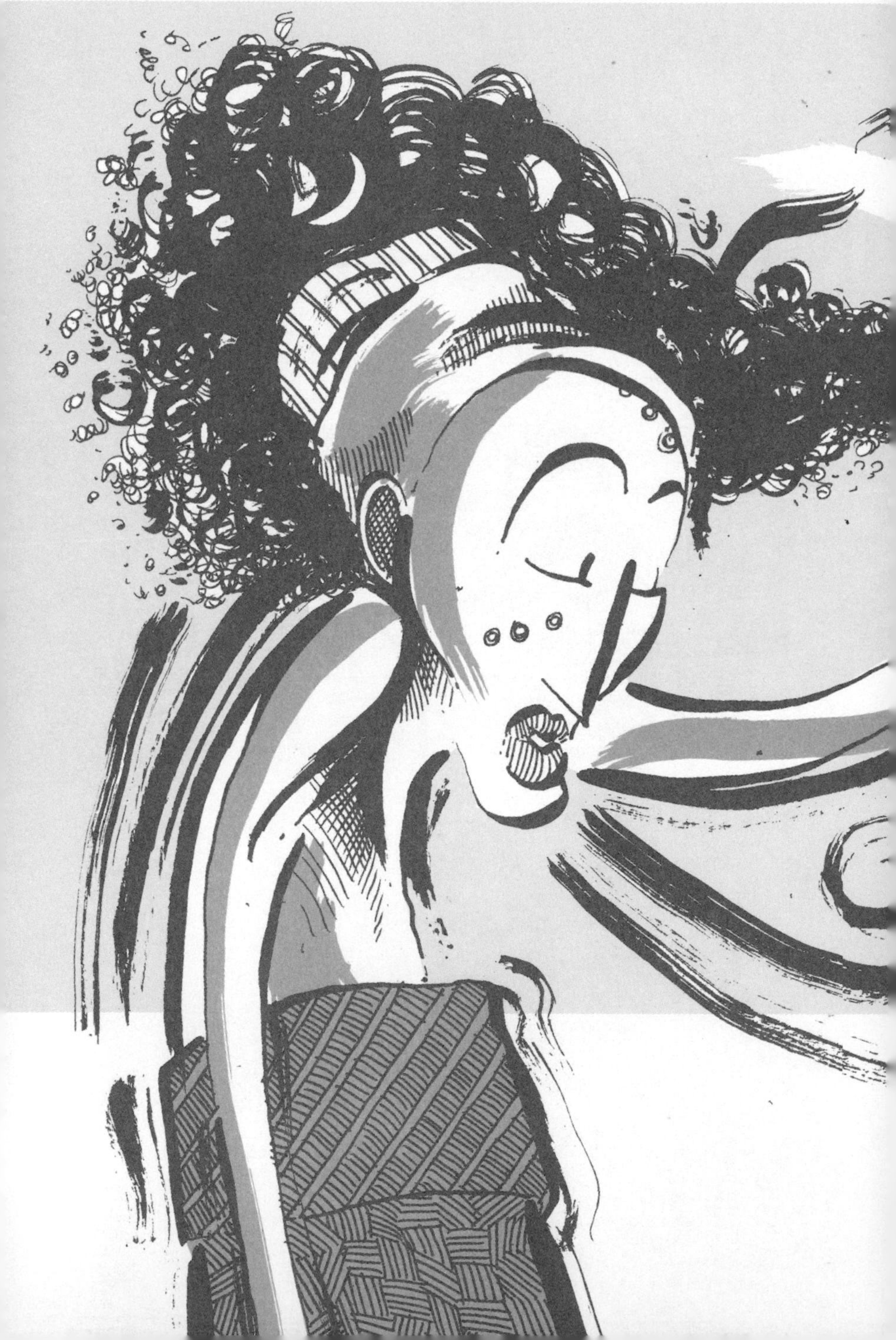

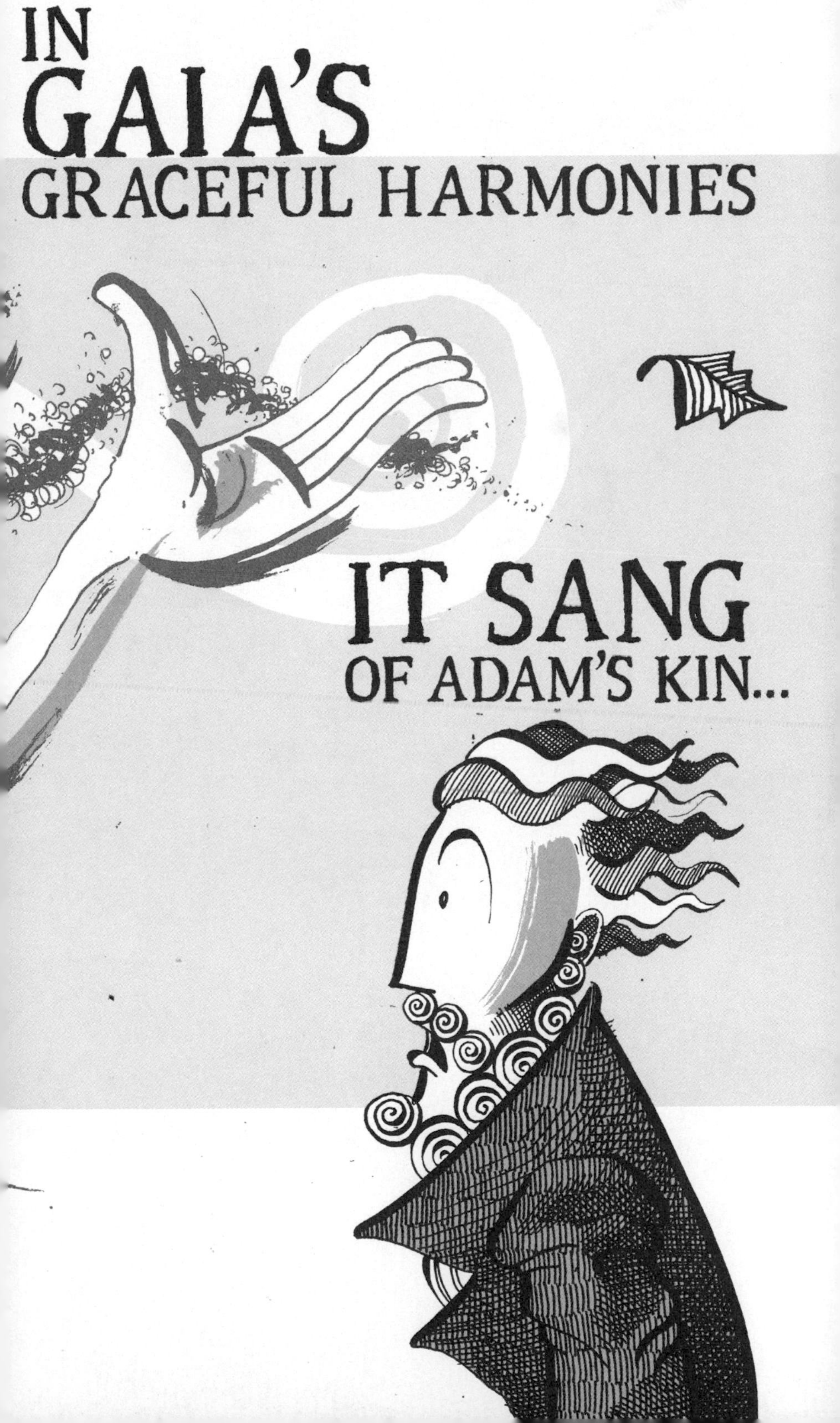
IN GAIA'S GRACEFUL HARMONIES
IT SANG OF ADAM'S KIN...

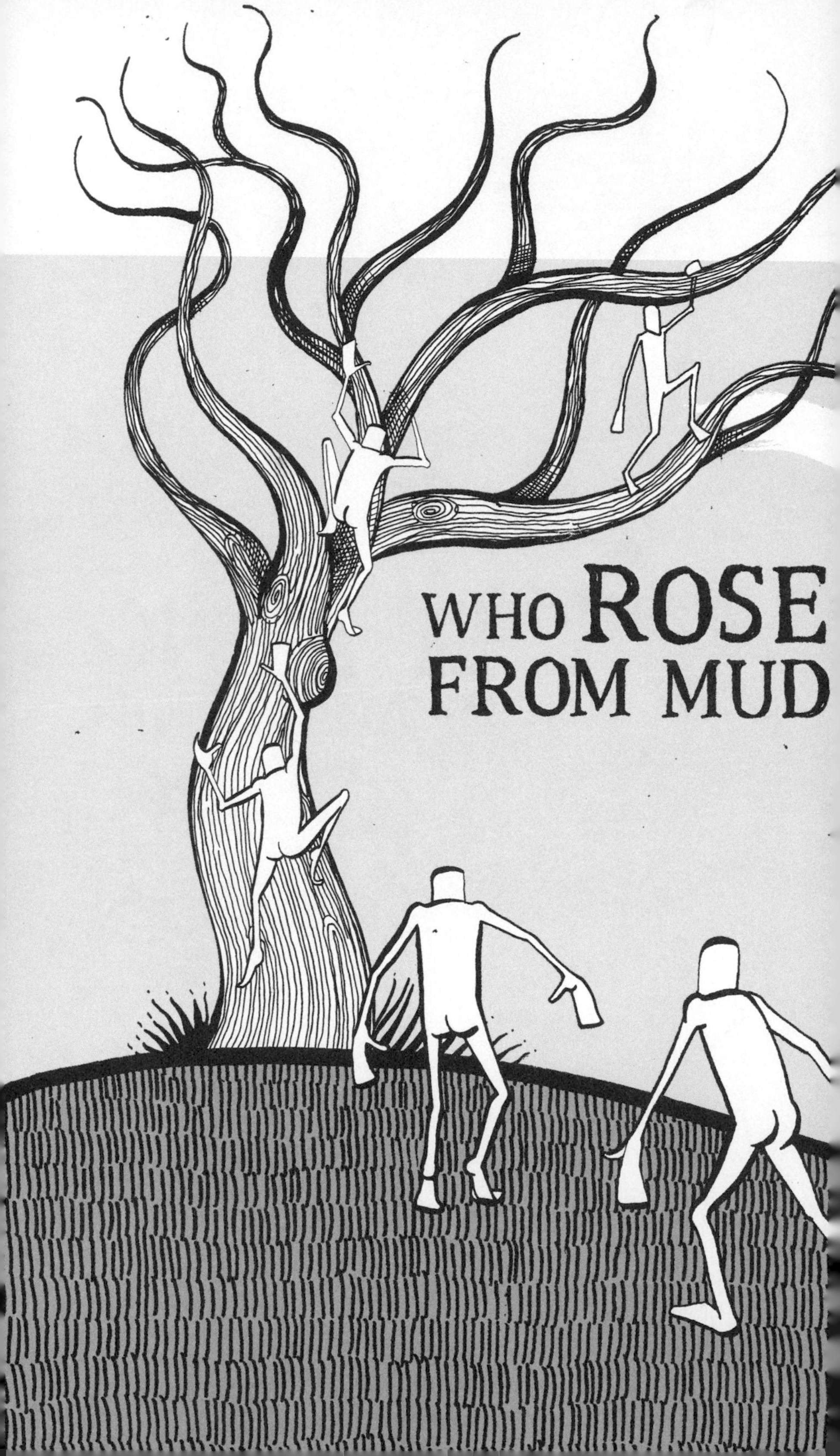
WHO ROSE
FROM MUD

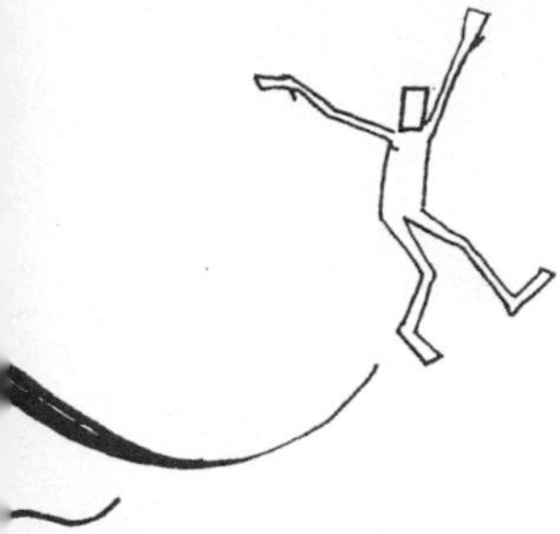

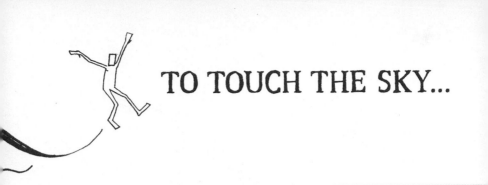

TO TOUCH THE SKY...

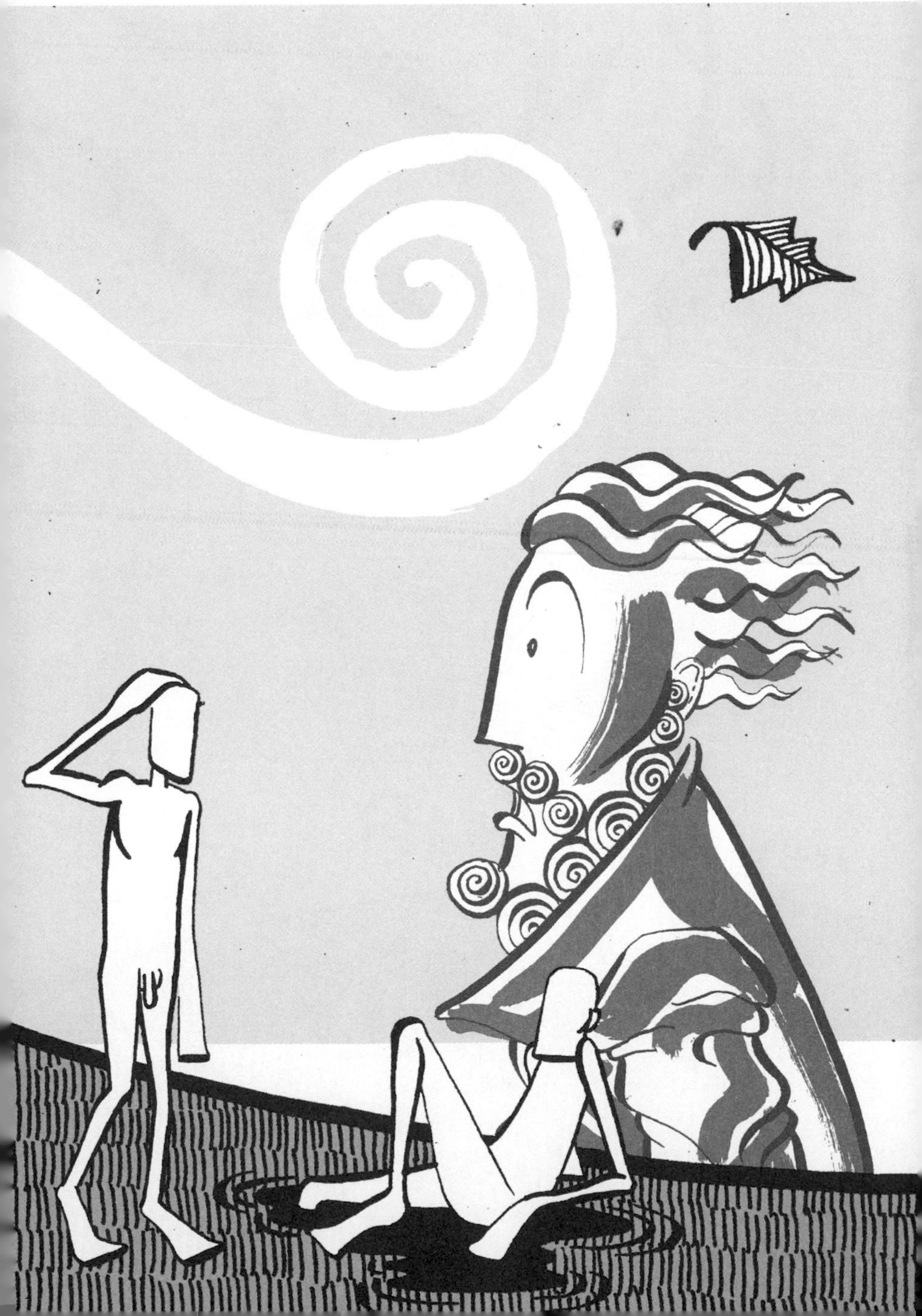

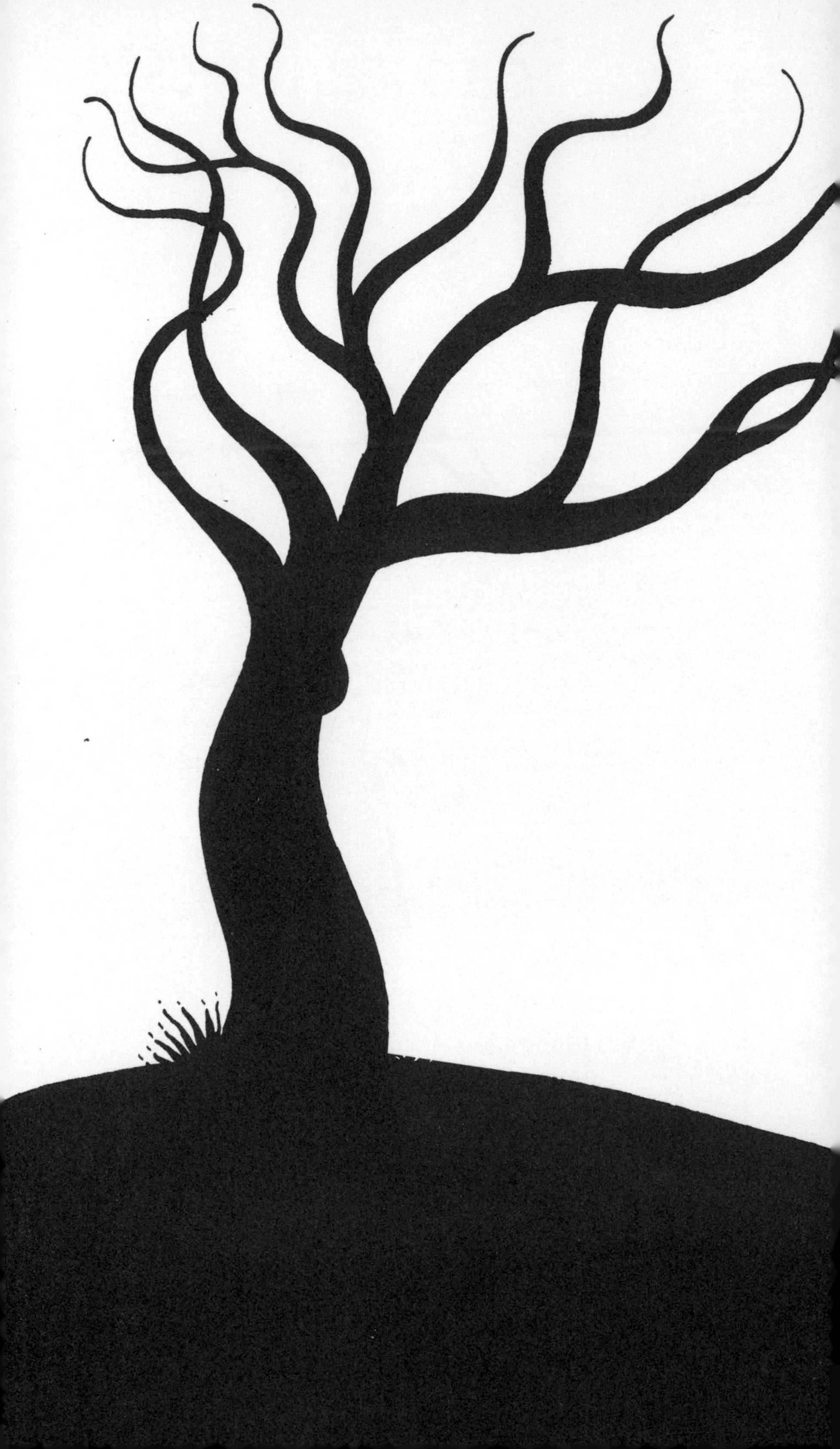

AND VANISHED...

...IN THE WIND.

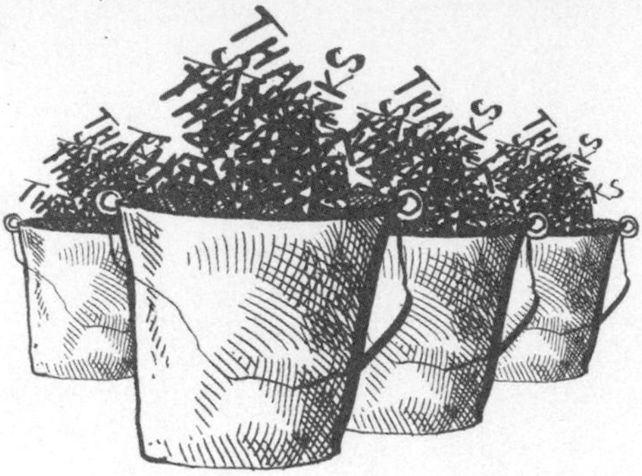
THANKS
THANKS
THANKS
THANKS

Bucket-loads of thanks to:

My dear mother and father, for, very simply, everything; to professor benny-boy hayes, for his jumper, tea, operatics, practical assistance in matters virtual, and for his love. To Martin Rowson, for his gracious patience with yet another pestering young tyke. To Andy James, for being my oracle on all things sequential. To Marcus Markou and the Dynamis crew, for their patronage. To Keiran Phelan, of the West Berks Arts council, for help and encouragement worthy of an embarrassingly large pay increase. To West Berks itself, its beechwoods and rooted secrets, and to its brewery, the holy West Berkshire Brewery, not just for its meaty ales, but also its golden spirit. To Barney Bardsley, for his wood lore, his sticks, and his gifted walnut, olive and box. To my country chums and my city chums, to whom this book is dedicated. To the spirit of Roger Deakin, Walnut tree Farm and to Titus, Jasmine, Electra and Anouk, for hospitality in our shrine, and more importantly, their home. To Rob Macfarlane, for his tireless and magical help, but most of all, for lighting, laying and walking the way.

And finally, to Nic Jones and Peter Bellamy, the voices in my head.

X